CATHOLIC
Sexual Ethics

A Summary, Explanation, & Defense
Third Edition

D0880033

CATHOLIC
Sexual Ethics

A Summary, Explanation, & Defense
Third Edition

William E. May,

Rev. Ronald Lawler, O.F.M. Cap.,

& Joseph Boyle, Jr.

Our Sunday Visitor Publishing Division
Our Sunday Visitor, Inc.
Huntington, IN 46750

Nihil Obstat
Msgr. Michael Heintz, Ph.D.
Censor Librorum

Imprimatur
✠ Kevin C. Rhoades
Bishop of Fort Wayne-South Bend
July 9, 2011

The *Nihil Obstat* and *Imprimatur* are official declarations that a book is free
from doctrinal or moral error. It is not implied that those who have granted
the *Nihil Obstat* and *Imprimatur* agree with the contents, opinions,
or statements expressed.

ISBN: 978-1-59276-083-1 (Inventory No. T1185)
LCCN: 2011931935

Cover design: Peggy Gerardot (updated by Amanda Falk)
Interior design: Sherri L. Hoffman

PRINTED IN THE UNITED STATES OF AMERICA

Acknowledgments

The authors and publisher are grateful to the following for the use of their materials appearing in this work:

- The Division of Christian Education of the National Council of the Churches of Christ for Scripture quotations taken from the *Revised Standard Version, Catholic Edition*, © 1965 and 1966 by the Division of Christian Education of the National Council of the Churches of Christ, except for those appearing in quoted sources such as *Vatican II: The Conciliar and Post Conciliar Documents* and in paraphrased material. All rights reserved. Where indicated, Scripture quotations are taken from the *New American Bible, Revised Edition* (NABRE) © 2010, 1991, 1986, 1970 Confraternity of Christian Doctrine, Inc. Washington, DC. All rights reserved.
- The Costello Publishing Company, Inc., for quotations taken from *Vatican II: The Conciliar and Post Conciliar Documents* and *Vatican Council II: More Post Conciliar Documents*, Austin Flannery, O.P., General Editor. Reprinted with permission of Costello Publishing Co., Inc., © 1975 by Costello Publishing Company, Inc., and Reverend Austin Flannery, O.P. All rights reserved.

A special debt of gratitude is owed those publishers, authors, etc., for the use of excerpts taken from the works cited in the chapter notes of this book, among them:

- Sheed and Ward, *Marriage: Human Reality and Saving Mystery*, by Edward Schillebeeckx, © 1965 by Sheed and Ward, Inc., reprinted with permission of Andrews McMeel & Parker,

Contents

Foreword to the Third Edition

In his call for the New Evangelization, Pope Benedict XVI urges us first to know and appropriate more deeply our Catholic faith and then have the confidence to share it with others. One particular area of life that requires thoughtful understanding and courageous living is human sexuality.

The Third Edition of *Catholic Sexual Ethics: A Summary, Explanation, & Defense* provides the reader with an accurate summary of the Church's teaching that is written in a way that guides readers to the truth of God's plan that sees each human as a unity of both bodily and spiritual dimensions. The need for this book grows out of the Church's perennial search to proclaim the truth but also out of the recognition that our understanding of gender, marriage, and family has been so consistently and persistently challenged by academia, media and the new norm — political correctness. Here, in this volume, we find a reasoned, calm, clear and well-thought-out response to the questions, How shall I live? What are the moral norms that should guide my life? How should I best see the ethics of human sexuality? William E. May, who revised the chapters of the Third Edition, offers the fruit of more than three decades of reflection on the teaching of Blessed John Paul II and Pope Benedict XVI on the gift of human sexuality and the noble purpose of marriage. The "Pastoral Conclusion," written by the late Ronald Lawler, O.F.M. Cap., is substantially unchanged from previous editions.

We are all aware that there is much confusion about the gift of human sexuality and rightly ordered sexual expression. At the same time, as Christians we recognize that there is more to life and human action than fleeting personal preference. Each person knows deep down, at the very core of human experience, that there is such a thing as right and wrong — that while the wrong choice may be alluring at the moment, it is a choice with lasting consequences. It is precisely in light of the consequences of sexual activity that the chapters on the virtue of chastity and the moral analysis of the requirements of chastity are of such welcome value. For a society faced with rising rates of addiction to pornography and sexual promiscuity among teens and young adults, the virtue of chastity is a beacon of clarity.

Where do we go to know right from wrong in all of the myriad forms that moral issues appear today? Jesus has not left us orphans. The pledge of the Holy Spirit is verified today, as it has been for 20 centuries, in the teaching office of the Church. In the many issues before us today, when decisions are presented with a range of good attached to each of the multiple choices, we need to listen to the sure and Spirit-led voice of the Church's teaching guiding us, particularly as we hear so many other voices offering so many other pathways.

Years ago, I had the privilege of reviewing the First Edition of *Catholic Sexual Ethics* in 1985. I rejoiced when the 1998 Second Edition appeared. This Third Edition builds upon the established reputation of this book. This edition of *Catholic Sexual Ethics* will be a valuable text for pastors, parents, catechists, and students who seek an ever-deeper appreciation for the gift of the Church's moral teaching and the knowledge and confidence to articulate its truth in family life, formation programs, and pastoral ministry.

✠ DONALD CARDINAL WUERL
Archbishop of Washington
June 29, 2011
Feast of SS. Peter and Paul

Introduction to the Third Edition

Thirteen eventful years have passed since publication of the Second Edition of this book. They witnessed the final seven years of the long pontificate of Blessed Pope John Paul the Great, who devoted tremendous attention to and thought about marriage, the family, and the significance of sex, from the time he was elected pope in 1978 until he died. They also witnessed the first six years of the pontificate of Pope Benedict XVI, who is not only a brilliant theologian but also, as Joseph Cardinal Ratzinger, served John Paul II so well as prefect of the Congregation for the Doctrine of the Faith, when his Congregation issued many important documents regarding marriage and the family and conjugal morality. Finally, these years have seen the growth of moral relativism, the repudiation by European countries of their Judeo-Christian roots, and the spread of the culture of death with its dualistic anthropology that divorces the "person" (= the consciously experiencing subject) from his or her body (which they believe is merely a privileged "instrument" of that subject but of no intrinsic value). These years have also witnessed the drive for same-sex unions along with a drastic redefinition of "marriage" and "family," along with attempts, largely successful, to prevent any exercise of religious freedom in expressing views affecting public policy. For all these reasons this new edition required quite substantive changes. I believe that what was said in the final paragraph of the "Introduction to the Second Edition" foreshadows many of the substantive changes made in this edition. There we read:

> [A]t the beginning of the new millennium, the idea that sex, gender, sexual morality, and the family itself are all the result of the social construction of morality and that the sexual "nature" of men and women is, as it were, the raw material for

such social construction is becoming more and more dominant among the elite of our society, and is likely to exert more
and more influence in the future on public debates over sex
and sexual morality. The challenges raised by the "responsible-relational" view of human sexuality and the "social con-
struction/deconstruction" view of sex, gender, morality, and
the family make it all the more imperative to know, appreciate,
and defend the Church's teaching on human sexuality, love,
marriage, and the meaning of man and woman.

I will here identify the major changes that I have made and why I
have done so.

Omission of Chapter 9 of the "updated" 1996 version of the First
Edition and kept in the Second Edition of 1998: The "expanded"
version of the First Edition, published in 1996, added this new chapter entitled "Recent Magisterial Teaching and 'Catholic Sexual Ethics.'" Although the new documents considered in Chapter 9 of the
"expanded" First Edition were integrated into the text in the Second
Edition and Chapter 9 was retained, I omit that chapter here. The
Second Edition added a further document in Chapter 9 published
after the "updated" First Edition had been prepared, namely, the Pontifical Council for the Family's *The Truth and Meaning of Human Sexuality: Guidelines for Education Within the Family.* Since 1998, when
the Second Edition was published, another very important document
was published: the Congregation for the Doctrine of the Faith's 2003
*Considerations Regarding Proposals to Give Legal Recognition to Unions
Between Homosexual Persons.* This document is of exceptional importance insofar as it addresses a very new issue, one not seriously considered until the very end of the twentieth and the beginning of the
twenty-first century after the secularization of marriage had taken
root in the Western World and after Europe had repudiated its Judeo-
Christian roots, namely, the claim that persons of the same sex can
marry and that to deny marriage to them is to be guilty of a crime
analogous to racism or sexism.

This issue is of such paramount significance that I have decided
to include a discussion of this great document and its importance
in Chapter 1, along with a presentation of principal elements in the

teaching of Pope Benedict XVI on marriage during the first years of his pontificate. I have also decided that salient material from the other documents that had been summarized at length in Chapter 9 can be integrated into other chapters when relevant. Many of these are relevant to Chapter 1 (and were to some extent considered in that chapter in the "expanded" 1996 draft of the First Edition, especially the *Catechism of the Catholic Church*). But here, too, I found it necessary to expand consideration of that document in order to call attention to and comment on its teaching that marriage is by its very nature "ordered to the *good of the spouses* and to the procreation and education of children."

I have in other ways also reworked Chapter 1 in an effort to clarify several sections, to deepen the consideration of marriage as a sacrament, and to introduce new considerations helpful in understanding the material this chapter covers.

I have made minor changes in Chapter 2, "The Biblical Teaching on Sex," in order to make this teaching clearer and to eliminate unnecessary or repetitious material and to integrate helpful matter from more recent studies. I have in particular integrated relevant material from Pope John Paul II's catecheses on the "theology of the body" into the text. To a large extent this kind of revision is true also of Chapter 3, "Sex in the Catholic Tradition" — although for this chapter I was principally concerned to make the text more readable. Chapter 4, "Patterns of Thinking in Moral Theology," required very substantive changes because the situation today is in many ways different from what it was when this book was first published (1985), and this chapter basically remained unchanged in both the "expanded" version of the First Edition and in the Second Edition. Although I have not completely rewritten this chapter, I have changed it very extensively so that in many ways it can be regarded as a new chapter. This chapter now has a shorter discussion of "proportionalism" and an added section on the "virtue-based ethics" advocated by many today. I have basically retained Chapter 5 on conscience and its meaning, etc. However, I have introduced and emphasized Pope Benedict XVI's provocative understanding of conscience as a kind of *anamnesis* or "remembering," and I have linked this understanding to some observations of Pope John Paul II and to ideas developed by some contemporary thinkers.

Chapter 6, "Chastity, Christian Marriage, and Virginity," has been left basically as it was, with minor changes. But I have substantively revised and rewritten Chapters 7 and 8 on the requirements of chastity within marriage and those requirements outside the covenant of marriage. I have, in fact, renamed these chapters so that Chapter 7 is now "Chastity and the 'Obligations' (Love-based Demands) of Married Persons," and Chapter 8 is now "Chastity and the 'Obligations' (Love-based Demands) of Unmarried Persons." I am somewhat opposed to speaking of the "requirements of chastity" because speaking in this way helps convey the false idea that Catholic sexual ethics is a series of "don'ts," of legalistic prohibitions, and it most definitely is not because it is liberating and a great "yes" to the God-given gift of sex and its orientation to life. In Chapter 7 I add a consideration of the debates over using condoms to protect sexual partners, including one's spouse, from contracting the AIDS virus. Chapter 8 required quite extensive revision in order to take into account the much more radical attitudes today regarding such issues as marriage and divorce, masturbation, homosexuality and homosexual acts common to both secular thinkers and those Catholic theologians and writers who regard magisterial teaching as false.

The Pastoral Conclusion, written by the late Ronald Lawler, O.F.M. Cap. (1926-2003), stays the same.

Finally, I want to express my profound gratitude to Mark Latkovic, one of my former students and now professor of moral theology at Sacred Heart Seminary in Detroit and a treasured friend, for the great care he took in reading the entire text of this Third Edition, making many excellent comments that have helped me to improve the text. He has also identified important recent literature on several issues and by doing so has helped bring the endnotes up to date and more helpful to readers.

WILLIAM E. MAY
January 17, 2011

Introduction to the Second Edition

This Second Edition of *Catholic Sexual Ethics* is intended primarily to bring the text, published originally in 1985, up to date. It does so, first of all, by integrating into the text and notes the relevant teaching of the magisterium found in documents promulgated after 1985. Here we should note that the "updated" text of the First Edition, published in 1996, featured a new chapter (Chapter 9), offering a summary of six magisterial documents of relevance to sexual ethics published between 1985 and 1995. This chapter, revised to the extent necessary to take into account the fact that the teaching of these documents has now been incorporated into the previous chapters, has been retained for the revised edition, and it now includes a summary of another relevant magisterial document — the Pontifical Council for the Family's *The Truth and Meaning of Human Sexuality: Guidelines for Education Within the Family,* published after the "updated" version of the text had been prepared.

The revision also brings the text up to date by taking into account some of the more significant scholarly literature on issues of sexual ethics and incorporating references to this literature throughout the work. The revised text also integrates our own efforts to develop and strengthen some of the evidence and arguments presented in the First Edition.

A major feature of the revised text is the reordering of the first three chapters. Chapter 1 is now given over to a presentation of the Church's teaching on sex; Chapter 2, to the biblical teaching on sex; and Chapter 3, to the understanding of sex in the Catholic theological tradition. In the First Edition the present Chapter 1 was Chapter 3, the present Chapter 2 was Chapter 1, and the present Chapter 3 was Chapter 2. We are now convinced that the order followed in the revised edition is the right order, since the Church's teaching on sex gives us an authoritative interpretation of Scripture and of the Catholic tradition. The chapters on the Church's teaching and on the biblical understanding of sex have been extensively rewritten. All the other chapters have been substantively revised in light of recent magisterial teaching, particularly that found in the new *Catechism of the Catholic Church* and in the major writings of Pope John Paul II such as *Veritatis Splendor*, more recent scholarly studies, and our own efforts to strengthen and develop the matter included in the First Edition. Of the co-authors, May was primarily responsible for preparing the revised edition; Lawler and Boyle, however, gave him inestimable advice and help on many specific matters. In revising the chapter on the biblical teaching on sex, May was helped greatly by advice given to him by Reverend Francis Martin, professor of Scripture at the John Paul II Institute for Studies on Marriage and Family in Washington, DC.

This "Introduction to the Second Edition" is followed by the original "Introduction." This has, however, been revised slightly to take into account, first of all, the ordering of chapters in this edition and the inclusion of the new chapter on recent magisterial documents of relevance to the subject. We have also decided to shorten the original introduction by cutting material no longer judged necessary. We believe that the "responsible-relational" view of human sexuality described in the original "Introduction" is still the dominant understanding of human sexuality in our culture. Moreover, now, at the beginning of the new millennium, the idea that sex, gender, sexual morality, and the family itself are all the result of the social construction of morality and that the sexual "nature" of men and women is, as it were, the raw material for such social construction is becoming more and more dominant among the elite of our society,* and is likely to exert more and more influence in the future on public debates over sex and sexual morality. The challenges raised by the "responsible-relational" view of human sexuality and the "social construction/ deconstruction" view of sex, gender, morality, and the family make it

---

* On this see *Sex, Preference and Family: Essays on Law and Nature*, ed. David M. Estlund and Martha C. Nussbaum (New York: Oxford University Press), 1997. (The titles of some essays are revealing: e.g., "Sexual Orientation and Gender, Dichotomizing Differences?"; "The Social Construction and Reconstruction of Care"; "Sexuality and Liberty: Making Room for Nature and Tradition?"; "Beyond Lesbian and Gay: Families We Choose"). See also Carol Levine, "AIDS and Changing Concepts of the Family," *Milbank Quarterly*, 68, Supplement 1 (1990), 30-46.

all the more imperative to know, appreciate, and defend the Church's teaching on human sexuality, love, marriage, and the meaning of man and woman. We hope that the revised text of *Catholic Sexual Ethics* will help satisfy this need.

Introduction to the First Edition

The purpose of this book is to present the teachings of the Catholic Church on questions of sexual morality.

A presentation of Catholic teaching on sexual morality is needed today because many Catholics and non-Catholics alike do not have a clear overall view of this teaching. Even those who know the Church's position on the various controverted issues in sexual ethics do not understand the roots of this teaching and its real human value. Many see it as a set of rules or taboos created by human authorities, or as vestiges of a culture which no longer serves any human needs.

The true character of the Church's teaching on sexual ethics can be understood only if its genuinely personalistic emphasis is grasped. With remarkable uniformity and insistence the Church, over many centuries, has taught that sex is fundamentally a good and wonderful gift of God, and that intelligently ordered sexual activity can be a humanly perfecting and even sanctifying thing. The condemnation of certain kinds of acts, choices, and attitudes bearing on the sexual domain is the result of this conviction about the basic goodness and importance of sexuality, for those things condemned by the Church are the sexual acts and attitudes which harm the human goods at stake in sexual activity. They are treated as gravely wrong because these goods are so central to the person's self-integrity, to the most intimate and fundamental relationships between persons, and to the person's relationship to God.

The Christian view of sexuality stands in stark contrast to many views that have become widely accepted in our culture. Perry London, for example, summarized the change in attitude toward various sexual activities which has occurred over the past few decades. He reported that there have been revolutionary changes in attitude and practice concerning things that have until recently been considered immoral.

He concluded that sexual legitimacy is no longer confined to marriage, and that sexual prohibitions might well follow in the way of the now abandoned prohibitions concerning various kinds of food: "If sexual norms were to follow a similar course, then common attitudes and behavior connected with it, like those predominant today with food, might become matters of preference, of health and manners, not of religion and morals."[1] Thus, he says: "It is unclear whether sex will long remain a topic for ethical concerns of any kind in our society."[2]

London, however, is not willing to endorse this trend without some kind of qualification. He believes that there might still be a need to regulate the sex appetite. He argues: "The most important characteristics of sex may finally be that it is so deeply intertwined with affection and that it is still the chief human instrument for making progeny, and these may suggest some limits on its exercise, though they do not reveal the contents of those limits."[3]

From the perspective of Catholic sexual ethics, London's observations are instructive. Intelligent reflection, even from an entirely secular perspective, must acknowledge that sexual activity cannot be treated as a trivial matter, and that the current permissiveness in sexual matters does trivialize sex. Sex is simply too important a part of life to be left as a matter of taste or mere preference.

There are many views about how sexuality is to be regulated so as to avoid its trivialization. Some might wish to see a revival of Victorian prudery or a puritanical denial of the real goodness of human sexuality. Such views, however, involve a denial of what most people correctly see as important human values. A more dominant view nowadays is that sexuality is governed by moral norms, and that these are requirements of its interpersonal character. On this view, the relational character of sexual activity is its most important feature,[4] and thus provides a moral criterion for evaluating sexual behavior. This criterion is the quality of the relationships established and expressed in the sexual activity. By this standard, degrading and exploitative sexual relationships are excluded. Some would add the further condition that the relationship be responsible — that it show care and concern for one's sexual partner, and that it be contraceptive unless a child is expressly desired.[5]

This view of sexual morality might be called the "responsible-relational" view. Besides upholding the conviction that moral norms do bear on sexual activity, this view has the merit of focusing on an undeniably important part of sexual morality, for human beings do establish the most intimate of their interpersonal relationships sexually. However, all human relationships should be responsible and nonexploitative, so this view provides no specific guidance on sexual matters as such. It fails to highlight the special moral responsibilities that flow from concern for the human goods toward which sexuality itself is ordered. It pays insufficient attention to the connection between sexual activity, marital love, and children. It is not surprising, therefore, that this view tends to approve, in many kinds of circumstances, premarital sex, masturbation, homosexual activity, and so on, and simply has nothing to say about questions of purity of thought. Its view of personal relations is not broad or deep enough to allow a realistic account of what is specifically at stake in sexual activity.

It is surprising, therefore, to note how much of the responsible-relational view some Catholic writers have accepted. Most of these writers have stated their views in a careful and circumscribed way. But they have denied some teachings very insistently affirmed by the Church, and have proposed a view of sexuality more in keeping with the responsible-relational view. Catholic writers, of course, are concerned to preserve the special place of marriage in the sexual domain. But even here some are willing to allow — at least as a possibility — the legitimacy of sexual activity outside marriage.[6] These writers also allow the permissibility of contraception,[7] and some would count homosexual behavior in some circumstances as morally acceptable or even praiseworthy.[8]

For many Catholics nowadays, the clear light of the Church's teaching is not brought to bear on the problems of sexual life. The only moral tempering of the sexual exploitation and hedonism of our culture is provided by the responsible-relational view, which can do little to articulate the real grandeur of sexuality or to protect it from the current onslaught. When Catholic moral teachers cannot show clearly what is distinctive about the Christian understanding of sexuality, Catholics are likely to be confused and misled.

It is essential, therefore, that the Church's teaching on sexual morality be presented in a way that reveals its truth and attractiveness. This book is part of the effort to do this — to fulfill the mandate of Pope John Paul II to reveal "the biblical foundations, the ethical grounds, and the personalistic" appropriateness of the good news about human sexuality which God has commanded the Church to proclaim.[9] Thus, this book will contain an extended exposition of the Church's teaching on sexual morality as well as a theological development of the arguments which support the Church's teaching. This theological argumentation will seek to relate the Church's teaching on sexual morality to the most fundamental concerns of Christian life, and to make clear within the perspective of Catholic faith why the Church's teaching on these matters is important and true.

To achieve these theological and pastoral aims, the book is divided into nine chapters and a conclusion. The first three chapters present a general account of the development of the Church's understanding of human sexuality. The first sets forth the authoritative teaching of the Church on sex; the second, the biblical understanding of sex; and the third, the development of the Catholic theological tradition on sex. The fourth and fifth chapters deal with general issues of moral theology which lie behind many of the specific issues in sexual morality. The fourth is a brief account of the foundations of moral theology; it provides a critique of the method of moral reasoning used by those Catholic writers who do not accept the received teaching on sexual morality. The fifth is a presentation of the Church's teaching on conscience; it focuses on the relationship between Church teaching and the conscience of the Catholic. The sixth chapter is an account of Christian marriage from a moral theological perspective. The next two chapters consider in some detail the specific requirements of chastity; Chapter 7 considers the requirements of chaste love within marriage; Chapter 8 considers the requirements of chastity for the unmarried. Chapter 9 offers an overview of seven major magisterial documents of relevance to understanding human sexuality promulgated between 1985 and 1995. Following the nine chapters the Pastoral Conclusion considers how the Christian message about sexuality is to be presented; it emphasizes both the seriousness of living chastely and the real possibility of living chastely given our union with the Risen Lord. His own example of dealing with fallen humankind is proposed as the model for pastoral problems in this area where so much weakness abounds.

This work was begun in 1978 at the urging of Ronald Lawler, O.F.M. Cap. Many unavoidable delays prevented its publication until

1985. It should be noted that these delays were largely beneficial. Perhaps the greatest of these benefits was the appearance of the great body of teaching on the issues at hand by the present pope, John Paul II. His statements and analyses have enriched every aspect of our work enormously. Most importantly, his *Familiaris Consortio* has made clear beyond any doubt that the received teachings of the Church — what the authors of this work have set out to explain and defend in this book — are indeed the authentic teachings of Christ's Church. Dissent on sexual matters is rejected — firmly and clearly — by the Church in this apostolic exhortation. This statement has exceptional authority, for in it John Paul II — as the authentic pastor of the whole Church and as the leader of the college of bishops — hands on received Catholic teaching. The collegiality of *Familiaris Consortio* is very real, since it is the pope's summary and response to the proposals made by the 1980 Synod of Bishops on the problems of the family.

Originally, the group of people involved in preparing this work was quite large. In addition to the authors, the following persons contributed material which has been used in some way in the development of the final product: Mark Dosh; John Harvey, O.S.F.S.; Frederick Jelly, O.P.; Mary Joyce; John Kippley; James Mohler, S.J.; Henry Sattler, C.Ss.R.; and William B. Smith. The authors thank these friends and colleagues for their irreplaceable help. The authors also thank Germain Grisez, whose insight on the issues addressed and whose work on fundamental moral theology and specific issues in sexual ethics has influenced this book greatly. In addition, the authors thank Barbara Boyle, who typed and retyped several versions of a number of the chapters, and Joseph Koterski, who entered a number of chapters into a word processor. The authors owe a great debt to the University of St. Thomas in Houston, Texas, and to the Basilian Fathers there, for providing word-processing equipment, hospitality, facilities for the authors' common work, and encouragement.

Finally, a word about the collaboration which led to this book is in order. Boyle and May drafted most of the chapters as they now appear. Drafts of early chapters often made use of materials provided by the collaborators listed above. Revisions were made on the basis of editorial work done by all three authors but primarily by Lawler. The final text, therefore, is the joint work of all three authors. All have read and agreed to the text as it appears, to the extent that it is very difficult to say who authored any individual sentence or came up with any specific argument or point. The authors hope that this work will prove invaluable to married and single people, to pastors and marriage counselors, and especially to those individuals who are seeking guidance concerning the Church's stand on sexual ethics.

ENDNOTES FOR INTRODUCTION TO THE FIRST EDITION

1. Perry London, "Sexual Behavior," in *Encyclopedia of Bioethics*, vol. 4, ed. Warren Reich (New York: Macmillan, 1978), p. 1567.

2. Ibid.

3. Ibid., p. 1569.

4. See Louis Janssens, "Considerations on *Humanae Vitae*," *Louvain Studies*, 2 (1969), 249. Janssens is a prominent Catholic moralist.

5. See Ashley Montagu, *Sex, Man, and Society* (New York: Putnam's, 1969), pp. 22-23.

6. See Philip S. Keane, S.S., *Sexual Morality: A Catholic Perspective* (New York: Paulist Press, 1977), pp. 100-110; Anthony Kosnik et al., *Human Sexuality: New Directions in American Catholic Thought* (New York: Paulist Press, 1977), pp. 148-149, 152-169.

7. See Daniel C. Maguire, "The Freedom to Die," in *The New Theology, No. 10*, ed. Martin E. Marty (New York: Macmillan, 1973), p. 189. See also Keane, *Sexual Morality*, pp. 109-110, for a justification of the use of contraceptives by nonmarried persons.

8. See Charles E. Curran, "Dialogue with the Homophile Movement," in his *Catholic Moral Theology in Dialogue* (Notre Dame, IN: Fides, 1972), pp. 184-219. See also John McNeill, S.J., *The Church and the Homosexual* (Kansas City, MO: Andrews and McMeel, 1976).

9. John Paul II, *Familiaris Consortio*, no. 31. [*NOTE*: Besides *Vatican Council II: The Conciliar and Post Conciliar Documents* and *Vatican Council II: More Post Conciliar Documents*, ed. Austin Flannery, O.P., excerpts from the conciliar and post-conciliar documents (such as *Familiaris Consortio*) can be found in a number of other sources, including *The Pope Speaks* and *NC Documentary Service*.]

CHAPTER ONE

The Church's Teaching on Sex

I. Moral Theology and the Magisterium

The purpose of this book is to summarize, explain, and defend the teaching of the Catholic Church on sexual ethics. This teaching, and the moral theology compatible with this teaching, is rooted in faith in Jesus Christ. The Gospels portray Christ telling his followers to teach all the nations "to observe all that I have commanded you; and lo, I am with you always, to the close of the age" (Mt 28:20).

Catholic faith is before all else faith in Christ, who remains with us through his Church, the "sacrament" of his own presence. Much of what we believe about the moral life and sexual ethics can also be shown to be true by good moral reasoning. Not all persons, however, are capable of freely assimilating such proofs, while the gift of faith in Christ is far more accessible and is more decisive than any philosophical argument.[1]

Christ is the one Teacher upon whose word all faith depends (Mt 7:29, 11:27). In a special way he himself teaches his faithful today through the teaching office (magisterium) he has willed to be in the Church until the end of time. He has given it authority to speak in his name. The mission of the magisterium is to guard and hand on, with divine authority, the saving truth brought to us by the Lord. The Second Vatican Council declared that the "task of giving an authentic interpretation to the Word of God... has been entrusted to the living teaching office of the Church alone" (*Dei Verbum*, no. 10). This teaching office, first given to St. Peter and the other apostles, is now, by the will of Christ, entrusted to the pope and the bishops who teach in communion with him.

The Church presents and always has presented many moral teachings with entire assurance, expecting her sons and daughters to believe and live by this teaching. She does not expect this because popes and bishops are so humanly wise, but because through them Christ himself guards the faith and its saving truths — truths necessary if we are to live worthily as children of God.

According to Catholic faith, the magisterium invested in the college of bishops under the headship of the pope *always* teaches with the authority of Christ — a more-than-human authority. At times this teaching office proposes matters, whether of faith or morals, infallibly, i.e., with divine assurance that what is proposed is absolutely true and is to be held definitively. Teachings proposed in this way are to be given the assent of faith (cf. *Lumen Gentium*, no. 25). At other times, it teaches matters of faith or morals *authoritatively and as true*, but not as divinely guaranteed to be true or as irrevocable. Although teachings proposed in this way do not require the assent of faith, they are to be received with a "religious assent of will and mind," and all the faithful, including pope, bishops, ordinary lay people, and theologians, are to accept these teachings as true and to shape their lives and actions in conformity with them.[2] (This matter will be taken up in more detail in Chapter 5).

The Church teaches infallibly in matters of faith and morals through the solemn definitions of councils and *ex cathedra* pronouncements of supreme pontiffs. But she also teaches infallibly through her ordinary teaching by the bishops of the Church in union with the pope, when they agree in teaching that something of faith or morals is to be held definitively.[3]

The Church's magisterium is capable of teaching infallibly and authoritatively precisely because it is the instrument by which the Spirit of Christ preserves the Church in his saving truth, and prevents the Church from wandering from this truth. The apostolic preaching, through which the saving truth given by our Lord was communicated to the apostolic Church, was, as Vatican Council II affirmed,

> To be preserved in a continuous line of succession until the end of time. Hence, the apostles, in handing on what they themselves had received, warn the faithful to maintain the traditions which they had learned either by word of mouth or

by letter (cf. 2 Thess 2:15); and they warn the faithful to fight hard for the faith that had been handed over to them once and for all (cf. Jude 3). What was handed on by the apostles comprises everything that serves to make the People of God live their lives in holiness and increase their faith. In this way, the Church, in her doctrine, life, and worship, perpetuates and transmits to every generation all that she herself is, all that she believes. (*Dei Verbum*, no. 8)

The Spirit's work within the Church is not, of course, limited to his guidance of the pope and bishops. The Spirit also guides and instructs the many people within the Church who seek to penetrate God's revelation more deeply and to live worthily as God's children. Theologians, philosophers, mystics, and ordinary good people are helped by the Spirit in their attempts to understand, live, and explain the faith. But they can hold and proclaim the faith securely and shape their lives in accord with its truths only when they take care to teach and live in conformity with the guidance of the teaching office of the Church, for that office alone has been charged with the supervision of public teaching in the Church, and it alone has the God-given authority to make secure, final judgment in matters of faith and morals. Christ has confided to the magisterium the task "to preserve God's people from deviations and defections and to guarantee them the objective possibility of professing the true faith without error" (*Catechism of the Catholic Church*, no. 890). It is for this reason that the Second Vatican Council declares that "in forming their consciences the faithful must pay careful attention to the sacred and certain teaching of the Church. For the Catholic Church is by the will of Christ the teacher of truth. It is her duty to proclaim and teach with authority the truth which is Christ and, at the same time, to declare and confirm by her authority the principles of the moral order which spring from human nature itself" (*Dignitatis Humanae*, no. 14).

Theologians have an indispensable role to play within the Church, for they can help all the faithful — including pope and bishops — come to a deeper and richer understanding of the faith and of the requirements of the Christian way of life. But they are *not* charged with the direct pastoral responsibility for the care of souls, for this has been entrusted to the magisterium. Theologians are not vested with the authority of Christ. The matter can perhaps be put this way: do not *believe* theologians; rather, consider the evidence and arguments that they offer to support their positions, and be grateful to them when well-founded positions they take help deepen one's faith; but do not listen to them if they take positions contrary to those proposed by Christ's shepherds. As St. Thomas Aquinas, surely a model for theologians and for the faithful, put the matter, "we must abide by the pope's judgment rather than by the opinion of any theologian, however well versed he may be in divine Scriptures."[4]

It is therefore critically important for us to summarize accurately what the teaching office of the Church has taught and does teach about marriage and sexual morality. It is necessary to consider the Church's teaching on sexual morality within the context provided by her teaching on marriage. This is so because the Church clearly recognizes that it is only within marriage that human persons, and the precious goods which human sexuality is to serve, can be respected and realized. We will show this in considerable detail in Chapters 6, 7, and 8 where we will develop a theological account of the Catholic view of marriage and the concrete requirements of chastity. In this chapter we will summarize what the Church teaches about the goodness and holiness of marriage, what the Church teaches about sexual activity within marriage, and what it teaches about the immorality of sexual activity that is not authentically marital. This will be done so as to highlight some of the essential points of Catholic sexual teaching, and to make clear the seriousness, constancy, and nonarbitrariness of this teaching.

II. Magisterial Teaching on the Goodness and Holiness of Marriage[5]

The Church has always taught that the union of man and woman in marriage is a good and holy thing. It is good because, as Scripture makes clear, God himself instituted marriage and gave it its defining characteristics. It is holy because the Lord Jesus made marriage a sacrament of his spousal union with his bride, the Church, and a source of grace. That is, the marriage of baptized persons, who through baptism have been irrevocably united for weal or woe with Jesus the Bridegroom, not only points to or signifies his bridal union with his bride the Church — a union that is love giving, life giving, and grace giving — but also *makes that union efficaciously present in the world here and now so long as the spouses put no obstacles in the way.*

The Church clearly affirmed the goodness of marriage in the face of the attacks on marriage by the various forms of Gnosticism which appeared through the centuries. As early as 340, a council of bishops meeting in Gangra (in Asia Minor, in what is now modern-day Turkey) stated: "If anyone disparages marriage, shuns a faithful and God-fearing wife who sleeps with her husband, and speaks as though she cannot enter the kingdom of God, let him be anathema."[6] Similarly, the Second and Fourth Councils of the Lateran in 1139 and 1215 defended the goodness of the marital union against the challenge of the medieval neo-Gnostics.[7] In 1208 Pope Innocent III insisted that Catholics "believe that the husband with his wife can be saved."[8] And these declarations from the local council of Gangra, the Second and Fourth Councils of the Lateran, and Pope Innocent III are simply illustrative of the universal teaching of the Church; other magisterial documents on marriage prior to the great Council of Trent contain the same praise for marriage as a good and holy reality.[9]

Although from her very beginning the Church has lived in virtue of the power of the seven sacraments instituted by Christ, time was needed for developing clearly, in the light of faith, what precisely a sacrament itself is, and which gifts of Christ are sacraments in that sense. Concretely, thanks to the witness of the Fathers, it is clear that marriage was always regarded as a source of the graces needed by spouses in order to live a holy life and that it is a symbol of the union between Christ and the Church. Nonetheless, the detailed development of the Church's teaching on the sacramentality of marriage took place over many centuries.[10] Long before the sacramentality of marriage was solemnly defined, marriage was recognized in the Church as a true sacrament. In 1439 the Council of Florence explicitly affirmed that marriage was not only humanly good but also one of the seven sacraments instituted by Christ. This council also affirmed as Catholic teaching that "three blessings are assigned to matrimony. The first is the procreation and education of children for the worship of God. The second is the fidelity that each of the spouses must observe towards the other. The third is the indissolubility of matrimony, indissoluble because it signifies the indivisible union of Christ and the Church."[11]

The Council of Trent in the sixteenth century was not faced with a challenge to the inherent goodness of marriage but rather with the denial of its sacramental character and indissolubility. In a solemn dogmatic proclamation, this Council reaffirmed the divine institution of marriage and its later elevation by Christ to the dignity of a sacrament. The decree *De doctrina sacramenti matrimonii* began by calling to mind the divine institution of marriage, at the very beginnings of the human race, established as a unique and indissoluble bond between one man and one woman: "The first parent of the human race, under the inspiration of the Divine Spirit, proclaimed the perpetual and indissoluble bond of matrimony when he said, 'This now is bone of my bones, and flesh of my flesh.... Wherefore a man shall leave father and mother and cleave to his wife: and they shall be two in one flesh' (Gen 2:23; see Eph 5:31)."

Moreover, in order to give spouses the help necessary, given man's fall from grace, to make marriage a road to holiness Christ raised the marriage of Christians to the dignity of a sacrament giving or increasing sanctifying grace, i.e., the grace that makes us holy: "Christ himself, who instituted the holy sacraments and brought them to perfection, merited for us by his passion the grace that brings natural love to perfection and strengthens the indissoluble unity, and sanctifies the spouses. The Apostle Paul intimates this when he says: 'Husbands, love your wives, just as Christ also loved the Church, and delivered himself up for her' (Eph 5:25); and he immediately adds: 'This is a great mystery — I mean in reference to Christ and to the Church' (Eph 5:32)."[12]

In the centuries since Trent there have been many challenges to the Catholic teaching on marriage. None of these until the latter years of the twentieth century explicitly denied that marriage is a good institution, but many of these challenges involve the belief that marriage is a purely human institution which can be changed by human decision so that it need not be regarded as permanent but can be considered as allowing for divorce and remarriage, or that it can be understood as a relationship between persons with no necessary order to the begetting and educating of children. Today, however, there are claims that marriage is possible between persons of the same sex. In addition, it is now common for many to claim that marriage is *not* good but is rather a form of slavery imposed on women by domineering males.

In response to these and other challenges, popes in recent centuries have reaffirmed the divine origin of marriage and the sacramental character of Christian marriage. They have done this to emphasize that the human meaning and the supernatural significance of marriage are threatened by the various proposals to change the character of marriage or to alter sexual morality. Thus, for example, Pope Leo XIII in 1880 affirmed very clearly that marriage was instituted by God, that it is indissoluble, and that as one of the seven sacraments it provides special graces to spouses.[13]

In 1930, fifty years later, Pope Pius XI issued his comprehensive encyclical on Christian marriage, *Casti Connubii*. He solemnly reaffirmed Catholic doctrine that God is the author of marriage, that Jesus raised Christian marriage to the dignity of a sacrament, that it is indissoluble and blessed with the goods of children, fidelity between the spouses, and indissolubility. Noting the errors and vices opposed to marriage and marital love, he repudiated as intrinsically immoral abortion, contraception, adultery, and divorce. He emphasized that the beauty and dignity of marriage can be secured only by adhering to the divine plan for marriage and doing so by having recourse to prayer and to the sacraments, by docility to magisterial teaching, and by preparing adequately for marriage.

A major element in *Casti Connubii* was Pius's teaching on the beauty of conjugal love, the "soil" which enables conjugal fidelity to flourish. This love, which is presented as the vital principle of marriage, is meant to inform the whole of married life and reaches its perfection in conjugal charity, which leads the spouses to imitate the holiness of Christ himself.[14]

Although he wrote no encyclicals on marriage, Pope Pius XII took up issues concerning marriage in many of his addresses, in particular his "Addresses to Newlyweds" and to various organizations of Christian families. He reaffirmed Catholic teaching on marriage as a divine institution and sacrament of the new law, considering in particular issues of conjugal sexual morality (see the following section).[15]

The Second Vatican Council, in response to the developing modern attitude that marriage is whatever society or individuals may choose to make it, attractively reaffirmed and developed Catholic teaching on marriage. First, it presented Christian marriage as a specific vocation to holiness, affirming that Christian "spouses are fortified and, as it were, consecrated for the duties and dignity of their state by a special sacrament; fulfilling their conjugal and family role by virtue of this sacrament, spouses are penetrated with the spirit of Christ and their whole life is suffused by faith, hope, and charity; thus they increasingly further *their own perfection and their mutual sanctification*, and together they render glory to God" (*Gaudium et Spes*, no. 48).

Second, it developed significantly the understanding of the role of conjugal love in the structure of marriage, clearly showing that this love is the animating principle of marriage. It is manifested at the very beginning of marriage in the act of marital consent, through which a man and woman give themselves unreservedly, completely, and irrevocably to each other as husband and wife. It is present in principle throughout the whole of married life, a love always possible for spouses to give and one that they are obliged to deepen and foster in their daily life.

Third, Vatican Council II insisted that there can be no true contradiction or conflict between the requirements of authentic marital love and the great good of having and raising children. It insisted that by its own inner dynamism conjugal love is ordered to the procreation and education of children, a gift crowning and perfecting the love of the spouses.

In continuity with the Catholic tradition the Second Vatican Council reaffirmed the truth that God is the author of marriage, that he has endowed it with "various benefits and ends in view" (*Gaudium et Spes*, no. 48) — namely, the procreation and education of children, spousal fidelity, and indissoluble unity.[16] While insisting that marriage comes to be only when a man and a woman freely consent *to be* husband and wife by giving themselves irrevocably to each other, the Council emphasized that the *nature* of marriage is not subject to human choices but has been definitively determined by God.[17] Consequently, the "sacred bond" of marriage, which comes into being when the man and the woman freely give themselves to each other through an "irrevocable" act of the will, perdures and is not "dependent on human will" (*Gaudium et Spes*, no. 48).

Pope Paul VI succinctly summarized the key elements of the Second Vatican Council's teaching on marriage in his 1968 encyclical *Humanae Vitae*. In his encyclical, Paul VI stressed the competence of the magisterium to interpret authoritatively the divine law, both natural and evangelical, and reaffirmed strongly Catholic teaching on contraception.[18]

Pope John Paul II, even prior to becoming Supreme Pontiff, had devoted himself extensively to the study of human sexuality, sexual morality, marriage, and the family.[19] Immediately upon becoming pope and in order to prepare for the Synod of Bishops in 1980 devoted to the theme "The Role of the Christian Family in the World Today," he began a series of papal Wednesday audiences given over to reflections on the "theology of the body," reflections concerned with human sexuality, the male-female relationship, marriage, and family.[20] Throughout his pontificate he gave hundreds of addresses on marriage and the family and sexual morality.[21] The most important and authoritative document on marriage and the family promulgated by John Paul II, however, is undoubtedly his 1981 apostolic exhortation *Familiaris Consortio*, "The Role of the Christian Family in the World Today." This document, which John Paul II himself described as a "*summa* of the teaching of the Church on the life, the tasks, the responsibilities, and the mission of marriage and of the family in the world today,"[22] is divided into four parts.[23] Parts Two and Three are doctrinal in character and beautifully summarize and develop Catholic teaching on marriage and family, particularly as deepened by the teaching of the Second Vatican Council. Pope John Paul II affirmed the goodness of marriage as a human reality created by God and takes special pains to explain its holiness. He emphasized that, by reason of their baptism, "man and woman are definitively placed within the new and eternal covenant, in the spousal covenant of Christ with the Church" (*Familiaris Consortio*, no. 13). Because of this "indestructible insertion" into the new covenant, married love is elevated and enriched by Christ's redeeming power. As a result, the Christian family is a "domestic Church" and, as John Paul II developed extensively in Part Three of *Familiaris Consortio*, is called to play an indispensable role in the redemptive mission of the Church.

In his 1994 *Letter to Families* John Paul II recapitulated many of the themes set forth in *Familiaris Consortio*, emphasizing that the family rooted in marriage has as its task the building up of the "civilization of love," a theme to which he returned in his 1995 encyclical *Evangelium Vitae*, where he stressed that the conjugal love of spouses enables the family to be the "sanctuary of life."[24]

Catholic magisterial teaching on marriage is concisely set forth in the 1994 *Catechism of the Catholic Church*. It begins its consideration of marriage by summarizing Catholic teaching on the meaning of marriage in God's wise and loving plan for human existence, considering marriage first in the order of creation as a gift from God, then marriage under the regime of sin and under the Mosaic law, and finally, it takes up marriage "in the Lord," that is, marriage as restored to its original dignity and, in addition, raised to the level of a sacrament of grace, insisting that "it is by following Christ, renouncing themselves, and taking up their crosses that spouses will be able to 'receive' the original meaning of marriage and live it with the help of Christ" (no. 1615). It considers the "goods" of marriage — the procreation and education of children, fidelity between the spouses, and indissolubility — as required by the nature of conjugal love, a love that leads to the sanctification of the spouses and, through them, of the world in which they live (cf. nos. 1643-1658). The *Catechism* also, following the teaching on marriage in the 1983 revision of canon law, teaches that "the matrimonial covenant, by which a man and a woman establish between themselves a partnership of the whole of life, is by its nature ordered toward the good of the spouses and the procreation and education of offspring."[25]

The "good of the spouses," it should be noted, is named prior to the "procreation and education of offspring" as the "end" of marriage or, as formulated, is named first as that toward which the matrimonial covenant is by nature ordered. But what is the "good of the spouses," and how is it related to the "procreation and education of offspring"? Scholars who have studied this matter carefully show that the "good of the spouses" ultimately consists in their sanctification and that this good, far from being in conflict or opposed to the "procreation and education of offspring," embraces or includes such procreation and education insofar as children are indeed the crowning gift of marriage and contribute to their parents' growth in holiness or sanctity.[26]

The genuine goodness and holiness of marriage is therefore a constant theme of Church teaching, whether in response to Gnostic claims that marriage is evil or in response to modern claims that its meaning is to be determined by human decision. The character of this God-given goodness is especially important today, because those who wish to change the Church's teaching on sexual morality fail to recognize that this morality is necessary to preserve great and indispensable human goods.

There are other sources of magisterial teaching on marriage, some issued during the long pontificate of Pope John Paul II, and in particular after *Familiaris Consortium*. There is also Pope Benedict XVI's encyclical *Deus Caritas Est* ("God Is Love"), a section of which, devoted to the "epitome of love," takes up marriage and conjugal love. In addition, some of his major addresses concern marriage and family.[27] There are also several documents from pontifical congregations or councils. Of the documents issued during the pontificate of Pope John Paul II, most consider subject matter taken up in later chapters, and I will integrate their teaching at the appropriate places in those chapters. But one document issued by the Congregation for the Doctrine of the Faith in 2003 is very important for this chapter insofar as it addresses the challenge to marriage raised by the vigorous efforts made today to recognize the "marriage" of same-sex persons; the document in question is *Considerations Regarding Proposals to Give Legal Recognition to Unions Between Homosexual Persons*. I will summarize the teaching of that document here and then summarize Pope Benedict's teaching on marriage in *Deus Caritas Est* ("God Is Love") and in some of his major addresses.

Summary of the Congregation for the Doctrine of the Faith's *Considerations Regarding Proposals to Give Legal Recognition to Unions Between Homosexual Persons*

The document contains an introduction, four major sections, and a conclusion. The four major sections are: I. The Nature of Marriage and Its Inalienable Characteristics; II. Positions on the Problem of Homosexual Unions; III. Arguments from Reason Against Legal Recognition of Homosexual Unions; IV. Positions of Catholic Politicians with Regard to Legalization of Homosexual Unions. Section I summarizes Catholic teaching, rooted in the Catholic understanding of Sacred Scripture and tradition, showing that homosexual acts are objectively gravely immoral and that homosexual persons cannot marry because they cannot do what married couples are supposed to do and are capable of doing. Section II reviews a wide variety of contemporary positions. Section III, the longest in the document, is most relevant for this chapter; hence I will summarize its teaching.

Section IV takes up the subject matter identified and instructs Catholic politicians never to vote for legalization of homosexual unions and, if such have been given legal recognition, to do all they can to have this recognition revoked and, should this not be possible, to support proposals aimed at limiting the harm done or at lessening its negative consequences.

Section III, "Arguments from Reason…" presents arguments from four "orders": the order of *right reason;* the *biological and anthropological* order; the *social* order; and the *legal* order.

Considering the order of *right reason* the Congregation first emphasizes that civil laws are legitimate and just only if they are in conformity with the natural moral law and respect the inalienable rights of human persons. States giving legal guarantees analogous to marriage to homosexual unions fail in their duty to promote and defend marriage as an institution essential to the common good of the community. It is important to distinguish between homosexual behavior as a *private* phenomenon and the same behavior as a social relationship approved by the state as a legally sanctioned institution. The lifestyles and underlying presuppositions this expresses externally shape the life of the community and tend to mold the minds of youth, thereby obscuring basic moral values and devaluing the institution of marriage and failing to protect the rights of husbands and wives.

If we consider the *biological, anthropological* order, it is evident that homosexual unions totally lack the biological and anthropological characteristics of marriage and family and ought thus not to be legally recognized as such. Homosexual unions are not capable of contributing to the survival of the human race, nor do modern reproductive technologies remedy this very serious defect. In addition, the absence of sexual complementarity in such unions harms any children who might be placed in the care of such persons; they would have no proper role models for what mothers and fathers are and do. This even contradicts the United Nations' conventions on the rights of the child.[28]

Considering the *social* order, the document emphasizes that its continued survival depends on the family founded on marriage. If homosexual unions were legally recognized as marriages, marriage would of necessity be redefined and would become an institution devoid of features linked to heterosexuality, such as the procreation and education of children, and this would be to the detriment of the common good of society. Refusing to recognize homosexual unions as marriage is not a form of unjust discrimination; rather justice demands that such unions and other forms of sexual cohabitation that are not and cannot be marital not be recognized as such.

From the *legal* order, homosexual unions, which do not serve the society's common good but rather harm it, do not require the institutional recognition given marriage, which serves the common good or interest. Legal protection can be given to the *civil* rights of homosexual persons and of heterosexual persons who cohabitate without declaring their unions "marriage."[29]

Pope Benedict XVI's Encyclical *Deus Caritas Est* ("God Is Love")

In *Deus Caritas Est* Benedict declares that the "love between man and woman" is the "very epitome of love." The love he is talking about is the love between husband and wife, i.e., marital or conjugal love. This love, moreover, has an essentially *bodily* component: Thus in the text just cited, he emphasized that in this love between husband and wife "body and soul are inseparably joined" (no. 2). In another paragraph of the encyclical he stressed that "man is a being made up of body and soul... [and] is truly himself when his body and soul are intimately united; the challenge of *eros* can be said to be truly overcome when this unification is achieved.... [In addition] Christian faith... has always considered man a unity in duality, a reality in which spirit and matter compenetrate, and in which each is brought to a new nobility" (no. 5). Of great significance, too, is this passage from the encyclical: "Corresponding to the image of a monotheistic God is monogamous marriage. Marriage based on exclusive and definitive love becomes the icon of the relationship between God and his people and vice versa. God's way of loving becomes the measure of human love" (no. 11).

III. Sexual Activity Within the Covenant of Marriage

The Church clearly teaches that marital intercourse is good and holy when the choice to engage in such intercourse is properly marital. As Vatican II has stated: "Married love is uniquely expressed and perfected by the exercise of the acts proper to marriage. Hence the acts in marriage by which the intimate and chaste union of the spouses takes place are noble and honorable; the truly human performance of these acts fosters the self-giving they signify and enriches the spouses in joy and gratitude" (*Gaudium et Spes*, no. 49).

This teaching of the Second Vatican Council, as we shall show in the chapters to follow, is by no means new. It is rooted in the biblical understanding of the bodily, personal union between husband and wife (cf., for instance, the Song of Songs), and was clearly recognized by the great theologians of the Middle Ages. It gradually received greater attention in magisterial teaching over the last few centuries. Clearer teaching on this matter was occasioned by the development of modern secular humanism with its often distorted views about the goodness of sexual pleasure and other forms of human fulfillment. Especially in the twentieth century the popes have sought to clarify the authentic goods of human sexuality fostered and protected by the covenant of marriage in the face of the hedonistic and subjectivist values of secular humanism — Benedict XVI continues these efforts in the twenty-first century, and no doubt his successors will of necessity do so also. The secular humanist view of values has enough truth in it to make it appear initially plausible, and it has become dominant in much of modern Western society; but its shortcomings make it a real threat to the genuine humanism, rooted in a profound respect for the inviolable dignity of human persons, which the Church proclaims.

To stress the authentic goodness of marital love, Pope Pius XI taught that the decision of the spouses to engage in the marital act can be virtuous, even when they know that procreation is impossible. He recognized that "the cultivation of mutual love" is a worthy purpose in such circumstances.[30] Pius XII taught that spouses may rightly and gratefully seek the pleasure which accompanies their marital intercourse. He carefully distinguished his position from the condemned view that marital intercourse may be properly sought *solely* for the sake of pleasure.[31] He clearly taught, however, that the Creator in his goodness and wisdom has willed to make use of the work of the man and the woman to preserve and propagate the human race, by joining them in wedlock. The same Creator has arranged that the husband and wife find pleasure and happiness of mind and body in carrying out that noble mission. Consequently, the husband and wife do no wrong in seeking out and enjoying this pleasure. They are accepting what the Creator intended for them.[32]

Pius went on to articulate the Church's basic standard for evaluating these pleasures, which is, in fact, the Church's basic standard for evaluating sexual activity: "This, therefore, is the rule to be followed: the use of the natural, generative instinct and function is lawful in the married state only, and in the service of the purposes for which marriage exists. It follows from this that only in the married state and in the observation of these laws are the desires and enjoyment of that pleasure and satisfaction allowed."[33] The purposes to which he refers are, of course, the goods pursued in the marital act — the good of offspring and the good of faithful marital love. I have noted already and will do so later that these are the "goods" named in the *Catechism of the Catholic Church*, following the teaching of the 1983 *Code of Canon Law*, i.e., the "good of the spouses" and the "good of procreating and educating new life."

The moral norm stated by Pius XII was reaffirmed by the Second Vatican Council and subsequent popes. Vatican II emphasized that decisions about sexual activity within marriage should be guided by objective criteria "drawn from the nature of the human person and human action," and should "respect the total meaning of mutual self-giving and human procreation in the context of true love" (*Gaudium et Spes*, no. 51). The Council Fathers continued by stressing that spouses would be able to honor these criteria and respect these goods only by seriously practicing the virtue of marital chastity.

Paul VI makes a similar point in *Humanae Vitae*. He teaches that any marital act which separates the procreative from the unitive significance of marriage and the marital act is wrong. This separation is wrong because one cannot properly respect and foster these goods if one deliberately separates them, when one intentionally repudiates either one. Thus Paul VI rejected contraceptive acts because by freely choosing to contracept one intentionally repudiates the procreative meaning of the marital act, severing it from its unitive meaning, and by so doing harms both of them. He also rejected sexual acts imposed on one's spouse without regard for his or her condition or legitimate desires, since such sexual acts fail to respect the good of marital union.[34] The teaching of *Humanae Vitae* has been vigorously reaffirmed by John Paul II, most notably in *Familiaris Consortio*.[35]

John Paul II has provided a succinct, clear, and powerful summary of the Church's teaching on this matter in the following passage:

> Sexuality, by means of which man and woman give themselves to one another through the acts which are proper and exclusive to spouses, is by no means something purely biological, but concerns the innermost being of the human person as such. It is realized in a truly human way only if it is an integral part of the love by which a man and a woman commit themselves totally to one another until death. The total physical self-giving would be a lie if it were not the sign and fruit of a total personal self-giving, in which the whole person, including the temporal dimension, is present; if the person were to withhold something or reserve the possibility of deciding otherwise in the future, by this very fact he or she would not be giving totally. (*Familiaris Consortio*, no. 11)

The *Catechism of the Catholic Church,* as I noted earlier, in Part Two: "The Celebration of the Christian Mystery," Article Seven: "The Sacrament of Matrimony," declared that "the matrimonial covenant... is by its nature ordered toward the good of the spouses and the procreation... of offspring" (no. 1601). In Part Three: "Life in Christ," Section Two: "The Seven Sacraments of the Church," Article Six: "The Sixth Commandment," it declares: "Sexuality is ordered to the conjugal love of man and woman. In marriage the physical intimacy of the spouses becomes a sign and pledge of spiritual communion" (no. 2360). It then declares:

> The spouses' union achieves the twofold end of marriage: the good of the spouses themselves and the transmission of life. These two meanings or values of marriage cannot be separated without altering the couple's spiritual life and compromising the goods of marriage and the future of the family.
>
> The conjugal love of man and woman thus stands under the twofold obligation of fidelity and fecundity. (*CCC*, no. 2363)[36]

To conclude this section it is worth noting an observation of Pius XII which forms an important part of the evaluation of modern attitudes toward sexuality on the part of recent popes. Pius disputed the popular view that "happiness in married life is in direct proportion to the mutual enjoyment of marital relations." He recognizes, as we have seen, that sexual pleasure adds to the joy of marriage; but he also teaches that it is not basic. Marriage has far greater goods to rejoice in. "Happiness in marital life," he wrote, "is in direct ratio to the respect husband and wife have for each other, even in the intimate act of marriage."[37] They respect each other by treating each other as irreplaceable persons, committed to a common life in which each fosters the uniquely exclusive conjugal love for each other and the great goods of marriage.

IV. The Immorality of Sexual Activity Outside the Covenant of Marriage

In proclaiming the norms of sexual behavior rooted in God's law and in respect for the inviolable dignity of human persons and the goods of human sexuality, the magisterium has always taught, as the previous section has indicated, that it is seriously wrong to choose to engage in any sexual activity that is not authentically marital. From the first days of the Church, pastoral leaders taught, as Scripture had, that those who engage in fornication, gross indecency, and sexual irresponsibility "... shall not inherit the kingdom of God" (Gal 5:19-21). Moreover, the magisterium has always proposed its teaching on these matters as being the teaching of God himself, as revealed in Scripture. This is clearly shown by both the *Roman Catechism*, promulgated after the Council of Trent in the sixteenth century and in use until the present century, and by the *Catechism of the Catholic Church*, written in response to Vatican Council II and promulgated by John Paul II, who describes it as "a sure norm for teaching the faith."[38] The *Roman Catechism*, in condemning adultery, fornication, prostitution, and homosexual acts, listed them as violations of the sixth commandment — that is, as acts prohibited by Scripture.[39] The *Catechism of the Catholic Church* begins its treatment of the sixth commandment and its requirements by citing Exodus 20:14 and Deuteronomy 5:18, where we read, "You shall not commit adultery," and Matthew 5:27-28, where Jesus says, "You have heard that it was said, 'You shall not commit adultery.' But I say to you that every one who looks at a woman lustfully has already committed adultery with her in his heart." It goes on to condemn as absolutely immoral and opposed to the virtue of chastity and the dignity of marriage the sins of masturbation, fornication, pornography, prostitution, rape, homosexual acts, adultery, divorce, and polygamy, incest, and "free unions" (see the *Catechism of the Catholic Church*, nos. 2351-2359, 2380-2391, 2396, 2400). From earliest times the magisterium has regarded masturbation and contraception among the grossly indecent and sexually irresponsible acts which exclude their perpetrators from God's kingdom.[40]

The reasons for these teachings are spelled out in later chapters. But it is clear that the Church presents this teaching as based not only on the most serious of reasons but also on the basis of her faith in God's revelation. She has received a teaching from God which she must proclaim both to be true to her mission and to protect the dignity of human persons and human sexuality. This teaching expresses a loving concern to preserve the real meaning and goodness of marital love and to foster human dignity in intimate personal relations. Pope John Paul II has articulated these considerations as follows:

> The only "place" in which this self-giving [of man to woman] in its whole truth is made possible is marriage, the covenant of conjugal love freely and consciously chosen, whereby man and woman accept the intimate community of life and love willed by God Himself, which only in this light manifests its true meaning. The institution of marriage is not an undue... imposition of a form. Rather, it is an interior requirement of the covenant of conjugal love which is publicly affirmed as unique and exclusive, in order to live in complete fidelity to the plan of God, the Creator. A person's freedom, far from being restricted by this fidelity, is secured against every form of subjectivism or relativism and is made a sharer in creative Wisdom. (*Familiaris Consortio*, no. 11)

The kind of reasoning exhibited here will be developed further and applied to particular sexual activities in the final chapters of this work. The point here is simply that the Church's teaching on sexual matters is always presented both as the revealed will of God and also as eminently reasonable. The Catholic vision of sexuality teaches a way of living sexually which is liberating and genuinely good for human beings. Those who reflect carefully in the light of faith can see and experience this for themselves.

ENDNOTES FOR CHAPTER ONE

1. See St. Thomas Aquinas, *Summa Theologiae*, 1, q. 1, a. 1.

2. See Germain Grisez, *The Way of the Lord Jesus*, vol. 1, *Christian Moral Principles*, ch. 35, qq. F and G for a brief, clear, and accurate account of the assent due to teachings of this kind. See also William E. May, *An Introduction to Moral Theology*, 2nd ed. (Huntington, IN: Our Sunday Visitor, 2003), pp. 257-264.

The Congregation for the Doctrine of the Faith's 1990 *Instruction on the Ecclesial Vocation of the Theologian* discusses this issue in some detail, providing a helpful commentary on the nature of the "religious submission" that the Fathers of Vatican Council II said is to be given to such authoritative but noninfallibly proposed magisterial teachings. It clearly distinguishes between *questions* that can be raised about such teachings (nos. 24-31) and *dissent* from such teachings (nos. 32-41). It holds that questioning can be compatible with the "religious assent" required, but it firmly and decisively repudiates dissent from these teachings as incompatible with this required religious assent. It recognizes that one might, in a given instance, *suspend* or *withhold* assent, so long as this is accompanied by a willingness to submit one's questions to the magisterium and to accept the magisterium's judgment about these questions. But dissent is *not* compatible with this "religious submission."

Pope John Paul II rightly points out that "no damage must be done to the *harmony between faith and life: the unity of the Church* is damaged not only by Christians who reject or distort the truths of faith but also by those who disregard the moral obligations to which they are called by the Gospel (cf. 1 Cor 5:9-13)" (*Veritatis Splendor*, no. 26). He emphasizes that "*dissent... is opposed to ecclesial communion and to a correct understanding of the hierarchical constitution of the People of God*" (no. 113).

3. Vatican Council II, *Lumen Gentium*, no. 25: "Although the bishops, taken individually, do not enjoy the privilege of infallibility, they do, however, proclaim the doctrine of Christ infallibly on the following conditions: namely, when, even though dispersed throughout the entire world but preserving for all that amongst themselves and with Peter's successor the bond of communion, in their authoritative teaching concerning matters of faith or *morals*, they are in agreement

that a particular teaching is to be held definitively and absolutely"
(emphasis added; cf. Vatican Council I, *Dei Filius*, DS 3011 [DS
refers to *Enchiridion Symbolorum Definitionum et Declarationum de
Rebus Fidei et Morum*, ed. Henricus Denzinger and Adolphus Schön-
metzer, 36th ed. (Freiburg: Herder, 1976). Hereafter this volume will
be referred to as DS followed by the paragraph number or numbers
— in this case, for example, DS 3011.])

Some theologians today contend that no specific moral teachings
of the Church have been infallibly proposed. In fact, some claim that
the Church *cannot* propose specific moral norms infallibly. From this
claim they draw the conclusion that one may reject moral teachings
of the Church, such as those relating to sexual ethics, which have
been universally proposed as necessary for salvation if one judges he
has good reasons to do so. This question is examined in Chapter 5.
Representative statements of this position can be found in the following sources: Francis Sullivan, S.J., *Magisterium: Teaching Authority in
the Church* (New York: Paulist, 1983), ch. 6; Charles E. Curran et al.,
Dissent in and for the Church (New York: Sheed and Ward, 1969); and
Daniel Maguire, "Moral Absolutes and the Magisterium," pp. 57-107
of *Absolutes in Moral Theology?*, ed. Charles E. Curran (Washington,
DC: Corpus, 1968). This radical and spurious claim completely fails
to take into consideration the infallibility of the ordinary and universal magisterium as exercised by the bishops of the entire world, teaching in union with the pope that specific matters of the moral life must
be held definitively (cf. *Lumen Gentium*, no. 25). For detailed exposi-
tions of the serious deficiencies in the reasoning of these theologians
see the following: Germain Grisez, *The Way of the Lord Jesus*, vol. 1,
Christian Moral Principles (Chicago: Franciscan Herald Press, 1983),
ch. 35; William E. May, *An Introduction to Moral Theology*, 2nd ed.
(Huntington, IN: Our Sunday Visitor, 2003), pp. 257-264. For an
explanation of the background and theological context of *Lumen
Gentium*, no. 25, see John C. Ford, S.J., and Germain Grisez, "Contraception and the Infallibility of the Ordinary Magisterium," *Theological Studies*, 39 (1978), 263-267, reprinted in Germain Grisez et al.,
Humanae Vitae: A Defense of the Encyclical (San Francisco: Ignatius,
1998). On the competency of the magisterium in matters of morals
see Ronald D. Lawler, O.F.M. Cap., "The Magisterium and Catholic
Moral Teaching," in *Persona, Verità e Morale: Atti del Congresso Inter-*

nazionale di Teologia Morale (Roma, 7-12 aprile 1986) (Rome: Città Nuova Editrice, 1987), pp. 217-233; T. Lopez, "'Fides et Mores' en Trento," *Scripta theologica* 5 (1973), 175-221; Jacques Marie Aubert, "Le Magistère Morale de l'Église," *La foi et les temps* (August 1981), 311-333.

Moreover, the *Instruction on the Ecclesial Vocation of the Theologian*, issued by the Congregation for the Doctrine of the Faith on May 24, 1990, explicitly taught that "Revelation also contains moral teachings which *per se* could be known by natural reason. Access to them, however, is made difficult by man's sinful condition. *It is a doctrine of faith that these moral norms can be infallibly taught by the Magisterium*" (no. 16, with reference to Vatican Council I, Dogmatic Constitution *Dei Filius*, ch. 2, DS 3005).

Finally, in his 1995 encyclical *Evangelium Vitae* Pope John Paul II, invoking his papal authority and after consulting with all the bishops of the world, authoritatively reaffirmed as Catholic teaching the truth that all intentional killing of innocent human beings, all directly procured abortions, and all acts of mercy killing or euthanasia are gravely immoral, and each time he referred explicitly to the teaching of *Lumen Gentium*, no. 25, concerning the infallibility of the *universal and ordinary magisterium of the Church*. He clearly taught that these specific moral norms have been and are infallibly proposed by the magisterium (see *Evangelium Vitae*, nos. 57, 62, 65).

4. St. Thomas Aquinas, *Quodlibetum* IX, q. 8.

5. An exceptionally valuable source for magisterial teaching on marriage and family and sexual issues is provided by the six-volume work *Enchiridion Familiae: Textos del Magistero Pontificio y Conciliar sobre el Matrimonio y la Familia (Siglos I a XX)*. This work, edited by Augusto Sarmiento and Javier Escriva-Ivars, was published jointly in 1992 by the Instituto de Ciencias para la Familia of the University of Navarre and the Istituto Giovanni Paolo II per Studi su Matrimonio e Famiglia. This multi-volume work provides texts on marriage and family found in the papal and conciliar magisterium from the time of Pope Clement of Rome in A.D. 97 until 1988 during the pontificate of Pope John Paul II. Volume 1 includes material from Clement of Rome (97) up to and including Pius XI (1939); volume 2 incorporates texts from Pius XII (1939-1958) and John XXIII (1958-1963); volume 3 has texts from Paul VI (1963-1978), John Paul I (1978), and

John Paul II (1978-1980); volume 4 provides texts from John Paul II (1981-1982); and volume 5 texts from John Paul II (1983-1988). Volume 6 is a masterful index to the previous five volumes. The texts of the magisterium are given in their original language (Latin, Italian, French, Spanish, English, etc.) in the bottom half of the page and in a Spanish translation the first half of each page.

The finest single-volume study of marriage and family in the documents of the magisterium is that of Ramón García de Haro, *Marriage and the Family in the Documents of the Magisterium: A Course in the Theology of Marriage* (2nd ed.: San Francisco: Ignatius Press, 1993), tr. William E. May. Unfortunately this book is now out of print.

6. See *Enchiridion Familiae* [hereafter *EF*], 1.

7. See Lateran Council II, March 4, 1139, Canon 23 (DS 718; *EF* 1.104); Lateran Council IV, February 4, 1215, Canon 1 (DS 802; *EF* 1.125), "Not only virgins and the continent but also the married, pleasing to God by true faith and good action, will be judged worthy of attaining eternal beatitude."

8. Innocent III, "Letter to the Archbishop of Terragona," December 18, 1208, *Ejus Exemplo* (DS 795; *EF* 1.124).

9. Among other documents affirming the same truth are the following: First Council of Toledo, October 400, Canon 236 (DS 206; *EF* 1. 16); Council of Braga, May 1, 563, Canons 11 to 13 (DS 461-463; *EF* 1.41); Council of Florence, *Decree Pro Jacobitis*, February 4, 1442 (DS 1353; *EF* 1.139-140).

10. On this see G. H. Joyce, *Christian Marriage: History and Doctrine* (London: Sheed & Ward, 1933), and L. Godfroy, G. Le Bras, M. Jugie, article "Marriage," in *Dictionnaire de Théologie*, Vol. IX-2, 2040-2335. Although dated, these two sources remain two of the best and most comprehensive studies available. See also Edward Schillebeeckx, *Marriage: Human Reality and Saving Mystery*, tr. N. D. Smith (New York: Sheed and Ward, 1965), esp. pp. 244-260, and the fine study of G. Baldanza, "La grazia sacamentale matrimoniale al Concilio di Trento. Contributo per uno studio storico-critico," *Ephemerides Liturgicae* 98 (1983), 89-140.

11. Council of Florence, bull *Exultate*, November 22, 1439 (DS 1327; *EF* 1.139).

12. See Council of Trent, Session 24, 1563; DS 1797-1812; *EF* 1.141-146. In the canons following this dogmatic decree Trent sol-

emnly proclaimed the indissolubility of marriage — not even adultery can sever the bond between husband and wife — its sacramental character, and the Church's God-given authority over marriage. See ibid. An excellent analysis of the teaching of the Council of Trent on marriage is given by García de Haro, *Marriage and Family in the Documents of the Church*, pp. 64-79.

13. Pope Leo XIII, encyclical, *Arcanum Divinae Sapientiae*, in *Official Catholic Teachings: Love and Sexuality*, ed. Odile M. Liebard (Wilmington, NC: McGrath, 1978), nos. 3, 5, 6, pp. 2-3, 4-5. [*NOTE*: Hereafter *Official Catholic Teachings: Love and Sexuality* will be referred to as Liebard's *Love and Sexuality*.] See also *EF* 1.147-153.

14. A fine summary and analysis of *Casti Connubii* is given by García de Haro, *Marriage and Family in the Documents of the Magisterium*, pp. 107-145. The text of *Casti Connubii* is found in Liebard's *Love and Sexuality*, pp. 40-47, and in *EF* 1.709-794.

15. García de Haro, *Marriage and Family in the Documents of the Magisterium*, pp. 147-194, provides a detailed analysis of the teaching of Pope Pius XII on marriage.

16. It should be noted that the Council Fathers refer in a footnote at this point in the text to the threefold good of marriage originally articulated by St. Augustine and long since appropriated by the magisterium.

17. García de Haro offers an exceptionally comprehensive account and analysis of the teaching of Vatican Council II on marriage in his *Marriage and Family in the Documents of the Magisterium*, pp. 211-282.

18. See García de Haro, *Marriage and Family in the Documents of the Magisterium*, pp. 283-332, for a detailed analysis of the teaching of Paul VI on marriage and marital sexual morality.

19. In 1960, while still a professor of moral philosophy at the University of Lublin, he wrote a very probing study of human sexuality, sexual morality, marriage, and the family, *Love and Responsibility*. This book, translated by H. Willetts, was published in English in 1981 by Farrar, Straus, Giroux, and has since been republished by Ignatius Press.

20. The best contemporary English source for these audiences or "catecheses" is Pope John Paul II, *"Man and Woman He Created Them": A Theology of the Body*, translation, Introduction, and Index by Michael Waldstein (Boston: Pauline Books & Media, 2006), referred to hereafter as Waldstein *TOB*.

21. Here it is worth noting that of the 5,127 pages of text found in *Enchiridion Familiae,* more than 2,600 provide magisterial documents from the pontificate of John Paul II, and this series concludes with the year 1988.

22. Pope John Paul II, Address of December 22, 1981, in which John Paul II presented his new apostolic exhortation. Text in *EF*, 14.3415f.

23. Part One is entitled, "Bright Spots and Shadows for the Family Today," and offers both an analysis of the contemporary situation facing the family and presents anew the most important moral principles necessary for an adequate solution to modern problems. Part Two is called "The Plan of God for Marriage and the Family" and discusses the meaning of marriage and its fundamental structure as designed by God and integrated into the economy of grace by Jesus. Part Three, the longest of the document, is called "The Role of the Christian Family," and takes up in great depth the indispensable and necessary role that the Christian family plays in (1) forming a community of love, (2) serving life, (3) serving the wider human community, and (4) participating in the redemptive mission of the Church. The final part, Part Four, called "Pastoral Care of the Family: Stages, Structures, Agents and Situations," gives explicit attention to situations of greater difficulty confronting marriage and family life today.

24. See García de Haro, *Marriage and Family in the Documents of the Magisterium*, pp. 333-408, for an analysis of the teaching of John Paul II on marriage and family.

25. *Catechism of the Catholic Church*, no. 1601, citing *Code of Canon Law*, Canon 1055, par. 1.

26. See my essay, co-authored with my wife Patricia, "The 'Good of the Spouses' and Marriage as a Vocation to Holiness," in *The Church, Marriage, & The Family: Proceedings from the 27th Annual Convention of the Fellowship of Catholic Scholars*, September 24-26, 2004, Pittsburgh, PA, ed. Kenneth Whitehead (South Bend, IN: St. Augustine's Press, 2007), pp. 75-94. See also Dominic Kimengich, *The Bonum Coniugum: A Canonical Appraisal* (Romae: Pontificium Athenaeum Sanctae Crucis, 1997).

27. I believe that the following addresses given from 2005 to 2007 are most significant: 1. Address to Participants in the Ecclesial Diocesan Convention of Rome, June 6, 2005; 2. Address to Members of the

Pontifical John Paul II Institute for Studies on Marriage and Family on the 25th Anniversary of Its Founding, May 11, 2006; 3. Address to Participants in the Plenary Session of the Pontifical Council for the Family, May 13, 2006; 4. Address to the Fifth World Meeting of Families, Valencia, Spain, July 8, 2006; and 5. Address to Members of the Tribunal of the Roman Rota, January 27, 2007. In 2008, the 50th anniversary of Paul VI's *Humanae Vitae*, he gave many addresses in commemorating it and re-affirming the Church's teaching on the grave immorality of contraception.

28. See Rita Joseph, *Human Rights and the Unborn Child* (Leiden/ Boston: Martinus Nijhoff, 2009).

29. Congregation for the Doctrine of the Faith, *Considerations Regarding Proposals to Give Legal Recognition to Unions Between Homosexual Persons*, July 31, 2003.

30. Pius XI, *Casti Connubii*, in Liebard's *Love and Sexuality*, no. 84, p. 42.

31. The condemned view is that there is no fault whatsoever in seeking marital intercourse "solely for the sake of pleasure" — that is, without considering the goods to which marriage is ordered. For the condemnation, see "Decree of the Holy Office," March 2, 1679; DS 2109.

32. Pius XII, "Address to Midwives," October 29, 1951; in Liebard's *Love and Sexuality*, p. 119.

33. Ibid., pp. 119-120.

34. Paul VI, *Humanae Vitae*, nos. 12-13.

35. See John Paul II, *Familiaris Consortio*, nos. 28-32; the new *Code of Canon Law*, Canon 1061, no. 1, states that an act which consummates marriage must be one open both to the transmission of life and to the fostering of love. The new code was approved by John Paul II on January 25, 1983.

36. Thus the *Catechism of the Catholic Church* declares: "Sexuality is ordered to the conjugal love of man and woman. In marriage the physical intimacy of the spouses becomes a sign and pledge of spiritual communion.... The spouses' union achieves the twofold end of marriage: the good of the spouses themselves and the transmission of life. These two meanings or values of marriage cannot be separated without altering the couple's spiritual life and compromising the goods of marriage and the future of the family. The conjugal love of

man and woman thus stands under the twofold obligation of fidelity and fecundity" (nos. 2360, 2363).

37. Pius XII, "Address to Midwives," in Liebard's *Love and Sexuality*, p. 121.

38. John Paul II, *Fidei Depositum,* Part IV, Par. 1, available at http://www.vatican.va/holy_father/john_paul_ii/apost_constitutions /documents/hf_jp-ii_apc_19921011_fidei-depositum_en.html.

39. *Roman Catechism*, also known as *The Catechism of the Council of Trent,* Part Three: The Ten Commandments: The Sixth Commandment.

40. See St. Leo IX, "Letter to St. Peter Damian," 1054; DS 687-688; "Decree of the Holy Office," March 2, 1679; DS 2109. Congregation for the Doctrine of the Faith, *Declaration on Certain Questions Concerning Sexual Ethics*, December 29, 1975.

CHAPTER TWO

The Biblical Teaching on Sex

In its *Dogmatic Constitution on Divine Revelation* Vatican Council II declared: "All the preaching of the Church, as indeed the entire Christian religion, should be nourished and ruled by sacred Scripture" (*Dei Verbum*, no. 21).

The study of the biblical teaching on human sexuality is then appropriate and necessary, for Scripture is the primary fount of the Church's teaching. This chapter will offer a review of this teaching, based on the work of excellent contemporary exegetes and biblical theologians, and of other persons qualified to expound on the biblical teaching on human sexuality, marriage, and the morality of freely chosen sexual acts.

I. The Old Testament

The Old Testament is not, nor was it intended to be, a textbook either on morality in general or on sexual morality in particular. But it is the record, written under divine inspiration, of God's revelation to his chosen people, preparing them and the whole of humanity for his definitive revelation in and through the life, death, and resurrection of his only-begotten Son made man, Jesus Christ. As such, it articulates fundamental truths about God himself and the created universe, and in particular, about human life and destiny, and the special relationship of friendship that he wills to exist between himself and human beings and between men and women. It reveals to us, too, the source of "shame, both 'immanent' and 'sexual'" regarding the body. This source is the sinful concupiscence that entered the human heart as a result of original sin and the "veiling," as it were, of the "spousal significance" of the body.[1] Nonetheless, these Old Testament accounts of creation also point ahead to the One who will be our Redeemer. It is not surprising, therefore, that the Old Testament contains fundamental truths about human sexuality and its place in human life and the divine economy. These truths have lasting significance and are relevant today.

The Context of Old Testament Teaching on Sex

The proper perspective for understanding the Old Testament's teaching on sexual matters is provided by the fundamental concerns of this first stage of divine revelation. These concerns cluster around the Hebrew awareness of the reality of God, his holiness, and his covenant with the people Israel and, through them, with all humankind. The God of Israel, utterly unlike the "no gods" of their pagan neighbors, is a holy God. He is good, and he cares about the moral quality of our actions. Israel's conviction about the holiness and moral character of the one true God is reflected in the life of the people. The Old Testament itself explicitly claims that in sexual matters its ways are in sharp contrast to the practices of the surrounding peoples (cf. Lev 18:3, 24-30; cf. also Gen 34:7; Judg 19:30; 2 Sam 13:12).[2] Indeed, as John L. McKenzie has observed, "the *morality of sex* is far more rigorous in Israel than among its neighbors. It is not merely fanciful to see in this a reflection of the character of Yahweh himself in contrast to the gods and goddesses of the fertility cults. Sexual license profanes the holiness of a God who is above all sexual processes."[3]

The Hebrews saw sexuality primarily in moral terms, and they understood morality in the light of their faith in God and in the light of what was taught them in God's name. Morality thus understood was primarily a way of response to the love of the all-holy God as revealed to them in the various covenants God offered them. All of human life, including sexual life, was seen as a worshiping service of God. This was so because God, who gave to human persons the gift of life and of sexuality, wanted his people to be holy, as he is holy.

In this summary of Old Testament teaching on sex, attention will center first on the first two chapters of Genesis, the "beginning," to which Jesus himself referred in his response to the question about divorce posed to him by the Pharisees (cf. Mk 10:2-12; Mt 19:3-12). For these chapters describe God's original design for human existence, human sexuality, and human marriage. The third chapter of Genesis is also central inasmuch as it treats of the disobedience of our first parents, and the terrible effects of their sin on human existence, human sexuality, and the relationship between men and women. Following the analysis of these Genesis texts, other teachings of the Old Testament on sex will be summarized.

Genesis 1-2: Human Sexuality and Marriage

The first two chapters of Genesis, the "creation accounts," are central for understanding the teaching of the Old Testament on marriage and human sexuality. These chapters, which contain the stories of what Pope John Paul II has called the "beatifying beginning of human existence,"[4] have been shaped into a harmonious whole, although they include two distinct accounts — the Priestly narrative of Genesis 1:2-2:4a and the Yahwist narrative of Genesis 2:4b-25. Though these two accounts differ in many ways, they share certain central common themes. Thus, for instance, each was written in a deliberate effort to counter the stories of human origins current among Israel's pagan neighbors, in particular, the myth of Baal and its accompanying fertility cult. That account of human origins and of human life and sexuality was utterly incompatible with faith in the God of Abraham, Isaac, and Jacob because it divinized human sexuality and portrayed the gods as sexual beings, capable, like men, of the unrestrained passion of lust. Biblical scholar John L. McKenzie has brilliantly shown this.[5] Other features common to the two accounts will be noted below. But first we will summarize and comment on the key teachings of each account.

Genesis 1:1-31, 2:1-4a — The First Account of the Creation of the Universe and the Creation of Marriage

The narrative of Genesis 1:1-31, 2:1-4a, attributed to the Priestly tradition (chronologically later than the Yahwist tradition that is the source of Genesis 2:4b-25), expresses many great truths about human persons, human sexuality, and marriage.[6] First, it unequivocally affirms the fundamental equality of man and woman as persons made in the image and likeness of God, and uses the Hebrew word `adam (man) as a generic term, not a proper name, to refer to both the man and the woman: "So God created man [`adam] in his own image, in the image of God he created him; male and female he created them" (Gen 1:27). Each, the male and the female, is a different but complementary epiphany or revelation of God himself, whose full image is found in their communion.[7]

Another great truth expressed by Genesis 1 is that human sexual activity is not something divine. It is not something that God engages in, nor is it a means of currying favor from the gods, as it was understood to be in the fertility cults. Sexuality, rather, is a great and good gift of God to human persons, male and female. Through their sexuality men and women image him in the world.[8] Moreover, through their responsible exercise of their sexual powers in the pursuit of the great goods toward which sexuality is ordered, they honor God.

A third great truth of this account is that God is the author of marriage. Genesis 1 speaks not only of God's creation of man, male and female, but also of his creation of marriage. Indeed, it was in the first Adam, the first human beings, male and female, "that God himself constituted the essential structure of marriage between man and woman — the structure that we should expect to encounter in every marriage."[9]

A fourth great truth of this account of human origins is that human fertility is a blessing, not a curse: "And God blessed them, and God said to them, 'Be fruitful and multiply, and fill the earth and subdue it'" (Gen 1:28). The marital union is one upon which the blessing of fertility can descend. Children are a gift from God, the fruit of his blessing.[10]

Genesis 2:4b-25

The narrative in Genesis 2, stemming from the earlier Yahwist tradition, is more poetic in character. It, too, contains many truths about human existence, human sexuality, and marriage,[11] in poetic language and imagery. Unlike the text in Genesis 1, which speaks of the simultaneous creation of male and female and which uses the term `adam (man) to designate both, this passage speaks first of the creation of man as male and uses the word `adam to identify this male. This being is alone in the universe, utterly different from and superior to the other animals, and this is the first great truth of this narrative, namely, that *man* [and here "man" signifies both male and female beings], *unlike other animals, is alone before God in the visible universe.* None of these animals is his equal; he exercises authority over them all. This authority is symbolized by his being given the power to name all the animals (cf. Gen 2:19-20).[12] To give the first man a "helper fit for him," that is, a being equal in dignity to him, the Lord God then makes the "woman," fashioned from the man's own ribs.

A second magnificent truth that Genesis 2 articulates is *the complementary character of man and woman,* who are made for each other and meant to live in an intimate communion of persons. The very first words of the man (`adam*) in this text ("this at last is bone of my bones...") are a short poem expressing, in wondrous delight, a vision of the relation meant to exist between man and woman.[13] The helper, the woman, is a person equal to the man (`adam*), but she is not his clone. She is woman (*ishshah*) because she is taken from man (*ish*), but differs from him. Communion is between two likes who are yet unlike. In naming her, moreover, the man (`adam*) himself assumes a new name (*ish*). Sharing bone and flesh forms a totally human basis for an interpersonal and covenantal relationship made possible by God's action.[14] The woman is given to the man by God. Without her the man, in his solitude, is in a situation that is "not good." She is taken from him and given to him so that, together, they may be what they cannot be alone. There is a complementarity between them that permits them to form a true communion of persons when they become "one flesh," cleaving to each other as husband and wife.

"Cleaving" (Gen 2:24) implies a devotion and an unshakable faith between humans: it connotes a permanent attraction that transcends genital union, to which, nevertheless, it gives meaning. There can be no mistaking the author's intention. The author of Genesis 2 concludes his narrative by interpreting the divinely ordered sexual differentiation and the sexual drive within the perspective of a permanent social union between man and woman.

Genesis 2 also suggests the great truth that marriage comes into being when a man and a woman "give" themselves to each other by a free act of irrevocable personal consent. Pope John Paul II eloquently expresses this in his reflection on the text of Genesis 2:18-24, which describes in poetic terms the "creation" of woman. "When the first man exclaims at the sight of the woman: 'she is flesh from my flesh and bone from my bones' (Gen 2:23), he simply affirms," the pope says, "the human identity of both. By exclaiming this, he seems to say: *'Look, a body that expresses the person.'*" Genesis 2:24 then says that "a man leaves his father and his mother and clings to his wife, and the they become one flesh." Just as a man belongs by nature to his parents, so he belongs by *choice* to his wife and she to him.[15]

A third great truth about man and woman as created by God and prior to their disobedience is expressed in the remark that "... and the man and his wife were both naked, and were not ashamed" (Gen 2:25).[16] By stating that the man and the woman were naked and felt no shame, the sacred author refers to a mode of existence for the man and his wife beyond our experience. He indicates that they have a distinctive form of integrity, which permitted a spontaneous and unveiled communication between them. This truth, central to the teaching of Genesis 2, is what John Paul II seeks to communicate by speaking of the "spousal meaning" of the body.[17] Since the naked bodies of both the man and the woman, the husband and the wife, perfectly manifest their dignity as persons and, because of their complementarity, the "gift" that each is for the other, they feel no shame.[18]

Another truth that Genesis 2, like Genesis 1, makes clear is that God is the author of marriage. Genesis 2, as Johannes Bauer emphasizes, proclaims "monogamy as ordained and willed by God."[19] Genesis 2 does not explicitly talk about the procreative nature of the marital union, but it nonetheless presupposes it. Genesis 2 forms a literary unit with Genesis 3 and 4, and Genesis 4:1 affirms that "Now Adam knew Eve his wife, and she conceived and bore Cain, saying, 'I have gotten a man with the help of the LORD.'" This shows that "the establishment of the first family was the solution to the man's need for social life and for a race to fulfill his commission.... In creating woman and coupling her with the man, God created one flesh that could be the source of the family."[20]

Genesis 3

The third chapter of Genesis, also from the Yahwist tradition, tells of the primordial sin by the first man and woman. As a result of their sin — their rebellion against God — the man and the woman find themselves alienated from God, from each other, and even from their own sexuality. They now experience shame over their nakedness, for after their sin "... the eyes of both were opened, and they knew that they were naked" (Gen 3:7). Concupiscence had entered the human heart. As a result, one can truly say: "Man, alas, is not such a perfect being that the sight of the body of another person, especially a person of the other sex, can arouse in him merely a disinterested liking which develops into an innocent affection. In practice, it also arouses concupiscence, or a wish to enjoy concentrated on sexual values with no regard for the value of the person."[21]

The "spousal meaning" of the bodies of men and women has, as it were, been veiled; concupiscence makes itself felt.[22] The man begins to lord it over his wife, whose social and cultural oppression begins. The treatment of women as inferior to men within Israelite society is the consequence of sin.[23] In his original creation, God intended that man and woman should live harmoniously, in peace and unity. The evil which disrupted their daily lives, even in their most intimate aspects, was the result of human sin.[24]

Key Old Testament Teachings on Sex

First of all, throughout the Old Testament marriage is presented as something holy and good; and sexual union within marriage is portrayed as good when it is mindful of God and his covenant.[25] All this is brought out nicely in the prayer Tobias offers before consummating his union with Sarah:

> "You made Adam, and you made his wife Eve
>   to be his helper and support;
>   and from these two the human race has come.
> You said, 'It is not good for man to be alone;
>   let us make him a helper like himself.'
> Now, not with lust,
>   but with fidelity I take this kinswoman as my wife.
> Send down your mercy on me and on her,
>   and grant that we may grow old together."
>   (Tob 8:6-7, NABRE)

In addition, the prophets, beginning with Hosea and continuing through Isaiah, Jeremiah, and Ezekiel, saw in human marriage a fitting symbol of the covenant between God and his people. In using this image, the prophets were more interested in articulating the truth about God's love, forgiveness, and mercy than they were in spelling out the nature of a loving marriage. Nonetheless, as Schillebeeckx has pointed out, the use of this image by the prophets involves a "reciprocal illumination" of the human meaning of marriage. Their use of this image speaks to us not only of the utterly faithful love of God for his people but also the normative reality of marriage — the divinely intended, faithful, and exclusive union of husband and wife.[26]

It is true that the understanding of marriage among the Hebrews was imperfect. The husband was permitted to divorce his wife, but she was not permitted to divorce him; women were regarded as inferior to men; and there was a double standard for adultery. A married man committed adultery only if he had sexual relations with the wife of another man or with a maiden betrothed to another, but he was not judged guilty of adultery if he had sexual relations with an unbetrothed maiden, a harlot, or slave girl (cf. Deut 22:28-29). But any sexual relations on the part of a married woman or betrothed virgin with any man other than her husband was considered adultery.

These inequalities were rooted in socioeconomic factors within Hebrew society and reflect its patriarchal ethos.[27] While it is true that husbands who had intercourse with prostitutes, unbetrothed maidens, or slave girls were not considered to have committed adultery, their infidelity is severely criticized by the prophets (Mal 2:14-15) and in the Wisdom literature (e.g., Prov 5:15-20).[28] There is abundant evidence in the Old Testament that the very nature and purposes of human sexuality require husbands and wives to be faithful to one another.[29] The story of Joseph and Potiphar's wife (Gen 39), the episode of Abimelech and Sarah (Gen 20), and in particular the teaching set forth in the Wisdom literature give the reasons why adultery is incompatible with married life. Thus it is clear, for instance, from a reading of Proverbs 1-9 that "sexual fidelity is... a symbol of one's attachment to Lady Wisdom," and the upright Israelite man was urged to be attached to Lady Wisdom.[30]

Moreover, the insistence by the prophets (above all, Hosea, Isaiah, Jeremiah, Ezekiel) that the marriage of man and woman is a sign of God's utterly faithful love for his people led to the idea that fidelity was central to a covenanted marriage. This fidelity was so highly valued that restrictions were developed so that a wife could not be too easily abandoned by her spouse. "Marriage," above all, "was to be experienced from the standpoint of an unconditional faith and confidence in Yahweh, since this was the very core of the covenant of grace and it was in this way that man was to express his response to Yahweh's love."[31]

Although fornication is not explicitly condemned in the Old Testament, the rich meaning of sexual union was appreciated ever more deeply by the prophets and the authors of the Wisdom literature. The latter repeatedly counsels husbands and wives to be faithful to one another and speaks glowingly of the happiness of a marriage marked by lifelong fidelity. The advice given young men, especially in the Wisdom literature, strongly supports a negative evaluation of fornication or premarital sexual activity.[32]

The Old Testament vehemently condemns bestiality and homosexuality as reprehensible and abominable. Since human sexuality is ordered to the personal relationship of marriage and the good of children, sexual commerce with a beast is utterly repugnant. To engage in bestiality is to be guilty of a most grievous crime (Ex 22:19; Lev 18:23, 20:15-16; Deut 27:21).

Contemporary biblical scholars differ as to why homosexuality was so strongly condemned in the Old Testament (cf. Lev 18:22, 20:13), and offer different interpretations of the story of Sodom and Gomorrah in Genesis 19. The older Catholic tradition (Fathers, scholastics, manualists) frequently appealed to the Onan story (Gen 38:8-10) to show that the Old Testament condemned masturbation and contraception. A number of contemporary exegetes[33] suggest that the men of Sodom were punished because of inhospitality and that Onan was punished not because of any sexual sin but because he violated the Levirate law, according to which he was obliged to help his widowed sister-in-law Tamar have a child in order to continue his brother's line. This interpretation, although popular today, is sharply challenged by other scholars. Closely analyzing the language used to describe Onan's offense, they point out that God punished him both because of *what* Onan chose to do — to waste his seed on the ground was a perverse sexual act — and because he did this for a base purpose or *end*, namely, to deprive his dead brother of progeny.[34]

II. The New Testament

The principal message of the New Testament is that the long-awaited good news, heralded by the prophets, is now with us.

God himself, through the person of his only-begotten Son made man, Jesus Christ, is establishing his reign of justice, peace, and love, bringing his people and all humankind redemption and salvation. Indeed, God, in and through Jesus, in a most wonderful and unexpected way, is making possible a new kind of intimate friendship and life with himself. God has saved us, through the life, death, and resurrection of Jesus. In and through union with Jesus we are freed from the slavery of sin, and from the "hardness of heart" (cf. Mt 19:8; Mk 10:5) that had prevented post-Adamic man from honoring God's will regarding marriage. In and through union with Jesus we can overcome concupiscence and recover the "spousal meaning" of the body and live lives worthy of the holiness to which we are called.[35]

Here we will show how this new way of understanding the meaning of human existence impacted the New Testament's teaching on sex by considering (1) New Testament teaching on virginity, (2) Jesus' teaching on marriage and sexual morality, and (3) the teaching of St. Paul on marriage and sexual morality.

New Testament Teaching on Virginity

The new way of understanding human existence central to the Gospel — the "good news" of our redemption in and through Christ — is clearly manifested in the new evaluation of virginity and celibacy. The Jews of the first century — with the exception of the ascetic Essenes — believed that a life of celibacy was abnormal, perhaps even sinful. According to the rabbinical schools of the time "no man may abstain from keeping the Law, 'Be fruitful and multiply,' unless he already has children; according to the school of Shammai, two sons; according to the school of Hillel, a son and a daughter."[36] Yet Jesus was himself a virgin and highly commended virginity or celibacy for the Gospel's sake to his disciples. In like manner, St. Paul encourages those Christians of Corinth who were able to embrace the life of virginity for the sake of the kingdom, arguing that virginity, like marriage, is a great gift from God.

Today, some claim that the prominence given to the virginal state by Paul and other New Testament writers is simply a contingent, culturally conditioned aspect of the apostolic age. It was favored simply because the early Christians thought that Jesus' second coming was imminent — hence, why marry at all?[37] But this opinion is not supported by a careful study of the New Testament's teaching on virginity for the sake of the kingdom. The whole point of the New Testament teaching is that we must put first the requirements of God's kingdom — his reign of justice and love — and everything must be seen in this light. Jesus makes this clear in his teaching on the indissolubility of marriage (see below) and his absolute prohibition of divorce. How difficult his teaching must have appeared to husbands and wives abandoned by their spouses, but surely among the "eunuchs for the sake of the kingdom" were husbands and wives so abandoned. Yet, because of the requirements of the kingdom of God — of the requirements of his love — such persons had to remain celibate.[38]

Schillebeeckx notes the richness of New Testament teaching on virginity. Although Paul's views on the subject were set in the context of his expectation that Jesus would soon return in glory, his overriding concern was to impress upon his converts the radical transformation of human life effected by Jesus' saving deed and our new life in the Risen Lord. Thus, as Schillebeeckx accurately observes, Paul wanted to encourage Christians to be self-sacrificing enough to embark on the charism of total continence. It is inconceivable that some "'new existential experience,' the discovery of new aspects of marriage which escaped those who experienced it at an earlier period, should make the New Testament vision of Christian celibacy appear relative or incomplete in any respect.... Christianity will never be able to close its ears to the authentic biblical call to total abstinence as a possibility that forms an intrinsic and essential part of Christianity itself."[39]

This shows us that the basic perspective from which the New Testament approaches all questions of human existence, including those concerned with human sexuality, is that provided by our new life in Christ. With Christ we have "died" to sin and are risen to a new kind of life. This new and richer life is possible only because of his redemptive death and resurrection and our union with him through baptism. We are indeed "new creatures" for we have been regenerated through the waters of baptism. We are now, in, with, and through Christ, members of the divine family, led by his Spirit, able to call his Father "our Father," called to be holy even as the heavenly Father is holy.

New Testament Teaching on Marriage and Sexual Morality

The New Testament takes for granted Old Testament teaching on the goodness of sexuality and the beauty of faithful marriage. But the New Testament is concerned above all with showing how marriage, sexuality, and indeed everything human, have been inwardly transformed and deepened by the new life brought to us by Jesus.

Jesus' Teaching on Marriage and Sexual Morality

Jesus' teaching on these matters needs to be put into the context of his teaching on the moral life in general. This is provided by his Sermon on the Mount (Mt 5:1-7:28) and in particular his teaching on the Beatitudes.[40]

This is the framework within which Jesus set forth his teaching — brief but very significant — on marriage and sexual morality. In his teaching on divorce (Mt 19:3-12; Mk 10:2-12; Lk 16:18)[41] Jesus first reaffirms the goodness of sexuality and marriage as taught by Genesis. By including in their versions of our Lord's teaching explicit references to both Genesis 1:27 (Mt 19:4; Mk 10:6) and Genesis 2:24 (Mt 19:5; Mk 10:7), the evangelists indicate that for Jesus the sexual differentiation of man into male and female is part of God's plan of creation and that marriage is the only proper "place" for genital union to take place.[42]

Several features of Jesus' teaching here are particularly striking. First of all, he unequivocally condemns both divorce and remarriage. He insists that "remarriage" after divorce is not a marriage at all but adultery. As Schillebeeckx has rightly emphasized: "Christ not only expressly condemned divorce (showing, in other words, that the indissolubility of marriage is a *moral* obligation); he also said that any divorce that might possibly take place had no effect whatsoever on the bond of marriage itself (pointing out, in other words, that the indissolubility of marriage is an *objective* bond)."[43] Second, he clarified and developed the Old Testament teaching on the fundamental equality of woman. He stated that the one who divorced his wife and married another committed adultery against his wife. This is particularly clear in Mark's account: "Whoever divorces his wife and marries another, commits adultery against her" (Mk 10:11). Thus, any double standard of the sort tolerated in the Old Testament was firmly excluded: adultery was a very serious evil, and since remarriage after divorce was adultery, it was obviously a serious violation of God's wise and loving plan for human existence.[44]

Matthew's account of Jesus' teaching contains an *apparent* exception when it says "whoever divorces his wife [lewd conduct is a separate case]" (Mt 19:9). The Greek word translated here by "lewd" is *porneia* (cf. Mt 5:32). Traditionally, in the Fathers, Scholastics, and post-Tridentine manuals, it was understood that unchaste conduct could permit separation from bed and board, but not dissolution of the union with freedom to marry again. But modern scholarship has shown that in this text the Greek term *porneia* specifically refers to an *unlawful or invalid* marriage. As one scholar, Johannes Bauer, says: "*porneia* means an unlawful marriage, in particular marriage between blood relations, as was practiced among the gentiles and regarded among them as lawful. Such marriage relationships, which could sometimes be found among applicants for baptism, had to be dissolved, and this could give the impression of a divorce such as had been forbidden by Jesus. The Matthean redaction is an attempt to meet this problem as it arose in gentile Christian circles."[45]

Thus this text cannot be interpreted as an "exception clause" to the teaching of Jesus on the indissolubility of marriage.

Jesus and Woman's Equality With Man. Jesus' gracious dealings with women further illustrate his concern for their human and personal dignity and their fundamental equality with men. For example, his treatment of the Samaritan woman at the well reveals an open friendliness not expected in first-century Palestine (Jn 4:27). And his response to the woman taken in adultery, although it makes clear his firm teaching that adultery is seriously wrong, shows his kindness and mercy in a context in which righteous indignation was a more common reaction.

Jesus' Emphasis on Interior Attitudes and Dispositions. The focus on internal dispositions and the emphasis that morality comes from the "heart," from the inner core of a person, is absolutely central to Jesus' teaching on sexual morality. It is reflected in the catalog of vices Jesus presents (Mt 15:19; Mk 7:21-22). These vices proceed from the human heart and profoundly defile the human person in a way that eating "unclean food" could not. In the list provided by Mark there are several sexual sins, among them adultery (*moicheia*), fornication (*porneia*), and sensuality (*aselgeia*). The list found in Matthew includes adultery (*moicheia*) and fornication (*porneia*). New Testament scholars recognize that it is difficult to determine precisely the nature of the different kinds of sexual offenses designated by some of these terms, in particular by *porneia* ("fornication") and by *aselgeia* ("sensuality"). Nonetheless, it is clear that the authors of these Gospels present Jesus as teaching that adultery (*moicheia*, whose meaning is not disputed) is not the only act of a sexual nature that must be considered sinful and utterly opposed to God's wise and loving plan for human existence. There are many others. Moreover, although *porneia* was frequently used in the New Testament to speak of prostitution or incest, this term was definitely used in the New Testament to include acts properly designated by the English term *fornication*, which is today sometimes referred to as "premarital" sex. Such sexual behavior was certainly condemned by the New Testament.[46]

St. Paul on Marriage and Sexual Activity

The writings attributed to St. Paul provide another most important source of New Testament teaching on marriage and human sexuality. In his First Letter to the Corinthians, Paul, who is keenly aware of the effect of concupiscence on human persons and on our need for redemption, nonetheless reaffirms the basic goodness of human sexuality and the goodness and holiness of marriage. In 1 Corinthians 7 he clearly affirms that marriage is the way willed by God for men and women to exercise their sexuality. It is the only legitimate means of satisfying the call inscribed in nature and of mastering the disorder of the passions (cf. 1 Cor 7:2).

Moreover, in 1 Corinthians 7 Paul clearly recognizes that Christ's coming has inwardly affected the whole reality of marriage, so that it is now incorporated into God's economy of grace. This is reflected in the following passage: "If any brother has a wife who is an unbeliever but is willing to live with him, he must not divorce her. And if any woman has a husband who is an unbeliever but is willing to live with her, she must not divorce him. The unbelieving husband is consecrated [literally "made holy"] by his believing wife; the unbelieving wife is consecrated by her believing husband. If it were otherwise, your children should be unclean; but as it is, they are holy" (1 Cor 7:12-14).[47]

Paul says that if the unbelieving spouse wishes to separate, then the believing spouse can let him or her depart, but, speaking to those

who have married "in the Lord," he writes: "To those now married...
I give this command (though it is not mine; it is the Lord's): a wife
must not separate from her husband. If she does separate, she must
either remain unmarried or become reconciled to him again. Similarly, a husband must not divorce his wife" (1 Cor 7:10-11).[48] Commenting on this important passage, Pierre Benoit has justly said: "We
understand by this the prohibition of divorce such as we find it in
the Gospels on the lips of Jesus ... [who], returning to the will of the
Creator... declared that in the Kingdom of God he was inaugurating
divorce was not allowed. It is this command of the Lord that Paul
solemnly repeats with his apostolic authority. He knows that human
weakness can involve serious difficulties between married persons. He
admits, therefore, not without hesitation, the possibility of a separation, but without remarrying."[49]

The Letter to the Ephesians[50] (see 5:21-33) immeasurably deep-
ens the prophetic presentation of marriage as a reality symbolizing
the covenantal relationship between God and his chosen people.
It teaches that the marriages of those who marry "in the Lord" are
meant to symbolize and make present the life-giving, love-giving,
grace-giving union of Christ and his bride the Church. It is thus a
text that figures largely in the development of Catholic teaching on
the sacramentality of marriage.[51]

Other key texts of St. Paul dealing with human sexuality are 1 Corinthians 6:15-20[52] and 1 Thessalonians 4:3-6.[53] A key term in both of
these passages is the Greek word *porneia*, which, as we have seen, can
signify a wide range of immoral sexual acts or "lewd conduct," including incest and prostitution (which seems to be its central meaning in
1 Cor 6). But there can be no doubt, as important biblical scholars
(e.g., Silverio Zedda and others) have demonstrated[54] that this term is
used by St. Paul to exclude all non-marital genital intercourse.

*St. Paul and the Fundamental Reason Why Christians Must Avoid
Sexual Sins.* Moreover, and this is supremely important, the fundamental reason leading Paul to the judgment that all non-marital genital intercourse is gravely immoral and unbecoming a Christian is that
it is utterly irreconcilable with *the* most fundamental moral norm of
the Christian life, namely, our call *to be what we are!*, i.e., *children of
God himself, called to live worthily as those who have been "purchased at
a price" recreated in the image of Christ.* As new beings in Christ, we

must let Christ be formed in us and live in us, and we cannot do this if we freely choose to perform immoral sexual acts.[55]

Homosexuality. Paul's brief discussion of homosexuality in Romans 1 is also noteworthy. He does not argue that homosexuality is wrong. He sees that as evident. He treats homosexual practices as being both sinful in themselves and part of the punishment for disbelief. Homosexuality is therefore presented as an evil, a distortion of human life which follows from sin (Rom 1:26-27).

Summary

The New Testament teaches that chastity is required of every Christian, male or female, married or unmarried. Because sexuality is a good gift from God, God shows us in the fullness of his revelation in Jesus that its proper use is to be highly prized and its abuse severely condemned. The Letter to the Hebrews sums it up well: "marriage is to be held in honor by all; the marriage bed is to be kept undefiled; God will judge adulterers and fornicators (Heb 13:4)."[56]

ENDNOTES FOR CHAPTER TWO

1. Pope John Paul II, General Audience of May 28, 1980, in Pope John Paul II, *Man and Woman He Created Them: A Theology of the Body,* translation, introduction, and index by Michael Waldstein (Boston: Pauline Book & Media, 2006). This is the definitive translation of Pope John Paul II's "catecheses on the theology of the body," given from September 5, 1979 through November 28, 1984. In this definitive translation, hereafter referred to as Waldstein *TOB,* 133 such catecheses are given. References will be made to the number of the papal audience, the paragraph number of that audience, and the page on which it appears in Waldstein's translation. Thus here it is Waldstein *TOB* 28.1-5, pp. 242-246.

2. See Manuel Miguens, "Biblical Thoughts on 'Human Sexuality,'" in *Human Sexuality in Our Time: What the Church Teaches,* ed. George A. Kelly (Boston: St. Paul Editions, 1979), pp. 102-118, especially pp. 103-107.

3. John L. McKenzie, "Aspects of Old Testament Thought," *New Jerome Biblical Commentary,* eds. Raymond E. Brown, S.S., Joseph

Fitzmyer, S.J., and Roland E. Murphy, O.Carm. (Englewood Cliffs, NJ: Prentice-Hall, Inc., 1990), p. 1305, no. 123.

4. See Pope John Paul II, General Audience of January 9, 1980, in Waldstein *TOB*, 14.1-6, at 3, pp. 181-185, at 182. In this text Pope John Paul II is explicitly concerned with the account in Genesis 2, but the expression "beatifying beginning" can also be applied to the narrative in Genesis 1.

5. See John L. McKenzie's masterful account of the Baal myth and its attendant fertility cult in *The Two-Edged Sword: An Interpretation of the Old Testament* (New York: Doubleday Image, 1966), ch. 3: "The Gods of the Semites." On pp. 76-77 McKenzie "translates" this ancient myth into language understandable today: "the supreme good, the good life, consists in the satisfaction of human material needs. This is all we ask of the gods, and this is all they can give us. They bless us in full when they satisfy these needs not only in the minimum necessary for survival, but in abundance, so that we enjoy not only the simple life, but also the material comforts of life. . . . The highest of all pleasures is the pleasure of sex; life offers nothing finer, nothing which so raises a man to the level of the divine. Consequently, the difference of the sexes exists only that the male may have this supreme satisfaction; woman is his possession, and her noblest function is to satisfy his sexual appetite. When she does this, she is a goddess; otherwise, she is a high-grade domestic animal, a drudge, not fully a human being." He concludes by saying: "One suspects that many modern Europeans and Americans, if transported suddenly into the Babylon of the second millennium, after an initial adjustment to inconveniences in such things as language, travel, and plumbing, would find themselves spiritually at home. They would never feel at ease with the ancient Hebrews" (p. 77). The accounts of human origins and of human sexuality in Genesis 1 and 2 are deliberately framed to repudiate this understanding of these realities.

6. The relevant text from Genesis 1 reads as follows: "Then God said, 'Let us make man ['adam] in our image, after our likeness; and let them have dominion over the fish of the sea, and over the birds of the air, and over the cattle, and over all the earth, and over every creeping thing that creeps upon the earth.' So God created man ['adam] in his own image, in the image of God he created him, male and female he created them. And God blessed them and said to them, 'Be fruitful

and multiply, and fill the earth and subdue it; and have dominion over the fish of the sea and over the birds of the air and over every living thing that moves upon the earth'" (Gen 1:26-28).

7. On this see Francis Martin, "Male and Female He Created Them: A Summary of the Teaching of Genesis Chapter One," *Communio* 10 (Summer 1993), 257, 259-260. See also Pauline A. Viviano, "Genesis," in *Collegeville Bible Commentary: Old Testament* (Collegeville, MN: The Liturgical Press, 1992), pp. 35-78.

8. See Martin, pp. 254-255: "The first function of the description of `adam as male and female is to place sexual differentiation and sexuality itself within a world created by God and seen by him as good. Sex is not a means of cultivating cosmic powers, as in the fertility cults, nor is it an expression of an hubris that degrades it to the level of self-assertion and power and thus despises its modest but true place as something properly human. It is one expression of the way in which humans image God. As God creates in his image and likeness, Adam begets in his likeness and image, and Eve acquires a man-child with the help of Yhwh (see Gen. 4:1)."

9. Edward Schillebeeckx, *Marriage: Human Reality and Saving Mystery* (New York: Sheed and Ward, Inc. 1965), p. 16.

10. The Old Testament is replete with texts proclaiming that children are God's gift to married couples. Infertility and female barrenness were regarded as bad, not good. This great biblical idea, constantly taught by the Church, is poignantly described in Sara's great sadness that she cannot bear a child for Abram, and later in the New Testament in Elizabeth's inability to bear a child for Zachary and how God himself, for whom all things are possible, intervened and Elizabeth then conceived John. Shakespeare's King Lear eloquently expresses this truth when, to curse his treacherous daughter Goneril, he says to her: "Hear, nature, hear; dear goddess, hear! Suspend thy purpose, if thou didst intend to make this creature fruitful! Into her womb convey sterility! Dry up in her the organs of increase, and from her derogate body never spring a babe to honour her!" (Act I, scene 4, lines 281-287).

11. The relevant text follows: "then the LORD God formed man [`adam] of dust from the ground, and breathed into his nostrils the breath of life; and man [`adam] became a living being.... Then the LORD God said, 'It is not good that the man [`adam] should be alone; I will make him a helper fit for him.'... So the LORD God caused a

deep sleep to fall upon the man [`adam], and while he slept took one of his ribs and closed up its place with flesh; and the rib which the LORD God had taken from the man [`adam] he made into a woman [ishshah] and brought her to the man [`adam]. Then the man [`adam] said, 'This at last is bone of my bones and flesh of my flesh; she shall be called Woman [ishshah], because she was taken out of Man [ish].' Therefore a man [ish] leaves his father and his mother and cleaves to his wife [ishshah], and they become one flesh. And the man and his wife were both naked, and were not ashamed" (Gen 2:7, 18, 21-25).

12. Pope John Paul II has reflected deeply on the meaning of man's "original solitude." See his General Audience of October 10, 1979, in Waldstein TOB, 5.1-5, pp. 146-150. Commenting on Genesis 2:18 and its context, John Paul II shows that this text dramatically discloses the uniqueness — the solitude — of man (male and female) in the created universe. None of the other animals, over whom the man exercises authority (signified by his being given by God the power to "name" them; cf. Gen 2:19-20), is his equal. Man's "consciousness reveals him as the one *who possesses the power of knowing* with respect to the visible world. With this knowledge… *man* at the same time *reveals himself to himself in all the distinctiveness of his being.*… Man is alone because he is 'different' from the visible world, from the world of living beings. When we analyze the text of Genesis, we are in some way witnesses of how man, with the first act of consciousness, 'distinguishes himself' before God-Yahweh from the whole world of living beings (*animalia*), how he consequently reveals himself to himself and at the same time asserts himself in the visible world as a 'person' in the visible world" (5.5, p. 150).

13. Pope John Paul II, General Audience of January 9, 1980, Waldstein TOB, 14.1-6, pp. 181-185. There the Holy Father declares: "When the first man exclaims at the sight of the woman, 'she is flesh from my flesh and bone from my bones' (Gen 2:23), he simply affirms the human identity of both. By exclaiming this, he seems to say, *Look, a body that expresses the person!*… The body, which expresses femininity 'for' masculinity and, vice versa, masculinity 'for' femininity, manifests the reciprocity and the communion of persons. It expresses it through gift as the fundamental characteristic of personal existence. This is *the body*: *a witness* to creation as a fundamental gift, and therefore a witness to *Love as the source from which this same gift*

springs. Masculinity-femininity — namely, sex — is the original sign of a creative donation and at the same time the sign of a gift that man, male-female, becomes aware of as a gift lived so to speak in an original way. This is the meaning with which sex enters into the theology of the body" (14.4, p.183).

14. Several biblical scholars have noted the covenantal significance of the words "flesh" and "bone" in this text. See, for instance, Walter Brueggemann, "Of the Same Flesh and Bone (Gn 2:23a)," *Catholic Biblical Quarterly* 32 (1970): 532-542. See also Silvio José Báez, O.C.D., "L'uomo del progetto di Dio," in B. Moriconi, *Antropologia Cristiana: Bibbia, teologia, cultura* (Rome, Cittá Nuova, 2001), p. 185, footnote 80: "The phrase 'bone of my bone and flesh of my flesh' is a technical formula to indicate kinship (see Gen 29:14) or the covenant (see 2 Sam 5:19)."

15. Pope John Paul II, General Audience of January 9, 1980, Waldstein *TOB* 14.4, p. 183.

16. Perhaps the most probing analysis of the significance of original nakedness is provided by Pope John Paul II. See in particular the following addresses, all found in Waldstein *TOB*: (1) General Audience of December 12, 1979 (Waldstein *TOB* 11:1-6, pp. 169-173); (2) General Audience of December 19, 1979 (Waldstein *TOB* 12:1-5, pp. 173-177); (3) General Audience of January 2, 1980 (Waldstein *TOB* 13.1-4, pp. 17-181).

17. In older translations of John Paul II's audiences this meaning was called the "nuptial" meaning of the body. Waldstein believes that "spousal" better translates the text his research discovered. See Pope John Paul II's General Audience of January 9, 1980 (Waldstein *TOB* 1.41-6, pp. 181-185); General Audience of January 16, 1980 (Waldstein *TOB*, 15.1-5, pp. 185-190); General Audience of January 30, 1980 (Waldstein *TOB*, 16.1-5, pp.190-194. Richard M. Hogan ably summarizes John Paul II's notion of this meaning of the body in his essay, in *Natural Family Outreach,* 2003, available at http://www.nfpoutreach.org/; Retrieved 2006-07-14. See also, Richard Hogan, *The Theology of the Body* (Jamesville, MD: Word Among Us Press, 2007), chapter on nuptial meaning of body.

18. Such freedom from shame is, in the Old Testament, an eschatological promise linked to freedom from sin and the experience of God's saving power (cf. Is 45:17; Zeph 3:11).

19. Johannes Bauer, "Marriage," in *Sacramentum Verbi: An Encyclopedia of the Bible*, ed. Johannes Bauer (New York: Herder & Herder, 1985), 3.551. On this also see Schillebeeckx, *Marriage: Human Reality and Saving Mystery*, pp. 21-22.

20. Steven Clark, *Man and Woman in Christ: An Examination of the Roles of Men and Women in the Light of Scripture and the Social Sciences* (Ann Arbor, MI: Servant Books, 1980), p. 22. See also Pierre Grelot, *Man and Wife in Scripture* (New York: Herder & Herder, 1965), pp. 37-38.

21. Karol Wojtyla (Pope John Paul II), *Love and Responsibility*, tr. H. T. Willetts (New York: Farrar, Straus, Giroux, 1981), p. 190.

22. Pope John Paul II analyzes in depth the devastating effect of sinful concupiscence on human sexuality and the spousal meaning of the body in a lengthy series of catecheses: General Audience of April 30, 1980, in Waldstein *TOB* 26, 1-5, pp. 235-238; General Audience of May 14, 1980, in Waldstein *TOB* 27, 1-4, pp. 238-242; General Audience of May 28, 1980, in Waldstein *TOB* 28.1-6, pp. 242-246; General Audience of June 4, 1980, in Waldstein *TOB* 29.1-5, pp. 246-250; General Audience of June 18, 1980, in Waldstein *TOB* 30, 1-6, pp. 250-253; General Audience of June 25, 1980, in Waldstein *TOB* 31, 1-6, pp. 253-257; General Audience of July 23, 1980, in Waldstein *TOB* 32.1-6, pp. 257-260.

23. See *Catechism of the Catholic Church*, no. 404. See also Clark, *Man and Woman in Christ*, pp. 31-36.

24. A brief but excellent commentary by a biblical scholar on Genesis 3 (the Fall) and Genesis 4 (its effects on family life) is given by Michael Duggan, *The Consuming Fire: A Christian Introduction to the Old Testament* (San Francisco: Ignatius Press, 1991), pp. 76-79.

25. Francis Martin, "Marriage in the Old Testament and Intertestamental Period," in *Christian Marriage: A Historical Study*, ed. Glenn W. Olsen (New York: The Crossroad Publishing Co., 2001), pp. 1-49.

26. Schillebeeckx, *Marriage: Human Reality and Saving Mystery*, p. 33.

27. See Elaine Adler Goodfriend, "Adultery," in *The Anchor Bible Dictionary*, ed. David Noel Freedman et al. (New York: Doubleday, 1992), 1:82-86.

28. See ibid., 82.

29. Joseph Jensen, O.S.B., "The Relevance of the Old Testament," in *Dimensions of Human Sexuality*, ed. Dennis Doherty (Garden City, NY: Doubleday, 1979), pp. 1-8, at 6-7.

30. Roland E. Murphy, O.Carm., "Wisdom and Eros in Proverbs 1-9," *Catholic Biblical Quarterly* 50 (1988): 600-603, at 603.

31. Schillebeeckx, *Marriage: Human Reality and Saving Mystery*, pp. 42-43.

32. On this see Thomas McCreesch, "Wisdom as Wife: Proverbs 31:10-31," *Revue Biblique* 92 (1985), 25-46; see also the study by Claudia V. Camp, *Wisdom and the Feminine in the Book of Proverbs*, ed. David M. Gunn, Vol. 11, Bible and Literature Series (Decatur, GA: Scholars Press, 1985).

33. Those who claim that the sin of the men of Sodom was not homosexuality but inhospitality include Raymond Collins, *Christian Morality: Biblical Foundations* (Notre Dame, IN: University of Notre Dame Press, 1986), pp. 172-173; Richard B. Hayes, *The Moral Vision of the New Testament* (San Francisco: Harper Collins, 1996), p. 381. These authors and others, for instance, James B. Nelson, *Embodiment: An Approach to Sexuality and Christian Theology* (Minneapolis, MN: Augsburg, 1978), pp. 180-210, on "Gayness and Homosexuality," also claim that Onan's sin was not homosexual acts but a violation of the levirate law.

34. Manuel Miguens, "Biblical Thoughts on 'Human Sexuality,'" pp. 116-117 argues that it definitely was the sin of homosexuality. Richard J. Clifford suggests that the Sodomites were guilty of a two-fold crime, that of inhospitality and that of forbidden sex — and by referring here to Lev 18:22 Clifford makes it clear that the forbidden sex in question is homosexual activity. See his "Genesis," in *New Jerome Biblical Commentary*, p. 23, no. 30. On this question also see Jensen, "The Relevance of the Old Testament," p. 8. An excellent discussion of Old Testament teaching on the malice of homosexual acts is given by Maurice Gilbert, "La Bible et l'homosexualité," *Nouveau Revue Théologique* 109 (1987), 78-95. See also Brian Harrison, "The Sin of Onan Revisited," *Living Tradition: Organ of the Roman Theological Forum*, No. 67, November 1996, accessible at http://www.rtforum.org/lt/lt67.html; accessed November 18, 2010.

35. Schillebeeckx develops these ideas briefly and well in his *Marriage: Human Reality and Saving Mystery*, pp. 108-109, 125-140,

155-176. See also Manuel Miguens, "On Being a Christian and the Moral Life: Pauline Perspectives," in *Principles of Catholic Morality*, ed. William E. May (Chicago: Franciscan Herald Press, 1981); Germain Grisez, *The Way of the Lord Jesus*, vol. 1, *Christian Moral Principles* (Chicago: Franciscan Herald Press, 1983), pp. 551-682; Servais Pinckaers, *The Sources of Christian Ethics* (Washington, DC: The Catholic University of America Press, 1995), pp. 104-132. On recovering the "spousal meaning of the body," see Pope John Paul II, General Audience of December 3, 1980, in Waldstein *TOB*, 49.1-7, pp. 321-325.

36. This is a Mishnaic text cited by Collins, *Christian Morality*, p. 84.

37. This is the view taken by Anthony Kosnik et al. in *Human Sexuality: New Directions in American Catholic Thought* (New York: Paulist, 1977), p. 26.

38. On this see Quentin Quesnell, "Made Themselves Eunuchs for the Kingdom of Heaven," *Catholic Biblical Quarterly* 30 (1968): 335-358.

39. Schillebeeckx, *Marriage: Human Reality and Saving Mystery*, pp. 127, 131.

40. Long ago St. Augustine called our Lord's Sermon on the Mount the magna carta of the Christian life, indeed, the *"perfect pattern of the Christian life"* (see his *The Lord's Sermon on the Mount*, tr. John J. Jepson, S.S., in *Ancient Christian Writers*, no. 5 [Westminster, MD: Newman Press, 1948], p. 11). St. Thomas declared that the Lord's Sermon on the Mount "contains completely the information needed for the Christian life. In it the inner movements of the person are perfectly ordered" (*Summa Theologiae*, 1-2, 108, 3). Pope John Paul II says that in the Sermon on the Mount "Jesus brings the commandments to fulfillment... by interiorizing their demands and by bringing out their fullest meaning" (*Veritatis Splendor*, no. 15).

41. Matthew 19:3-12: "And Pharisees came up to him and tested him by asking, 'Is it lawful to divorce one's wife for any cause?' He answered, 'Have you not read that he who made them from the beginning made them male and female [cf. Gen 1:28] and said, "For this reason a man shall leave his father and mother and be joined to his wife, and the two shall become one?" [cf. Gen 2:24]. So they are no longer two but one. What therefore God has joined together, let no man put

asunder.' They said to him, 'Why then did Moses command one to give a certificate of divorce, and to put her away?' He said to them 'For your hardness of heart Moses allowed you to divorce your wives, but from the beginning it was not so. And I say to you: whoever divorces his wife, except for unchastity [lewd conduct (*porneia*) is a separate case], and marries another, commits adultery; and he who marries a divorced woman, commits adultery.' The disciples said to him, 'If such is the case of a man with his wife, it is not expedient to marry.' But he said to them, 'Not all men can receive this precept, but only those to whom it is given. For there are eunuchs who have been so from birth, and there are eunuchs who have been made eunuchs by men, and there are eunuchs who have made themselves eunuchs for the sake of the kingdom of heaven. He who is able to receive this, let him receive it.'"

Mark 10:2-12: "And Pharisees came up and in order to test him asked, 'Is it lawful for a man to divorce his wife?' He answered them, 'What did Moses command you?' They said, 'Moses allowed a man to write a certificate of divorce, and to put her away.' But Jesus said to them: 'For your hardness of heart he wrote you this command-ment. But from the beginning of creation, "God made them male and female" [cf. Gen 1:27]. "For this reason a man shall leave his father and mother and be joined to his wife, and the two shall become one. So they are no longer two but one" [cf. Gen 2:24]. What therefore God has joined together, let no man put asunder.' And in the house the disciples asked him again about this matter. And he said to them, 'Whoever divorces his wife and marries another commits adultery against her; and if she divorces her husband and marries another, she commits adultery.'"

Luke 16:18: "'Everyone who divorces his wife and marries another commits adultery, and he who marries a woman divorced from her husband commits adultery.'"

42. See Schillebeeckx, *Marriage: Human Reality and Saving Mystery*, p. 154ff; Grelot, *Man and Wife*, pp. 86-90.

43. Schillebeeckx, *Marriage, Human Reality and Saving Mystery*, p. 154.

44. See John J. O'Rourke, "Divorce in the New Testament," *Dimension: Journal of Pastoral Concern 1* (1969), 138-146.

45. J. Bauer, "Marriage," *Sacramentum Verbi* 2.552. See also Joseph Fitzmyer, S.J., "The Matthean Divorce Texts and Some New Palestin-

ian Evidence," *Theological Studies* 37 (1977): 197-226 (reprinted in Fitzmyer's *To Advance the Gospel: New Testament Studies* [New York: Crossroad, 1981], pp. 79-111) and also Schillebeeckx's analysis of the Matthean text in *Marriage: Human Reality and Saving Mystery*, pp. 141-154.

46. On this see Silverio Zedda, *Relativo e assoluto nella morale del San Paolo* (Brescia: Paideia, 1984), ch. 5. See also Joseph Jensen, O.S.B., "Does *Porneia* Mean Fornication? A Critique of Bruce Melina," *Novum Testamentum* 20 (1978), 161-184.

47. See Schillebeeckx, *Marriage: Human Reality and Saving Mystery*, pp. 160-162.

48. This is the source for what came to be known as the "Pauline Privilege," the dissolution of a nonsacramental marriage by the Church if the non-believing partner refuses to remain with the partner who has become a Christian.

49. Pierre Benoit, O.P., "Christian Marriage according to Saint Paul," *Clergy Review* 65 (1980): 314.

50. Today the Pauline authorship of this letter is denied by many, although some exegetes maintain Pauline authorship, at least indirectly (on this, cf. Benoit, work cited in previous endnote, p. 315f).

51. For comment, see Peter Elliott, *"What God Has Joined": The Sacramentality of Marriage* (New York: Alba House, 1990; paperback Wipf and Stock, 2010), pp. 46-72.

52. The full text of 1 Corinthians 6:15-20 reads: "Do you not know that your bodies are members of Christ? Shall I therefore take the members of Christ and make them the members of a prostitute? Never! Do you not know that he who joins himself to a prostitute becomes one body with her? For, as it is written, 'The two shall become one.' But he who is united to the Lord becomes one spirit with him. Shun immorality [*porneia*]. Every other sin which a man commits is outside the body, but the immoral man [*ho porneuon*] sins against his own body. Do you not know that your body is a temple of the Holy Spirit, within you, which you have from God? You are not your own; you were bought with a price. So glorify God in your body."

53. 1 Thessalonians 4:3-6 reads as follows: "For this is the will of God, your sanctification: that you abstain from immorality [*porneia*]; that each one of you know how to control his own body [member (wife?) *skeuos*] in holiness and honor, not in the passion of lust like

heathen who do not know God; that no man transgress, and wrong his brother in this manner, because the Lord is an avenger in all these things, as we solemnly forewarned you."

The Greek work *skeuos* in v. 4 literally means "vessel" or "dish." Some biblical scholars provide cogent arguments to hold that in this text the term refers to one's "wife." On this see, for instance, the arguments given by O. Larry Yarbrough, *Not Like the Gentiles: Marriage Rules in the Letters of Paul* (Atlanta, GA: Scholars Press, 1985; Dissertation Series No. 80), pp. 68-76. Others, however, offer good reasons for translating it as "member" or one's own "body." See, for instance, Silverio Zedda, S.J., *Relativo e assoluto nella morale del San Paolo*, pp. 61-64. No matter what the translation, scholars agree that this is a key text giving Paul's teaching on sexual morality.

54. One of the most careful and penetrating studies of this matter is given by Zedda in his *Relativo e assoluto nella morale del San Paolo*, ch. 5. See also John J. O'Rourke, "Does the New Testament Condemn Sexual Intercourse Outside of Marriage?" *Theological Studies* 37 (1976): 478-479; Joseph Jensen, O.S.B., "Does *Porneia* Mean Fornication? A Critique of Bruce Malina," *Novum Testamentum* 20 (1978): 161-184.

55. The basic norm of Christian life, as summarized in the text, is the way Zedda proposes it in his study of Paul's thought. See his *Relativo e assoluto nella morale di San Paolo,* pp. 34-35. He then shows, massively, that sexual immorality (*porneia*), which includes all non-marital sexual acts, violates this norm. Cf. ibid., ch. 5, pp. 63-85. On this see also Yarbrough, *Not Like the Gentiles*, pp. 123-127. Yarbrough uses somewhat different language, but his principal conclusion after studying St. Paul's texts very minutely, is that sexual immorality (non-marital sex) violates God's will for the Christian.

56. Francis Martin, "Marriage in the New Testament Period," in *Christian Marriage*, ed. Olsen, pp. 50-100 for a fine overview of the teaching of Jesus and Paul on marriage and sex.

CHAPTER THREE

Sex in the Catholic Tradition

Catholics are the heirs of a long theological tradition. Over the centuries there has been careful reflection on human sexuality and sexual morality in the light of the Scriptures. From apostolic times to the present, Catholic scholars, saints, and pastoral leaders have sought to understand, in the light of God's revealing word, the meaning of human sexuality and the norms of sexual morality, i.e., the *truths* in whose light we can make true judgments of what we are to do and, in doing them, make ourselves *to be* the kind of persons we are. During this long history, errors have unquestionably been made. It is, however, important to note the *kind* of errors made by the tradition, and the kind not made. Thus, for instance, some of the Fathers of the Church mistakenly believed, for a variety of reasons, that sexuality would never have been used in a state of innocence. But errors of this kind did not mislead the Christian people in their efforts to lead chaste lives. None of the Fathers, none of the Scholastics, indeed no theologian in the Catholic tradition up to the very recent past, ever claimed that the Church is in error in saying that fornication or adultery or masturbation is always gravely wrong. While it is not surprising to discover some rather strange opinions by theologians over such a long period of time and in the development of a complex history, what is truly remarkable and striking is the profound unity one discovers: the same basic Catholic teaching on sex everywhere. This history is also a story of the development in doctrine toward a clearer understanding of the nature of sexuality as revealed by God and uncovered by human reflection. The growth in the Church's understanding of human sexuality has not been haphazard but systematic, for it has been directed by an awareness of fundamental truths about human nature and destiny, which are grounded in Scripture, proclaimed by the teaching authority of the Church, and gradually refined by the developing theological tradition.

This tradition teaches now, and has always taught, that the union of man and woman in marriage is good, indeed holy. It teaches now, and has always taught, that the virtue of chastity is necessary for all persons, male and female, married and unmarried, so that they might fully have freedom of self-possession and not be controlled by unworthy sexual desire. It teaches now, and has always taught, that some specific sorts of sexual activity — fornication, adultery, contraception, and sodomy, for instance — are simply incompatible with the way of life appropriate for and required of a person who has become one body with Christ through baptism, and whose body is a living tabernacle of God.

It is, of course, impossible in a brief section of a book such as this to provide a detailed history of the developing Catholic theological tradition on sex. A satisfactory history on this subject has never, in fact, been written.[1] Still, it is possible to note the major claims about human sexuality and sexual morality that have been central to this developing tradition, and to specify some of the principal developments that have taken place.

I. Early Christian and Patristic Thought

To understand the sexual attitudes expressed by the earliest Christian writers, one must be aware of the context in which they wrote. They lived in an age of great sexual licentiousness — an age whose similarities to our own are unmistakable. The early Christian writers were keenly aware that the teachings of the New Testament on marriage, virginity, and chastity were radically opposed to the sexual outlook and practice of the pagan world. Thus, their thought must be understood in the context of their interaction with a society in which prostitution was widespread; divorce, contraception, abortion, and infanticide were common; and chastity for males was considered out of the question.[2]

In addition to the debauchery and disregard for human life prevalent in the Greco-Roman world of the time, the early Christians likewise faced a religious challenge in the various Gnostic movements of the day. Gnosticism at times posed as a variant of the Gospel, but it was a mystery religion more influenced by contemporary philosophical ideas than by the Gospel. It claimed a "saving" knowledge quite opposed to the Christian message. The Gnostics were metaphysical dualists, and therefore held that matter itself was evil. Consequently, they held that the human body and sexuality were evil. They despised marriage and, in particular, the procreation of new life through marital union. Although they advocated sexual abstinence for the "elite," they did so not because they thought that such abstinence might be required by God's will or by a proper regard for the goods of human nature but because they regarded sexual union as defiling. Since total abstinence was difficult for most people, however, some Gnostics conveniently taught that the non-elite could freely engage in all kinds of sexual activities for the sake of the exquisite experience of pleasure that they might bring, as long as they took care to ensure that no new life was generated.[3]

Facing these two evils, the early Christian writers drew on the teaching of the Gospels and Paul to instruct the faithful and to articulate Christian attitudes toward sex. While extolling a virginity chosen for the sake of God's kingdom, they taught that marriage itself was something good because it had been divinely instituted and had been blessed by Jesus' presence at the wedding feast of Cana (Jn 2). Irenaeus, for example, writing in the second century, repudiated the views of the Gnostics, saying: "Saturninus and Marcion, who are called 'the Continent,' preach abstinence from marriage, frustrating the age-old creation of God and implicitly finding fault with Him who made human beings male and female so that they could reproduce themselves. They introduced abstinence from what they describe as 'animal-like,' ungrateful as they are to Him who made everything, God."[4] In similar fashion St. Clement of Alexandria wrote: "if marriage... is a sin, I do not see how a person can say he knows God when he says that the law of God is a sin. But if 'the law is holy,' then marriage is holy."[5]

In their desire both to encourage the faithful to live chastely and to repudiate Gnostic dualism, the early Christians stressed the procreative purpose of marriage and of human sexuality. Thus, Justin the Martyr, another second-century apologist, declared that "we Christians either marry with but one thought, to beget children, or, if we refuse to marry, we are completely continent."[6] Similarly, Athenagoras of Athens[7] and Clement of Alexandria wrote that marriage is for the sake of children. Clement, writing from a center of Gnosticism and a city notorious for its sexual licentiousness, appealed to the teaching of the Stoic philosophers in stressing the procreative purpose of marriage. Yet it needs to be said that Clement and other Christians who appealed to Stoic thought were not themselves Stoics. They were Christians, and they had already adopted the view that marriage and sex are meant for procreation from their reading of the Scriptures.[8] Clement, who with other Fathers praised virginity as a preferable state of life for Christians, also noted that married persons have more trials. But these trials could themselves serve growth in virtue.[9]

The great value of virginity and the procreative purposefulness of sex and marriage were also emphasized by the Fathers of the fourth and fifth centuries. Athanasius is typical of them in his encouragement of the young to choose a life of virginity for the sake of the Gospel. All of these writers — including Jerome and Augustine in the West, and John Chrysostom and Gregory Nazianzus in the East — see Christ as the founder of Christian virginity. They teach that the life of the virgin is to be preferred to marriage insofar as those who choose the virginal state rightly have fixed their concern on eternal realities and are already living in the anticipated end time.[10]

While they praised highly a life of virginity, these Fathers nonetheless recognized that marriage, too, is good, and that proper sexual relations within marriage can be morally good. Like earlier writers, they commonly found marital relations good precisely because they can lead to the procreation of children. In their reading of Genesis they saw the good of procreating children as *the* purpose of marriage. As several of them noted, it was, after all, in view of generating human life that God had given Eve — a woman — to Adam as his helpmate instead of another male.[11] There was nonetheless in these Fathers an anxiety about sex. This anxiety was caused not only by the sexual depravity they witnessed in the lives of the pagans but also by their understanding of Scripture, in particular the story of the fall of our first parents. In the third chapter of Genesis, Adam and Eve are described as being ashamed of their nakedness after eating the forbidden fruit. The Fathers saw in this a sign that sexual appetite in particular had been wounded by sin.[12]

Some of the Fathers were so suspicious of the sexual appetite that they believed it became operative only after the fall. These Fathers — among them Gregory of Nyssa, John Chrysostom, Theodoret, and John Damascene[13] — believed that God had originally intended to generate life in some nonsexual way. Foreseeing, however, that Adam and Eve would fall, he had providentially endowed them with sexual powers that would be used after the fall. This view, to be sure, was not commonly held, and was vigorously repudiated by many, including Augustine. Still, its presence in some of the Fathers is sufficient to show us the caution with which some of them regarded sexual activity. This caution was not based on the conviction that sexual activity was evil in itself but on the conviction that it had been profoundly wounded by mankind's fall.

These Fathers saw sexuality as lying at the root of the conflict so eloquently spoken of by Paul when he described his inability to do the good he willed, and when he distinguished between the law of his mind and the law of his members. The Fathers blamed the loss of rational control over sexual activity on the impairment brought about by original sin. In sexual matters desires frequently seemed to overpower reason. Thus, even within marriage there is need to make sure that reason dominates, lest man be led to sin by unruly desires. Clement of Alexandria wrote: "The man who has taken a wife in order to have children should also practice continence, not even seeking pleasure from his own wife, whom he ought to love, but with honorable and moderate desire, having but one intention, children."[14] The Fathers were thus led to stress the procreative end, or purpose, of marriage, for this wonderful purpose provides married couples with a reasonable ground for the choice to have sexual relations. With this purpose in mind they can moderate their desires and bring them under reason's rule.

Still, there was in Scripture, particularly in the teaching of Paul on marriage in 1 Corinthians, another purpose of marriage. Paul suggested that marriage could allay the concupiscence experienced by humankind as a result of Adam's sin. Among the Fathers, Lactantius in the West and John Chrysostom in the East explicitly affirm that marital relations for the purpose of avoiding concupiscence are licit.[15] These authors do not expressly affirm that marital relations may be chosen as a way of fostering or expressing love between the spouses, but they do say that marital relations may rightfully be chosen in order to alleviate sexual desire and to avoid fornication. In addition, Chrysostom wrote beautifully about Christian marriage as an image of Christ's bridal union with the Church.[16]

What all this shows is that it was difficult for these Fathers to articulate a balanced sexual morality within the context provided by the twin evils of sexual licentiousness and Gnostic hatred of matter and marriage. The whole aim of the Fathers was to instruct the faithful in the Gospel of salvation. They saw, and rightly so, that sexual immorality, to which humankind is easily inclined, is a form of idolatry, for it is, as Paul had taught, a desecration of a human person who has become, through baptism, one body with Christ and a living temple of the Holy Spirit. Likewise, the Fathers believed that sex in itself, as created by God, is good, as is marriage.

From the Scriptures they had likewise learned that through Adam's sin all men had been harmed, for now the power of sin enslaved all mankind, disrupting the interior harmony of the human person and rendering humans incapable of ordering their desires — in particular, their sexual desires — as they must be if evil is to be avoided. Thus, in their efforts to combat, on the one hand, sexual immorality, and, on the other, Gnostic contempt for marriage and the generation of human life, they quite naturally found it necessary to stress one important truth about sexuality and marriage, namely, that these good gifts of God are intended for the generation of new human life.[17]

St. Augustine

The thought of St. Augustine is especially important for several reasons. First of all, Augustine wrote more extensively about sexual and marital issues than did other Fathers.[18] Second, his influence, particularly on later theologians in the Western Church, has been and continues to be profound. It is fashionable today to portray Augustine as something of a pessimistic villain in the history of Christian theological reflection on sex, with some even accusing him of a latent Manicheism — that is, of an essentially Gnostic viewpoint which regarded sex as evil.[19] But these charges are unfair. There were, as shall be noted, limitations in Augustine's thought. But they are far from gross errors, and they should not cause us to forget the important contributions he has made to our understanding of human sexuality and of marriage.

In his early writings as a Catholic, Augustine was inclined to accept the view of some Greek Fathers that marriage and the sexual generation of human life would not have existed in Paradise (the Garden of Eden).[20] But the mature Augustine rejected this opinion, saying: "I do not see what could prevent there having been honorable marriage and an immaculate marriage bed in Paradise.... God could have arranged that, without any restless burning of sexual desire,... children would be born."[21] Obviously Augustine did not believe sex and sexual desire as such to be evil, though some claim that he did.[22] Following the Letter to the Hebrews, Augustine believes that marriage is to be held in honor, but he also shares this epistle's concern that the marriage bed "be undefiled" (Heb 13:4). He believes that this defilement occurs when desire is disordered, when it is a "restless burning."

Augustine held that concupiscence is the source of this restless burning. Concupiscence, which exists in us as a result of Adam's transgression, is not the same as original sin.[23] Rather, concupiscence is *caused* by original sin and *inclines* us to sin. Original sin itself, from which concupiscence arises, is clearly distinct from concupiscence because baptism completely removes original sin, whereas its effect and punishment, concupiscence, remains.[24] Augustine clarifies the relationship between concupiscence and actual sins of human beings in his commentary on a passage from the Letter of James in which we are told that "everyone is tempted by being drawn away and enticed by his own concupiscence. Once concupiscence has conceived, it gives birth to sin" (Jas 1:14-15). "These words," Augustine wrote, "distinguish the thing brought forth from the one giving birth. But concupiscence gives not birth unless it conceives; it does not conceive unless it entices, that is, unless it obtains willing consent to commit evil."[25] Thus, concupiscence may be called sin "by a certain figure of speech" (that is, by metonymy), since it comes from sin and leads to sin.[26] But since sin as such exists only in the will, it is not sin in the strict sense.[27]

According to Augustine, concupiscence distorts all our natural desires. These desires are good in themselves; but, as a result of original sin, they are now prone to seek their own proper objectives in a disordered way. Thus, for Augustine, concupiscence is a privation whereby our natural appetites or desires are bereft of their proper subordination to the rule of reason, and, thus deprived, tend to lead human beings away from God to the pursuit of worldly things in a sinful way.[28]

Augustine taught that, in virtue of our freedom and the grace of God poured forth in our hearts through Christ,[29] we are capable of resisting the enticements of concupiscent desire and of choosing and doing the good. We choose what is good when we "use" created goods, including our natural desires, for the purposes for which they have been created. Such "use" is not to be understood in any narrow utilitarian sense but simply in the sense that things to be used must be treated in a way that recognizes their true worth. The goods of this world are to be used and not "enjoyed" as if they were the final objects of human desire, for these are created and limited goods in which our hearts are not to take final rest. These created goods are ordered among themselves and are ordered ultimately to the Uncreated Good, God. He alone is our end — the one in whom our hearts will find rest. He alone is the Being that is to be "enjoyed" in the true sense of that word.[30]

Augustine explains how the goods of human sexuality are to be properly used in his discussion of marriage, for it is within marriage that these goods can be realized fully and rationally. Marriage, for Augustine, is a very good thing, and the goods of marriage provide the standard for proper sexual activity. His classification of the goods of marriage as the good of offspring, the good of fidelity, and the good of indissoluble unity became a classic source for subsequent theological reflection on marriage and chastity.[31]

Before taking up Augustine's teaching on the goods of marriage, however, it is most important to emphasize that he clearly distinguished *pleasure*, including *sexual pleasure*, from the evil of sinful concupiscence. He insisted that sexual pleasure, sought temperately and rationally, is not and cannot be termed concupiscence.[32] And he contrasts the lawful pleasure of the conjugal embrace with the unlawful pleasure of fornication.[33] In short, Augustine is not, as some people like to portray him, a pessimist who condemned all sexual pleasure as evil.[34]

For Augustine, offspring is the first and most obvious good of marriage. "What food is to the health of man, intercourse is to the health of the race."[35] This good does not consist merely in the physical generation of life. "Marriage was instituted so that the chastity of women would make children known to their fathers and fathers known to their children. True, it was possible for men to be born of promiscuous and random intercourse with any women at all, but there could not have been a bond of kinship between fathers and children."[36] The good of offspring, for Augustine, means the giving of life to persons who are called to a life of surpassing joy and friendship with God. Augustine says: "By offspring is meant not merely their begetting, but the receiving of them lovingly, the nourishing of them humanely, and the educating of them religiously."[37]

The great good of marital fidelity required, for Augustine, not only fidelity in sexual intercourse for the sake of procreating children but also mutual service in sustaining each other's weakness so that each may avoid illicit intercourse.[38] It is in conjunction with these two goods of marriage that Augustine discusses the morality of sexual union within marriage. Since procreation is "the primary, natural, and legitimate purpose of marriage,"[39] it is evident that conjugal union chosen to serve this good is completely without any fault. It is, indeed, a "chaste activity."[40]

The good of fidelity requires that spouses be faithful to each other, avoiding fornication and adultery. Augustine, like Lactantius and Chrysostom, is mindful of Paul's teaching in 1 Corinthians that people are to marry if they cannot exercise self-control, for "it is better to marry than to burn [with concupiscent desire]" (1 Cor 7:9), and that married couples are "not to deprive each other, except perhaps by consent, for a time that [they] may give themselves to prayer and return together again lest Satan tempt them because they lack self-control. But this I say by way of concession, not commandment" (1 Cor 7:5-6). But whereas Lactantius, Chrysostom, and Damascene — in speaking of the rightfulness of marital union "to avoid fornication" — imply that marital union for this purpose is unqualifiedly good, Augustine teaches that a spouse who requests marital relations precisely in order to avoid fornication is guilty of a venial sin. By "venial sin" Augustine means the sort of sin to which all of us are daily susceptible and of which we cannot claim to be free without lying (cf. 1 Jn 1:8); it is the sort of sin that is forgiven when we recite the Lord's prayer.[41] "In marriage, intercourse for the purpose of procreation has no fault attached to it; but intercourse for the purpose of satisfying concupiscence, provided it is with a spouse, is but venial fault because of fidelity; adultery or fornication, however, is a mortal sin."[42]

Many find this teaching of Augustine distasteful and demeaning to marriage. Yet Augustine's teaching perhaps shows a deeper appreciation of the human reality of marriage than does that of Lactantius, Chrysostom, and Damascene, for in holding that there is some minor fault when spousal relations are sought for the precise purpose of allaying desires and avoiding fornication, Augustine suggests that a basic good of marriage is itself not directly being sought but only indirectly fostered by avoidance of an activity that is seriously disordered. What is being sought in this type of intercourse is precisely the allaying of a desire and the avoiding of an evil to which the desire may lead. It is hardly an act which precisely expresses conjugal fidelity or, in modern terms, conjugal love. Augustine did clearly teach that the spouse who serves the good of conjugal fidelity by consenting to marital relations to meet the need of the spouse seeking relations for this purpose is choosing something perfectly good, for this spouse is choosing to serve the good of marital fidelity. Marital intercourse in the service of a real good is itself good.

Where Augustine can be faulted is in his failure to consider that spouses can choose to have marital relations for the precise purpose of expressing their fidelity, their love. With his predecessors, he sees as the possible purposes of marital union (1) the generation of children and (2) the serving of the good of fidelity when one spouse blamelessly agrees to marital union when the other spouse seeks it, with venial fault, expressly as a way of avoiding illicit intercourse. He does not explicitly entertain the possibility that both spouses might choose marital relations precisely as a way of showing their fidelity, their love.

Nevertheless, there is some evidence that if Augustine had considered this possibility, he would have approved it. For instance, in one place he wrote: "Surely we must see that God gives us some goods which are to be sought for their own sakes, such as wisdom, health, friendship; others which are necessary for something else, such as learning, food, drink, sleep, marriage, sexual intercourse. Certain of these are necessary for the sake of wisdom, such as learning; *others for the sake of friendship, such as marriage or intercourse*"[43] (emphasis added). Obviously, there is here the suggestion, one that will be made explicit in the development of the Catholic theological tradition, that spouses can rightly choose marital union as a way of showing their friendship. This would involve no unworthy motive and no sin. Unfortunately, however, Augustine himself did not proceed in this way. Rather, he conceived marriage not as something good in itself, like wisdom and friendship, but only as something instrumentally good, specifically as a means toward friendship. Moreover, the friendship he had in mind was the friendship that could exist between fathers and their sons, not the friendship between husband and wife.[44]

The third good of marriage discussed by Augustine is the bond of indissoluble unity between husband and wife. Although he did not use his term for this bond — the Latin word *sacramentum* — in precisely the same sense in which the Church now uses the word "sacrament," Augustine nonetheless attributed to marriage two characteristics which make it a true sacrament. First, he taught that Jesus Christ himself instituted this symbolic representation of his union with the Church,[45] and second, he taught that grace is given to the spouses in virtue of this institution.[46]

In his own understanding of the good of *sacramentum* in marriage Augustine first stressed that it was a holy bond. He based the permanence of marriage on the moral obligation of married persons to honor this sacramental bond, but this holy bond is itself rooted in the sacramental sign which reveals the meaning of marriage. Marriage is a human reality pointing toward the mystery of God's love for man, a love made real by Christ's indissoluble union with his bride, the Church.[47] Marriage symbolizes and draws strength from that union.

Augustine taught that every marriage has a natural bond requiring that it not be dissolved, but the marriage of Christians has more than this natural bond. Its indissolubility is also rooted in something even more profound; for Christians, marriage is a reality profoundly touched by the love between Christ and his Church. Christian marriage must be as indissoluble as this love.[48]

Augustine held that any act of adultery or faithlessness violated the good of fidelity, but such an act could not rupture the indissoluble unity between the spouses. The good of fidelity requires the spouses to be faithful to each other and to abstain from any form of sexual immorality; the good of the *sacramentum* excludes that adultery which would be involved in an invalid marriage after separation.[49]

Augustine's analysis of the goods of marriage has provided the Church with a powerful analytical device for understanding both the human significance and the salvific importance of marriage and human sexuality. Later theologians and the magisterium even till the present time make use of a framework whose full implications

Augustine did not grasp.[50] Augustine's study of sexual morality therefore, even though it has limitations, is an important step in the development of the Church's understanding of sexual morality.

II. The Teaching of the Medieval Theologians

Between the death of Augustine in 430 and the flowering of scholarship in the universities of the twelfth and thirteenth centuries, Western Europe experienced great social upheaval and disarray as a result of the fall of the Roman Empire and the migrations of the Germanic, Frankish, and Celtic peoples. During these centuries, dedicated communities of monks both preserved the cultural heritage of the past and worked to evangelize the pagan peoples and to instruct the Catholic faithful in the Christian way of life.

These monks, as the penitential books they wrote show, regarded marriage as good and holy. They informed the people of the immorality of nonmarital sex, and instructed couples about the immorality of contraceptive, anal, and oral intercourse, and the wickedness of abortion.[51] Some of their views were too rigoristic — for instance, their prohibition of marital intercourse during certain seasons of the year, on holy days, and prior to receiving communion.[52] However, these positions were only peripheral to their central teaching, and can perhaps be understood as a function of the difficult times in which they lived. The core of their teaching on sexual matters was not something specific to their cultural situation but rather a set of admonitions and prohibitions which were already present in patristic and scriptural times. Thus, for example, the condemnation of sexual activity outside of marriage is not unique to the monks and their penitentials but was already the common teaching of the Church and was proposed as such by the monks. The teaching of the Fathers of the Church on sexual matters as well as their understanding of the relevant biblical texts had already become normative for Christian life.

The great contribution of the medieval Church to the developing understanding of human sexuality came during the period of the High Middle Ages, when theological activity reached a high point of creative achievement, especially in the works of Doctors of the Church like St. Thomas Aquinas and St. Bonaventure in the thirteenth century. Although their cultural situation was very different from that of the

Fathers of the Church almost a millennium before, some of the challenges they faced were quite similar to those the Fathers had to deal with. A new form of Gnosticism developed during the High Middle Ages, particularly in the south of France. Albigensianism, Catharism, and Bogomilism constituted a movement which, like the older forms of Gnosticism, held marriage in contempt. This contempt had the standard Gnostic rationale: matter was taken to be evil, and marriage was bad because it was the basis for the generation of new life.

The great medieval theologians also faced a challenge not unlike that presented to the Fathers in the form of pagan sexual licentiousness. The ideal of "pure" or "romantic" love proposed by some of the troubadours was, in effect, an endorsement of romantic sexual activity separated from marriage and procreation, for these troubadours not only emphasized something very good — the love between man and woman — they also glorified sexual pleasure within the context of romance. Far more important, they showed no appreciation for the good of procreation. In this last respect they were influenced by the Gnosticism of the age.[53] This movement had considerable appeal, especially to the wealthier classes, and had the effect of creating within medieval culture a kind of neopaganism.

These two challenges — of Gnosticism and neopagan licentiousness — form the background for the thought of the medieval theologians on sexual morality. Their creative responses to these challenges led them to develop a body of work that deepened the Church's understanding of human sexuality in a real way, for their response to the anti-humanism of the Cathars and Albigenses required an affirmation of the Church's concern for human values, and their response to the hedonism of the heterodox troubadours required a careful sifting of opinions about what really is good for human beings.

Furthermore, this work of clarification took place within the context of an unprecedented effort to systematize the teaching of the Church and to present it as a coherent whole. Thus, in the great theologians of the Middle Ages, there is not only a creative response to serious challenges to Christian life and teaching but also an attempt to see this response within an overall account of Christian doctrine. This effort was carried out within the context of acceptance of the Church's received teachings on moral matters, and of heavy reliance on the Fathers of the Church, and especially on St. Augustine.

Augustine's teaching on sexual morality was particularly influential, and his discussion of the goods of marriage was the framework for thinking about marriage. It is not surprising, therefore, that the medieval theologians unanimously affirmed the goodness of marriage and the excellence of properly ordered sexual activity, and that they unanimously condemned those acts which attacked the great goods of marriage. They counted all such disordered acts as "unnatural."

The Evil of Acts Which Attack the Goods of Marriage

Three principal lines of argument were developed by medieval theologians to show the moral evil of nonmarital and "unnatural" sexual activity. The first was an argument from the authority of the Scriptures and the Fathers. This was advanced, for instance, by the twelfth-century theologian and bishop Peter Lombard, whose *Sentences* were used as a textbook for teaching theology from 1157 until 1550, and were commented on by all the great theologians of the thirteenth century. In discussing the sixth commandment, Lombard observed, citing Augustine, that this commandment required one not to have sexual union except within the marital covenant.[54] He also held that any sexual activity fully contrary to the purpose of marriage and of the sexual differentiation of the species into male and female was a gravely sinful violation of this commandment.[55]

A second line of argument, developed at length by the medieval theologians in their discussion of the natural law written in the hearts of mankind and discernible by right reason, was that the prohibited forms of sexual activity violated not only the law divinely revealed by God but also the natural moral law written in our hearts.[56] Bestiality, sodomy, contraceptive intercourse, and other forms of "unnatural sex" were judged to be wrongful in a special way insofar as they violated the order God had called into being by making humankind a species sexually differentiated into male and female and therefore capable of giving life to new human beings through acts of sexual intercourse.[57] These sins were judged to be unnatural in a stronger sense than other sins, including other sexual sins. All evil actions were held to be unnatural insofar as they are contrary to the order of right reason, that is, to the demands of rationally ordered activity which properly respects the goods of human nature. But unlike other sins, these particular sexual sins were held to be unnatural in a further sense, since they violated the most basic, God-given purpose of human sexuality. For this reason, they were held to be more seriously wrong than acts of sexual intercourse outside of marriage. These latter sins, too, were judged to be gravely sinful because such acts as adultery and fornication contradicted both God's divine law and the requirements of right reason. But sins of sodomy and the like were judged to be more gravely sinful because their peculiar unnaturalness violated divine and natural law in a radical way.

The teaching of medieval theologians that such sexual sins as masturbation, sodomy, and contraception are more perverse, as sexual sins, than fornication or adultery or even rape (the former were said to be *contra naturam* whereas the latter were said to be *praeter naturam*), angers many people today. But this teaching must be understood properly. The medieval theologians are claiming that certain kinds of sexual sins more seriously offend the virtue of chastity than do others. They are not saying that these sins are for this reason less grave as sins than adultery or rape, for instance. After all, adultery and rape are very serious violations of the virtue of justice, as well as being violations of the virtue of chastity. Thus, as a sin, rape is far more serious than masturbation or homosexual sodomy because it not only offends chastity but also gravely violates justice.

Thomas Aquinas, in arguing that nonmarital sexual union is contrary to the demands of the natural law insofar as it acts against the good of offspring, provides an argument characteristic of this second line of reasoning: "The end [or purpose] of the exercise of the genital organs is the generation and education of children; therefore, every exercise of these powers which is not properly ordered (*proportionatus*) to the generation of children and the education to which they have a right is of itself disordered."[58] Thus, sexual intercourse outside of marriage is excluded, for it is only in marriage that human life can properly be given, nurtured, and educated in the love and worship of God.

The medieval theologians also taught that nonmarital sexual behavior violated the fidelity spouses owe to each other. Bonaventure presents this teaching in a passage which reveals the growing appreciation by the medieval theologians of the love that is meant to exist between husband and wife: "In matrimony there is indeed a singular kind of love (*amor singularis*) which is not possible to be shared with others; naturally, therefore, a husband is jealous of his wife with respect to this, that she love no one else and that she love him in this act, and similarly the wife is naturally jealous of her husband in this respect."[59]

A third line of argument used by some of the medieval theologians to show that every kind of sexual union outside marriage and every kind of "unnatural" sexual act is morally wicked was based on the nature of concupiscent desire. This argument, which they believed to be rooted in biblical and patristic teaching, focused on the inclination to evil that exists in human beings as a result of original sin. According to this view — one expressed by many authors, including Lombard, Aquinas, Bonaventure, Albert the Great, and the authors of the *Summa of Brother Alexander*[60] — all our desires, good in themselves, have been corrupted by original sin. But sexual desires, they held, have been corrupted and indeed infected by original sin in a special way. Of itself the disorderliness of human sexual desire is not a moral evil, for moral evil can arise only when free personal consent is given to evil. But it is an evil we experience as a penalty. This restless itching for sexual gratification in a disorderly way exists in us as a result of original sin.[61] As a result of this we are tempted to do evil deeds in order to satisfy disorderly desires.

But according to the argument advanced, particularly by writers like Peter Lombard and Bonaventure,[62] God has in his goodness given us a remedy to help us avoid the evil to which we are prone as a result of this restless itching. That remedy is marriage. Before the fall, it had been instituted — as Lombard says — to be an office of nature, something good. Indeed now, as Paul and the Fathers had taught, it exists as a holy sign or sacrament pointing to the mystery of Christ's love for his Church. But in our present state, as Paul taught in 1 Corinthians 7, marriage also serves as a remedy for allaying the burning desires of concupiscence.[63] The great goods of marriage noted by Augustine, and, in particular, the good of offspring, serve to rectify sexual desires.[64] These goods cannot be properly and adequately realized outside of marriage, for children can be conceived but not properly cherished outside of marriage, and a kind of fidelity is possible but not the reality of a firm and unshakable union in a single life. Consequently, this argument continued, any choice to exercise one's sexual powers outside of marriage is morally wrong. Such acts may satisfy strong and natural desires; but they are not the remedy which God has provided.[65]

These three lines of argument advanced by the medieval theologians to explain the Church's received teaching on sexual morality were not meant to provide a rationalistic proof of the immorality of nonmarital and unnatural sexual activity. They do not seek to replace faith by philosophical argumentation. Rather, these arguments were proposed as a way of understanding, from within the faith, the sexual teaching based on Scripture and handed down through the Church. If these arguments are taken on their own terms they are very weighty, even if some of their details must be revised or even rejected. The power of these arguments within the perspective of Catholic faith becomes even clearer when their connection with the Church's affirmation of the goodness of marriage is spelled out.

The Goodness of Marriage

As the inheritors of Christian tradition, the medieval theologians unequivocally affirm the goodness of marriage. Like the Fathers they regard this matter as settled in Scripture. God himself instituted marriage by creating humankind as he did; and Christ blessed it at the marriage feast of Cana. This theme is sounded throughout the period. It was clearly articulated by Peter Lombard. When discussing the question of the goodness of marriage, he is content to refer simply to the patristic teaching, ably summed up by Hugh of St. Victor, the first medieval theologian to set forth in detail a theology of marriage.[66] Hugh had written: "That marriage is a good thing is proved not only from the fact that the Lord is said to have instituted it in creating our first parents but also because Christ himself took part in the marriage feast at Cana, commending the nuptials with a miracle by changing water into wine.... Therefore it is quite evident that marriage is a good thing."[67]

Thus far the medieval theologians reaffirm and make their own the patristic teaching on the goodness of marriage. Where they go beyond the Fathers is in developing a deeper appreciation for all the goods of marriage and conjugal intercourse.

The Goods of Marriage and the Meaning of the Marital Act

Augustine's teaching on the threefold good of marriage — progeny, fidelity, and indissoluble unity — was, as noted already, fully accepted by the medieval theologians. They regarded the indissoluble unity to be the good that marriage is, the good that man and woman bring into being when they freely choose to be husband and wife.[68] The medieval theologians saw the bond of unity not only as a moral obligation but also as having ontological significance. This bond is not only a sign of the indissoluble unity between Christ and his Church but also a reality within marriage. The marriage really participates in this mystery of divine love. It becomes a union so profound that only death can dissolve it. Moreover, it is accompanied by graces intended to assist spouses in living their marriages faithfully and generously. There was, however, a debate among medieval theologians whether the grace the sacrament of marriage conferred was "remedial" or "sanctifying." Lombard and many others held that it was only "remedial." In his earliest writings on marriage Aquinas held it "more probable" that marriage confers sanctifying grace, and in his later writing on marriage, in his *Summa contra gentes* he held that this is certain precisely *because the Church teaches that marriage is a true sacrament and that the sacraments of the new law give sanctifying grace.* It is for this reason, the medieval theologians taught, that marriage between Christians is a true sacrament of the Church.[69] This teaching, as indicated already, was affirmed by the Church.[70]

The other two goods of marriage — fidelity and progeny — were held to be the goods that marriage *intends*, that is, they are goods which the spouses promise to give and honor in their shared lives as they make the free consent that constitutes them as husband and wife and brings into being their indissoluble unity.[71] Adultery and contraceptive intercourse violate the goods of fidelity and progeny by undermining and wounding them. Such deeds violate the good of the indissoluble bond of marriage as well, but since this bond is the very reality of marriage itself, it cannot be broken by them. Marriage itself cannot be dissolved by these or any other sins.[72]

The medieval theologians, with Augustine and the other Fathers, held that marital intercourse for the sake of having children — that is, with the intention of begetting progeny — is completely justifiable. Indeed, they commonly taught that the conjugal act ordered to this good was an act of the virtue of religion, insofar as its end was the generation of life that was to be brought up in the love and worship of God.[73]

Likewise, the medieval theologians followed Augustine in teaching that it was a venial sin for a spouse to seek sexual union merely as a way to avoid fornication, while the spouse who consented to marital union for this purpose was free of all sin.[74]

But the medieval theologians developed Augustine's teaching in this matter by focusing on an idea only implicit in his writings — namely, that the spouses could rightly choose to unite in marital coition in order to foster and express the good of fidelity. To choose marital union for this purpose, writers like Thomas Aquinas and Bonaventure maintained, is a truly virtuous act, an act of the virtue of justice.[75] In fact, Aquinas argued that a husband ought to anticipate his wife's desires in this matter and offer to give himself to her in sexual union in order to cherish this good.[76]

There is even, on Aquinas's account, a suggestion that the sexual expression of the good of fidelity by husband and wife participates in the sacramental character of the marriage. Thus, St. Thomas writes: "A human act is good in two ways. In one way, by moral goodness, which the act has from the goods which make it a right act. In the case of the marital act, fidelity and progeny do this.... In another way, by sacramental goodness: this factor causes an act to be not simply good but also holy. And the marital act has this goodness from the indissolubility of the union, for in this regard it is a sign of the union of Christ and the Church."[77] It is not surprising, therefore, that Aquinas regarded sexual intercourse for the sake of fidelity to be a meritorious act.[78]

A procreative intent is not, then, necessary for marital acts to be virtuous, holy, and meritorious. To choose conjugal intercourse for the sake of the good of fidelity is to choose to do something exceedingly good. Of course, Aquinas and other writers who justified marital union as an expression of the good of fidelity regarded it as wicked to act *contrary* to the good of offspring — that is, to act contraceptively. But in the medieval theologians there is clear and explicit recognition of the "non-procreative" purposes of marital sexual union.

It is true that Aquinas, Bonaventure, and other medieval theologians who justified marital union as a way of fostering the good of fidelity taught that the act in question was an act of the virtue of justice, of the justice that husband and wife owe each other. They did not, ordinarily, speak of it as an act of conjugal love, but their thought was clearly open to fuller development in this direction. This is strongly suggested by Bonaventure when he speaks of the "singular love that is meant to exist between husband and wife, a love expressed in that act," namely, in the marital act. In this passage love is explicitly related to marital union. St. Thomas Aquinas speaks in a similar way about the special character of the friendship between spouses. He affirms this to be the highest friendship, and clearly supposes that marital intercourse is integral to it; his concern is to affirm that sexual intercourse is not the whole of marital friendship.[79]

A similar emphasis can be found in the teaching of the *Summa Fratris Alexandri*. This work is specially significant because it is not the work of an individual author (Alexander of Hales, to whom it was attributed) but is rather the compilation of many theologians representing "the spirit of the Franciscan thirteenth-century school of theology at the University of Paris."[80] The authors of this work consider an objection to the appropriateness of the human race's derivation from the first pair of humans by way of sexual intercourse. The objection is that this mode of derivation only serves to increase the intensity of carnal love, which is an "impediment" to spiritual love. To answer this objection the authors of the *Summa Fratris Alexandri* distinguish three types of love: carnal love, natural love, and spiritual love. They maintain that "natural love," which is carnal love purged of all lust, is no obstacle to spiritual love; on the contrary, "spiritual love should come to be through natural love, and natural love is meant in turn to be perfected by the spiritual love toward which it disposes."[81] The authors of this work go on to speak of the loving embrace of husband and wife — obviously a reference to sexual union between spouses — as symbolizing the union of the soul with God "both as to the intensity of that union and its fruitfulness."[82]

It is clear, therefore, that the medieval theologians enhanced the Church's understanding of the values involved in marriage by their development of the teaching that fidelity was one of the goods of marriage, and by their explicit recognition of the value of marital friendship and its relationship to sexual intercourse.

These developments quite naturally led to a more positive evaluation of the status of sexual pleasure than Christian tradition had accepted, but the medieval theologians did not, for the most part, articulate these implications. Thomas Aquinas, however, did make several points that are important in the development of a more balanced view of the moral status of sexual pleasure. Like the other medieval theologians, Aquinas affirmed the common teaching of the Church that sexual intercourse solely for the sake of pleasure was sinful. He maintained that it would be mortally sinful if one's sexual interest in one's wife would be so exclusively aimed at finding pleasure that he viewed her really as only a sex object or object of lust, not as a wife, as one with whom he was lovingly committed to honoring the great goods of marriage. But he rejected as absurd the more rigorous position that it is better to repudiate or merely tolerate the pleasure of marital intercourse.[83] His view on this matter follows from his realistic and warmly human evaluation of pleasure and its role in human life. With Aristotle, he held that pleasure is a natural accompaniment and perfection of a human action. As such, the moral character depends on the moral status of the action it accompanies. Thus, the pleasure of a morally good act is itself morally good and worthy of pursuit as part of a good activity. The pursuit of pleasure becomes morally suspect only if it inclines one to act in ways that are somehow unreasonable or disordered. Aquinas's analysis of pleasure provides the ground for a more realistic appreciation of sexual pleasure.[84]

III. Post-Medieval Catholic Thought

In this section our purpose is by no means to attempt even a brief history of the development of Catholic theological thought on sexual morality from the Middle Ages to the present. Rather, we hope only to indicate the continuity of the Catholic theological tradition, and to note briefly some of the principal developments that have taken place since the end of the age of high Scholasticism.

The continuity of the Catholic theological tradition from the death of St. Thomas Aquinas in 1274 until the 1960s is remarkable. For nearly eight hundred years Catholic tradition has affirmed unanimously and with one voice that marriage is good; that genital sexual activity outside marriage, whether through adultery, fornication, masturbation, homosexual activity, or bestiality, is gravely sinful; and that within marriage some sexual acts — notably contraception and acts leading to orgasm apart from sexual intercourse — are seriously wrong. Germain Grisez and John Ford, S.J., surveyed forty-two manuals on moral theology in common use during the nineteenth and twentieth centuries for their teaching on contraceptive intercourse. All the authors studied unanimously held that such behavior was gravely sinful.[85] Nor is it surprising that these authors taught as they did, for in branding contraceptive intercourse as seriously wrong they were simply reaffirming the centuries-old teaching of the Church, a teaching which the Fathers, the Scholastics, and their modern successors found rooted in the Scriptures as understood by the Church.[86]

The same authors examined by Ford and Grisez likewise unanimously teach that all forms of nonmarital sexual activity (fornication, adultery, rape, sodomy, masturbation, etc.) are serious moral evils, contrary both to the natural moral law and to the law divinely revealed by God. Again, there is nothing surprising in this teaching.

In the 1960s some Catholic theologians began to question the received teaching on contraception; and in 1966 several prominent moral theologians — in preparing a report for the Papal Commission for the Study of Problems of Population, Family, and Birthrate — urged that contraceptive intercourse could be morally justifiable for married couples.[87] In advocating this view, these authors rejected the claim that the principles upon which they justified contraception for married couples could be used to justify anal or oral intercourse for married couples.[88] These theologians held, in accord with the theological tradition, that nonmarital modes of sexual activity were immoral. Likewise, they agreed that sexual activity between spouses must be directed toward sexual intercourse — that seeking orgasm outside of natural intercourse was seriously wrong even for married couples. They thought that allowing contraception for married couples under narrowly described circumstances would not compromise the rationale for these proscriptions.

Recent history shows that they were mistaken, for subsequent Catholic theologians — among them Michael Valente[89] and the authors of *Human Sexuality: New Directions in American Catholic Thought*[90] — were willing to draw the conclusion that the principles justifying contraceptive intercourse for married couples likewise can be used to justify nonmarital sexual activity and deviant sexual activity within marriage. As Charles E. Curran has noted: "History has clearly shown that those who were afraid that a change in the teaching on contraception would lead to other changes [in the teaching on sexual morality] were quite accurate."[91] Curran seems to have recognized that a radical change in principle was needed to justify contraception, and that such a change is bound to have wide effects.

It is not our purpose here to enter into the current dispute concerning the morality of contraception and other types of sexual activity. Subsequent chapters of this volume will be concerned with these issues. What is relevant here is that those contemporary theologians who justify contraception, and with it various kinds of sexual activity condemned by the received teaching of the Church, themselves recognize that their teaching markedly contrasts with the theological tradition as expressed in the writings of theologians prior to the 1960s. No theologian, from the time of the apostolic writers until the 1960s, even suggested that sexual activities of the kinds justified by these writers could be morally legitimate.

This aberrant development is not, however, the only development in the Church's sexual teaching in recent centuries and decades, for there has been a genuine development in the Church's understanding of the purpose of human sexuality *within* marriage on the part of post-medieval theologians. There has been, throughout the modern period, a deepening appreciation of the significance of marital intercourse as an expression of love. This growing appreciation of marital love in no way contradicts the theological tradition but authentically develops themes which were suggested by the medieval theologians and present in Christian consciousness from the start.

As noted above, the medieval theologians clearly recognized that procreative intent was not necessary for marital intercourse to be morally good, and even meritorious and holy.[92] The medieval teaching that marital intercourse undertaken in order to express the good of marital fidelity developed through the modern period into the explicit recognition that marital intercourse can be rightly chosen as a way to foster and nourish spousal love.

Even before the medieval period came to an end, Nicolas Oresme, a theologian who became bishop of Lisieux, wrote warmly about the love between husband and wife, a love that is displayed in their marital act. The teaching of Oresme, who wrote about the middle of the fourteenth century, has been summarized as follows:

> The union between man and woman in marriage is fully
> natural. It is meant to spring from love and to be grounded

upon love — a love that is productive of an intensity of joy and pleasure, that makes equals of man and woman and makes each to be supreme in the other's affections. The marriage act is good if decently and lovingly engaged in. It has purposes beyond generation.... Sin may enter into the union, but if the union is of reason and is basically good, there is no need to worry about it. It is only when love becomes "bestial" — when one is intent only upon his isolated pleasure — that there is cause for concern.[93]

Oresme's conception of the value of sexual intercourse between spouses as expressive of their mutual love is foreshadowed by the work of St. Thomas Aquinas, St. Bonaventure, and other medieval writers. It was to be developed and more fully articulated only in the nineteenth and twentieth centuries in the works of thinkers like Jean Gury and Dietrich von Hildebrand.[94]

Another element in the development of Catholic theologians' appreciation of marital intercourse has been the explicit recognition that spouses may legitimately seek pleasure in the marital act. Here, too, there is a development anticipated by medieval authors. We have already noted that the principles of Thomas Aquinas are open to this recognition, and his great commentator, Thomas Cardinal Cajetan (1469-1534), explicitly recognized that spouses may legitimately seek pleasure in conjugal union. Like Aquinas, he taught that spouses were obliged to seek conjugal union as spouses, that is, as acting for one or the other of the goods of marriage, and that pleasure is the natural perfection of the act, as beauty is the bloom of youth. But he added that spouses ought to give God thanks for the pleasure that marital union brings, thus suggesting that sexual pleasure was a legitimate object of marital activity.[95] He taught, however, that an explicit or actual intent to foster one or the other of the goods of marriage, such as the aim of nourishing faithful love, also had to be present for the act to be morally good.

Subsequent theologians like Thomas Sanchez (1550-1610) and Alphonsus Liguori (1696-1787) taught that this last condition was too stringent. They held that it was sufficient for the proper respect for these goods, and thus for the moral goodness of marital intercourse, that spouses seek marital union *as spouses*.[96] Their teaching became the common heritage of nineteenth- and twentieth-century theologians. In other words, spouses need not *explicitly* intend their marital act to further either the good of procreation or of marital fidelity. A habitual intent to respect these goods — to seek marital union as spouses — was sufficient, although of course, it would be seriously wrong for them to repudiate either the good of *proles* or the good of *fides*.

In short, there has been development since the time of the Middle Ages in the Church's understanding of human sexuality and the role, within marriage, of conjugal intercourse. As one would expect in the legitimate development of God's revelation, this development has many antecedents in the earlier tradition. The medieval notion that spouses could rightly choose marital union as a way of expressing their marital fidelity was a development of ideas found in St. Augustine. The more modern teachings that marital union is a way of expressing the singular love between the spouses and that it is by no means wicked for spouses to take delight in their conjugal union but that it is rather quite proper for them to seek this pleasure *as spouses* are foreshadowed by and rooted in the teaching of the great Scholastics. Another sign of the real continuity and legitimacy of the post-medieval theological developments in sexual morality is the unwillingness of a great many contemporary theologians to question or compromise the received teaching that it is seriously wrong to seek sexual union within or outside of marriage in ways that deliberately fail to honor any of the goods of marriage.[97]

In sum, even the briefest of surveys of the theological tradition's developing teaching on sexual morality shows beyond all doubt that there is real continuity and development in the Church's understanding of human sexuality.[98] This development has taken place within a framework of moral norms which are not questioned or rejected but better understood as the moral thinking of the Church unfolds in response to new situations. This framework is never presented as a mere imposition of divine or human authority but as an inherent requirement of authentic human life. One of the most important aspects of the development of doctrine on sexual matters has been the ever-clearer articulation of the connection between the specific requirements of Christian sexual morality and the basic moral principles of Christian living. Today it has become clearer than ever before that Christian sexual morality is no more and no less than the implication of the logic of love — what love of God and of neighbor requires in this area of human life.

ENDNOTES FOR CHAPTER THREE

1. Several works can be noted here, but none can be recommended without qualification, and none, of course, is an attempt at a systematic history of the Catholic theological treatment of human sexuality or sexual morality: see Derrick S. Bailey, *The Male-Female Relationship in Christian Thought* (New York: Harper and Row, 1968); John T. Noonan, Jr., *Contraception: A History of Its Treatment by Catholic Theologians and Canonists* (Cambridge, MA: Harvard University Press, 1965); Joseph Kern, *The Theology of Marriage: The Historical Development of Christian Attitudes Toward Sex and Sanctity in Marriage* (New York: Sheed and Ward, 1964). In addition to these works there is a number of works on the theological study of sexuality by various saints and doctors of the Church. Some of these will be cited in this chapter. There is a wealth of useful material in the relevant articles in the *Dictionnaire de Théologie Catholique*, ed. A. Vacant, E. Manganot, and A. Amann (Paris: Librairie Letouzey et Ane, 1902-1950), 15 vols. In 2008, David Cloutier's *Love, Reason, and God's Story: An Introduction to Catholic Sexual Ethics* (Winona, MN: St. Mary's Press, 2008), which offers a history of Catholic sexual ethics, particularly from the 19th century until the present, was published. This is a useful work, but it does not help readers to know the Catholic tradition before the 19th century to any degree more than the present text. However, John S. Grabowski, *Sex and Virtue: An Introduction to Sexual Ethics* (Washington, DC: Catholic University of America Press, 2003), ch. 4, "Sex and Chastity," pp. 71-95 has a brief useful summary.

2. See Noonan, *Contraception*, pp. 56-106; Arno Karlen, *Sexuality and Homosexuality* (New York: Morrow, 1972); F. Van der Meer, *Augustine the Bishop: The Life and Work of a Father of the Church* (New York: Sheed and Ward, 1962), ch. 1. See also James F. Jeffers, *The Greco-Roman world of the New Testament Era,* (Downers Grove, IL: Intervarsity Press, 1999) ch. 12. Luke Timothy Johnson, *Among the Gentiles: Greco-Roman Religion and Christianity* (The Anchor Yale Bible Reference Library) (New Haven: Yale University Press, 2009).

Everett Ferguson, *Backgrounds of Early Christianity* (3rd ed. Grand Rapids, MI: Eerdmans, 2003) 70-80.

3. See Noonan, *Contraception*, pp. 57-70, for an account of Gnosticism.

4. Irenaeus, *Adversus Haereses*, I.28 (PG 7.690). [*NOTE*: In referring to the writings of the Fathers of the Church, the title of work will first be given, followed by book and chapter number (in this instance, I.28), or book, chapter, and section number (for some Fathers). Reference will then be given to the pertinent volume and column, in the famous collection of patristic sources provided by J. P. Migne. Migne collected the works of the Greek-writing Fathers into 161 volumes, published in a town near Paris between 1857-1866. In this collection he provided the Greek text with a Latin translation in parallel columns. The reference is to the volume of this collection and to the column containing the Greek text. Thus the text of Irenaeus to which reference is made is found in Migne's *Patrologiae Cursus Completus: Series Graeca* (hereafter PG), vol. 7, col. 690. Migne likewise collected the writings of the Fathers who wrote in Latin into 221 volumes, which he published originally between 1844 and 1855. These volumes, called *Patrologiae Cursus Completus: Series Latina* (hereafter PL), provide the Latin texts of the Fathers in pages made up of two columns, and the reference is to the volume of this collection and the column or columns concerned. Thus a reference such as PL 34.394 in endnote 11 below means vol. 34 of Migne's collection of Latin texts, col. 394.]

5. Clement of Alexandria, *Stromata*, 3, 12.83 (PG 8.1176).

6. Justin Martyr, *Apologia*, 1.29 (PG 6.373).

7. Athenagoras of Athens, *Legatio*, 33 (PG 6.965, 968).

8. See Noonan, *Contraception*, p. 75; here, the appeals to nature by these Fathers are said to be a way of reinforcing positions held on other grounds.

9. See Clement of Alexandria, *Stromata*, 3.12.84 (PG 8.1177, on procreation and marriage); 7.12.70 (PG 9.497, on marital virtue).

10. See L. Godefroy, "Le Marriage au Temps des Pères," *Dictionnaire de Théologie Catholique*, 9.2, cots. 2077-2123.

11. See Theodoret, *Quaestiones in Genesi*, c. 3, q. 37 (PG 80.136); Augustine, *De Genesi ad Litteram*, 9.3 (PL 34.394); John Damascene, *De Fide Orthodoxa*, 2.30 (PG 94.976).

12. See Kern, *Theology of Marriage*, pp. 41-60.

13. Gregory of Nyssa, *De Opificio Hominis*, 17 (PG 44.187); John Chrysostom, *De Virginitate*, 17 (PG 48.546); *Homilia in Genesi*, 18 (PG 53.153); Theodoret, *Quaestiones in Genesi*, c. 3, q. 37 (PG 80.136); Damascene, *De Fide Orthodoxa*, 2.30 (PG 94.976).

14. Clement of Alexandria, *Stromata*, 3.7 (PG 8.1162).

15. Lactantius, *Divinarum Institutionum*, 6.23 (PL 6.715f): "Whoever cannot control his affections, let him keep them within the confines of the marriage bed." Chrysostom, *De Verbis Illis Apostoli, "Propter Fornicationem"* (PG 51.210): "There are two reasons why marriage was instituted, that we may live chastely and that we may become parents."

16. On this see St. John Chrysostom, *On Marriage and Family Life*, trs. Catherine P. Roth and David Anderson (Crestwood, NY: St. Vladimir's Seminary Press, 1986). This small work contains short but beautiful texts of Chrysostom on the goodness of marriage and family life: Homily 19 on 1 Corinthians 7; Homily 20 on Ephesians 5:22-33; Homily 21 on Ephesians 6:1-4; Homily 12 on Colossians 4:18; Sermon on Marriage; and How to Choose a Wife.

17. Developing Catholic doctrine has made it clear that the procreative good is not the only good at stake in marriage; but this development has in no way suggested that this good is not essential. See *Gaudium et Spes*, nos. 48, 50.

18. Among Augustine's explicit treatments of marriage are *De Bono Conjugale* (PL 40.373-394), *De Nuptiis et Concupiscentia* (PL 44.413-474), and *De Conjugiis Adulterinis* (PL 40.451-486). Glenn Olsen, "Progeny, Faithfulness, Sacred Bond: Marriage in the Age of Augustine," in *Christian Marriage: A Historical Study*, ed. Glenn Olsen (New York: The Crossroad Publishing Co., 2001), pp. 101-145, provides a good overview of Augustine's three goods; see especially pp. 121-126.

19. For criticisms of these misrepresentations of Augustine, see John Hugo, *St. Augustine on Nature, Sex, and Marriage* (Chicago: Scepter Press, 1969). See Eugene Portalié, *A Guide to the Thought of St. Augustine* (Chicago: Henry Regnery, 1960). D. Paul, "Saint Augustine on Marriage," *Augustinus* 12 (1967): 165-180; J. Thonnard, "La morale conjugale selon saint Augustin," *Revue des Etudes Augustiniennes* 15 (1969), 113-131; Cormac Burke, "Saint Augustine and Conjugal Sexuality," *Communio,* 17 (Winter 1990): 545-565.

20. On this see the very excellent study of Philip Lyndon Reynolds, *Marriage in the Western Church: The Christianization of Marriage During the Patristic and Early Medieval Periods*, vol. 24 of Supplements to Vigiliae Christianae: Texts and Studies of Early Christian Life and Language (Leiden/New York/Cologne: E. J. Brill, 1994), pp. 241-251, where he shows that in his early writing *De Genesis contra Manichaeos* Augustine was attracted to this position, although in his more mature writings (e.g., *De civitate Dei*) he definitively rejected this notion.

21. *Opus Imperfectum Contra Julianum*, 6.30 (PL 45.1582).

22. See, for example, Louis Dupré, *Contraception and Catholics* (Baltimore: Helicon, 1964), pp. 26-27. But see the article by Cormac Burke in endnote 19.

23. See Portalié, *A Guide to the Thought of St. Augustine*, pp. 297-313; Hugo, *St. Augustine on Nature, Sex, and Marriage*, pp. 52-67.

24. See Ibid.

25. *Contra Julianum*, 6.15.47 (PL 44.849).

26. *De Nuptiis et Concupiscentia*, 1.25 (PL 44.429-430).

27. For Augustine, sin as such is only in the will; see *Confessions*, 8, chs. 5, 9-10; *The City of God*, 22, ch. 24.

28. Perhaps the best study of St. Augustine's understanding of concupiscence is provided by F.-J. Thonnard, "La notion de concupiscence en philosophie augustinienne," *Recherches Augustiniennes* 3 (1965), 90-99.

29. See *De Natura et Gratia*, 43.50 (PL 44.271): "God does not command the impossible, but by commanding He admonishes you that you should do what you can and beg Him for what you cannot." This text is cited by the Council of Trent (DS 1536).

30. For the Augustinian distinction between use and enjoyment and its application in articulating the proper attitude toward God and earthly things, see *De Vera Religione*, 24.45 (PL 34.165-166) and *De Doctrina Christiana*, 1.35.39 (PL 34:42).

31. See *De Bono Conjugali, De Nuptiis et Concupiscentia*, passim. On the permanent value of Augustine's understanding of the goods of marriage see Augustine Reagan, C.Ss.R., "The Perennial Value of Augustine's Theology of the Goods of Marriage," *Studia Moralia* (1981), 351-377.

32. *De Bono Coniugali*, c. 16, no. 18 (PL 40, 385): "and neither [nourishment nor generation] can take place without carnal pleasure,

which, however, when moderated and used naturally, cannot be the same as concupiscence."

33. *Sermo* 159, c. 2, no. 2 (PL 38, 868-869): "Conjugal embraces give delight; so too do the embraces of prostitutes. But the former are legitimate, the latter not."

34. On this whole question see Burke, "St. Augustine and Conjugal Chastity," *Communio* 17, 1990: 545-565.

35. *De Bono Conjugali*, 16.18 (PL 40.385-386).

36. *Contra Julianum*, 5.9 (PL 44.806).

37. *De Genesi ad Litteram*, 9.7 (PL 34.397).

38. *De Bono Conjugali*, 6 (PL 40.377-378).

39. *De Conjugiis Adulterinis*, 1.12 (PL 40.459); *De Nuptiis et Concupiscentia*, 1.17 (PL 44.424-425); *De Bono Conjugali*, 6 (PL 40.377-378).

40. *Enarratio in Psalmos*, 50.7 (PL 36.591-592). The complete text says: "It is not therefore because it is sin to have to do with wives that men are conceived in iniquity.... This chaste operation (*opus hoc castum*) in a married person has no sin, but the origin of sin brings with it condign punishment."

41. *De Gratia Christi et Peccato Originali*, 2.43 (PL 44.407-408); see *De Nuptiis et Concupiscentia*, 1.16 (PL 44.424).

42. *De Bono Conjugali*, 6 (PL 40.377-378).

43. Ibid., 9 (PL 40.380). Augustine follows this point by noting the connection between marital friendship and procreation: "For from these come the propagation of the human race in which friendly association is a great good."

44. On this see Reynolds, *Marriage in the Western Church*, ch. 12.

45. *In Johannis Evangelium*, 9.2 (PL 31.1458-1459).

46. *De Bono Conjugali*, 24.32 (PL 40.394-395).

47. Ibid.

48. See Edward Schillebeeckx, *Marriage: Human Reality and Saving Mystery* (New York: Sheed and Ward, 1965), p. 286.

49. Ibid., p. 283.

50. Vatican Council II, for example, makes use of Augustine's teaching on the three goods of marriage; see *Gaudium et Spes*, no. 48.

51. See John T. NcNeill and Helena Gamer, "Records of Civilization," in *Medieval Handbooks of Penance: A Translation of the Principal Libri Poenitentiales*, vol. 29 (New York: Columbia University Press,

1938). See also John T. McNeill, *The Celtic Penitentials and Their Influence on Continental Christianity* (Paris: 1938). Noonan, *Contraception*, pp. 152-170, provides an account of the penitential materials relevant to sexual morality.

52. These proscriptions were rooted in the belief that the corruption of the sexual appetites by original sin required abstinence from sexual activity to show the proper respect for God within the worship of the Church. Thus, it is unlikely that these proscriptions are the result of Stoic or Manichean influences on the authors of the penitentials, but rather arise from their reading of Scripture.

53. See Noonan, *Contraception*, pp. 179-193, for an account of medieval Gnosticism, the ideal of romantic love, and their connection. See also Teresa Olsen Pierre, "Marriage, Body, and Sacrament in the Age of Hugh of St. Victor," in *Christian Marriage*, ed. Glenn W. Olsen, pp. 213-268.

54. Peter Lombard, *Libri IV Sententiarum*, III, d. 37, c. iv: "Non moechaberis, 'id est, ne cuilibet miscearis, excepto foedere matrimonii. A parte enim totum intelligitur. Nomine igitur *moechiae* omnis concubitus illicitus illorumque membrorum non legitimus usus prohibitus debet intelligi.'" The internal quote is from Augustine, *Quaestiones in Exodi*, q. 71, no. 4, PL 31.622.

55. Peter Lombard, Ibid., IV, d. 28, c. ii.

56. See, for example, Bonaventure, *In IV Sententiarum*, d. 33, a. 1, qq. 1, 2; *Summa Fratris Alexandri*, P. III, q. 35, m. 4; P. II, q. 147, m. 2; Albert the Great, *In IV Sententiarium*, d. 33, a. 5; Thomas Aquinas, *In IV Sententiarum*, d. 33, q. 1, aa. 1-3 (= *Summa Theologiae*, Supplement, q. 65, aa. 1-5).

57. It was the unanimous opinion of the medieval theologians that the distinction of humankind into man and woman was for the sake of procreation. This point was made by Peter Lombard, *Liber Sententiarum*, II, d. 18, c. 1; the commentaries on this text reinforce the point. See, for example, Aquinas, *In II Sententiarum*, d. 20, q. 1, a. 1; *Summa Theologiae*, I, q. 98, a.2, sed contra.

58. *De Malo*, q. 15, a. 1: "Finis autem usus genitalium membrorum est generatio et educatio prolis; et ideo omnis usus praedictorum membrorum qui non est proportionatus generationi prolis et debitae ejus educationi, est secundum se inordinatus." See also *Summa Theologiae*, II-II, q. 153, a. 2; *Summa Contra Gentiles*, bk. III, ch. 122.

59. Bonaventure, *In IV Sententiarum*, d. 33, a. 1: "In matrimonio est quidam amor singularis, in quo non communicet alienus: unde naturaliter omnis vir zelet uxorem quantum ad hoc, ut nullum alium diligat, ut diligat ipsum in actu illo: et omnis uxor similiter zelet virum ad hoc.... Caritate adveniente, quae facit omnia communia, numquam facit uxorem communem propter privatum amorem qui debet esse in matrimonio." See Sister Paula Jean Miller, F.S.E., *Marriage: The Sacrament of the Divine-Human Communion*, vol. 1, *A Commentary on St. Bonaventure's Breviloquium* (Quincy, IL: Franciscan Press, 1996).

60. See endnote 80 below on the authorship of this work.

61. See Lombard, *Liber Sententiarum*, II, d. 31, c. 2, and the commentaries on this text. See also Aquinas, *Summa Theologiae*, I-II, q. 83, a. 4; *De Veritate*, q. 25, a. 6.

62. Lombard, *Libri IV Sententiarum*, II, d. 31, c. 4; IV, d. 26, cc. 2-4; Bonaventure, *In II Sententiarum*, d. 31, a. 1, q. 3.

63. See ibid.

64. The medieval theologians often spoke of the goods of marriage as "excusing" marital intercourse, but they regarded these goods as intrinsic perfections of marriage. Aquinas, for example, says the following: "Ista bona, quae matrimonium honestant, sunt de ratione matrimonii; et ideo non indiget eis quasi exterioribus quibusdam ad honestandum, sed quasi causantibus in ipso honestatem, quae ei secundum se competit." *In IV Sententiarum*, d. 31, q. 1, a. 2, ad 2 (= *Summa Theologiae*, Supplement, q. 49, a. 1, ad 2).

65. See Bonaventure, *In IV Sententiarum*, d. 31, a. 2, ad 1, 2, 3.

66. See Hugh of St. Victor, *De Sacramentis*, II, P. XI (PL 176.479-520). See Schillebeeckx, *Marriage*, pp. 320-324, for a summary.

67. Hugh of St. Victor, *Summa Sententiarum*, tr. 7, c. 2, PL 176.155. This is cited by Lombard, *Libri IV Sententiarum*, IV, d. 26, c. 5.

68. See Fabian Parmisano, O.P., "Love and Marriage in the Middle Ages I," *New Blackfriars*, 50 (1969), 604. For an analysis of Thomas Aquinas's discussion of this matter, see Germain Grisez, "Marriage: Reflections Based on St. Thomas and Vatican II," *Catholic Mind*, 64 (1966), 4-19.

69. The doctrine that marriage was one of the seven sacraments developed during the Middle Ages; Aquinas, following Lombard, held

that it was one of the sacraments but, as we have seen in the text, held that it conferred only "remedial" and not "sanctifying" grace. In the Supplement to his *Summa Theologiae,* q. 41, a. 3, Aquinas held it more probable that it confers sanctifying grace (this question is taken from his early Commentary on Lombard's *Sentences*). But in his *Summa Contra Gentes,* bk. 4, ch. 78, he says that it is certain that marriage gives sanctifying grace because this is what the Church teaches.

70. See the Fourth Lateran Council of 1215. The sacramentality of marriage was clearly taught also by Pope Innocent IV in his profession of faith for Waldenses in 1208.

71. The medieval theologians realized, of course, that not all couples could have children because of sterility. But they held that sterile spouses need not repudiate the good of offspring. Such an intention in the exchange of marriage vows would vitiate the marital consent.

72. See Parmisano, "Love and Marriage in the Middle Ages II," *New Blackfriars,* 50 (1969), 649-660.

73. See Aquinas, *In IV Sententiarum,* d. 26, q. 1, aa. 3, 4 (= *Summa Theologiae,* Supplement, q. 41, aa. 3, 4); Bonaventure, *In IV Sententiarum,* d. 26, q. 1, a. 3; d. 31, a. 2, q. 1.

74. See, for example, Lombard, *Libri IV Sententiarum,* IV, d. 31, c. 5; Bonaventure, *In IV Sententiarum,* d. 31, a. 2, q. 2; Aquinas, *In IV Sententiarum,* d. 31, q. 2, a. 3 (= *Summa Theologiae,* Supplement, q. 49, a. 6).

75. See texts cited above in endnote 73.

76. See *In IV Sententiarum,* d. 32, q. 1, a. 1 (= *Summa Theologiae,* Supplement, q. 64, a. 2).

77. *In IV Sententiarum,* d. 31, q. 2, a. 2 (= *Summa Theologiae,* Supplement, q. 49, a. 4); it should be noted that in the very next article Aquinas states that the third good of marriage — the indissoluble bond — pertains to the essence of marriage and not to its use, and therefore makes marriage to be upright but not the act of marriage.

78. See *In IV Sententiarum,* d. 26, q. 1, a. 4 (= *Summa Theologiae,* Supplement, q. 64, a. 2).

79. See *Summa Theologiae,* II-II, q. 26, a. 11. In *Summa Contra Gentiles,* bk. 3, ch. 123, Aquinas says: "Inter virum et uxorem maxima amicitia esse videtur; adunantur enim non solum in actu carnalis copulae, quae inter bestias quamdam suavem amicitiam facit, sed ad totius domesticae conversationis consortium." In ch. 125, he writes

of the great union between spouses which leads them to love each other more fervently. For an account of the various kinds of friendship in Aquinas, and the particular form found in marriage, see Guy Durand, *Anthropologie Sexuelle et Marriage Chez Thomas d'Aquin* (Lyon: Université de Lyon, 1966-1967), pp. 150-172.

80. Étienne Gilson, *A History of Christian Philosophy in the Middle Ages* (New York: Random House, 1955), p. 327.

81. See Alexander of Hales, *Summa Theologica* (= *Summa Fratris Alexandri*), II, 1, Inq. IV, tr. II, Sect. II, q. 2; see Parmisano, "Love and Marriage in the Middle Ages II," 684-685.

82. Ibid.

83. See *In IV Sententiarum*, d. 31, q. 2, a. 3 (= *Summa Theologiae*, Supplement, q. 49, a. 6). The view Aquinas rejects here is that of William of Auxerre, *Summa Aurea*, IV, tract. *De Matrimonio*, q. Utrum bona matrimonii excusent... (folio 287r of the Paris edition of 1500).

84. *Summa Theologiae*, I-II, q. 31, aa. 1, 2; q. 33, a. 4; q. 34, a. 4; see also Durand, *Anthropologie Sexuelle*, pp. 176-183.

85. See John C. Ford, S.J., and Germain Grisez, "Contraception and the Infallibility of the Ordinary Magisterium," *Theological Studies*, 39 (1978): 258-312, at 277-286.

86. The universality of the condemnation of contraception is demonstrated by Noonan, *Contraception*, p. 6.

87. See "The Question Is Not Closed: The Liberals Reply" and "On Responsible Parenthood," in *The Birth Control Debate*, ed. Robert G. Hoyt (Kansas City, MO: *National Catholic Reporter*, 1969).

88. "The Question Is Not Closed," p. 76.

89. Michael Valente, *Sex: The Radical View of a Catholic Theologian* (New York: Bruce-Macmillan, 1970).

90. Anthony Kosnik et al., *Human Sexuality: New Directions in American Catholic Thought* (New York: Paulist Press, 1977).

91. Charles E. Curran, "Divorce in the Light of the Revised Moral Theology," in his *Ongoing Revision: Studies in Moral Theology* (Notre Dame, IN: Fides, 1975), pp. 77-78; Curran favors the change in Catholic teaching on contraception and proposes that the logical consequences for other areas of sexual morality be frankly admitted.

92. Noonan, *Contraception*, mistakenly supposes that the medieval theologians required procreative intent as a condition for marital intercourse to be wholly good. He praises the position of Martin Le

Maistre, a 15-century writer who held that there was no prohibition of intercourse on the part of a husband who is "scarcely master of himself because of the vehemence of the desire of lust." His wife is "given to him for the sake of solace and remedy." This sexist position is clearly opposed to the realistic and balanced position of the medievals who taught that marital relations thus motivated were venially sinful.

93. Parmisano, "Love and Marriage in the Middle Ages I," 603.

94. See J. B. Gury, S.J., *Compendium Theologiae Moralis* (Turin: M.D. Autia, 1852), no. 688. This is an early edition of one of the most reedited and influential manuals of moral theology. Gury taught that spouses may rightly seek marital intercourse out of "the desire of fostering or bringing about decent friendship." See also Dietrich von Hildebrand, *In Defense of Purity* (New York: Sheed and Ward, 1935). For a careful summary and evaluation of Hildebrand's position and that of other influential authors of the 20th century, see John C. Ford, S.J., and Gerald Kelly, S.J., *Contemporary Moral Theology*, vol. 1, *Marriage Questions* (Westminster, MD: The Newman Press, 1963). This volume makes clear that it had become the common teaching of theologians prior to Vatican II that marital intercourse was morally legitimate insofar as it expressed marital love.

95. Cajetan, *Commentarium in II-II*, q. 153, a. 2: "Unde non debet persona de hujusmodi delectatione recepta dolere, sed potius Deo gratias agere." See Louis Vereecke, C.Ss.R., "L'éthique Sexuelle des Moralistes Post-Trindentins," *Studia Moralia*, 13 (1975), 175-196, at 178-181.

96. See Vereecke, "L'éthique Sexuelle," 182-185.

97. Thus in 1988 a multiday conference was held in Rome, co-sponsored by the Pope John Paul II Institute for the Study of Marriage and Family (an integral part of the Pontificia Universitá Lateranense University) and by the Centro Accademico della Santa Croce (now the Pontificia Universitá della Santa Croce) and at that time part of the Universidad de Navarra, entitled *"Humanae Vitae" Vent'Anni Dopo: Atti del II Congresso Internazionale di Teologia Morale* (Roma, 9-12 Novembre 1988) to celebrate the 20th anniversary of Pope Paul VI's encyclical *Humanae Vitae*. Hundreds of theologians participated in this Congress and 18 masterful papers were given by internationally renowned theologians, a score of excellent written contributions were presented orally at the conference and later published in the

proceedings in the volume *"Humanae Vitae" Vent'Anni Dopo: Atti del II Congresso Internazionale di Teologia Morale* (Roma, 9-12 Novembre 1988) (Milan: Edizione Ares, 1989). The first such International Congress of Moral Theology had been held in Rome in 1986, with the papers published under the title *Persona, Veritá, e Morale.*

Undoubtedly, the most significant development in the Catholic understanding of marriage and human sexuality in the last quarter of the 20th century was the teaching of Pope John Paul II, particularly in the catecheses he gave to General Audiences from September 5, 1979 through September 28, 1984 on the "theology of the body."

98. Germain Grisez makes this clear in his *The Way of the Lord Jesus*, Vol. 2: *Living a Christian Life* (Quincy, IL: Franciscan Press, 1993), pp. 555-574.

CHAPTER FOUR

Patterns of Thinking in Moral Theology

Christian life is not primarily the following of a moral code. It is, most fundamentally, living as adopted sons and daughters of God. This new life is made possible by Jesus' redemptive act. By dying and rising with him when we are baptized, we are literally divinized and made members of the divine family. We now share in Jesus' divine life as he shares our human life. The grace we receive through baptism is indeed *sanctifying* grace; it makes us holy as God is holy.[1]

Christian Life and Morality

Although not primarily the following of a moral code, Christian life involves a morality. We are to act as Christians; we are to love our neighbors not only as we love ourselves (this is a requirement of the natural law or our own intelligent participation in God's eternal law); Jesus has given us a *new* commandment: "love one another... as I have loved you" (Jn 13:34), that is, with a redemptive kind of love, the kind of love with which God himself loves us and makes manifest in Jesus Christ our Lord (see Rom 8:38-39). Specific ways of living are appropriate and required for those who are to love in this way, and some ways of living, some choices and actions, are simply incompatible with this life. There is in reality a *unity* between the spiritual and moral life of a Christian. All Christians are called to be holy, as the heavenly Father is holy.[2] The new Gospel law to love others even as Jesus loves us with his redeeming love not only empowers us to *know* the truth about what we are to do as Christians and human persons but also to *do* the good we know and avoid whatever is opposed to the Christian life. In this it differs from the "natural law" inscribed in our being as our participation in God's eternal law; this law empowers us to know the truth but does not enable us to *do* good or avoid evil, whereas the new "law" of grace enables us both to know and to *do* good and avoid evil.[3] The moral implications of Jesus' message are so central to it that they appear prominently in the original proclamation of the Gospel; they appear in the heavily moral emphasis of the early Pauline epistles, as they do in all later Catholic teaching.

Jesus came to redeem sinners by his teaching and by his life and saving death and resurrection and in this was to give them power to live a new life. Those who would respond to Jesus' invitation to new life were required to have a change of heart, a conversion. The free cooperation of those who would follow Jesus must include repentance for their sins (Acts 2:38), and a resolve to live unselfish and upright lives, doing all that love requires (1 Jn 3). The Christian life is a unity of the moral and spiritual life; it includes a moral element, and this element is integrally related to the spiritual, divine life of the Christian. The Christian, like Christ himself, must shape his life in accord with the commands of the Father and in this way live as befits a child of God, of one who shares in divine life. Christian faith offers important helps toward living as authentic love requires. First, it helps believers to know what God's will is. Then it gives power to live in the good ways in which God wishes us freely to walk.

The Church has always taught the moral vision of Christianity with confidence, for the Church is convinced that authentic Catholic morality is true and good, that this morality serves love, reveres the person, intelligently resolves difficult problems, and faithfully responds to Gospel requirements. In this chapter we cannot provide an exhaustive study of the principles underlying this moral vision.[4] But it is possible — and sufficient for our purposes — to consider the most basic principles of Christian morality in order to show their truth and relevance. These principles provide a rationale for understanding the received teaching of the Church on sexual morality. Moreover, they make it plain that current challenges to this teaching, both by various groups outside the Church and by some Catholics, is neither rationally defensive nor compatible with basic truths of revelation and of sound reasoning.

This chapter contains four major sections. The first is a discussion of the most basic principles of Christian morality. The second is an account of the human values or goods, recognized by human intelligence and celebrated in Scripture, which are the grounds for moral norms. The third considers how moral norms are based upon the goods discussed in the second section. There is considerable debate among Catholic theologians about how moral norms are justified and applied. After presenting the proportionalist method of moral reasoning and showing why it is both unreasonable and incompatible with Catholic teaching (as Pope John Paul II showed in his encyclical *Veritatis Splendor*), we will examine more recent developments in the debates among Catholic theologians, in particular, the views of those advocating a virtue ethic as preferable to a morality of principles and the debates this has stimulated. The fourth section is a discussion of the importance of human actions and choices in the economy of salvation and for our spiritual life.

I. The Basic Principles of Catholic Moral Reasoning

To understand Christian morality one must reflect on the importance of free choice and the reality of divine and human love. A correct understanding of these two principles is especially important in a treatment of sexual morality, for mistaken ideas about love and freedom are often at the root of people's distorted views about human sexuality.

Freedom. The word "freedom" has several related senses.[5] Two of these are especially important for the Christian, namely, the liberty of the children of God and free choice. The "liberty of the children of God" speaks of God's merciful gifts of grace which enable the Christian to escape from the dominance of sinful desire and selfishness. Free choice is a gift. It is an endowment given by God to all human beings; it is not an achievement. It is presupposed by the Judeo-Christian notion of moral responsibility. It would be useless to study sexual ethics if human beings were so dominated by irrational forces that they could not come to know and to choose intelligent and good ways to direct their sexual lives, or if God did not provide the power for people to live in these excellent ways. Both kinds of freedom are therefore important. We will focus on free choice in its relation to moral principles.

A person makes a free choice when he or she selects one from a set of practical options, that is, a set of actions that are possible for him to do. A choice is free when the person's own choosing determines which of the available options the person will select. In other words, all the factors determining the outcome of the choice, other than the person's own choosing, are not sufficient to determine which selection is made. A free choice is made when a person could choose this or that, and the person himself determines which alternative he will adopt.[6]

Free Choice in Scripture and Tradition

The reality of free choice is explicitly affirmed in Scripture: "It was he who created man in the beginning, and he left him in the power of his own inclination. If you will, you can keep the commandments, and to act faithfully is a matter of your own choice. He has placed before you fire and water: stretch out your hand for whichever you wish. Before a man are life and death, and whichever he chooses will be given to him" (Sir 15:14-17). This biblical teaching has also been explicitly affirmed by the authentic teaching of the Church.[7] Furthermore, free choice is implicit in a number of biblical themes: sin and punishment, conversion and repentance — all presuppose free choice. As St. Thomas Aquinas noted: "Counsels, exhortations, precepts, prohibitions, rewards, and punishments would be in vain" if mankind lacked free choice.[8] In his encyclical *Veritatis Splendor*, Pope John Paul II emphasized the truth that human acts have moral significance because at their heart is a free, self-determining choice. They "do not produce a change merely in the state of affairs outside of man, but *to the extent that they are deliberate choices,* they give moral definition to the person who performs them, determining his *profound spiritual traits.*"[9] Indeed, it is in and through free choices that one shapes one's own life.[10]

We rightly prize freedom. God wishes us to live in freedom, for it is above all by virtue of free actions that we please God and shape good lives in time and for eternity. Freedom is not opposed to that law which directs one to what is really good and fulfilling, that empowers us, gives us freedom to do what is best for us.[11] Freedom does not mean the power or right to "make good" what is not good. God is the author of the moral law; but it is not an arbitrary law, alien to our hopes. God enables us to see the goodness of it, both naturally (in the gift of awareness of the natural law) and through the gift of divine revelation.

Grace. The biblical affirmation of free choice is not opposed to the equally strong biblical emphasis on the importance of God's grace and the inability of fallen human beings consistently to do good without God's help. Human free choice can be exercised for good or for evil, but in the present condition of mankind when he is subject to concupiscence as a result of original sin, it cannot be consistently used for good without the help of God's grace. However, the effect of God's grace on human lives does not override or cancel human freedom. God works through human freedom as he does through all the capacities of human nature.

Limitations on Free Choice. Similarly, the truth that we can make free, self-determining choices does not involve the denial that many factors affect human behavior and inhibit the exercise of free choice. The work of social scientists in recent decades confirms the common-sense judgment that pressures of various kinds often limit human freedom. The Christian tradition recognizes that not all human behavior is free. Sexual conduct is especially affected by passions and pressures, and at times it is difficult to know that one has freely chosen sexual acts that are morally evil.[12]

Nevertheless, the view that all or most human behavior is determined by factors other than choice has no basis in experience and is irreconcilable with the revealed truth that people are in fact responsible for their acts and the basic direction of their lives. Even in this world of many pressures, God made human beings capable of free choice.

The Law of Love. The moral teachings of Christianity express the requirements of love. Both the Old and the New Testaments insist that love is the foundation of all morality. Jesus declared unequivocally that every other commandment flows from the two greatest commands: that we should love God above all things and our neighbor as ourselves (Mt 22:34-40). Moreover, Jesus has given us a new commandment: "love one another... as I have loved you" (Jn 13:34). As St. Paul said, "Indeed, only with difficulty does one die for a just person, though perhaps for a good person one might even find courage to die. *But God proves his love for us in that while we were still sinners Christ died for us* (Rom 5:7-8, emphasis added, NABRE). And this is the kind of love that we, now truly his children, the adopted brothers and sisters of Jesus, are to show to others, even to those who hate us and do evil to us.

The love commandments play a central part in God's providential plan for mankind, for they direct human beings to a sharing of life and good things with God and with other human beings that is closely related to God's loving purpose in creating mankind. He who is Love itself — sharing divine goodness within the perfect community of the Trinity — wishes to share this love with us creatures by making us his children. This love between God and creatures cannot be realized unless human beings live in such a way as to be open to this wonderful fellowship.

The basic norms of Christian morality are therefore in no way arbitrary. They do not restrict our freedom but are addressed to it.[13] They are proposed to us by a loving God to assist us to live as intelligent love would choose to live.

To make clear the connection between specific moral norms and the love commandments — thus revealing the necessity and nonarbitrariness of these specific requirements — we shall reflect on the human goods, the basic perfections of human nature which God desires us to promote and respect.

II. The Human Good

God loves us and wishes us to flourish in all that is really good. He wishes our lives and actions to be good, for authentic love always wishes the beloved to flourish in what truly enriches and fulfills the beloved. This perfection cannot be merely something that happens to intelligent creatures — but rather is something persons must freely and intelligently achieve by their own actions. Hence, God's love for us must include the demand that we show an intelligent concern for what is truly good for us.

Today there is much pessimism about the fundamental roots of a good life. Skepticism and relativism lead many to hold that nothing is really good, or knowable as really good. Christian faith, however, confidently teaches human beings what is really good. It also teaches that we can know the nature of goodness, even without the help of revelation, and that people can know the real goods that are so precious that they make all moral striving worthwhile.

The Nature of Goodness. Difficult moral questions, like those in sexual ethics, cannot be resolved without an understanding of the most basic ideas, such as "good" and "bad," and without a grasp of the richness of the human values that underlie all our striving. Reflection upon why we call some things, thoughts, actions, or experiences good and others bad makes clear that the meaning and application of the terms "good" and "bad" are not arbitrary. "Good" does not refer simply to whatever a person prefers or recommends or likes. Most people have asked, or at least can understand, the question, "I like it, but is it good?" This question supposes that the goodness of something is not simply constituted by one's liking it.

Thus, common sense, reflection, and experience support what Christian faith affirms on this matter: there are reasons rooted in reality for calling some things "good" and others "bad." God, the Creator of all, has willed that human beings should be able to participate in his creative activity by their free actions. This is possible only because he has created an intelligible order in which some realities can be recognized as truly valuable and worthwhile. Life, truth, beauty, friendship, peace, and so on are good; what undermines, harms, and attacks them is bad.

The Objectivity of Goodness. Human creativity operates within this divinely established set of values. It cannot create the very goodness of these values. But human beings can grasp the real goodness of these values, and by choosing rightly can create worthy human lives in which the goodness God made accessible can flourish. Thus, human beings can choose to do certain things and to live in a certain way; by their choices they make themselves the kinds of persons they become, but they cannot by their willing it make any kind of action whatsoever to be good.[14] Whatever they choose must have at least some appearance of good; but a good human action, one that tends to make the one who does it a good person, requires, as we shall see, much more.

What Makes Human Life Good? A good human life therefore is one in which a person is fully perfected in all the dimensions of his or her personality. It is a rich life of human flourishing. Whatever contributes to that flourishing is to that extent good.[15] Being a good person is an essential part of this full human perfection, for one is a good person in virtue of making morally good choices, and this is the part of human flourishing that is most properly human, most properly a form of self-perfection. Moral norms are the standards for choosing well. They are the guidelines for that part of human flourishing that is within our own power to realize. This is why being moral is the same in the end as being good. Being moral is not, in the last analysis, a matter of rules and regulations but of the demands of our own self-perfection, a perfection that God desires because it is good for us.

The Nature of Evil. This general account of the meaning of goodness throws light on the problem of evil. Christian faith believes that all things are made by an infinitely good God who is free and loves our freedom. There are evil deeds, persons, and things, but evil does not have the substantial reality of goodness. Evil in any reality is not a positive and substantial factor in it. But evil is not an illusion; it is real, but real as the *privation* of a good due to some reality. The evil in any reality is the lack of its proper perfection, an absence of the good that should be present. It is not an evil that a rock cannot see; but it is an evil if a dog cannot see. There is evil in the world because things can fail to have the fullness of reality they were meant by their Creator to possess. The worst and most bitter of evils — the evil of deliberate, malicious actions — flows not from God's creative will but from the refusal of the creature to let his or her free acts have the fullness of being that God commands and makes possible but does not force upon the person. It would be a serious mistake to imagine that any sexual sin is evil because sex itself, or pleasure, or passion, is inherently evil or suspect. The things God made are very good. This understanding of the relationship of good and evil is important for Christian ethics generally and for sexual ethics in particular. Any form of Gnosticism which denies the fundamental goodness of physical reality or of human bodily life must be rejected as inconsistent with the basic truth that all of God's creation is very good.

The Goods of Human Nature. The human good is that which perfects and completes human nature. Human persons are dynamic, reaching their fulfillment by actively participating in real goods like truth and friendship. This section is concerned with developing an account of those objective values that make up this human good. These values — basic goods of human nature — are revealed by reflection on the basic motives of human action. Some of them are noted in *Gaudium et Spes*, no. 39:

> When we have spread on earth the fruits of our nature and
> our enterprise — human dignity, brotherly communion, and

freedom — according to the command of the Lord and in his Spirit, we will find them once again, cleansed this time from the stain of sin, illuminated and transfigured, when Christ presents to his Father an eternal and universal kingdom "of truth and life, a kingdom of holiness and grace, a kingdom of justice, love and peace." Here on earth the kingdom is mysteriously present; when the Lord comes, it will enter into its perfection.[16]

This powerful manifesto of Christian humanism lists as intrinsic components of the Lord's kingdom a number of basic human concerns which are not unique to Christians. All persons and cultures pursue goods like these. Truth, life, justice, love, and holiness are not valued by Christians only but by all men and women. These values are not always properly realized and respected in the individual and social activities of humankind, but they do comprise a good deal of the basic motivation for human action and enterprise. These values motivate us at this basic level precisely because they are the basic components of human perfection. By doing things which realize these values we are perfected and completed as human beings.

The Goods of Human Communities. Perhaps the most obvious of these basic goods are those realized in the relations between persons and within communities. Such things as love and friendship, justice and peace, are among the most basic concerns of all persons. They are also among the most highly regarded human realities in Scripture.[17] These values are characteristics of persons and communities based on the relationships the persons establish among themselves and with those outside the community and with God himself. It is clear that these goods are realized primarily in the commitments of persons to relate decently to one another and to have good and friendly relationships. It is also clear that these goods can be, and often are, sought not as a means to any further goal but as part of what makes life rich and meaningful. Even those who treat others unjustly by manipulating or oppressing them desire some genuine friends and some real human mutuality. The deep human significance of the charge that one does not really care for another but is merely using the other, shows that people understand that a true human relationship is meant to be a basic, noninstrumental value within human life, precious in itself and not a mere means of pursuing other goals. Clearly, the interpersonal goods perfect a dimension of human nature, for we are by nature social beings; a satisfactory human life without friends and decent relationships is simply unthinkable.[18]

Other Basic Goods. Goods perfect other aspects of human nature. Since human beings are complex creatures made up of intellects and wills, minds and bodies, emotions and convictions, it is part of human perfection to harmonize and integrate these elements. This good has a number of aspects, so it is called variously self-integration, authenticity, integrity, practical reasonableness, or, simply, peace.[19] It is the good realized in the cardinal virtues of prudence, temperance, and courage.[20] Consequently, this good is very important for sexual morality, since this good is almost always affected when decisions about sex are made.

Knowing the truth is also a basic human good. Human persons pursue truth not only for pragmatic reasons but also for its own sake, simply because it is good to know; and it is good because the capacity to know is a basic aspect of human nature. Scripture and Church teaching clearly endorse the goodness of knowledge.[21]

Finally, human life itself is a basic good of human nature. Without life the human person does not exist. This does not mean, however, that life has value only as a means or as the context for the realization of other goods. Life is good in itself. To be alive is good, and to flourish in biological life by being healthy and by passing life on to new generations is a perfection of this basic good. The goodness of human life is explicitly and implicitly affirmed in Scripture and in the lives of faithful believers down through the centuries.[22]

This listing of basic human goods is not meant to be exhaustive.[23] It is, however, sufficient for present purposes because it reveals the goods that are most often at stake in sexual activity. Moreover, this discussion makes clear that the human good is not a specific finite goal or achievement but something that is realized in different ways in the actions of individuals and communities. No individual or group can realize all the human goods. That is why choices are necessary. Still, it is possible to make our choices in a way that shows proper regard for all that is humanly good. Moral norms show the way to this proper regard.

The Goodness of Pleasure. Our discussion of the human goods up to this point is obviously incomplete, for we have not yet considered pleasure. Common experience indicates the basic goodness of pleasure. All human beings desire pleasure in one form or another. Thus, unless human desire is utterly perverse, pleasure must be good. It is unthinkable that God, who created mankind out of love, should have created us with utterly perverse desires.

But common experience also reveals another, darker side of pleasure. For the lure of fleeting, empty, and even destructive satisfactions is an undeniable part of the human condition. Many spouses have deeply hurt those they love, and wounded their own lives, by servile pursuit of adulterous pleasure. The desire for pleasure can lead us away from things we know to be good — even from good things to which we would like to remain deeply committed. Pleasure, in short, can enslave us.

Thus, pleasure has a complex character: it is a good thing but one which — more than other good things — can lead us astray. Consequently, any account of pleasure which implies that it is essentially a bad thing, or that it is always entirely good, must be rejected as oversimplified.

Hedonism. The tendency in our culture is toward an uncritical overestimation of the goodness of pleasure. This cultural tendency has found a number of theoretical formulations. Perhaps the most important of these is the familiar philosophical doctrine of hedonism. For the hedonist, the point of all human effort and action is pleasure of some sort. Thus, pleasure is not simply the highest good; it is the only thing that is desirable for its own sake. Nothing is counted as good except to the extent that it causes pleasure.

This doctrine correctly emphasizes the goodness of pleasure; but, like all extreme views, it vastly oversimplifies the human experience of this complex phenomenon. As careful students of human motivation from the time of Plato and Aristotle have noted, the goodness of the desirable things in life cannot be explained simply in terms of their capacity to cause pleasure. Some good things are not pleasurable, at least not in most circumstances; and they are good and desirable even when they do not give pleasure, even when they are quite unpleasant. It is good to struggle to protect one's friend, even when the pain and tension of the effort are so great that one cannot enjoy the nobility or praiseworthiness of one's fidelity.

Moreover, other things than pleasure are truly good. Pleasure simply is not the ultimate point of all human action, the basis for all motivation.[24] It is good to pursue and honor truth and justice, even when one's efforts have no pleasurable resonance. Ideally the pursuit and realization of these and other human goods will be pleasant, but they are not recognized as good only to the extent that they lead to pleasure. Trials, hardship, and pain must be endured by one who truly cherishes the goods of human persons. The fidelity of Job and the obedience of Jesus unto death show how good persons pursue what is really good without expecting to taste pleasure in their efforts.

Examples like these show that the direction of Christian thought about pleasure is profoundly anti-hedonist. But being opposed to hedonism is not being opposed to pleasure, for hedonism says that only pleasure is ultimately good, and this is a false theory. It does not follow that pleasure is not fundamentally a good thing.[25] Thus, the Christian evaluation of pleasure is not a rejection of its goodness but a critical, realistic understanding of its complex reality and motivational complexity.

Evaluating Pleasure. According to this understanding, the good actions and efforts in human life can be and ideally are pleasurable. But they are not good because they give pleasure. Such activities tend to give pleasure because they perfect some dimension of the human person. So, pleasure is a good thing, but it is not the very meaning of goodness nor is it an independent principle of goodness.

This does not mean that actions are always pleasurable in proportion to their goodness, for the amount of pleasure any activity causes depends on many variable conditions.[26] People must work even when they are tired and distracted. Even when the work is noble, they may find no pleasure in it. People must struggle against divided selves — trying to do good when emotion, laziness, or passion is pulling in another direction. So, good activities which under ideal conditions would be pleasant are in fact often not so.

Conversely, activities that are intensely pleasurable can often be destructive and immoral. The adulterer may take great pleasure in acts he knows are destroying his life. Evil but pleasurable acts do have something good about them. They do fulfill some human potentiality but not in an ordered and integrated way. To the extent that such actions are good, they can be pleasant; but to the extent that they block or destroy the full goodness of persons, the associated pleasures will fail to be deeply and enduringly satisfying.

This evaluation of pleasure is based on an understanding of pleasure as a kind of accompaniment to a good activity which completes and crowns the activity. Pleasure, therefore, is closely related to what is good, but it is not the primary component in the goodness of humanly good activities. The presence of pleasure indicates something good in the activity, though not necessarily total goodness. Its absence does not indicate a lack of real goodness. In determining the goodness of an action, therefore, the emphasis must be on the character of the action itself and not on the quality of the accompanying experiences of pleasure and pain.[27] This is the case in the sexual domain as elsewhere. A morally good sexual act is in no way suspect because of its great pleasure. This pleasure is an appropriate concomitant of the act's overall goodness. Similarly, the pleasure of an immoral sexual act is not itself bad. What is bad is the act itself, and the willingness to yield to disordered desire for gratification in acts that by striking against the authentic goods of human persons are unreasonable.

III. From Human Goods to Moral Norms

The good person acts out of love, pursuing what is really good out of love of God, of neighbor, and a right love of self. Since it is possible to pursue good things in evil ways, the task of moral thinking is to discover how to love good things rightly, and to pursue them properly.

The Second Vatican Council urged moral theologians to show more clearly how Christian morality is based upon the Scriptures, and how moral theology throws light on the vocation of Christians and the obligation to bring forth fruit in charity for the life of the world; it in essence urged moral theologians to show the unity of the moral and spiritual life (*Optatam Totius*, no. 16). Thus, the Council Fathers called for a renewal in moral theology which would make clearer its connection with the fundamental realities of Christian life. This call for renewal presupposed recognition that there were deficiencies in the ways many theologians of recent centuries explained the moral teachings proclaimed by the Church. In the decades and centuries prior to the Vatican Council, the moral teachings of the Church, especially her insistence on moral absolutes, were sometimes presented as legalistic restraints on living which impose merely extrinsic limitations on persons, telling them only the minimum necessary for escaping grave sin.[28]

As the Fathers of Vatican II suggest, the shortcomings of moral theology in the years prior to the Council are not problems in Catholic moral teaching itself but in its presentation and theological explanation. The basic way of overcoming these difficulties is a thoroughgoing recognition that moral norms are, as the Gospel insists, requirements of intelligent love of what is really good. Once this point is accepted, the objection that traditional moral teaching is some form of authoritarian imposition loses its force. This objection might be true of some theological presentations of morality, but it cannot be said of the substance of Catholic moral teaching.

Making Good Moral Choices. The problem facing us in this section concerns the standards and procedures for arriving at the judgment that a certain choice — a certain proposed human act — is morally good or bad. We have already seen that the love commandments require a concern and respect for human goods, but we have yet to see how that concern is translated into specific practical norms and procedures of moral thinking.

Since Pope John Paul II explicitly addressed this problem in his encyclical *Veritatis Splendor*, we will begin by noting pertinent teaching of that encyclical.

The Teaching of Pope John Paul II

Early in his encyclical John Paul II emphasizes that the commandments of the so-called "second tablet" of the Decalogue, those concerned with our neighbor, are rooted in the more basic commandment to love our neighbor, and he explicitly relates love of neighbor to unyielding respect for basic human goods. "The different commandments of the Decalogue," he writes, "are really only so many reflections of the one commandment about the good of the person, at the level of the many different goods which characterize his identity as a spiritual and bodily being in relationship with God, with his neighbor, and with the material world.... The commandments... are meant to safeguard *the good* of the person, the image of God, by protecting his *goods.*"[29]

Later on he says that reason attests that certain kinds of human acts, specified by the object freely chosen,[30] "are by their nature 'incapable of being ordered' to God." Why? Because "they radically contradict the good of the person made in his image. These are the acts which, in the Church's moral tradition, have been termed 'intrinsically evil' (*intrinsece malum*); they are such *always and per se*, in other words, on account of their very object, and apart from the ulterior intentions of the one acting and the circumstances."[31] Corresponding to these intrinsically evil acts are absolute moral norms, i.e., specific moral norms that admit of no exceptions, e.g., the norms prohibiting adultery, the intentional killing of innocent human persons, etc.[32] In fact, John Paul II says that the "central theme" of his encyclical is the reaffirmation of the universality and immutability of absolute norms proscribing intrinsically evil acts.[33]

Consequently, in this encyclical John Paul rejects the thesis, sustained by those defending consequentialist and proportionalist moral theories, "which holds that it is impossible to qualify as morally evil according to its species — its 'object' — the deliberate choice of certain kinds of behavior or specific acts, apart from a consideration of the intention for which the choice is made or the totality of the foreseeable consequences of that act for all persons concerned."[34]

Proportionalism (cf. Endnote 36)

In *Veritatis Splendor*, John Paul II repudiated two kinds of moral theories denying the reality of moral absolutes and intrinsically evil acts in the sense in which these terms are understood by the magisterium of the Church, identifying these theories as "consequentialism" and "proportionalism."[35] Our attention will focus on proportionalism because this is an accurate term for describing the position of Catholic theologians holding the views regarding moral absolutes and intrinsically evil acts rejected by Pope John Paul II.[36] The theory is called "proportionalism" because of its emphasis on the proportion of good and evil in actions. According to proportionalism, an act that would otherwise be immoral can be justified morally if the overall good or evil involved in doing the action compares favorably with the overall good or evil which the available alternatives would bring about. Thus, its basic principle can be called the principle of the greater good, or more commonly, the principle of the lesser evil. Or, to put it another way, *one ought to choose that alternative promising the greater good or, in situations where only evil can result from one's choice, the lesser evil.* Proportionalists believe it reasonable to assess all the good and evil involved in different alternatives of action in order to determine, prior to choice, which alternative promises the greater good or lesser evil. This is the alternative we ought to choose.[37]

Proportionalists typically hold that no kinds of acts, when defined in purely descriptive language, that is, language that includes no morally evaluative terms, are *always* wrong, or *intrinsically evil in a strong sense*. If one were to mean by murder an *unjust* slaying of an innocent person, then they would agree that every murder is indeed wrong, for the characterization of the killing as unjust is sufficient to settle its immorality. But the intentional killing of an innocent person is not held to be intrinsically wrong in every possible circumstance. Such an act does not include evaluative terms in its description, and it is conceivable that in some extreme circumstances such an act would be determined to be the lesser evil. In those circumstances killing would be a morally good act. The same is true of adultery *if* this is described *morally* as "intercourse with the *wrong* woman," as this is always and cannot not be a "wrongful act." But if one describes adultery in nonmoral terms as "sex with someone who is the spouse of another," then such a deed could be subject to an exception and could be justified as the greater good or lesser evil. In other words, proportionalism provides an "unlessment clause" for norms prohibiting as always wrong acts described in non-morally evaluative terms. Thus to the norm *it is always wrong to have sex with another person's wife* it in effect attaches the following: *unless having sex with another person's wife will bring about a greater good or avoid a greater evil.*

Proportionalists recognize, of course, that there are some alternatives for action that, although not excluded because they are by definition morally bad, are likely to cause greater harm in almost all circumstances. To use one of their examples, it would be wrong to force a retarded child to have sexual relations. Such a norm is a "practical absolute" which is "virtually exceptionless." But, as these phrases suggest, the norm here is not absolute in principle. This, or any other act characterized in purely descriptive terms, might under some circumstances we cannot now think of be thought to be the lesser evil, and thus the correct thing to do.[38]

The Basic Argument for Proportionalism. This is the claim that the fundamental principle of proportionalism is *evidently true*. Proportionalists argue that if one were not required to choose the greater good, or the lesser evil, the alternative would be that one would be obliged to choose the lesser good or greater evil. This alternative is patently absurd.[39] The self-evidence of the proportionalist principle is said to be confirmed by the fact that it is the natural, obvious way to determine the right course of action, as the actual moral thinking of good people reveals. The good person will certainly concede that he ought not do what leads to a greater balance of evil over good; that is to say, he instinctively judges as a proportionalist. The reason for this conviction is that morally serious persons care about what is really good, and this concern, if it is to be thoroughly reasonable, must justify the principle of the lesser evil.

Critique of This Basic Argument. The claim that the proportionalist principle of the lesser evil is self-evidently true cannot be sustained. This principle supposes that it is possible to determine which alternative has the better or the less bad effects overall. To make this determination it must be possible to "commensurate" in an unambiguous way the goods and evils at stake in human actions. It must be possible, in other words, to rank, measure, or compare the goods and evils at stake. One must be able to tell how much harm to one good is offset by the realization of some other good. Unless one can do this, the proportionalist method simply cannot work as a rational procedure of moral decision-making. This commensurating of goods, however, cannot be rationally carried out. As Pope John Paul II says, "everyone recognizes the difficulty, or rather the impossibility, of evaluating all the good and evil consequences and effects — defined as pre-moral — of one's own acts: an exhaustive rational calculation is not possible. How then can one go about establishing proportions which depend on a measuring, the criteria of which remains obscure?"[40]

Thinkers within the broad tradition of consequentialism have tried for centuries to show how human goods are commensurable but have never provided an account which is both analytically satisfactory and consonant with the common experiences of deliberation and choice. On the contrary, common experience shows that the goods at stake when a person must make a choice — the very situation in which moral guidance is needed — are not commensurable. It is because the goods between which we must choose are incommensurable that we must in the end settle what we shall do by choosing. Powerful philosophical and theological arguments have been developed which show that the common experience of the incommensurability of goods must of necessity reflect the reality of human motivation and choice.[41]

A leading proportionalist tries to deal with the incommensurability of the goods problem as follows: "In fear and trembling we commensurate"; "we *adopt* a hierarchy."[42] This approach seems to concede that there is no rational way to determine the lesser evil. It proposes that one adopt, that one choose for oneself, a hierarchy of goods, as a way of rating the worth of the various goods. One cannot do it objectively; but one *decides* how one will weigh alternatives; then one chooses in the light of the subjective evaluation that one has given. What this means is that one does not discover what is morally good; one decides what one shall call "good" by an arbitrary assessment.

The experience of our time shows how much human rights are threatened when small exceptions to necessary defenses of rights are allowed. For instance, few people wished the massive abortions now overwhelming the world. At first it was urged that some abortions be permitted "for very good reasons." But if abortions are permissible when the calculation of goods and harms permits it (a calculation that cannot be objectively valid; a calculation that will be mightily affected by hopes and fears), then the nonobjective nature of the calculation called for almost certainly leads to the terrible consequences brought about by abortion. Clearly, as John Paul II rightly insists,[43] there can be no inalienable rights when there are no exceptionless duties.

Virtue Ethics and the Making of Good Moral Choices

Historical Background in St. Thomas Aquinas

The entire Second Part of St. Thomas's *Summa Theologiae* is concerned with our moral-spiritual life. The 114 questions of the First Part of the Second Part of *Prima Secundae* (I-II) consider man's last end, the factors to be taken into account in determining whether actions are morally good or bad, the different passions or emotions that can affect one's judgment, the meaning of virtue (both supernatural and acquired) and vice, the role of law (eternal, natural, human or civil, the Old Law and the New Law). It treated virtues and vices in general in questions 55-67, including the three theological virtues of faith, hope, and charity, and the acquired moral or cardinal virtues of prudence, justice, fortitude, and temperance. In q. 63, a. 3 he says that God infuses the moral virtues of prudence, justice, fortitude, and temperance along with the theological supernatural virtues.

Thomas then organized the first 170 questions of the massive *Secunda Secundae* (II-II) — it treats a total of 189 questions — around a detailed presentation of the virtues, beginning with the supernatural virtues of faith, hope, and charity, continuing with the same kind of presentation of the four cardinal virtues of prudence, justice, fortitude, and temperance, their integral and associated virtues (chastity as integral to temperance), acts commanded by them, the vices opposed to them, the gifts and graces corresponding to them. Questions 171-178 take up special gifts such as prophecy, rapture, speaking with tongues, miracles, and questions 179-189 are concerned with different states of life — active, contemplative, ordained, lay, religious. Thus, this lengthy part of the *Summa Theologiae* focuses on the virtues, both supernatural and acquired (the cardinal virtues), as the core of our moral-spiritual life. Virtuous actions flow from the virtues that inwardly perfect the operative powers of the person, and those actions make the person morally good. Moral principles of themselves do not.

An in-depth study of Aquinas's teaching on virtue is not possible here. In brief it can perhaps be summarized as follows. According to Aquinas, the virtues are stable dispositions perfecting the powers of the soul that are the active principles of action, enabling the person to do something well. Thus, intellectual virtues perfect the intellect, and the principal *moral* virtue perfecting the intellect is prudence, supernaturally infused or acquired; justice perfects the will, fortitude perfects what he called the irascible appetite, and temperance the concupiscible appetite. He "seated" the virtues in the powers they perfect. Thus a chaste person (chastity is part of the cardinal virtue of temperance) not only knows intellectually what he must do or not do but "feels" that way, finding repugnant what is opposed to chastity and attractive what is in accord with it.[44]

Contemporary Developments in Virtue Ethics

Prompted in large measure by the stimulating and provocative work of Alisdair MacIntyre,[45] there is today an emergence of a strong movement advocating a virtue-based ethic as preferable to a morality of principles. Among the authors advocating this approach are Romanus Cessario, O.P., Jean Porter, Martin Rhonheimer, Livio Melina, and William C. Mattison III.[46]

According to these authors, knowledge of moral principles and of norms derived from them neither makes a person a morally good person, nor does a person who knows these principles and how to apply them necessarily choose to act in accordance with them and may choose to violate them. For instance, a professor of moral theology may have an excellent grasp of these principles and norms derived from them and still act immorally, and indeed this can happen. A virtuous person, or morally good person, on the other hand, is inwardly disposed and habituated to make good moral choices and to do them. After all, did not Jesus say, "A good person brings forth good out of a store of goodness" (Mt 12:35, NABRE; see Mk 7:21-23; Lk 6:45). In addition, did not St. Thomas advise us that, in cases of doubt when we are not clear as to what the morally good option is, we should ask a virtuous person to tell us? In fact, St. Thomas explicitly taught that the "remote conclusions" from the "first and common principles of natural law" are known only to the wise and that in God's providence other members of society are to come to know these precepts or norms "through the discipline of the wise" (*Summa Theologiae,* I-II, q. 100, a.3). And by the "wise" St. Thomas did not mean Ph.D.'s from Harvard or doctorates in sacred theology from some Pontifical University in Rome, but rather "saints." Surely, if one were perplexed about homologous *in vitro* fertilization, I think the person would get good advice from a person like Mother Teresa and not from Masters and Johnson.

Critical Reflections on Virtue-based Ethics

We fully appreciate and acknowledge the truths about human life and existence central to virtue ethics, but believe that it is wrong to oppose virtue ethics to the morality of principles. Both are needed. But which takes precedence? We believe that the morality of principles (this will be presented at length in the following section of this chapter) does so. First of all, we can ask how one acquires a virtue? One acquires the virtue by acting virtuously, that is, in accordance with reason, in accordance with true moral principles and norms derived therefrom and known to us through our intelligent participation in "the highest norm of human life," i.e., "the divine law-eternal, objective and universal — whereby God orders, directs, and governs the entire universe and all the ways of the human community by a plan conceived in wisdom and love. Man has been made by God to participate in this law, with the result that, under the gentle disposition of divine Providence, he can come to perceive ever more fully the truth that is unchanging."[47]

In addition, it is possible for virtuous persons to disagree among themselves, and at times their disagreements are contradictory so that one view must be true and the other false. For instance, I know some persons who are very virtuous and vigorously disagree whether it is morally permissible for a married woman and her husband to "adopt" a frozen and abandoned unborn baby "left over" from *in vitro* fertilization. Some judge this to be inherently bad; others morally justifiable and not inherently bad. These judgments are contradictory; one must be true, the other must be false. Were a married couple, perplexed about what they should do, to ask them for advice on this matter they would still be perplexed.[48] We think that what one must do then is to examine the *arguments* rooted in moral principles and norms relevant to this situation to see which party has rightly grasped and applied these principles and norms after settling relevant factual matters. Or in other words, which side has done its homework? Thus the need and priority of a morality of principles to which we shall now turn.

The Morality of Principles

We give the name "morality of principles" to the broad approach within Catholic moral theology which, on the one hand, seeks to meet the challenge of Vatican II for renewal in moral theology and, on the other hand, seeks to maintain continuity with the received teaching of the Church on moral matters and with the best of the moral thinking in the theological tradition.

This approach might also be called the "natural law" approach, and this is the way John Paul II and the *Catechism of the Catholic Church* identify it.[49] We identify it as "the morality of principles" to distinguish our approach, which is definitely based on St. Thomas's teaching on natural law,[50] from other theories of moral law also bearing the name of "natural law" approaches, for instance, the kind of natural-law theory rooted in the thought of Francis Suarez.

The primary way in which the morality of principles maintains continuity with the tradition of Catholic moral teaching is by insisting on the truth and centrality of moral absolutes. This approach holds that the specific moral norms taught by Christian tradition as valid in every instance do indeed have such universal applicability. Such norms as "never directly kill the innocent" and "never commit adultery" are held to be true, always binding, and nontrivial. There can never be any objectively good reasons for violating specific principles such as these. This, of course, is not taken to imply that no moral norms have exceptions. Most norms do have exceptions. "Keep your promises" and "obey all just civil laws" are true general norms, but there are certainly circumstances in which the good person recognizes that they do not apply.

The renewal of moral theology must be rooted in the morality of principles as an effort of deeper understanding and fuller appreciation of the significance of moral life within the economy of salvation. It is an effort to see how moral activity relates to the saving work of Christ, to the eternal destiny of Christians, and to the true humanism which faith has always held and Vatican II explicitly proclaimed. Thus understood, renewal in moral theology looks deeper into the sources of faith and into Catholic tradition to overcome a presentation of morality either as merely legalistic rules and regulations imposed by God or the Church, or as a set of directives which rationalistic arguments might establish.

The morality of principles, therefore, does not defend Christian moral teaching, including the teaching on moral absolutes, in a legalistic way. One must not avoid blasphemy or homosexual acts regardless of the consequences of one's faithfulness to the rule simply because one superstitiously venerates rules. Nor is the universality of the rule grounded merely in some command of God, who perhaps inexplicably demands faithfulness, even when more harm than good would appear to follow from faithfulness to the precept in a given situation.

Faith confirms that there are moral absolutes but also insists that moral absolutes are the requirements of love. The moral absolutes taught by the Church are not rules or laws imposed on persons by an external authority or nonrational demands. They are intelligent directives or truths of the practical reason participating in God's eternal law or "loving providence," guiding us to live in accord with the requirements of love for neighbor and reverence for what is really good. Hence, proponents of the morality of principles point out that it is always wrong to do such deeds as faith has proscribed absolutely because acts such as these are incompatible with the good of persons whom God calls us to love and absolutely respect. To do such acts is always to act in ways contrary to the full perfection of human persons and communities, and so it is to act in ways unworthy of persons created in God's image and called to act as he does — never willing evil, never harming love, and always respecting the dignity of persons. Human goods are not ideals that dwell apart; they are the fulfillment of human persons, and flourish only in persons. Hence, to act so as deliberately to harm a basic human good is to act against the fulfillment of a human person. And that is incompatible with loving the person.

The preceding argument in defense of moral absolutes is characteristic of the approach taken by those who hold for the morality of principles. But since this is a broad approach and not a single theory, not all who take this approach would develop the argument in exactly this way. Some would emphasize the dignity of persons, and how this dignity cannot be respected unless certain absolute rights and obligations are honored. Others would perhaps focus more on the precious human relationships and meanings that will be distorted unless these absolutes are accepted. But all versions of the morality of principles hold that moral absolutes protect what is most precious, lasting, and valuable in human life. In this sense they are all profoundly humanistic; all are variations on the theme that genuine love requires a care and respect for persons which absolutely excludes certain kinds of actions, namely, those that harm persons by attacking the goods prefective of them, or that manipulate them, or disregard their true dignity.

The morality of principles is serious about not harming human goods, and demands that in our acts we respect and honor each of them. Of course, we cannot in a given act immediately promote and pursue all that is humanly good; but we can always do acts in such a way that all the goods of human nature are respected and honored. Our fidelity to the whole good of human persons is often revealed not so much by the goods we seek but how we respect the goods that are not our immediate concern. The basic principle of the morality of principles, expressed in religious terms by the love commandment, can be formulated therefore as a principle of respect for the entire human good. We must always act in such a way as to be open to integral human fulfillment, that is, open to all the goods of human persons and to the persons in whom these goods are meant to flourish.[51]

Concern for the goods of persons is not therefore realized by trying, as it were, to create a world in which the maximum possible amount of good is realized but in making ourselves persons who humbly cherish and respect all that is good. This is not an attitude of contempt for the harms and tragedies which befall human beings, nor is it an attitude of self-righteousness that cares only for moral rectitude and not at all for human problems. It is, rather, realism about the multifarious character of the human good and our limited ability to make the world good. It is humility which recognizes that the solution to the problem of evil is not human action but God's healing re-creation. It is confidence that God will restore all that is really good and that we shall be part of the re-creation if only we cooperate by maintaining the steadfast loyalty revealed by Jesus and his saints, even in the face of failure and tragedy.

The morality of principles, therefore, is a form of humanism; but it is one in which the true good of man is seen in its full and proper perspective — the perspective of the kingdom of God made possible by Jesus' human acts and God's loving response to them. Thus, it is an approach to moral thinking which is fully open to the larger and deeper meaning of human existence made possible by the revelation of Jesus. It is a morality inherently united to our spiritual life as children of God.

Moral absolutes are only one ingredient in a morality of principles; but they have always had a distinctive place in Catholic moral thought. Even the most corrupt societies have known that adultery is generally harmful, and that divorce is destructive of the basic human community. But Christian thought has been distinctive in teaching that one should never commit adultery (have sex with someone else's wife), slay the innocent, or seek divorce and remarry even for the most splendid reasons, even to avoid the most bitter consequences. Catholic faith has seen that there are in fact evil kinds of deeds, deeds that always involve assaults upon the love of persons. Such deeds must never be done; there can be no "proportionate reason" for doing them.

We must not do evil that good may come of it (cf. Rom 3:8). We must not do even a small evil because a great good seems destined to come of it, or because a great harm can be avoided by doing it. (St. Thomas More was right in judging that he should not affirm by oath false statements already so affirmed by virtually all the religious leaders of England, even though it seemed that little harm and slight additional scandal would come of it, and even though his own life, his family's hopes, and the possibility of influencing the king for the better might be salvaged by doing the evil.) John Paul II has made explicit the connection between moral absolutes and martyrdom.[52] He also repeats the teaching of twentieth-century popes that moral absolutes are necessary for a decent society in which basic human rights are recognized, cherished, and protected.[53]

The morality of principles respects the rich complexity of serious moral thinking. It realizes that a good moral act involves more than doing a good kind of deed, or avoiding a perverse kind. It involves more than having good intentions in what we do, and more than seeking to avoid harmful consequences. St. Thomas Aquinas articulated what might be called a "principle of completeness" for evaluating human actions which required that good actions (like good persons and good realities of every kind) must be complete in their goodness.[54] According to this principle, clearly affirmed by the *Catechism of the Catholic Church* and by John Paul II,[55] every aspect of the act must be morally good: a single moral flaw, whether in the kind of action one does (i.e., its "object"), or in the intentions with which it is done, or in the circumstances in which it is done, is sufficient to render the act morally bad.

This principle does not prohibit actions because they have a tragic or unfortunate aspect to them; that would make most actions in this fallen world impossible. The integrity required is the integrity of a wholly upright will, of one who is unwilling to do whatever is contrary to a complete and intelligent respect for what is really good. Acts and other realities are morally bad to the extent that they lack any essential trait needed for their integrity and fulfillment. Thus, for example, if an act promises so much harm, and to do little good, in its outcomes, one who respects the Golden Rule will not do the act even if it be of a good kind and done with a good intention. One cannot merge these factors together and judge that one may do a bad kind of act, or approve an act done for a perverse intention, if one perceives that the act, considered in all its features, will have a greater balance of good consequences or aspects over bad ones. *Each* of the moral determinants must be good, or the act will not be a good one; it will not otherwise be faithful enough to what love requires.

IV. Good Deeds and Good Consequences

Christian faith has always been more concerned that the faithful do excellent actions and so live morally excellent lives than that they produce many good effects in the world, or have wonderful things occur in their lives. Our lives are constituted far more by what we do than by what happens to us.

Many people in today's world find this aspect of Christian faith to be very puzzling. Modern secular humanists and, in particular, secular consequentialists reject it altogether, for consequentialists believe that it is not actions but the overall effects of actions that are morally most important. Christian ethics, of course, does not deny that we have some responsibility for the predictable effects of our actions but maintains that our actions themselves are the center of moral life.

The Centrality of the Chosen Action. Classical Catholic thought stresses the centrality of action because our free actions are the existential center of our lives. In our freely chosen acts we not only affect the world and other persons but also shape our own personalities and character. By choosing to do certain actions we determine ourselves to be one kind of person rather than another; we make ourselves to be friends of God by responding to his grace and freely loving all that is good, or we choose actions incompatible with love of God and fellowman.[56]

Of course, we do not choose only actions in the narrow sense. We also make large-scale choices that tend to establish the broader outlines of our lives: our vocations, our professional identities, and our basic relationships with other persons. And the measure of the responsibility we have for the wide range of consequences of our actions varies with the ways we relate ourselves to those consequences.

Intended Actions and Unintended Side Effects. What we deliberately choose to do and the ends we deliberately make our own have an especially great importance. Clearly we do not, in every free choice and action, deliberately choose all that flows from such choices and acts:

all the side effects, all the other things left undone, and so on. What is foreseen to come about as a result of our choices — but is not itself chosen — is voluntary in a way; but it is not itself freely chosen. It is accepted or permitted but not positively willed. The voluntary acceptance of side effects is not self-determining in the way free choices of the objects and ends of our acts are.[57]

This difference is the basis for the crucial distinction in Catholic morality between what is directly willed or intended and what is indirectly willed or outside the person's intention. To deny the moral significance of this distinction, as many do today, is to deny something fundamental to Catholic morality.[58] For if one rejects this distinction, and holds that there is no moral difference between directly willing or doing evil and indirectly causing it, one would have to concede that it is permissible at times to do evil, and that there really are no moral absolutes. For it is scarcely deniable that even good people do, and cannot escape doing, acts from which bad effects flow. A parent who saves his or her child from the violent assault of an attacker may be able to do this only by a protective act that causes great harm or death to the assailant, however unintended that harm may be. But if every act that causes harm is morally indistinguishable from an act in which the harm is directly done or intended by the agent, then the absolute moral prohibition of directly doing evil would be meaningless.

To deny the moral significance of the distinction between directly doing and indirectly causing (or permitting) evil is unreasonable. Anyone can see how different is the personal attitude toward evil in two cases: one in which the agent chooses only good, and allows evil to happen as the unintended effect of his or her actions when there are weighty reasons for doing so; and the very different case in which one fixes the heart upon doing or achieving the evil as a means toward some end. Even God, in creating this good world, which is filled with adventures of freedom and responsibility, permitted the free evil deeds of his creatures (which he in no way directly willed to bring about). If there is no difference between permitting evil and setting one's heart on it, God must set his heart on evil. But such a conclusion is not only absurd, it is blasphemous. It is possible for persons to set their hearts only on good. Permitting evil is not choosing it. Choosing evil can never be justified; permitting evil, while obviously not always justified, can sometimes be justified.

Thus, it is not necessarily a violation of the Thomistic principle of completeness to accept bad consequences of actions. One should, of course, avoid acts having very harmful consequences, if one can morally do so. But if the alternative to accepting bad consequences is to choose to do an immoral act, one must endure the bad consequences, for to choose to do evil is to set one's heart against what is good, and to determine oneself as a person who rejects what the love of God and neighbor requires.

The End Does Not Justify the Means. Catholic teaching has always held that it is a terrible flaw in an action — and a horrible tragedy for the one who does it — to do evil directly for any reason. Even if the most precious and necessary goods could not be achieved except by doing a deed that directly does even a small evil, the good man should not do that deed. He must care to make the world good; but the most important good he is to do, the most pressing service he has, in making the world good, is to make his own heart good, by doing only good actions. If he cannot achieve goods he loves by good actions, he has no morally good way to achieve them. Yet he can rightly hope in God, if, living rightly, he does what good he can do well, and trusts God to realize the goods that he himself cannot achieve in acting well.[59]

Good Actions, Good Character, and Fundamental Option. Some protest against the traditional emphasis on freely chosen actions. They argue that actions alone are not the center of moral life. Character, or the basic and enduring moral orientation of the person, has a more profound significance. This has led some moral theologians to locate the basic self-determination of persons, not in free choices, but in a fundamental or transcendental freedom which cannot be found in any discrete choice but rather in the fundamental orientation of a person's entire life. This fundamental option, and not our free choices, is said to be what determines our basic response to God, our very moral identities, and thus our eternal destiny.[60]

This theory is correct in emphasizing that our lives can and should be organized by a fundamental commitment which shapes and orders all our life in response to God's call. But, as Pope John Paul II has taught, fundamental option theory is mistaken in holding that this basic commitment does not flow from the free, deliberate choices of our ordinary moral life but is rather the fruit of an allegedly profound, somewhat mysterious act at a deeper and ineffable level of freedom.[61]

Choices are spiritual realities and not physical events like the performances that carry them out. As Pope John Paul II has made clear, our free actions have not only a transitive aspect in which an event in the world is caused but also a nontransitive aspect which remains in the human self and determines the kind of person the agent is.[62]

Free choices, therefore, have enduring effects, and this enduring aspect is the basis for the virtues which form the fabric of a good life. The virtuous person is fundamentally one who has made the right free choices, and has made them in such a way that his or her entire personality, desires, reactions, and beliefs are integrated around these good choices.[63] So Christian morality is not too "act-oriented" but recognizes the importance of a life of integrated and stable commitment to the Lord's work.

Still, the Church also emphasizes that the discrete choices of a person's life are the root of personal self-determination and responsibility. Human action is trivialized if we fancy that a single choice moved by grace cannot be important enough to merit salvation or tragic enough to lose it.[64] Thus, a single free choice can change the fundamental orientation of a person's life, as the Good Thief changed his fundamental option on Good Friday.

The freedom of our choices is that whereby we determine ourselves; it is the locus of the "soul making" which is the center of the moral life. It is the part of our natures which perhaps most fully images the supremely free Creator of all; it is the part of us which allows us to be friends of God, not because we were in any way constrained or forced to be such but because we ourselves choose to be his friends. This freedom, however, has its burdens that make us want to hide from its full reality. We must, as the Church has always taught, use that freedom well; we must make hard choices but only good ones — choices to do actions that intelligently show that we love and cherish all that is good.

ENDNOTES FOR CHAPTER FOUR

1. See Second Vatican Council, *Dogmatic Constitution on the Church* (*Lumen Gentium*), ch. V, in particular, no. 40: "The followers of Christ, called by God not in virtue of their works but by his design

and grace, and justified in the Lord Jesus, have been made sons of God in the baptism of faith and partakers of the divine nature, and so are truly sanctified."

2. "You, therefore, must be perfect, as your heavenly Father is perfect" (Mt 5:48).

3. On this see St. Thomas Aquinas, *Summa Theologiae*, III, q. 69, a. 5.

4. See Germain Grisez, *The Way of the Lord Jesus*, vol. 1, *Christian Moral Principles* (Chicago: Franciscan Herald Press, 1983), for a systematic treatment of the foundations of Christian ethics, which incorporates the teaching of Vatican Council II.

5. See Joseph M. Boyle, Jr., Germain Grisez, and Olaf Tollefsen, *Free Choice: A Self-Referential Argument* (Notre Dame, IN: University of Notre Dame Press, 1976), pp. 8-10.

6. See ibid., pp. 11-12.

7. See DS 1521, 1554, 1939, 1941, and 1966; see *Catechism of the Catholic Church*, no. 1731; see also Grisez, *Christian Moral Principles*, ch. 2, q. B, and app. 1, for a fuller account of Church teaching on free choice.

8. *Summa Theologiae*, I, q. 83, a. 1.

9. Pope John Paul II, *Veritatis Splendor,* no. 71. Later in this number the pope cites a beautiful passage from St. Gregory of Nyssa's *De Vita Moysis* (II, 2-3): "All things subject to change and to becoming never remain constant, but continually pass from one state to another, for better or worse.... Now human life is always subject to change; it needs to be born ever anew.... But here birth does not come about by a foreign intervention, as is the case with bodily beings... it is the result of a free choice. Thus we *are* in a certain way our own parents, creating ourselves as we will, by our decisions."

10. See *Catechism of the Catholic Church*, no. 1731.

11. On this see John Paul II, *Veritatis Splendor*, nos. 35-53.

12. For the three conditions needed for mortal sin (grave matter, sufficient reflection, and full consent of the will), see St. Thomas Aquinas, *Summa Theologiae*, I-II, q. 88, aa. 2-6. Grisez offers an extended discussion of the meaning of "sufficient reflection," "full consent," and problems resulting from "quasi-compulsive sins of weakness" in *Christian Moral Principles,* ch. 17, pp. 411-433. Regarding "full consent of the will," one either freely consents to an act or does not; there is no middle ground, just as a woman is either pregnant or not pregnant.

13. The view that morality is an expression of an arbitrary divine will is called "the divine command theory," or "theological voluntarism." This view is rejected by the great teachers of the Church. Aquinas makes the classical rebuttal in *De Veritate*, 23, 6; for a modern discussion, see William K. Frankena, *Ethics*, 2nd ed. (Englewood Cliffs, NJ: Prentice-Hall, 1973), pp. 28-30.

14. The view that human choices create the goodness of things can be called "existentialism." This view is associated with the writings of the French philosopher Jean Paul Sartre; a somewhat similar position is developed in the work of English philosopher R. M. Hare. For critiques, see Alvin Plantinga, "An Existentialist's Ethics," in *The Review of Metaphysics*, 12 (1958), 235-256; Henry B. Veatch, *For an Ontology of Morals* (Evanston, IL: Northwestern University Press, 1971), pp. 19-84.

15. Aristotle, *Nicomachean Ethics*, 1, ch. 7, provides the classical formulation of the perfectionist account of goodness. Aquinas developed Aristotle's idea; throughout his ethical writing he defines the good as "fullness of being" and as perfection; see *Summa Theologiae*, I-II, q. 18, a. 1. See also Grisez, *Christian Moral Principles*, ch. 5, q. A.

16. The internal quote is from the Preface of the Mass of the Solemnity of Christ the King.

17. See Xavier Léon-Dufour, *Dictionary of Biblical Theology*, 2nd ed. (New York: Desclée, 1973), entries on Justice, Love, and Peace.

18. See *Gaudium et Spes*, ch. 2, and the social encyclicals of the last 120 years, for authoritative teaching on justice and related goods.

19. See Léon-Dufour, *Dictionary of Biblical Theology*, entries on Peace, Truth, and Wisdom.

20. The cowardly, imprudent, or intemperate person does establish a kind of relationship between the various elements of the self. These relations are unstable and profoundly unsatisfactory even by the standards a non-virtuous person might set. This is so because not every kind of self-integration truly contributes to one's perfection as a human being.

21. In Scripture, truth is primarily a matter of trustworthiness; knowledge a matter of intimate experience and fellowship; and wisdom a matter of practical reasonableness or prudence; see Léon-Dufour, *Dictionary of Biblical Theology*, entries on Truth, Knowledge, and Wisdom. Still, knowledge as the grasping of truth, and wisdom as

the understanding of reality, are valued in the Scriptures, especially in the Wisdom literature. Until recently, the value of theoretical understanding has been expressed more in the life of the Church than in its explicit teaching — for example, in the honor given to thinkers like Augustine and Aquinas, and implicitly to the vocation of the intellectual life they pursued. For recent, explicit endorsements of the pursuit of truth, see *Gaudium et Spes*, no. 15; *Dignitatis Humanae*, nos. 1-2.

22. See Léon-Dufour, *Dictionary of Biblical Theology*, entry on Life.

23. This listing of human goods is rooted in the list given by Aquinas, *Summa Theologiae*, I-II, q. 94, a. 2. See also Grisez, *Christian Moral Principles*, ch. 5, q. D. In *The Way of the Lord Jesus*, vol. 2, *Living a Christian Life,* (Quincy, Ill.: Franciscan Press, 1993), Grisez, rooting his thought in the teaching of the magisterium, shows that marriage must be regarded a distinct basic human good (pp. 555-569). Among magisterial sources showing that we need to consider marriage as a unique good are Pius XI's 1930 encyclical *Casti Connubii*, Pius XII's many addresses on marriage, the teaching of Vatican Council II in *Gaudium et Spes*, no. 48, and many documents from John Paul II. John Finnis has also shown that St. Thomas's teaching on the goods perfective of persons in *Summa Theologiae,* I-II, q. 94, a. 2, clearly identifies marriage as such a good. See Finnis, *Aquinas: Moral, Political, and Legal Philosophy* (Oxford and New York: Oxford University Press, 1998). The meaning of marriage as a basic good is central to some arguments regarding sexual acts, as will be shown in Chapters 7 and 8 below. Thus, St. Thomas himself, in *Summa Theologiae,* I-II, q. 94, a. 3, identifies as a basic good acting in accordance with reason.

24. See John Finnis, *Natural Law and Natural Rights* (New York: Oxford University Press, 1980), pp. 95-97, for a development of this point (the second edition, published in 2011, contains an extensive Postscript). The critique of hedonism is as old as Western philosophy; see Plato, *Philebus*, 20e-22e, 27d, 60a-61b, 67a; Aristotle, *Nicomachean Ethics*, X, 1172b, 10-25.

25. This point is overlooked by many popular criticisms of the Church's teaching on sexual morality; see, for example, the parody of the traditional teaching on sexual pleasure in Anthony Kosnik et al., *Human Sexuality: New Directions in American Catholic Thought* (New York: Paulist Press, 1977), pp. 24-25, 34, 40.

26. See Aristotle, *Nicomachean Ethics*, X, 1174b, 14-1175a, 10.

27. See Aquinas, *Summa Contra Gentiles*, bk. 3, ch. 26, for a statement of the dependence of pleasure on the thing which the pleasure accompanies.

28. See Grisez, *Christian Moral Principles*, ch. 1, qs. D and E, and the literature cited there, for the shortcomings of what Grisez calls "classical moral theology."

29. Pope John Paul II, *Veritatis Splendor*, no. 13.

30. On the meaning of the object of a human act that specifies it, see ibid., no. 78. See also St. Thomas Aquinas, *Summa Theologiae*, 1-2, q. 18.

31. *Veritatis Splendor*, no. 80.

32. See ibid., nos. 80, 81.

33. Ibid., no. 115.

34. Ibid., no. 79.

35. Ibid., no. 74.

36. In the Second Edition of this work, almost eight pages (pages 80-88) were devoted to a presentation and critique of proportionalism. Proportionalism, I believe, remains the view of a majority of moral theologians who are members of the Catholic Theological Society of America and the College Theology Society. In addition, several major contemporary and highly influential Catholic moral theologians, among them James Keenan, S.J., Margaret Farley, S.M., and Joseph Selling, are still active, along with others very sympathetic to proportionalism but whose own theory differs somewhat from theirs, for instance, Charles E. Curran. Nonetheless, the leading defenders and exponents of proportionalism from the late 1960s through the rest of the 20th century are deceased — Richard McCormick, Joseph Fuchs, Bernard Haering and Louis Janssens. In addition, new movements in moral philosophy and theology have emerged, in particular different forms of "virtue ethics" in distinction to "the morality of principles." I have thus decided to offer a more abbreviated presentation and critique of proportionalism in order to provide a discussion of "virtue ethics" and to revise the presentation of the morality of principles that was found in the Second Edition. For post-*Veritatis Splendor* defenses of proportionalism or presentations of works adopting the proportionalist way of arguing, see Joseph Selling and Jan Jans, eds., *The Splendor of Accuracy: An Examination of the Assertions*

Made in Veritatis Splendor (New York: Continuum, 1995), a collection of essays, including one by Selling and one by his mentor Janssens, attacking, misrepresenting, and disparaging the encyclical; Margaret Farley, *Just Love: A Framework for Christian Sexual Ethics* (New York: Continuum, 2006); James Keenan and Jon D. Fuller, "The Vatican's New Insights on Condoms for H.I.V. Prevention," *America: The National Catholic Weekly*, Sept. 23, 2010, and *Catholic Ethicists on HIV/AIDS Prevention* (New York: Continuum, 2000). In 2005 Curran published *The Moral Theology of Pope John Paul II* (Washington, DC: Georgetown University Press), a masterpiece of falsifying the Holy Father's thought and defending proportionalists from his attacks. See the reply to Curran by E. Christian Brugger and William E. May, "John Paul II's Moral Theology on Trial: A Reply to Charles E. Curran," *The Thomist* 69.2 (April 2005) 279-312.

37. See the following for presentations of proportionalist thought: Richard A. McCormick, *Notes on Moral Theology: 1965 Through 1980* (Washington, DC: University Press of America, 1981), pp. 350-355, 578-580, *Ambiguity in Moral Choice: Père Marquette Lecture for 1972* (Milwaukee: Marquette University Press, 1972); Louis Janssens, "Ontic Evil and Moral Evil," *Louvain Studies,* 4 (1972), 115-156, "Norms and Priorities in a Love Ethic," *Louvain Studies*, 6 (1977), 207-231; Joseph Fuchs, *Personal Responsibility and Christian Morality* (Washington, DC: Georgetown University Press, 1983), *Christian Ethics in a Secular Arena* (Washington, DC: Georgetown University Press, 1984); Garth Hallett, *Christian Moral Reasoning: An Analytical Guide* (Notre Dame, IN: University of Notre Dame Press, 1983), p. 46; Timothy E. O'Connell, *Principles for a Catholic Morality* (New York: Seabury, 1978), p. 153. For two handy collections of proportionalist thought, see *Proportionalism: For and Against*, ed. Christopher Kaczor (Milwaukee: Marquette University Press, 1999); *Readings in Moral Theology No. 1: Moral Norms and Catholic Tradition*, ed. Charles E. Curran and Richard A. McCormick (New York: Paulist Press, 1978); this includes essays by Janssens, Fuchs, McCormick (the most prominent and influential proportionalists) and others. See also Lisa Sowle Cahill, "Contemporary Challenges to Exceptionless Moral Norms," in *Moral Theology Today: Certitudes and Doubts* (St. Louis: The Pope John Center, 1984), pp. 121-135, for a clear statement of the

restrictions on the use of the proportionalist method by one who is sympathetic to it.

38. On practical absolutes, see Daniel Maguire, *Death by Choice* (New York: Doubleday, 1974), p. 99; on virtually exceptionless norms, see Richard A. McCormick, *Ambiguity in Moral Choice* (Milwaukee: Marquette University Press, 1973), p. 73.

39. McCormick, *Ambiguity in Moral Choice*, pp. 78-79. Another argument favored by Catholic proportionalists is that just as serious individuals make use of the proportionalist principle in their moral thinking so also does the Church. Thus, the adoption of proportionalism by Catholic thinkers, they claim, is a modest and legitimate development of moral themes already used by the Church, even if only implicitly. This argument is often supported by examples of the role of proportionality in the just-war theory and as one of the conditions of the principle of double effect. The most serious attempts by proportionalists to find this mode of moral reasoning in St. Thomas are those of John Milhaven, John Dedek, and Louis Janssens. See Milhaven's "Moral Absolutes in Thomas Aquinas," in *Absolutes in Moral Theology?*, ed. Charles E. Curran (Washington, DC: Corpus, 1968), 154-185, reprinted in Milhaven's *Toward a New Catholic Morality* (New York: Doubleday, 1972), pp. 135-167, 228-236; Dedek's "Intrinsically Evil Acts: An Historical Study of the Mind of St. Thomas," *The Thomist*, 43 (1979): 385-413; Janssens' "Ontic Evil and Moral Evil," *Louvain Studies*, 4 (1972): 115-156, reprinted in *Readings in Moral Theology No. 1: Norms and the Catholic Tradition*, ed. Charles E. Curran and Richard A. McCormick (New York: Paulist Press, 1979), pp. 40-93, as well as Janssens' "Norms and Priorities in a Love Ethic," *Louvain Studies*, 6 (1977): 207-238, and "St. Thomas Aquinas and the Question of Proportionality," *Louvain Studies*, 9 (1982): 26-46. For a critique of the interpretation of Aquinas given by Dedek and Milhaven, see Patrick Lee, "Permanence of the Ten Commandments: St. Thomas and His Commentators," *Theological Studies*, 42 (1981): 422-433. For a critique of Janssens' interpretation of Aquinas, see William E. May, "Aquinas and Janssens on the Moral Meaning of Human Acts," *The Thomist*, 48 (1984): 566-606. For attempts to find proportionalism in past Catholic thought, particularly in the just-war theory, see O'Connell, *Principles for a Catholic Morality*, p. 153.

40. See John Paul II, *Veritatis Splendor*, no. 75.

41. This argument has been developed extensively by Germain Grisez in a number of his works; for a recent summary of the argument along with relevant references to earlier analyses, see his *Christian Moral Principles*, ch. 6, q. F; see also John Finnis, *Fundamentals of Ethics,* Chapter IV, "Utilitarianism, Consequentialism... Proportionalism... or Ethics," pp. 80-106.

42. Richard A. McCormick, "A Commentary on the Commentaries," in *Doing Evil to Achieve Good*, ed. Richard McCormick and Paul Ramsey (Chicago: Loyola University Press, 1978), p. 277. This volume contains McCormick's *Ambiguity in Moral Choice*, already referred to above, along with responses by several moralists, including an important critical essay by Paul Ramsey and McCormick's responses to the essays.

43. See John Paul II, *Veritatis Splendor*, nos. 96-97; see also John Finnis, *Natural Law and Natural Rights,* ch. 8, on rights, where he shows the great difference between a "liberty right" and a "right in the strict sense."

44. One of the best and clearest — and relatively brief — presentations of St. Thomas's teaching on virtues in my judgment is that of Shane Defcinski, "A Very Short Primer of St. Thomas Aquinas' Account of the Various Virtues," accessible at http://www.uwplatt.edu/~drefcins/233AquinasVirtues.html. A modern interpreter of Aquinas's thought, Josef Pieper (1904-1997), is well known for his excellent studies of the virtues in St. Thomas. His presentation of the cardinal virtues of prudence, justice, fortitude, and temperance is given in the book *The Four Cardinal Virtues: Prudence, Justice, Fortitude, and Temperance* (Notre Dame, IN: University of Notre Dame Press, 1966) — a reprint of three books, one on prudence, one of justice, a third on fortitude and temperance, published originally in the 1950s by Pantheon Books of New York. Pieper also wrote books on the theological virtues called *Belief and Faith* (New York: Pantheon, 1963), *Hope* (San Francisco: Ignatius Press, 1986), and *About Love* (Chicago: Franciscan Herald Press, 1978). In 1997 Ignatius Press published these three works under the title *Faith, Hope, and Love.*

45. Alistair MacIntyre, *After Virtue*, 2nd ed. (Notre Dame, IN: University of Notre Dame Press, 1984; originally published 1981), *Whose Justice?, Whose Rationality?* (Notre Dame, IN: University of

Notre Dame Press, 1983), and other books. The pre-conciliar essay of Elizabeth Anscombe (1919-2001), "Modern Moral Philosophy," should also be cited as influential. It was originally published in *Philosophy*, Vol. 33, No. 124 (January 1958): 1-19.

46. For Romanus Cessario, O.P., see his *The Moral Virtues and Theological Ethics* (Notre Dame, IN: University of Notre Dame Press, 1991) and *The Virtues or the Examined Life* (New York: Continuum Books, 2002). For Jean Porter, see her *The Recovery of Virtue* (Philadelphia: Westminster Press, 1991). For Livio Melina, see his *Sharing in Christ's Virtues: For a Renewal of Moral Theology in the Light of Veritatis Splendor*, trans. William E. May (Washington, DC: The Catholic University of America Press, 2001). For Martin Rhonheimer, see *Natural Law and Practical Reason: A Thomist View of Moral Autonomy*, trans. Gerald Marlsbury (New York: Fordham University Press, 2000), especially pp. 279 ff. For William C. Mattison, III, see his *New Wine, New Wineskins: A Next Generation's Reflections Regarding Key Issues in Catholic Moral Theology* (New York: Rowman, Littlefield and Co., 2005) and *Introducing Moral Theology: True Happiness and the Virtues* (Grand Rapids, MI: Brazos Press, an imprint of Baker House, 2008). Of these authors Mattison — and others associated with him — seem to regard as misplaced in some way the debates noted already between proportionalist and defenders of the Church's teaching that some acts, specified by their moral objects, are intrinsically evil and that norms prohibiting them are absolute and without any exceptions.

47. Vatican Council II, *Declaration on Religious Freedom* (*Dignitatis Humanae*), no. 3.

48. On this see the different views of Catholic authors, all noted for their fidelity to magisterial teaching, in *Human Embryo Adoption: Biotechnology, Marriage, and the Right to Life*, eds. Thomas V. Berg, L.C., and Edward J. Furton (Philadelphia and Thornton, NY: National Catholic Bioethics Center and The Westchester Institute for Ethics & the Human Person, 2006).

Some scholars and others claim that *Dignitas Personae* (published by the Congregation for the Doctrine of the Faith in 2008) rejected embryo adoption in no. 19. But this is not the case. Archbishop Rino Fisichella, who was president of the Pontifical Academy of Life when *DP* was published and the United States Conference of Catholic Bishops both declared that the question is "open"(Fisichella's statement is accessible at http://forum.catholic.org/viewtopic.php?f=76&t=53774. The statement of the United States Conference of Catholic Bishops is found at http://usccb.org/comm/archives/2008/08-196.shtml.

See also the articles by Luke Gormally (against) and John Finnis (for) in E. Christian Brugger, "Symposium on Dignitas Personae," *National Catholic Bioethics Quarterly*, 9.3 (Autumn 2009): 470-478.

49. See John Paul II, *Veritatis Splendor*, no. 12; *Catechism of the Catholic Church*, nos. 1954-1960.

50. On this see William E. May, *An Introduction to Moral Theology*, 2nd ed. (Huntington, IN: Our Sunday Visitor, 2003), pp. 94-97, 135-139.

51. This statement of the first moral principle is adapted from Grisez, *Christian Moral Principles*, ch. 7, q. F; for a different formulation, compatible with the one stated here, see Karol Wojtyla (John Paul II), *Love and Responsibility*, tr. H. T. Willetts (New York: Farrar, Straus, and Giroux, 1981), p. 41; Wojtyla calls the basic principle "the personalistic norm" and explicates its meaning by contrasting it with utilitarianism and relating it to the love commandments. "The norm, in its negative aspect, states that the person is the kind of good that does not admit of use and cannot be treated as an object of use and as such the means to an end. In its positive form the personalistic norm confirms this: the person is a good towards which the only proper and adequate attitude is love. The positive content of the personalistic norm is precisely what the commandment to love teaches."

52. John Paul II, *Veritatis Splendor*, nos. 90-95.

53. Ibid., nos. 95-98; see also John Paul II, *Evangelium Vitae*, nos. 57-58.

54. See *Summa Theologiae*, I-II, q. 18, a. 4, ad 3; this principle was adopted by later moral theologians and stated in the following pithy formula, which is almost impossible to render meaningfully in a literal translation: "Bonum ex integra causa; malum ex quocumque defectu."

55. *Catechism of the Catholic Church*, nos. 1650-1761; *Veritatis Splendor*, nos. 75, 77-78.

56. See John Paul II, *Veritatis Splendor*, no. 71; cf. no. 80.

57. See Joseph M. Boyle, Jr., "Toward Understanding the Principle of Double Effect," *Ethics*, 90 (1980), 527-538; and "The Principle of

Double Effect: Good Actions Entangled in Evil," in *Moral Theology Today*, pp. 243-260.

58. For a discussion of this denial, see McCormick, *Ambiguity in Moral Choice*, pp. 72-83.

59. See *Veritatis Splendor*, nos. 76, 78.

60. See, for example, Josef Fuchs, S.J., "Basic Freedom and Morality," in his *Human Values and Christian Morality* (Dublin: Gill, 1970), pp. 92-111. For references to other statements of fundamental-option theory along with a critical analysis, see Joseph M. Boyle, Jr., "Freedom, the Human Person, and Human Action," in *Principles of Catholic Moral Life*, ed. William E. May (Chicago: Franciscan Herald Press, 1981), pp. 237-266. The articles by Ronald Lawler, O.F.M. Cap., and John R. Connery, S.J., in this volume provide further discussion and references on this matter. See also the remarks on this matter by John Paul II in *Reconciliatio et Paenitentia* (December 2, 1984), no. 17.

61. John Paul II, *Veritatis Splendor*, nos. 65-68. The pope's particular concern is using the idea of fundamental option to excuse the deliberate choice of gravely evil actions. This, he teaches, is contrary to Scripture and Tradition.

62. John Paul II, *Veritatis Splendor*, no. 71. In his philosophical writings, John Paul II developed at length the self-determining character of a person's choices. See Karol Wojtyla (John Paul II), *The Acting Person* (New York: Springer, 1979).

63. See Grisez, *Christian Moral Principles*, ch. 2, q. I.

64. See Sacred Congregation for the Doctrine of the Faith, *Declaration on Certain Questions Concerning Sexual Ethics* (*Persona Humana*), December 29, 1975.

CHAPTER FIVE

Conscience: Its Meaning, Formation, and Relationship to Church Authority

"But every person must follow his own conscience!" Christian faith holds that this statement expresses an important truth about morality.

This statement, unfortunately, is often misunderstood. Many take it to imply that personal conscience is the only thing a responsible person must be concerned with; in other words, that one need not be concerned with the objective principles of morality discussed in the previous chapter.

This implication is entirely unwarranted. The good person will care very much that his or her conscience guides him or her correctly to what is really good to the extent that he or she can discover it. For the upright person is concerned with doing authentically good actions, not only actions that now seem right or appear good. Such a person is concerned with knowing and doing what is truly good.

In this chapter we shall first note certain important distinctions in the uses of the word "conscience." Then we shall consider the duty to follow one's conscience. We shall then consider conscience as *anamnesis* or a "remembering." Finally, we shall treat of the principles for forming a Christian conscience, of the relationship between the personal conscience of a Catholic and the authoritative teaching of the Church, and the question of dissent.[1]

I. Different Meanings of the Term "Conscience"

The word "conscience" has a number of distinct but related meanings. In this section we will first consider conscience in the psychological sense — the conscience described by psychologists as related to parental norms, guilt feelings, and other nonrational factors. Second, we will analyze conscience as the moral evaluation of a particular action. Third, we will consider conscience as a personal grasp of correct moral principles and ways of thinking morally. Finally, we will consider a current account of the relation between moral principles and specific moral judgments — the theory of transcendental conscience.

Psychological Conscience. "Psychological conscience" is essentially related to feelings of moral approval or disapproval. Virtually everyone experiences at times — at least with respect to some important actions — either the security of some inner approval of one's decision, or the anxiety of a condemnation within the depths of one's own being. For example, a woman who had been trained from childhood to be submissive might feel that she is being immoral if she does not do just what her husband desires. This emotional self-condemnation might persist even if upon critical reflection she judges it right to behave as she does.

Guilt feelings stirred up by the inner mechanisms of psychological conscience have a great impact on one's life, and they have been widely discussed by psychiatrists. Freud's notion of the superego is one explanation of psychological conscience.[2] Conscience in this sense involves the internalization of parental and social norms and even of traditional taboos. Thus, conscience in this sense is the result of a process of psychological conditioning. The spontaneous reactions, impulses, and feelings associated with psychological conscience may, of course, be more or less healthy and realistic; they may at times be pathological.

Because conscience in this sense is shaped largely by nonrational factors, and is frequently found to condemn what is not wrong or to approve what is wrong, it cannot of itself provide decisive moral guidance. There can be no obligation to obey conscience in this sense. But psychological conscience is one of the factors that a mature and conscientious person will evaluate in the light of moral principles. A person's critical moral judgment must determine the validity of the impulses of psychological conscience.

Particular Moral Conscience. Sometimes "conscience" refers to one's considered judgment about the morality of a particular act. This judgment is the result of the attempt to know what is truly right, and it is this judgment that Catholic moral tradition most often calls "conscience." Conscience in this sense does not refer to feelings of approval or disapproval but to reflective moral judgment. Since the judgment of conscience is the result of the thoughtful evaluation a person makes about the moral goodness or badness of a particular action, it can be called "particular moral conscience." The judgment involved can be about an act one is considering doing (technically called *antecedent conscience*) or about an act that one has already done (*consequent conscience*).[3] In each case one is attempting to speak the moral truth about some action of one's own: "Is this particular act really a morally good act or is it an evil act?" The person responds to such questions in judgments of conscience like these: "I should not do this, because it would be wrong" or "What I did was good." It is in this sense — in the sense of a judgment about the rightness or wrongness of particular acts that St. Thomas Aquinas and much of Catholic tradition after him use the term "conscience."[4] Conscience in this sense can be defined as one's best judgment as to what in the circumstances is the morally right thing to do. Thus the *Catechism of the Catholic Church* says: "Conscience is a judgment of reason whereby the human person recognizes the moral quality of a concrete act that he is going to perform, is in the process of performing, or has already completed."[5] Similarly, Pope John Paul II writes: "The judgment of conscience is a *practical judgment*, a judgment which makes known what man must do or not do, or which assesses an act already performed by him. It is a judgment which applies to a concrete situation the conviction that one must love and do good and avoid evil."[6]

It is important to note that since the judgment of conscience is an act of the intellect, it cannot merely be a feeling or a personal decision to act or live in a certain way. This is not to say that the affective or existential dimension is unimportant in the moral life or that the feelings of an upright and integrated person are irrelevant in making judgments of conscience.[7] The point is simply that living morally requires the conviction that given acts either are or are not truly in accord with correct moral standards. Concern for the truth is essential. Intelligent judgments, not feelings or choices, should direct the lives of mature persons.

It is precisely because the judgment of conscience is one's best judgment about what one should do that a person is morally obliged to act in accord with his or her conscience.[8] We shall consider this matter more fully in our discussion of the duty to follow conscience.

General Moral Conscience. A person's awareness of the basic principles for making moral judgments is also often called "conscience." In this sense, conscience is one's personal awareness of the most basic moral truths.[9] It is in this sense of the term that one's conscience can be said to be an awareness of the law of God written in the human heart (Rom 2:14-16), and it is in this sense too that conscience refers to our awareness of ourselves as moral beings, summoned to seek the truth about our lives and to live them in accord with this knowledge. This dynamic thrust of our personality is called "transcendental conscience" and will be discussed below. Vatican II refers to conscience in this general sense when it affirms that conscience is that through which man "sees and recognizes the demands of the divine law" (*Dignitatis Humanae*, no. 3).[10]

Conscience in this sense grasps the norms that will guide one in evaluating particular actions. Thus, it is by this general conscience that a person knows that one should do good and avoid evil; that one should aim at harming no one; that one should love God and neighbor; and that one must never do deeds that are of their nature base, that always attack basic goods in ourselves or other persons.[11] Conscience likewise knows that the Ten Commandments follow from these basic principles and must be understood in the bracing way that faith has understood them.[12] The mature and responsible person grasps also, in intelligent conscientious reflection, more detailed moral precepts that can be seen to be true from a right understanding of basic moral principles and of the Ten Commandments. Thus, typical adult Catholics grasp personally not only the broad truth that killing innocent people is wrong but also the more specific truths that abortion and suicide are always wrong.

In a famous paragraph of the *Pastoral Constitution on the Church in the Modern World*, the Fathers of Vatican II stated the importance of conscience in the sense we are now discussing. They also make reference to the particular judgment of conscience and show its connection with our awareness of the moral law and of ourselves as moral subjects impelled to seek the truth. The Council Fathers say:

> Deep within his conscience man discovers a law which he has not laid upon himself but which he must obey. Its voice

[that is, the voice of this law],[13] ever calling him to love and to do what is good and to avoid evil, tells him inwardly at the right moment: do this, shun that. For man has in his heart a law inscribed by God. His dignity lies in observing this law, and by it he will be judged. His conscience is man's most secret core, and his sanctuary. There he is alone with God whose voice echoes in his depths. By conscience, in a wonderful way, that law is made known which is fulfilled in the love of God and of one's neighbor.... Hence, the more a correct conscience prevails, the more do persons and groups turn aside from blind choice and try to be guided by the objective standards of moral conduct. Yet it often happens that conscience goes astray through ignorance which it is unable to avoid, without thereby losing its dignity. This cannot be said of the man who takes little trouble to find out what is true and good, or when conscience is by degrees almost blinded through the habit of committing sin.[14]

This statement by the Council sums up many of the points we have been considering. First, conscience involves an awareness of something objective and truly good — a law which man does not give himself but discovers. Second, moral conscience, in the sense of man's best judgment about what he is to do, must be obeyed — even when it is mistaken. Man will be judged according to the law which conscience knows, and the very dignity of man consists in submitting to this law, that is, in doing what he perceives to be good. Third, the invincible ignorance which causes the conscience of an upright person to err is firmly distinguished from the ignorance of one who does not sufficiently care about finding the truth concerning what is right, and from the blindness of one whose conscience is dulled by habitual sin.

Conscience, understood in this sense, presents us with an objective standard of morality. We have a duty to obey this standard precisely because we perceive in the light of faith and of natural intelligence that it is directing us toward what is authentically good. It is, of course, possible for us to be ignorant of at least some part of this standard, or to make use of it in inadequate ways. But we cannot escape responsibility for these shortcomings if we are not serious about discovering what is truly right. "Certainly," as John Paul II says, "in order to have a 'good conscience' (1 Tim 1:5), man must seek the truth and must make judgments in accordance with the same truth."[15]

Transcendental Conscience. The morally mature person recognizes that feelings and social conventions do not determine what is morally right and morally wrong. We know that our own moral feelings can be misguided and that societies can be more or less corrupt, and at times incline us to approve what no truly good person should approve. The morally serious person is convinced that questions of right and wrong cannot be settled arbitrarily but need to be determined in accordance with the truth. Precisely because of this realization that moral conscience in its authentic sense is concerned with moral truth, some contemporary theologians have developed an account of moral awareness which they call "transcendental conscience." One of the leading proponents of this theological view, Walter E. Conn, has suggested that conscience can best be considered as "the dynamic thrust toward self-transcendence at the core of a person's very subjectivity, revealing itself... as a demand for responsible decision in accord with reasonable judgment."[16] Summarizing the work of developmental psychologists such as Erik Erikson, Jean Piaget, and Lawrence Kohlberg, and relying heavily on the philosophical and theological studies of Bernard Lonergan, Conn properly rejects any normative significance to conscience understood in a merely psychological sense. In his opinion, the term "conscience" refers basically to the *whole person* as a moral self, as a being inwardly impelled to act responsibly in accordance with the truth.

Conn and theologians like him are surely correct in emphasizing that conscience, in its moral sense, is intimately linked to our quest for truth. Human persons are unique in that they are question-asking beings, anxious to discover the truth not only about the physical world in which they live but even more the truth about what they are to do if they are to become fully the beings they are meant to be. In her teaching, the Church clearly recognizes this unique characteristic of human existence. More significantly, she explicitly uses the term "conscience" in speaking of the human person's inner drive to discover the truth about human action and being. In a remarkable passage in Vatican Council II's *Declaration on Religious Liberty*, the Council Fathers first note that "the highest norm of human life is the divine law itself — eternal, objective, and universal, by which

God orders, directs, and governs the whole world and the ways of the human community." Then they continue by saying:

> God has enabled man to participate in this law of his so that, under the gentle disposition of divine providence, man may be able to arrive at a deeper and deeper knowledge of unchangeable truth.... It is through his conscience that man sees and recognizes the demands of the divine law. (*Dignitatis Humanae*, no. 3)[17]

Thus, there are grounds for saying that conscience refers to the inner dynamism of the human person, impelling the individual to discover the truth about what is to be done and what he or she is to be. Conscience is therefore "a special and very fundamental mode of self-awareness — the awareness of 'how it is with oneself.'"[18] But conscience does more than reveal the gap between what we are and what we ought to become. It is also a summons to realize our full humanity.[19]

The vision supporting this understanding of conscience seems to be behind Pope Pius XII's metaphorical description of conscience as the "inner core and sanctuary of a man, where he is alone with God,"[20] a description which both the Second Vatican Council and Pope John Paul II have made their own.[21]

The theory of transcendental conscience focuses on several essential aspects of general moral conscience. Despite this, however, the theory of transcendental conscience, as proposed by Conn and others, does not adequately explain the whole of moral awareness. The fundamental weakness in Conn's position is this: it misrepresents the relation between the particular judgment of conscience and the knowledge of basic moral principles. An uncritical acceptance of certain popular philosophical assumptions leads the proponents of this theory to suppose that the natural awareness of morality does not contain any principles having definite implications. Conn argues that the judgment of conscience, while it is not arbitrary, cannot be derived in an objective way from the general principles of conscience.[22] Instead, he argues that authentic moral living "is determined neither by absolute principles nor by arbitrary creativity relative to each situation: authentic living, rather, is defined by a normative structure of consciousness which demands that a person respond to the values in each situation with creativity that is at once sensitive, critical, responsible, and loving."[23]

No one, of course, would advocate responding to moral situations in ways that are insensitive, uncritical, irresponsible, or unloving. But the question concerns the *criteria*, or *norms*, whereby one can know whether one's response is critical, responsible, sensitive, and loving. And Conn's position seems to make conscience itself the norm. It makes conscience altogether autonomous and beyond criticism, because in rejecting the proper role of principles it makes conscience an almost mystical and unanalyzable component of the person. However, one may acknowledge the dynamic thrust of basic moral awareness and yet hold that the basic structures of moral consciousness grasp principles of the sort the Church has held all along to be the basis of moral judgment. Unless there are such principles, it is hard to see how the "dynamic thrust toward self-transcendence" could be determined to be a movement toward authentic self-transcendence, for without critical principles it could become a dynamism toward self-destruction or self-deception.

Moreover, if there is no definite connection between the basic demands of being fully human and particular actions, it is hard to see how one of the basic facts of moral experience can be explained, for the phenomenon of moral evil is essentially one in which one is aware that one is choosing contrary to the concrete implications of the moral law. If the moral law has no definite implications, and all we have to guide our choices is the dynamic thrust of consciousness, it is difficult to grasp any intelligent patterns whatsoever in the workings of conscience.[24]

II. The Duty to Follow One's Conscience

As we have already seen, a person has the moral duty to act in accordance with his or her own judgment of conscience. "The judgment of conscience," Pope John Paul II writes, "has an imperative character: man must act in accordance with it."[25] Surely a good person must do what he or she decisively judges he or she truly should do. Nonetheless, since the obligation to follow one's conscience is so frequently misunderstood, it will be of value to extend our discussion of this important topic.

Even if one thinks that one would suffer great losses, or fail to gain important goods if one should follow the demands of conscience, one's duty is to act as one has conscientiously judged one must act. Even if the most august authorities, political or religious, should command one to act in a way that conscience — understood as one's firm and honest moral judgment — forbids, then such authorities should not be obeyed. This evident truth, one clearly affirmed by Catholic theological tradition and by the teaching authority of the Church,[26] must, however, be clearly distinguished from the question whether one who is *inclined* to make a particular moral judgment of conscience ought not be prepared to change it if any authoritative teaching of Christ or his Church begins to make one aware that one's own former opinion was incorrect.

It is important to recognize that the duty to follow one's conscience is intelligible only when conscience is understood in the sense of a *judgment of conscience* — the best judgment one can make about the truly good thing to do in the circumstances. Merely psychological conscience can generate no such duty.

It is, moreover, important to recognize that a person's judgment of conscience can be more or less mistaken. Any judgment is the result of a person's attempt to discover the truth. Such attempts can fail, especially when one attempts to discover the truth about complex matters. Of course, this is not to say that our attempts to discover the truth about particular moral matters always fail; we are often justifiably certain that we have succeeded.[27]

Our judgments of conscience are not therefore *infallible*.[28] One might perhaps be inclined to think of one's judgment of conscience as infallible if one thought of conscience as a kind of "moral sense" which grasps or intuits the moral qualities of acts, except that this intuitionistic view of conscience is not defensible. It is inconsistent with the common experience of the complexity of the process leading to the judgment of conscience, and with the awareness each of us has of noting and correcting mistakes in the formation of his or her conscience. Clearly, it conflicts with the approach to moral thinking taken by the greatest Catholic teachers and endorsed by the magisterium.[29] Moreover, the moral qualities of acts are not like the observable features of physical things and events: the rightness or wrongness of a particular act is not an observable feature of the act in the way that the size of this page is an observable feature of this page, and cannot be as simply observed as such features can be.

Thus, one's judgment of conscience can be mistaken. However, this does not change the fact that a person is obliged to follow his or her final judgment of conscience, for in such a case one honestly believes that a certain course of action is morally required, and to refuse to act in accord with one's judgment in such a case would be to refuse to act in the way one personally believes to be morally required.[30] The morally upright person will, of course, earnestly seek to see to it that his or her judgments of conscience are true. Such a person will seek to ground his or her judgments of conscience upon a solid basis of moral principles understood in the light of faith. Thus, "it is always from truth that the dignity of conscience derives. In the case of the correct conscience, it is a question of the *objective truth* received by man; in the case of the erroneous conscience, it is a question of what man, mistakenly, *subjectively* considers to be true."[31] Moreover, such a person will, when unable to reach secure answers personally, seek counsel from those he knows to be trustworthy and wise guides to good moral life.

If a person does not make efforts of this kind, he or she bears the responsibility for his or her mistaken judgments of conscience. The mistake in such a person's judgment is attributable to his or her own neglect. At times this mistake may be attributable to previous bad choices that an individual has made. Such sinful choices, as Vatican Council II reminds us in the passage cited previously, can frequently "blind" conscience, and the blindness in question is voluntary, at least in its cause. Thus, a seriously convinced — even "sincere" — racist is not innocent if his racist sentiments and judgments are the result either of his own negligence in seeking the truth about this matter, or of his deliberate choices not to discover this truth.[32]

Thus, the duty to follow one's conscience means that we have an obligation to act in accordance with our own best judgment of what is right in the circumstances. This obligation also requires that in arriving at this judgment, we have struggled to discover the truth, that we have sought to inform our conscience. As the American bishops put the matter in their pastoral letter on the moral life:

> We must have a rightly informed conscience and follow it. But our judgments are human and can be mistaken; we may

be blinded by the power of sin in our lives or misled by the strength of our desires. "Beloved, do not trust every spirit, but put the spirits to a test to see if they belong to God" [1 John 4.1]. Clearly, then, we must do everything in our power to see to it that our judgments of conscience are informed and in accord with the moral order of which God is creator. Common sense requires that conscientious people be open and humble, ready to learn from the experience and insight of others, willing to acknowledge prejudices and even change their judgments in light of better instruction.[33]

We shall now turn to consider conscience as a special kind of "remembering" that Pope Benedict identifies as *"anamnesis."*

III. Conscience as *"Anamnesis"*

Before his election as pope in 2005 the then Cardinal Ratzinger gave an address "On Conscience" to the American Bishops in 1991.[34] In his essay "Conscience and Truth," Ratzinger used the thought of Cardinal Newman, Socrates, and Plato to develop what he regards as the central anthropological and ontological meaning of conscience as *anamnesis*.

After first showing the falsity and solipsistic subjectivism at the heart of the understanding of "conscience" espoused by dissenting Catholic theologians who make one's own conscience "infallible," and how this notion of conscience was that held by the Nazi Gestapo, Ratzinger appealed to the thought of John Cardinal Newman and the Platonic Socrates in his battle against the Sophists to focus on what he calls conscience as *anamnesis*, which he regarded as its *central anthropological and ontological meaning*.

He cited the famous citation from Newman's *Letter to the Duke of Norfolk*: "I shall drink — to the Pope, if you please — still, to Conscience first, and to the Pope afterwards." In declaring this, Newman was not belittling the Pope or putting conscience above him. But in contrast to Gladstone and other Anglicans, he was showing that the papacy is correctly conceived only when viewed together with the primacy of conscience — "a papacy not put in opposition to the primacy of conscience but based on it and guaranteeing it." Most important was that for Newman, the middle term connecting authority with subjectivity is the truth. "The centrality of the concept *conscience* for Newman," Ratzinger wrote, "is linked to the prior centrality of the concept *truth*." Conscience is the demanding presence of the voice of truth in the subject. "Two standards become apparent for ascertaining the presence of a real voice of conscience. First, conscience is not identical to personal wishes and taste. Second, conscience cannot be reduced to social advantage, to group consensus, or to the demands of political and social power." Ratzinger saw the contemporary relativistic understanding of conscience paralleled by the Socratic-Platonic battle with sophistry. On one side, Socrates and Plato were confident that man has the ability to grasp truth; on the other, the Sophists were relativists who made each individual the measure of all things. Ratzinger taught that the "final meaning of the Socratic search and the profoundest element in the witness of all martyrs is that what characterizes man as man is not that he asks about the 'can' but about the 'should,' and that he opens himself to the voice and demands of truth."

He then contrasted the medieval notion of "conscience" with "*anamnesis*." The medieval tradition rightly recognized that two levels of conscience, while distinct, must be related to each other and that many unacceptable views of conscience result from neglecting either the difference or the connection between the two. "Mainstream scholasticism" expressed these two levels as *synderesis* and *conscientia*. The term *synderesis* entered medieval thought through the Stoic doctrine of the microcosm, but its exact meaning was not clear and therefore became a hindrance to understanding conscience. Ratzinger proposed replacing this problematic word with the clearly defined Platonic concept of *anamnesis*, a term in harmony with key motifs of biblical thought and anthropology, e.g., the thought expressed by Paul in Romans 2:14-15 and by Sts. Augustine and Basil. He then wrote:

> the first so-called ontological level of the phenomenon conscience consists in the fact that something like an original memory of the good and the true (they are identical) has been implanted in us, that there is an inner ontological tendency within man, who is created in the image and likeness of God, toward the divine…. This anamnesis of the origin, which results from the god-like constitution of our being, is not a

conceptually articulated knowing, a store of retrievable contents. It is . . . as inner sense, a capacity to recall, so that the
one whom it addresses, if he is not turned in on himself, hears
its echo from within. The possibility for and right to mission
rest on this anamnesis of the Creator, which is identical to the
ground of our existence. The gospel . . . must be proclaimed to
the pagans, because they themselves are yearning for it in the
hidden recesses of their souls.

"We can now," Ratzinger continued, "appreciate Newman's toast
first to conscience and then to the pope. The pope cannot impose
commandments on faithful Catholics because he wants to or finds
it expedient. Such a modern, voluntaristic concept of authority can
only distort the true theological meaning of the papacy. . . . the situation is really quite different according to the anthropology of conscience, of which we have tried to come to an appreciation in these
reflections. The anamnesis instilled in our being needs, one might say,
assistance from without so that it can become aware of itself. But this
'from without' is not something set in opposition to anamnesis but is
ordered to it. It has a maieutic function . . . [bringing] to fruition what
is proper to anamnesis, namely, its interior openness to truth."

Because here we are dealing with the faith and the Church, Ratzinger told the bishops that we must take into account another dimension treated particularly in Johannine writings:

John is familiar with the anamnesis of the new "we," which
is granted to us in the incorporation into Christ (one body,
that is, one "I" with him). In remembering, they knew him. . . .
The original encounter with Jesus gave the disciples what all
generations thereafter receive in their foundational encounter with the Lord in baptism and the Eucharist, namely, the
new anamnesis of faith, which unfolds, like the anamnesis of
creation, in constant dialogue between *within* and *without*. . . .
It does signify the sureness of the Christian memory. . . . One
can comprehend the primacy of the pope and its correlation to
Christian conscience only in this connection. The true sense
of the teaching authority of the pope consists in its being the
advocate of the Christian memory. The pope does not impose
from without. Rather, he elucidates the Christian memory and

defends it.... All the power that the papacy has is the power of conscience. It is service to the double memory on which the faith is based [creation/redemption] and which again and again must be purified, expanded, and defended against the destruction of memory....

What Ratzinger said to the American bishops should be read, we believe, in the light of the passage from Pope John Paul II's encyclical *Veritatis Splendor* in which he declared: *"the Magisterium does not bring to the Christian conscience truths which are extraneous to it; rather it brings to light the truths which it ought already to possess, developing them from the starting point of the primordial act of faith"* (emphasis added).[35] This is surely an instance of what Ratzinger called *anamnesis*, and it is surely of great importance for the Christian moral life.

IV. The Formation of a Catholic Conscience

As noted earlier, the goal of the judgment of conscience is to arrive at a knowledge of what truly is to be done in the concrete. An essential basis for this judgment is each person's awareness of the general principles of the moral law, already discussed above (under the heading of "General Moral Conscience"). These general principles, however, need to be specified and applied to the concrete circumstances of a person's life. While some applications are relatively easy, others are very complex. If one realizes that every intentional killing of an innocent person is wrong, and if a given act is readily seen to be an instance of intentionally killing an innocent person, then it is clear that this act is wrong. But there are cases in which it is very difficult to tell whether the killing is intentional or the person innocent in the relevant sense. Moreover, many moral norms are nonabsolute. For example, there are times when the rule that just civil laws are to be obeyed does not apply. Thus, guidance for the concrete choices which make up a person's life does not follow simply from general moral principles.[36]

Forming one's conscience, therefore, involves two types of activity. First, one must grasp the implications of the basic principles of morality; second, sensitive to all the significant features of one's situation, one must learn how to apply these norms so as to form reasonable judgments of conscience.

Every person must use thoughtful intelligence in making such judgments. The Catholic, knowing that one of the central purposes of revelation is to assist him or her in seeing how to live wisely, will accept what Christ teaches through his Church. As the Fathers of Vatican II state: "However, in forming their consciences the faithful must pay careful attention to the sacred and certain teaching of the Church. For the Catholic Church is by the will of Christ the teacher of truth. It is her duty to proclaim and teach with authority the truth which is Christ and, at the same time, to declare and confirm by her authority the principles of the moral order which spring from human nature itself."[37]

Thus, God's revelation in Scripture and Christian tradition as explained and articulated in the teaching of the Church, together with the expression of this teaching in the example of the saints, and the struggles of our ancestors in faith, as well as the Catholic's natural insight into morality — all these together provide the Catholic with reliable guides to form his or her conscience.

Moreover, in making use of these various elements by which God reveals his plan, the Catholic will treat them as forming an integral whole. Such a person will read Scripture as a Catholic and will understand the demands of his or her natural insight into moral issues in light of the whole of revelation and the Church's actual living of the faith.

These sources are not regarded by the Catholic as extrinsic sources of information or as external constraints upon his or her conscience. The revelation of Jesus is accepted by an intelligent and mature believer as the fundamental framework in which he or she organizes his or her life and understands his or her existence. "The authority of the Church," as John Paul II says:

> When she pronounces on moral questions, in no way undermines the freedom of conscience of Christians. This is so not only because freedom of conscience is never freedom "from" the truth but always and only freedom "in" the truth, but also because the magisterium does not bring to the Christian conscience truths which are extraneous to it; rather, it brings to light the truths which it ought already to possess, developing them from the starting point of the primordial act of faith. The Church puts herself always and only at the *service of conscience*, helping it to avoid being tossed to and fro by every wind of

doctrine proposed by human deceit (cf. Eph 4:14) and helping it not to swerve from the truth about the good of man, but rather, especially in more difficult questions, to attain the truth with certainly and to abide in it.[38]

The moral law is not an alien law. For each person, it expresses the demands of his or her own humanity. The divine law is not an extrinsic and foreign ordinance.[39] Rather, it presents the moral requirements of the Gospel, to which the believer is freely and gladly committed. In other words, the divine law presents requirements that lie at the heart of a believer's inner life.

Cardinal Newman, in his famous *Letter to the Duke of Norfolk*, points out how precious is the service of the Church in clarifying for us the bracing law of God:

> The sense of right and wrong, which is the first element in religion, is so delicate, so fitful, so easily puzzled, obscured, perverted, so subtle in its argumentative methods, so impressible by education, so biased by pride and passion, so unsteady in its course, that, in the struggle for existence amid the various exercises and triumphs of the human intellect, this sense is at once the highest of all teachers, yet the least luminous; *and the Church, the Pope, the hierarchy are, in the divine purpose, the supply of an urgent demand* [emphasis added].[40]

Thus, the appropriation of these sources by Catholics seeking to form their consciences is a development of their initial Catholic commitment. If one is to be a Catholic, one cannot form one's conscience in any other way. The bishops of Ireland observed: "It is impossible to separate allegiance to Christ from obedience to the teaching Church. One cannot be his disciple while disregarding those to whom he has given a share in proclaiming and teaching his Gospel."[41]

V. The Relationship Between Catholic Conscience and Catholic Teaching

The well-formed Catholic conscience, as we have just seen, draws light from the Scriptures and Christian tradition as these are understood and proclaimed by the magisterium and witnessed by the lives of good Christian people. It is thus unlikely that faithful Catholics will discover any serious conflict between the teaching of the Church and their particular judgments of conscience or their general approach toward making such judgments. And surely, as the *Catechism of the Catholic Church* reminds us, "personal conscience and reason should not be set in opposition to the moral law or the Magisterium of the Church."[42]

Furthermore, if a Catholic finds a measure of conflict between some of his or her convictions and the teaching of the Church, this conflict will be *within* that person's conscience, and not a conflict between the person's conscience and an alien authority. This is true because the teachings of the Church — as far as the believing Catholic is concerned — are teachings of a faith he or she has freely accepted and made his or her own. They enter into the formation of the believing Catholic's conscience.

But if this is so, how can we explain why many Catholics today — according to various surveys — have accepted moral views, particularly regarding matters of sexual morality, that contradict Church teaching? Several factors are relevant. The Church's teaching on contraception, for example, has not been effectively presented by many priests and theologians in recent years. Moved by the pressures of the world, it is easy for people to cease believing what is not earnestly preached. Moreover, while many Catholics realize that the Church *officially prohibits* contraception and other disordered sexual activities, still those same Catholics may not perceive that the Church firmly *teaches* in the name of Christ that such conduct is immoral. Some, indeed, may have been induced to think that "official" proscriptions of the magisterium are not Church teachings in the strict sense. They are said to lag behind the "real" mind of the Church, which is allegedly found in the experience of select members of the faithful, especially that of those Catholics who have rejected insistent teachings of the magisterium.[43]

Before examining these confusing situations, it is important to note the essential freedom and autonomy of the mature Catholic. He or she draws light from faith, but this does not mean blind acceptance of the judgments of Church leaders. There are many pronouncements by pastors, theologians, and even by bishops, that are merely private opinions which a conscientious Catholic might, after sufficient reflection, appropriately set aside.

Moreover, the precepts of the moral law taught by faith are always in some measure general precepts which can be applied in the concrete circumstances of life only through the conscientious deliberation of the individual person. Often this deliberation will have a creative element which cannot be anticipated in general precepts. While this personal deliberation is sometimes simple, the necessary reflection is at times much more difficult. For example, most people have a number of positive duties — to work at one's profession, to say one's prayers, to teach one's children, and so on. In many instances one must judge which duty one is to act on now, if many real duties seem to require attention at the same time. The individual himself or herself must make the judgment in such cases.[44]

In cases such as these the individual's judgment of conscience cannot be deduced from the general norms taught by the Church. One must learn prudence to guide one's life; no simple rules given by authority can substitute for this practical thinking. But there is no genuine *conflict* here between such a person's conscience and the teaching of the Church.

Conflict between personal conscience and Church teaching arises only when a person judges in a way he or she knows to be contrary to the firm teaching of the Church. When conflict arises, the person faces a difficult choice: either follow the Church's teaching, which, when it has been personally appropriated, becomes a living factor within that person's conscience, or reject that teaching — that part of one's own conscience — in favor of the personal judgment that opposes it. In the next section we will consider how it is reasonable for a Catholic to resolve such conflicts.

VI. May Personal Judgment Be Preferred to the Teaching of the Church?

There has been much talk in recent years of the problem of conflicts between personal conscience and the teaching of the Church. Great care must be taken to state this problem precisely. For one who has Catholic faith, who has acquired a happy, personal certainty that the Lord teaches and guides us in the teaching of the Church, the insistent message of Catholic faith is not something alien to conscience. Thus, one does not first form one's conscientious judgment, and then compare that with the teaching of the Church, and finally make another judgment about what to do. Church teaching is there from the beginning in the formation of conscience.

The difficulty arises concretely in something like the following scenario: A couple is faced with a decision about family planning and considers contraception as a possibility. The spouses become aware that the Church teaches that contraception is always gravely wrong, but they also become aware that many people do not believe this — including Catholics. They know that some people argue against the Church's teaching, and make the case that the use of contraception can be responsible, liberating, and even enriching. The question really facing such a couple is a decision about how the two of them should form their consciences. Should they form their conscience in accord with insistent Church teaching? Or should they shape it in the light of opinions they might favor, or might find persuasive, even though they contradict the teaching of the Church? The question therefore is not simply whether one may follow conscience when it contradicts Catholic teaching — it is the more fundamental question of how one is to form one's conscience. Should conscience be shaped by Church teaching, or by opinions contrary to this teaching?

Before 1960 there was unanimity among Catholic theologians and pastors on this point. It was common teaching that one who has the gift of faith must form his or her conscience in the light of faith's teachings. Since such faith is known by the believer to be true and to guide us toward what is really good, it would be unreasonable, foolish, and wrong for one to live in ways contrary to the teachings of the Church. It would be contrary to one's deepest interests to do so. Vatican II, expressing the received teaching of the Church on this matter, tells us:

> Bishops who teach in communion with the Roman Pontiff are to be revered by all as witnesses of divine and Catholic truth; the faithful, for their part, are obliged to submit to their bishops' decision, made in the name of Christ, in matters of faith and morals, and to adhere to it with a ready and respectful allegiance of mind. This loyal submission of the will and intellect must be given, in a special way, to the authentic teaching authority of the Roman Pontiff, even when he does

not speak *ex cathedra* in such wise, indeed, that his supreme teaching authority be acknowledged with respect, and sincere assent be given to decisions made by him, conformably with his manifest mind and intention. (*Lumen Gentium*, no. 25)

Moreover, the Council made it clear by the way it taught that the moral teaching of the Church includes not only very general principles but also specific moral norms. For example, its own teachings on sinful forms of family planning, and on crimes against human life such as abortion, euthanasia, and genocide, are stated in specific and categorical terms which are unmistakably intended to guide consciences and are proposed in the name of Christ.[45]

There can be times, of course, when the Catholic is strongly inclined to form his or her conscience in accord with principles which would be much more convenient than the teachings of the Church, or which would accord with philosophies in some way alien to Catholic belief. When tempted to consider whether it might be permissible to commit adultery in some circumstances, one might very much want to use the principle that adultery can be justified when there are good enough reasons, and might be inclined to think that in the situation those reasons were present. The question, however, is not whether such situations arise but whether it can ever be justified to adopt principles of the kind mentioned. The American bishops, following Vatican II, answer this question negatively, and provide the basic reason which faith always has held:

The Holy Father and the bishops in communion with him have been anointed by the Holy Spirit to be the official and authentic teachers of Christian life. For Jesus "established His holy Church by sending forth the apostles as He Himself had been sent by the Father" (cf. Jn 20:21). He willed that their successors, namely the bishops, should be shepherds in His Church "even to the consummation of the world" [*Lumen Gentium*, no. 18]. It is their office and duty to express the teaching of Christ on moral questions and matters of belief. This special teaching office within the Catholic Church is a gift of the Lord Jesus for the benefit of all His followers in their efforts to know what He teaches, value as He values, and live as free, responsible, loving, and holy persons. As Christ says, "He who hears you, hears Me" [Lk 10:16]. The authoritative moral teachings of the Church enlighten personal conscience and are to be regarded as certain and binding norms of morality.[46]

Moreover, the *Catechism of the Catholic Church* insists that "the law of God entrusted to the Church is taught to the faithful as the way of life and truth. The faithful therefore have the *right* to be instructed in the saving divine precepts that purify judgement and, with grace, heal wounded human reason. They have the *duty* of observing the constitutions and decrees conveyed by the legitimate authority of the Church."[47]

In the face of this clear teaching of the Church, a number of contemporary theologians have argued that in the formation of conscience it is permissible to follow personal opinions that contradict the teaching of the Church. Most of these have been developed by theologians who reject the firm teaching of the Church on various questions in sexual ethics.

In support of their position, these revisionist thinkers advance the following arguments. (1) The Church has, in fact, never infallibly proposed any specific moral norm. (2) It is, in fact, beyond the competency of the Church to teach infallibly on specific moral issues. (3) The authoritative but noninfallibly proposed teachings of the Church may be mistaken, and so Catholics have the right to reject them, i.e., dissent, when they are conscientiously convinced that the teachings are wrong.

Infallible Teaching and Specific Moral Norms

Those who encourage dissent from the Church's insistent moral teaching ordinarily suppose that they are urging changes in the non-infallibly proposed teaching of the Church. In arguing that some acts of contraception or adultery are permissible, they recognize that the Church has taught acts of those kinds to be seriously wrong, but they take it for granted that this teaching is not infallible. Frequently, they point out that it has not been the practice of the Church to make solemn definitions about specific moral points, and it is true that the great body of Catholic moral teaching has not been solemnly defined.[48]

However, as Vatican II has pointed out, there is a form of infallible teaching distinct from proclaiming solemn definitions. The bishops of the Church teach infallibly when they teach authoritatively in matters of faith and morals; "they are in agreement that a particular teaching is to be held definitively and absolutely," even though they are "dispersed throughout the world but preserving... amongst themselves and with Peter's successor the bond of communion" (*Lumen Gentium*, no. 25). Indeed, appealing to this precise text of *Lumen Gentium*, Pope John Paul II has made it lucidly clear in his encyclical *Evangelium Vitae* that the Church's teaching on the absolute inviolability of innocent human life from direct, intentional attack, and the intrinsically grave evil of all intentional killing of innocent human beings, as in abortion and euthanasia, has been infallibly proposed by the ordinary and universal magisterium.[49]

Clearly, it is one of the chief duties of the Church to teach the faithful "how they are to live and please God" (1 Thess 4:1). The Church's teaching on basic issues in sexual ethics in her ordinary magisterium has been most firm over the centuries. The Church has regularly insisted that her teaching about divorce, contraception, fornication, and the like is not a mere teaching of men but a teaching of the Lord himself.[50] With virtual unanimity the teachers of the Church have held and handed on the received teachings on sexual morality, and have presented them as unconditional requirements of salvation. When the Church teaches with such firmness and unanimity in the name of the Lord, it seems inescapable that she is exercising the infallibility of the ordinary magisterium as delineated by Vatican II.

For this reason, highly respected theologians have argued at length that the Church's ordinary magisterium concerning contraception meets these conditions for infallible teaching spelled out by Vatican II.[51] Hence, as we shall see more fully in Chapter 7, the Church's teaching on the immorality of contraception is in all likelihood infallible. And the arguments used by these theologians would seem to apply to other teachings of the Church on sexual matters, for the bishops of the Church have taught with equal firmness, with the same kind of unanimity over centuries, and as teachers who hand on what Christ requires for salvation, when they have taught on topics like adultery, masturbation, and so on.

A Supposed Lack of Competency. A few theologians respond that the Church is simply not competent to teach infallibly about the morality of specific kinds of action. They would admit that the Church could infallibly teach general principles of morality, such as that people must love one another, or that the faithful must put fidelity to the Gospel before worldly success. But they insist that the Church cannot infallibly teach such specific norms as adultery is always wrong or one must never directly kill the innocent.[52]

Aside from the fact that this position is clearly incompatible with the teaching of Pope John Paul II in *Evangelium Vitae*,[53] the arguments for this position are surprisingly weak. They rely too much on the supposed authority of a relatively small group of dissenting scholars, and on assumptions about moral teaching that presuppose proportionalism. The main argument is that it is impossible for a universally stated Church teaching to take into account all the details needed for a judgment that adultery or contraception is always wrong. If proportionalism were a correct way of understanding moral thinking, then it would be impossible for the Church to absolutely exclude certain kinds of acts as immoral. If a particular act of adultery could be upright when the good effects of doing it in its concrete circumstances outweighed the bad consequences, then the Church would have to look into all the details of every conceivable act of adultery before she could reasonably teach that every act of adultery is seriously wrong. But the Church does not suppose that the mistaken theory of proportionalism is correct, and then proceed to teach only those things which proportionalism can justify. She teaches instead, and has always taught, that there are moral absolutes. Some acts, just by being the human acts they are, are disordered; they cannot be acts of intelligent and faithful love.[54]

Serious reflection on the history of the Church's moral teaching shows that her most firm and insistent moral teachings have been concerned with the specific moral issues about which the dissenting theologians think decisive teaching is impossible. If anything is characteristic of the whole tradition of Catholic moral teaching, it is the constant and insistent proclamation that certain kinds of acts — adultery, contraception, abortion, direct killing of the innocent, and so on — are always seriously wrong. Her teaching on the broad moral principles which justify specific norms has often been less insistent and precise. Scholars have been allowed great discretion in explaining how specific norms follow from the basic principles of love, and why they are always binding. But these variations in theological reasoning have always been carried out within the conviction of the Church that the moral absolutes proclaimed are always true.

If there are more general principles that have been insistently taught by the Church, none has been more firmly taught than this: that one must never do evil that good might come of it (cf. Rom 3:8). This principle is appealed to again and again as part of the defense of moral absolutes. It is the reason why moral absolutes may not be set aside when the consequences of following them are very difficult to accept. In other words, it is the basis for rejecting the proportionalism which denies the competency of the Church to teach infallibly on specific moral questions.

A Supposed Lack of Connection With Revelation. Another reason given to support the claim that the Church cannot teach infallibly on specific moral questions is that such teachings cannot have the clear connection with divine revelation that is required for infallible teaching.[55] But there are two major flaws in this claim. First, this claim supposes that no specific choice can be essential for salvation. However, the Church, reading Scripture in the light of Christian tradition and with the aid of the Holy Spirit, judges that specific choices are essential to Christian life. In particular, the Church holds that some specific choices fail to show the love the Gospel requires in such a way that they exclude from membership in the community of divine love those who make the choices and refuse to repent. Even if there is no independent argument to show how and why such choices must separate one from the love of God, it cannot be denied that the Church has held that they do.

The second flaw in this position is suggested by the first, for the position supposes that unless one can demonstrate how and why a given teaching is related to divine revelation, one is not justified in thinking that it is. The fact that the Church presents it as such is not taken as decisive evidence that a teaching is essentially related to revelation; independent theological explanation of the connection is necessary. This assumption is rationalistic in a way that is contrary to the actual practice of the Church. When there is some dispute about whether something is of revelation — for example, whether Jesus is consubstantial with the Father — the Church does not seek to settle the question by consulting scholarly opinion. In fact, in such disputes there is often a lack of scholarly consensus, and even a body of scholarly opinion favoring the view that the teaching in question is not essentially related to revelation. To settle such questions the Church must rely on the exercise of the teaching office of the pope and bishops. Their determination settles whether or not a point of Christian teaching is essentially connected with revelation. The task of the theologians is to articulate this connection, to help us understand it, and not to determine whether or not it exists.[56]

In short, it would not be responsible to assume that the Church's most firm teaching about specific moral matters is not infallibly proposed by the Church's ordinary magisterium. As the *Catechism of the Catholic Church* says: "The authority of the Magisterium extends also to the specific precepts of the *natural law*, because their observance, demanded by the Creator, is necessary for salvation. In recalling the prescriptions of the natural law, the Magisterium of the Church exercises an essential part of its prophetic office of proclaiming to men what they truly are and reminding them of what they should be before God."[57]

Dissent From Authoritative Teaching

The focus of theological dissent in the last forty years has been on the authoritative moral teaching of the Church. In spite of the fact that in recent years competent theologians have made a powerful case that the teachings rejected are for the most part infallibly proposed by the exercise of the ordinary and universal magisterium according to the criteria set forth in *Lumen Gentium,* no. 25, most dissenters have not even considered the possibility that what they reject might be infallible. This possibility completely changes the contour of the debate about the status of the Church's received teachings on sexual matters. Clearly, it deserves continuing, careful study. Another question, however, must also be considered, namely, whether the dissenters are correct in thinking that dissent from authoritative but noninfallibly proposed teaching is justified.

Until the disputes of the last forty years, all theologians acknowledged that the authoritative judgments of the Holy See in moral matters were practically decisive. Even when its teachings were not infallibly proposed, they were taken to be binding on the consciences of the faithful, who were required to give them internal religious assent. Not surprisingly, such teachings were not lightly made. They were understood as the teachings of Christ, proclaimed by his vicar, the pope, for the sake of guarding the whole Church from serious moral harm.

But in recent decades some theologians have formulated arguments to justify both doctrinal dissent from authoritative teaching and practical dissent which allows formation of conscience in ways contrary to this teaching. We will consider briefly three of the central arguments for the position that such rejection of authoritative Church teaching is justifiably proposed.

An Alleged "Right" to Dissent. The first argument asserts boldly: "It is the common teaching of the Church that Catholics may dissent from authoritative, noninfallible teachings of the magisterium when sufficient reasons for doing so exist."[58] However, this assertion finds no justification within Church teaching or widely accepted theological opinion other than the recent opinions of those very theologians who wish to justify their own dissent from received teaching. Appeal is often made to the teaching of the "approved authors," and, in particular, of the approved authors who wrote on the binding force of authentic teaching in the years prior to Vatican II. During the Council a discussion of the binding character of noninfallibly proposed teachings took place. It was part of the discussion leading to the articulation of *Lumen Gentium*, no. 25. Conciliar officials referred to the teachings of the approved authors as normative in this matter. But when we examine the writings of these approved authors,[59] we find that they do not speak of a *right to dissent*, or of a right to guide consciences in ways opposed to authentic teaching. To be sure, they do argue that one might justifiably *withhold assent* provisionally from noninfallibly proposed teaching under certain stringently defined conditions. But withholding a positive act of assent provisionally, while continuing to study the matter with a willingness to accept magisterial teachings on the issues in question, is very different from dissenting actively from these teachings.[60]

Here it is worth noting the teaching found in the 1990 *Instruction on the Ecclesial Vocation of the Theologian* issued by the Congregation for the Doctrine of the Faith. This document clearly distinguishes between *questions* that theologians (and others) may raise about such Church teaching and *dissent* from such teaching. It judges that questioning can be compatible with the "religious submission of will and intellect" which Vatican II requires, but it firmly and unconditionally repudiates dissent from such teaching as incompatible with "religious submission" and irreconcilable with the vocation of the theologian.[61]

The So-called "Spirit" of Vatican II. The second argument given to justify dissent from authoritative but noninfallibly proposed Church teaching was that the "atmosphere," or "spirit," of Vatican II made such great changes in the Church that dissent could now be justified. This claim, however, has proved impossible to sustain in the face of what Vatican II actually says — namely, that the faithful are to assent "with a ready and respectful allegiance of the mind" to the authoritative teaching of the Church even when it is not proposed infallibly.[62] Admitting that the explicit teaching of the conciliar documents — in particular, of *Lumen Gentium*, no. 25 — forbids dissent, some argue that this conciliar teaching represented "a very dated and very discussable notion of the Church's teaching office."[63] That is, matters have changed since Vatican II spoke. But since the Council, the magisterium has continued to teach that one may not dissent from authentic teaching. Thus, the teaching of the Church on this question remains what was proclaimed at the Council, what has always been held within the Church: the faithful are expected to give internal assent to authoritatively proclaimed teachings in faith and morals.[64]

The Claim of the "Fallibility" of Noninfallible Teachings. A third line of reasoning to justify dissent from noninfallibly proposed but authoritative Church teaching is that good sense and integrity permit such dissent. This line of reasoning seems to underlie much of the theological dissent of recent years, although explicit arguments for it are not well developed. Noninfallibly proposed teachings, it is argued, are fallible — that is, they can be mistaken. Hence, it would be foolish and wrong to demand conformity to them from intelligent people who are reasonably convinced by arguments for contrary positions.

This familiar argument is remarkably weak if evaluated in the light of faith. In matters which touch salvation it is essential that the faithful be able to walk in secure ways. Faith knows that there is no more secure way of discovering how we are to live and to please God than by attending to what the Church has constantly taught. This is not to say that there are not reasons that many find plausible for accepting opinions contrary to constant and insistent Church teaching. Those who defend the permissibility of some acts of fornication or some homosexual acts can give reasons for these positions that many people find persuasive. But it would surely be an exaggeration to pretend that such arguments give to anyone a real certainty that the enduring teachings of the Church, which also have strong rational defenses, are mistaken.

The conviction that the Church's teachings on moral matters are mistaken is not based on irrefutable rational arguments. This conviction has a number of sources. It can be based on the appeal of persuasive but far from infallible forms of secular thinking, on cultural and social pressures, and on an uncertain hope that life might be happier if Church teaching were set aside. None of these or similar sources provide a reliable basis for rejecting Church teaching. Thus, the requirement that one follow the Church's teaching does not involve a demand that a person violate what his or her own intelligence has discovered. The grounds for rejecting Church teaching are far more fallible than the reasons a believer has for accepting this teaching.

Even if the teaching of the Church on a given point is not infallibly proposed, it is presented in a way that makes it a far more reliable guide than any other a Catholic might have. Moral debates, in areas in which persons have an emotional stake, are notoriously difficult. Where faith does not give guidance, we see astonishing and virtually irreconcilable differences on even the most basic moral issues. Those who believe that Christ the Lord remains always with his Church, teaching and guiding through those he authorizes to speak in his name, have far better reasons for accepting the teaching of the Church than they could ever have for accepting the novel and dubious arguments whose persuasive power is largely based on the insecure prejudices of a secular culture.

We pointed out earlier that a person has an obligation to follow his or her conscience, even though a person's conscience is not infallible. The reason is that a rightly formed conscience provides the best, though still imperfect, guide for action that a person can have. The role of the authoritative but noninfallible teachings of the Church in the formation of conscience is analogous. This teaching is not infallible, but it is the best guidance a person could have. To set it aside in favor of more pleasing but less sure guides is irresponsible; it is a failure to form one's conscience in the way most likely to lead to judgments that are true.

Many fail to formulate the issue this way because they suppose the Church's teaching on moral issues is not a matter of Christ's truth but rather of policies, decisions, or rules laid down by ecclesiastical leaders. This misunderstanding of the Church's teaching is a form of legalism. The Church's moral teaching is not simply a set of rules adopted by men. It is teaching based on prayerful and thoughtful reflection of the whole Church on the moral guidance found in divine revelation. It is proclaimed by those who have a duty to hand on and guard what God entrusted to the Church for the salvation of mankind; and it is teaching guided and protected by the Spirit Jesus promised to his Church. Thus, even when the teaching in question is not infallibly proposed, it should be thought of in terms of truth — not simply in terms of decisions which are more or less sensible. In these terms, the authoritative teaching of the Church makes a powerful, rational claim on the loyalty of believers, for this teaching is most likely to be true.

Other Arguments to Justify Rejecting Authentic Church Teaching

The two general positions just considered — the claim that Church teaching on specific moral questions is never infallible, and that dissent from noninfallibly proposed teaching is legitimate — are the basic reasons given for preferring personal judgment to Church teaching. There are, however, other arguments for this conclusion which are often used in conjunction with the two central arguments. We will consider four such arguments briefly.

"Physicalism." The first of these is based on the claim that the Church's traditional teaching on questions on sexual ethics is "physicalist" or "biologistic." The objection is that the natural-law theory on which traditional teaching is based left "moral man at the mercy of his biology. He had no choice but to conform to the rhythms of his physical nature and to accept its determinations obediently."[65] That is, the arguments for many of the Church's moral teachings proceed according to the following faulty pattern: since nature tends to act in this way, men have a duty to act in this way (that is, according to the way nature acts). While it can be admitted that some of the theological arguments used in the past to show that certain types of actions were immoral were poor,[66] this does not of itself show that the *conclusions* to which those arguments led were false, for a Catholic is to give

assent to Church teachings, not because of the philosophical-theological arguments scholars in any age use to support this teaching but because this teaching is proposed by those who have been divinely appointed as the authentic interpreters of the "Word of God, whether in its written form or in the form of Tradition" (*Dei Verbum*, no. 10).

Moreover, it is by no means the case that all who have developed arguments for the Church's received teaching have employed some form of objectionable physicalism. The writings on sexual morality by Pope John Paul II, which are used throughout this book, are clearly not physicalistic; they articulate a form of Christian personalism. In fact, in his encyclical *Veritatis Splendor*, Pope John Paul II directly confronted the claim that the Church's moral teaching, particularly on questions of human life and sexual ethics, is physicalistic. He compared the claim to "certain ancient errors [Gnosticism, Manicheism] always... opposed by the Church," and judged it incompatible with the Church's teaching on the unity of the human person and on the respect due to such basic human goods as bodily life and integrity.[67] The arguments of St. Thomas Aquinas, often strangely taken as the paradigm of physicalism by opponents of traditional teaching, do not follow the flawed logic of physicalism, for the main concern in these arguments is not the physical structure of acts as such but their finality, and the way they relate to the human goods at stake. For example, disordered sexual behavior is called unnatural because one engaging in such acts is unreasonably choosing in a way that harms or ignores the human good of procreation.

"The Dignity of Conscience." The second of the arguments for rejecting Church teaching in the formation of conscience is that the dignity of conscience requires it.[68] Of course, one morally ought to do what one finally judges to be right. It is also true that governments and other institutions having coercive power should not use this power to force people to act in ways opposed to their conscience. It is this obligation to respect individual conscience — especially in religious matters — which the *Declaration on Religious Liberty* of Vatican Council II articulates so forcefully.

Neither of these truths is, however, relevant to the justification of a Catholic's preferring his or her personal judgment to the teaching of the Church, for the liberty of conscience to which the Council document refers is not a liberty of the individual Catholic to set aside the teaching of the Church. As we have seen, the relationship of the teaching of the Church to the individual conscience is in no way analogous to that of the power of public authority and the individual conscience. The teaching of the Church is not a power alien to the conscience of the Catholic; it enters essentially into the formation of a Catholic's conscience. Moreover, there is no question here of coercion; the question is about the legitimacy of the procedure of one who is a Catholic and who nevertheless sets aside the teaching of the Church.

The "dignity" to which the Fathers of Vatican II refer is the dignity of a person who obeys in a Catholic way the law revealed by conscience.[69] One who accepts a moral teaching opposed to the teaching of the Church is not clearly behaving in a Catholic way, unless, of course, one is truly in invincible ignorance. For a Catholic, a primary source in seeking the truth in moral matters *is* the teaching of the Church.

"The Sense of the Faithful." The third line of argumentation for preferring personal judgment is that the "sense" of the faithful, or their practical experience, provides a better source for knowing what faith requires of them in their moral lives than does the "official" teaching of the "hierarchical" magisterium.[70] It is true that the *sensus fidelium* — the lived, experienced consent of the faithful to the truths of Catholic faith — is one source of our knowledge of the faith and its requirements. But the notion of "consent or sense of the faithful" needs careful analysis. It does not mean that any opinion of any believer is to be taken as normative, for members of the Church can be tempted to forsake the teachings of the Church and to conform to the pressures of the world around them, sometimes with excellent intentions. Nor does *"sensus fidelium"* refer to the opinions of some believers when they disagree with others, and especially when they disagree with the multitude of believers who still hold fast to what has been held by the overwhelming number of the faithful to be God's word down through the centuries.[71] To say that the sense of the faithful meant either of these things would be to replace doctrinal faith with some sort of relativism. It would pretend that what the Church over many centuries has taught to be the enduring word of God is in our age unacceptable. The sense of the faithful must reflect what the believers have in common; it is a sense true to the faith that has been authentically proclaimed in the Church. It is not to be confused

with transient convictions rooted in philosophies and visions of life received from sources alien to the Church.

"The Magisterium of Theologians." The final argument to support preference for personal judgment to Church teachings is based on an appeal to the "magisterium of theologians." This argument rightly supposes that theologians have a kind of teaching office within the Church based on their scholarly competence. But the argument wrongly proceeds to give the theologians an authority similar in practice to that of the magisterium of pope and bishops. Thus, some insist that the hierarchy must not teach in a binding way if the consensus of theologians is not in agreement with them. Lacking such agreement, the pronouncements of the magisterium are not binding.[72]

Some have suggested that when the hierarchy and the theologians disagree, the faithful may follow a new version of probabilism — that is, when some scholars reject authentic teaching, one may live by their opinions. However, classical probabilism taught that scholarly opinion lost its authority if it was opposed to the teaching of the Holy See.[73]

This argument supposes that the theological community is in overwhelming agreement in rejecting received teachings of the Church on sexual matters. But this supposition is false. There is nothing like a true consensus of theologians favoring theological dissent. Increasingly, theologians have come to recognize that their mission is to serve the magisterium of the Church, and that this mission cannot be carried out unless they responsibly accept the authentic teaching of the Church.[74]

Theologians do have a special office within the Church, and it is not improper to call this office a *magisterium*.[75] However, positions which contradict the received teachings of the Church simply cannot have normative status within the Church, for while there is an authentic mission for theologians within the Church, and while they can indeed teach us in significant ways, their role within the Church is clearly subordinate to that of those who are divinely appointed teachers of the faith, namely, the pope and the bishops in communion with him. The life of faith is not primarily guarded by scholars. It is a gift of God, proclaimed first of all by the authentic witnesses who are successors to his apostles. One of the greatest theologians of all time expressed this point precisely. Addressing the issue of conflict between theological opinions and the teachings of those divinely appointed to express the mind of Christ within the Church, St. Thomas Aquinas unambiguously declared: "We must abide rather by the pope's judgment than by the opinion of any of the theologians, however well versed he may be in divine Scriptures."[76] He speaks here the judgment of the great family of Catholic theologians.

Thus, the effort to justify a Catholic's putting aside the firm teaching of the Church in favor of his or her own judgment does not succeed. The final moral evaluation of an action by a Catholic must be the judgment of his or her Catholic conscience. There is no way to maintain the authenticity of this conscience without holding faithfully to the insistent moral teaching of the Church. In the light of what faith teaches, the mature Catholic freely and intelligently guides his or her conscience toward what is really good — what following Christ requires.

ENDNOTES FOR CHAPTER FIVE

1. Major documents of the universal magisterium concerned with conscience are the following: Vatican Council II, *Gaudium et Spes*, nos. 16-17; Vatican Council II, *Dignitatis Humanae*, nos. 2-3, 14; *Catechism of the Catholic Church*, Part 3, Section 1, Chapter 1, Article 6, nos. 1776-1802; Pope John Paul II, *Veritatis Splendor*, Chapter Two, Section II, nos. 54-64. In its treatment of conscience the *Catechism of the Catholic Church* considers: (I) the judgment of conscience, (II) the formation of conscience, (III) to choose in accord with conscience, and (IV) erroneous conscience.

Other relevant magisterial documents include: Sacred Congregation of the Holy Office, Instruction on "Situation Ethics": *Contra Doctrinam* (February 2, 1956); Canadian Catholic Conference, *Statement on the Formation of Conscience*, December 1, 1973 (available in pamphlet form from the Daughters of St. Paul, St. Paul Publications, Boston, 1974); Irish Episcopal Conference, *Conscience and Morality: A Doctrinal Statement of the Irish Episcopal Conference*, February 22, 1980 (also available in pamphlet form from the Daughters of St. Paul, St. Paul Publications, Boston, 1980).

Useful theological literature on conscience includes: Philippe Delhaye, *The Christian Conscience* (New York: Desclee, 1968); *Conscience:*

Its Freedom and Limitations, ed. William C. Bier, S.J. (New York: Fordham University Press, 1971); William B. Smith, "The Meaning of Conscience," in *Principles of Catholic Moral Life*, ed. William E. May (Chicago: Franciscan Herald Press, 1981), pp. 361-382; Germain Grisez, "The Duty and Right to Follow One's Judgement of Conscience," in *"Humanae Vitae": 20 Anni Dopo: Atti del II Congresso Internazionale di Teologia Morale* (Milan: Edizioni Ares, 1989), pp. 211-222.

2. See John Macquarrie, *Three Issues in Ethics* (New York: Harper and Row, 1970), pp. 113-114.

3. The use of "conscience" in the New Testament was apparently limited to the judgment of one's own past acts. See James C. Turro, "Conscience in the Bible," in *Conscience: Its Freedom and Limitations*, ed. W. C. Bier (Bronx, NY: Fordham University Press, 1971), pp. 3-8; but see Eric D'Arcy, *Conscience and Its Right to Freedom* (New York: Sheed and Ward, 1961), pp. 8-12, for an interesting argument by a philosopher that St. Paul has a directive or legislative sense of conscience as well.

4. See Thomas Aquinas, *Summa Theologiae*, I, q. 79, a. 13; Canadian Catholic Conference, *Statement on the Formation of Conscience*, no. 6; Irish Episcopal Conference, *Conscience and Morality*, no. 2; National Conference of Catholic Bishops, *To Live in Christ Jesus: A Pastoral Reflection on the Moral Life* (Washington, DC: U.S. Catholic Conference, 1976), p. 10.

5. *Catechism of the Catholic Church*, no. 1778.

6. Pope John Paul II, *Veritatis Splendor*, no. 59.

7. See Germain Grisez, *The Way of the Lord Jesus*, vol. 1, *Christian Moral Principles* (Chicago: Franciscan Herald Press, 1983), ch. 10, q. D; ch. 31, q. E.

8. This is the common teaching of the tradition. See Aquinas, *De Veritate*, q. 17, a. 3; D'Arcy, *Conscience and Its Right to Freedom*, pp. 87-112, provides a commentary.

9. Conscience in this sense is called *"synderesis"* by Aquinas and much of the subsequent tradition; see *Summa Theologiae*, I, q. 79, a. 12.

10. See also *Catechism of the Catholic Church*, no. 1780: "Conscience includes the perception of the principles of morality (synderesis), their application in the given circumstances by practical

discernment of reasons and goods, and finally judgment about concrete acts yet to be performed or already performed."

11. See *Summa Theologiae*, I-II, q. 100, aa. 1, 3, ad 1.

12. *Summa Theologiae*, I-II, q. 100, a. 1.

13. The Abbott translation of *Gaudium et Spes* mistakenly translates "voice of this law" as "voice of conscience."

14. *Gaudium et Spes*, no. 16.

15. Pope John Paul II, *Veritatis Splendor*, no. 62.

16. Walter E. Conn, *Conscience: Development and Self-Transcendence* (Birmingham, AL.: Religious Education Press, 1981), p. 205.

17. See John M. Finnis, "Natural Law, Objective Morality, and Vatican Council II," in *Principles of Catholic Moral Life*, ed. William E. May, pp. 113-150, especially pp. 114-121, for an explanation of the teaching of Vatican II on conscience; see also William E. May, "Conscience, the Natural Law and Developmental Psychology," *Communio*, 2.1 (1975).

18. Macquarrie, *Three Issues in Ethics*, p. 114.

19. Ibid.

20. Pius XII, "Radio Message on Rightly Forming Conscience in Christian Youth," March 23, 1952, *Acta Apostolica Sedis*, 44 (1952), 271. [*NOTE*: Hereafter *Acta Apostolica Sedis* will be referred to as AAS followed by volume and page numbers — in this case, for example, AAS 44.271.]

21. *Gaudium et Spes*, no. 16; John Paul II, *Veritatis Splendor*, no. 58.

22. Conn, *Conscience*, p. 205.

23. Ibid., p. 213.

24. See ibid., p. 209f. Conn develops an analogy between ethics and esthetics. He says: "Because the ethical analyst realizes that decisions are made in particular situations according to the subject's best *creative* understanding of the complex concreteness of the situation, he or she does not regard interpretations of general problem areas like abortion as applicable in a *deductive* way to particular cases, any more than a literary critic pretends to offer the author a formula on how to compose a fine poem or a first-rate novel." In response, it should be noted first that creativity does have a proper role in the moral thinking of a mature and conscientious person; such a person will seek to find ways to carry out all his or her responsibilities so as to best serve human goods and the often conflicting requirements of

188 | CATHOLIC SEXUAL ETHICS

common life. However, such creativity as is clearly a part of moral life does not exclude rigorous application of moral principles to cases in such a way as to absolutely exclude some kinds of acts. It is a parody of this application, which finds its formal development in casuistry, to say that it is deductive in the sense that it takes no real thinking or creative understanding.

25. John Paul II, *Veritatis Splendor*, no. 60.

26. For the theological tradition, see the sources cited above in endnote 8; for magisterial teaching, see *Gaudium et Spes,* no. 16; *Dignitatis Humanae*, no. 2; *Catechism of the Catholic Church*, no. 1778; Pope John Paul II, *Veritatis Splendor*, no. 60.

27. Sometimes we arrive at a doubtful judgment of conscience; since it is wrong to be willing to do what might be wrong, one must not follow a doubtful conscience but must instead seek to resolve the doubt. The traditional "moral systems" provide a reflexive device for doing this. In this context, "doubtful" means having a real question as to whether an action is morally good or bad. Its opposite is "moral certainty," which is not the certainty of strict proof. See Delhaye, *The Christian Conscience*, pp. 213-242, for a summary of the traditional discussion of doubtful conscience.

28. See Timothy E. O'Connell, *Principles for a Catholic Morality* (New York: Seabury, 1978), pp. 91-92; O'Connell says that one's conscience is infallible. This confuses the absolute obligation to follow a certain conscience with the truth status of that judgment. One must follow one's conscience, but that does not imply that its judgment is beyond criticism. Moreover, if one's conscience is in error, and it is one's fault that it is, one is culpable for the error. Thus, one may have an obligation to follow an erroneous conscience, but nonetheless commit sin in so doing because one has not taken proper care to form his conscience responsibly. One reason why some mistakenly suppose that conscience is infallible is that they misunderstand the teaching that God speaks to persons in the depths of their conscience. The correct sense of this teaching does not imply that what God reveals to people in this way has the infallibility of faith itself, for God thus speaks to us through the natural and fallible resources of our hearts and minds.

29. Thus, in *Veritatis Splendor*, no. 62, Pope John Paul II, recapitulating Catholic tradition, writes: "Conscience *is not an infallible judge*; it can make mistakes."

30. See *De Veritate*, q. 17, a. 4; *Summa Theologiae*, I-II, q. 19, a. 5.

31. Pope John II, *Veritatis Splendor*, no. 63.

32. See *Summa Theologiae*, I-II, q. 19, a. 6.

33. *To Live in Christ Jesus*, p. 10.

34. Joseph Cardinal Ratzinger, "Conscience and Truth." This originally appeared in *Catholic Conscience Foundation and Formation* (Proceedings of the Tenth Bishops' Workshop), ed. Russell Smith (Braintree, MA: Pope John XXIII Medical-Moral Research and Education Center, 1991). It was reprinted as *Conscience and Truth* by Joseph Cardinal Ratzinger (Boston: National Catholic Bioethics Center, 2000). It was later reprinted as "Conscience and Truth," in *On Conscience: Two Essays by Joseph Ratzinger* (San Francisco: Ignatius Press/Philadelphia: National Catholic Bioethics Center, 2007), pp.11-41.

35. Pope John Paul II, *Veritatis Splendor*, no. 64.

36. See *Summa Theologiae*, I-II, q. 100, a. 3.

37. *Dignitatis Humanae*, no. 14. The *Catechism of the Catholic Church* puts it this way: "In forming our conscience we are assisted by the gifts of the Holy Spirit, aided by the witness or advice of others, and guided by the authoritative teaching of the Church" (no. 1785). See also nos. 2030-2051 on "The Church, Mother and Teacher."

38. Pope John Paul II, *Veritatis Splendor*, no. 64.

39. See *Summa Theologiae*, I-II, q. 91, a. 2; for Aquinas the natural law is a participation in the eternal law by which God providentially guides the universe. The divine law is the law of God made known by revelation. This also includes the natural law, which is included within both the Mosaic law and the new covenant of Jesus. See also *Dignitatis Humanae*, no. 3.

40. John Henry Newman, *Letter to the Duke of Norfolk*, cited in the Irish Episcopal Conference's *Conscience and Morality*, no. 20.

41. *Conscience and Morality*, no. 11.

42. *Catechism of the Catholic Church*, no. 2039.

43. See Charles E. Curran, *Ongoing Revision: Studies in Moral Theology* (Notre Dame, IN: Fides, 1975), pp. 76-87; Curran argues that contraception is now recognized as morally good by married persons themselves, even though officially condemned by the Church. He goes on to apply this same line of reasoning to the indissolubility of marriage.

44. For an analysis of moral dilemmas of this kind, see Germain Grisez, *The Way of the Lord Jesus* vol. 2, *Living a Christian Life*, (Quincy, IL: Franciscan Press, 1993), ch. 5.

45. See *Gaudium et Spes*, nos. 27, 51.

46. *To Live in Christ Jesus*, p. 12.

47. *Catechism of the Catholic Church*, no. 2037.

48. Some specific moral teachings have been defined. The Council of Trent's condemnation of polygamy is a clear case (DS 1802). This Council's affirmation of the indissolubility of marriage also seems to be a solemn definition of a specific moral precept (DS 1805, 1807).

49. Pope John Paul II, *Evangelium Vitae*, nos. 57, 62, and 65.

50. See Grisez, *Christian Moral Principles*, ch. 35, qs. D and E, for an explanation of this point.

51. See John C. Ford, S.J., and Germain Grisez, "Contraception and the Infallibility of the Ordinary Magisterium," *Theological Studies*, 39 (1978): 258-312; Marcellinus Zalba, S.J., "Infallibilità del Magistero Ordinario e Contraccezione," *Renovatio*, 14 (1979): 79-90.

52. See Francis A. Sullivan, S.J., *Magisterium: Teaching Authority in the Catholic Church* (New York: Paulist Press, 1983), pp. 148-152, for a recent summary of this position by one who accepts it.

53. As we have seen, John Paul II, explicitly referring to *Lumen Gentium*, no. 15, clearly taught in that encyclical that the teaching of the Church on the absolute inviolability of innocent human life from direct attack and on the intrinsic evil of every intentional act of abortion and euthanasia has been infallibly proposed by the ordinary and universal magisterium of the Church.

54. Sullivan, *Magisterium*, pp. 148-152, 227-228, does not explicitly accept proportionalism. However, most of the moralists he cites are proportionalists; the list contains well-known dissenters from Church teaching on sexual morality, and no theologians known for support of the magisterium on these matters. For a typical account by a proportionalist, see Philip S. Keane, S.S., *Sexual Morality: A Catholic Perspective* (New York: Paulist Press, 1977), p. 54: "If we accept the notion that the ultimate morality of an action comes from the action in its total concreteness, the Church can never catch up with this total concreteness in such a way as to make infallible or fully absolute decisions on all aspects of concrete or specific moral cases." This argument fails to distinguish between the concreteness of an individual act and

the specificity of a kind of act. Every individual act is some kind of act, and some kinds of acts have been taught by the Church to be wrong. Thus, the phrase "ultimate morality of an action" is ambiguous. In some sense, of course, a decisive evaluation of an act requires a consideration of all the concrete circumstances of the act. One who wishes to evaluate fully the entire goodness or badness of an action must take into account not only the kind of act but also the intentions with which it was done as well as all the morally relevant circumstances. But it is not true that one must consider all these features before making *any* decisive judgment about the act. If one knows that a given act was an act of rape or of abortion or a contraceptive act, one knows that this is objectively a gravely evil kind of act and that every concrete act that would be an exemplification of this kind of act is objectively wrong and ought not to be done. Such a judgment is not final in the sense of taking into full account every morally relevant aspect of the case. But that does not prevent the judgment from being decisive. Proportionalists, as we saw in Chapter 4, do not accept the traditional teaching that acts of certain kinds are always wrong, i.e., intrinsically evil.

55. See Sullivan, *Magisterium*, pp. 143-145. Here, Sullivan disputes what he supposes to be Ford's and Grisez' effort to demonstrate that the received teaching on contraception is part of the secondary object of infallible teaching. What he says here could easily be applied to other areas of the Church's teaching on sexual morality. On this, see John Paul II, *Reconciliatio et Paenitentia* (December 2, 1984), no. 17.

56. See Germain Grisez, "Infallibility and Specific Moral Norms: A Reply to Francis A. Sullivan, S.J.," *The Thomist*, 49 (1985).

57. *Catechism of the Catholic Church*, no. 2036.

58. Charles E. Curran et al., *Dissent in and for the Church* (New York: Sheed and Ward, 1969), p. 26; in "Ten Years Later," *Commonweal*, 105 (1978): 429, Curran affirmed the more general thesis that dissent can be legitimate with respect to any specific moral teaching.

59. See J. R. Lerch, "Teaching Authority of the Church (Magisterium)," *New Catholic Encyclopedia*, 13.965; Francisco A. Sullivan, S.J., *De Ecclesia*, vol. 1, *Quaestiones Theologiae Fundamentalis* (Rome: Gregorian University Press, 1963), p. 354; I. Salaverri, S.J., *Sacrae Theologiae Summa*, vol. 1, *Theologiae Fundamentalis*, 5th ed. (Madrid: Biblioteca de Autores Cristianos, 1952), p. 708, no. 699; L. Lercher,

Institutiones Theologiae Dogmaticae, vol. 1, 5th ed. (Innsbruck: Rauch, 1951), p. 297.

60. Sullivan, *Magisterium*, p. 167, one of those who claim that the standard position of the approved authors is to allow dissent from authoritative but noninfallible teaching, cites Lercher, *Institutiones*, p. 297, in support of dissent. What Lercher actually says is this: "If the Roman Pontiff, using his authority but not to its highest degree, obliges all to give their assent to something as true (whether as revealed or as connected with revelation), it does not seem that in principle he is infallible, nor must we say that the Holy Spirit will never permit him to issue an erroneous decree. Certainly, the Holy Spirit will never permit it to happen that by such a decree the Church would be led into error. The way in which the error would be excluded more probably consists in the assistance of the Holy Spirit given to the head of the Church, by which such an erroneous decree would be prevented. However, it is not unthinkable that an error should be excluded by the Holy Spirit in this way: that the subjects recognize the decree to be erroneous and cease to give their assent to it." This is hardly a rationale for public dissent.

61. See Congregation for the Doctrine of the Faith, *Instruction on the Ecclesial Vocation of the Theologian*, nos. 21-41.

62. *Lumen Gentium*, no. 25. Sullivan, *Magisterium*, pp. 155-156, provides a recent example of the kind of argumentation to which we refer here. He argues that, because one of the schemata preparatory to *Lumen Gentium* was dropped from consideration by the Council, there is evidence that the Council meant to weaken restrictions on dissent. The schema in question referred to Pius XII's strong rejection of theological dissent in the encyclical *Humani Generis* (DS 3885). However, the very text of Pius XII which Sullivan supposes the Council meant to reject is explicitly referred to in *Optatam Totius*, no. 16. As Avery Dulles, *A Church to Believe In* (New York: Seabury, 1982), p. 124, has said: "The position of Pius XII to this effect [that the decisive judgment of a pontiff ends theological debate] in *Humani Generis* (DS 3885), even though not explicitly repeated by Vatican II, still seems to stand as official teaching, especially in view of its reaffirmation by Paul VI."

63. Richard A. McCormick, S.J., *Notes On Moral Theology: 1965 Through 1980* (Washington, DC: University Press of America, 1981), p. 667.

64. In *Veritatis Splendor*, no. 113, Pope John Paul II emphasized that "dissent... is opposed to ecclesial communion and to a correct understanding of the hierarchical constitution of the People of God. Opposition to the teaching of the Church's Pastors cannot be seen as a legitimate expression either of Christian freedom or of the diversity of the Spirit's gifts." See also John Paul II, *Familiaris Consortio*, no. 73; *Code of Canon Law* (1983), Canons 752-754, 823, 1371.

65. Daniel C. Maguire, "The Freedom to Die," in *The New Theology No. 10,* ed. Martin E. Marty and Dean Peerman (New York: Macmillan, 1973), p. 18. Charles Curran argues this position in many of his writings on sexual morality; see *Themes in Fundamental Moral Theology*, pp. 27-80, especially pp. 64-69; *Issues in Sexual and Medical Ethics* (Notre Dame, IN: University of Notre Dame Press, 1978), pp. 38-39, and continues to do so in some of his more recent writings.

66. See Germain Grisez, *Contraception and the Natural Law* (Milwaukee: Bruce, 1964), pp. 47-53.

67. Pope John Paul II, *Veritatis Splendor*, nos. 48-49.

68. See Keane, *Sexual Morality*, pp. 52-54; O'Connell, *Principles for a Catholic Morality*, pp. 91-92.

69. See *Gaudium et Spes*, no. 16; see Finnis's commentary cited above in endnote 17.

70. Curran uses the terms "hierarchical" and "papal" to describe the Church's magisterium; he calls the teaching office of professional theologians the "doctrinal magisterium," and maintains for theologians a source of teaching authority independent of the papal and episcopal magisterium; see *Ongoing Revision*, pp. 45-48, 75-87.

71. See Grisez, *Christian Moral Principles*, ch. 35, q. A, for a positive account of the sense of the faithful.

72. See Richard McCormick, *Notes on Moral Theology*, pp. 784-786; the late Avery Dulles, S.J., is the theologian perhaps best-known for the position of the twofold magisterium. However, Dulles's remarks are guarded. He rightly emphasizes that the theologians have a teaching office, and certainly never draws the conclusion which we are disputing. See his *Survival of Dogma* (New York: Doubleday, 1973), pp. 98-108; "The Theologian and the Magisterium," *Catholic Theological Society of America: Proceedings of the Thirty-First Annual Convention*, 31 (1976), 335-346; *A Church to Believe In*, pp. 110-111,

194 CATHOLIC SEXUAL ETHICS

and especially his more cautious remarks on the twofold magisterium, pp. 118-132. Dulles was created a cardinal in 2001.

73. Maguire, "Of Sex and Ethical Methodology," in *Dimensions of Human Sexuality*, ed. Dennis Doherty (New York: Doubleday, 1979), pp. 139-140. Richard Roach, S.J., provides a critique of Maguire's misuse of probabilism in his review of this volume in *Fidelity*, 2.8 (1983): 23-25. Probabilism was never used to justify dissent from magisterial teaching but was a basis for preferring one from a number of theological opinions on matters not settled by the magisterium.

74. This is implicitly admitted by McCormick in his lament in "Notes On Moral Theology: 1983," *Theological Studies*, 45 (1984): 84, that many theologians have rejected the position of dissent and instead follow the magisterium.

75. See Yves Congar, O.P., "Pour Une Histoire Semantique du Terme 'Magisterium,'" *Revue des Sciences Philosophiques et Théologiques*, 60 (1976): 85-98.

76. Aquinas, *Quodlibetum*, IX, q. 8, corp.

CHAPTER SIX

Chastity, Christian Marriage, and Virginity

The first three chapters of this book summarized the teaching of the Church, of Scripture, and of the Catholic moral tradition on marriage and questions of sexual morality. The fourth and fifth chapters considered the general moral issues which must be faced by those trying to reach responsible and true judgments about how they should act, not simply in the sexual area but in all the areas of human existence. These teachings of God and his Church, as well as these general moral considerations about moral reasoning and decision making, must be brought to a focus to make it clear how they provide the needed guidance for making correct decisions about sexual matters. This application of Catholic teaching to particular questions of sexual ethics will be carried out in some detail in Chapters 7 and 8.

Before developing this detailed application to specific moral questions, however, it is necessary to consider the virtue of chastity and its relationship to the basic vocations of Christian life. This consideration is necessary because chastity is the virtue by which a person integrates his or her sexuality into his or her own Christian life. All Christians, of course, have the common vocation to holiness, to be saints (*Lumen Gentium,* nos. 39-42). But each individual Christian has his or her own unique personal vocation, his or her own indispensable part to play in carrying on the redemptive work of Christ. Pope John Paul II points this out clearly in his apostolic exhortation *Christifideles Laici,* where he writes: "God calls me and sends me forth as a laborer in his vineyard. He calls me and sends me forth.... This *personal* vocation and mission defines the dignity and the responsibility of each member of the lay faithful" (emphasis added).[1] One's personal vocation is one's particular way of responding to God's call and of following Christ; it should be the organizing factor in the life of each Christian. One of the dimensions of our lives which must be integrated with our personal vocation is our sexuality, for sexuality is a powerful force within us. It can be used intelligently in the service of Christian love; but it can also be used for self-gratification, and then it becomes a source of personal disintegration, which compromises the organization of life in response to vocation. The virtue of chastity is, therefore, necessary for mature Christian living.

Of course, the chastity of a consecrated religious or of a single person in the world is very different from that of a married person. But they are not totally different realities: both require that sexual desire be permeated by love and guarded by self-possession; both involve the appreciation of sexuality as a gift to be used intelligently in the service of what is really good.

This chapter, therefore, will consider the virtue of chastity in general and its realization in the two most fundamental vocations of Christian life: marriage and virginity, whether voluntarily chosen for the sake of the kingdom or freely accepted as God's way of calling one to fulfill one's vocation. Thus, this chapter will provide the immediate framework for the discussion of the specific questions of sexual morality which will complete this work.

I. Chastity and Our Sexual Life

It is a commonplace saying that human persons are sexual beings. Human beings are members of a species that is sexual: every human being is either a male or a female. This biological fact about human nature is not, however, simply of biological significance — for sexuality, as Pope John Paul II has noted, is "by no means something purely biological, but concerns the innermost being of the human person as such."[2] In other words, being male or female is not simply an accidental or unimportant aspect of a human person, nor is it something whose significance is simply cultural. The sexuality of men and women affects them not only in obvious physical ways but also psychically, intellectually, and spiritually. Sexual differences make possible the complementarity and special friendship between men and women — relationships that in a host of ways are connected to the economy of salvation: man and woman he made them; in his image he made them.

Human persons are not spirits who happen to have bodies attached. Each one is a living flesh of a kind that is inherently sexual. This is not to deny that the human person has an immortal soul, a spiritual dimension which other animals lack. It is to say, rather, that this soul is a part or dimension of the entire human person — a part that is essentially related to the bodily reality of which it is a principle. The soul of a man is his soul and thus inherently male; the soul of a woman is her soul and thus inherently female. Thus, human sexuality is a modality affecting our entire being as persons.

Sexuality is, in fact, "a fundamental component of personality, one of its modes of being, of manifestation, of communicating with others, of feeling, of expressing and of living human love."[3] This capacity for love as self-giving, rooted in the being of man and woman as sexual persons, is incarnated, as it were, in their bodies. As John Paul II has said, "The human body, with its sex, and its masculinity and femininity, seen in the very mystery of creation... contains right 'from the beginning' the 'spousal' attribute, that is, the *power to express love: precisely that love in which the human person becomes a gift* and — through this gift — fulfills the very meaning of his being and existence"[4] (emphasis in original). The sexuality of man and woman is, thus, complementary in character.[5]

Human sexuality is not, of course, simply a fact about human nature that must be observed objectively, from the outside, as it were. It is experienced — long before it is analyzed or understood — as a dynamic tendency or urge within us. We experience it as an impulse orienting us toward love and affection with other persons, particularly to persons of the other sex. We experience it, too, as a dynamic tendency having existential significance, inasmuch as it is bound up with the being or existence of the entire human species, with the generation of new human persons.[6] Obviously, sexuality as experienced in this way has a specifically genital component which is distinct from, although by no means separated from, our generic sexuality.

Because we are sexual, genital beings, it is natural that we respond to the sexual values incarnate in other persons, particularly in those of the opposite sex. It is natural, too, that there should arise within us sexual desires, accompanied at times by intense feelings of affection. These natural desires are in themselves good, for they are a part of our human nature created by God, and, when properly integrated into the personal vocation to which God calls every person, they play an irreducible role in the self-perfection which is each person's contribution to the kingdom of Christ.

These desires, however, also present a challenge because they elicit powerful emotions which sometimes resist rational control, particularly because of concupiscence. Our sexual desires, indeed, our sensuality or natural tendency to respond to the sexual values of the body, in particular, the body of a person of the opposite sex, are natural to us as bodily, sexual beings. But as a result of original sin concupiscence has entered the human heart. Because of concupiscence human beings, male and female, are inclined to "hanker after" these sexual values, divorcing them from the person and viewing them as objects of potential enjoyment.[7] In other words, our sensuality and sexual desires, under the influence of sinful concupiscence, can lead us to treat persons as objects of sexual gratification and not as irreplaceable and nonsubstitutable persons with whom we must join in a community that respects the dignity of all.

There is likewise the danger that sentimentality and superficial feelings of affection may blind us to reality and cause us to lose sight of the authentic goods at stake in sexual activity. We may, because of sentimental affection, be prompted to say "I love you," when in reality what we love is the feeling of warmth and affection that we experience in a particular person's presence.[8] There is also the danger that we will become possessed by our sexual desires and inclined to act in accord with them and not in accord with the objective demands of intelligent love. Possession by such desires is incompatible with the self-possession of the mature and integrated person, and makes impossible the use of sexuality as part of a free and intelligent gift of self. What is compelled by passion cannot be a free gift.

Sexual desire and emotional affectivity are part of the raw stuff out of which authentic human love can be shaped, but this material needs to be shaped intelligently if it is to become integrally and fully a component of love.

To achieve this goal the virtue of chastity is necessary. Put briefly but neatly, chastity is a virtue that "frees love from selfishness and aggression."[9] It can be more fully described as a virtue concerned with the intelligent and loving integration of our sexual desires and affections into our being as persons, enabling us to come into possession of ourselves as sexual beings so that we can love well — and so that we can touch others and allow ourselves to be touched in ways that respect fully the goods of human existence, and the irreplaceable persons in whom these goods are meant to flourish. A brief explanation of this description will now be given.

Chastity is a virtue. A virtue is a stable character trait or disposition. Virtues, therefore, are not actions or feelings, for these are passing and often momentary. Virtues last, and like other traits that are not naturally given, they must be acquired over a period of time and are not readily lost. Virtues are those character traits which enable a person to do well what is morally good. Virtues enable a person to know what is right and to do it without excessive struggle. Thus, virtues are the extension of a person's morally good choices throughout his or her entire personality; they integrate a good person's entire self around what is best and most central in his or her personality.[10]

Our powers of intellect and will must be developed; they must put on muscle if they are to properly guide our lives. The virtues are the developed orientations of the self which enable these powers to do their proper jobs. But virtues are not only traits of the mind and will; they also develop and perfect the other aspects of our personalities so that they are able to respond readily and joyfully to the directions of our intelligence and will.[11]

The mark of a virtuous person is not simply that he or she does the right things. To be virtuous a person must do the just or courageous or temperate thing in the way a just or courageous or temperate person would do it — that is, with the promptitude and joy that mark such a person's good actions.[12] Thus, a virtuous person does not act from fear and out of a merely automatic routine but freely and autonomously.[13] Likewise, the virtuous person does not act from external constraint, or out of a conditioned response, but because the virtuous person wants to do the right thing and delights in doing it well.[14]

This can be illustrated if we consider two employers and the justice each exhibits in dealing with employees. One pays his employees a just wage and provides decent working conditions. So this employer does the just thing. But he does so reluctantly, with no real willingness, perhaps because laws require him to provide decent working conditions, or because economic forces constrain him to pay a just wage. This employer lacks the virtue of justice. The other employer does the same things, but he does so because he wants to; he does so willingly, freely, and with enthusiasm. This employer does the just thing justly, that is, virtuously. For him, justice is not an extrinsic constraint but an orientation of his own personality.

The virtue of chastity is an aspect of the cardinal virtue of temperance, which has as its subject matter the pleasures of eating, drinking, and sex. Chastity is the form of temperance concerned with the pleasures of sex. These pleasures are essentially related to touch — in particular, touches involving the exercise of one's genital sexuality — and secondarily all the pleasures which prepare them by stimulating the desire for them.[15]

These pleasures and the desire for them are, as we have already seen, natural. The clamor to satisfy these desires is often vehement. The point of the virtue of chastity is not to flee from these pleasures or to suppress the desire for them. Thus, those who despise chastity as being a renunciation or denial of sexuality are mistaken. Chastity does not deny the goodness of these pleasures or suppress desire for them because chastity, like all virtue, is reasonable. To be reasonable is to care for the goods of human nature, and sexuality is meant to promote and respect these goods. The reasonable person therefore sees in the desires and feelings of our sentient nature something good that can serve the entire good of the human person if intelligently integrated into a life of commitment to what is really good.[16]

Chastity, therefore, does not seek to suppress or deny sexuality but rather enables a person to put a loving and intelligent order into his passional life, to take possession of his desires so that the whole self can be integrated and at peace. Thus, in a certain way, the emotions and desires themselves participate actively in the moderation coming from intelligence. This moderation becomes, as it were, a kind of connatural eagerness on their part. Our will and intellect do not dictate from without to restless passion. But our emotions and desires spontaneously, as it were, order themselves to the authentic goods of human persons, which the person grasps through intelligence and loves through his will. Thus, it is a mockery of chastity to regard it as a life of constant warfare between unruly passion and imperious reason. Chastity, once achieved, is a basis for inner peace and personal integration.[17]

As Karol Wojtyla says, far from being something negative, chastity is above all positive and affirming. Its essence "consists in quickness to affirm the value of the person in every situation, and in raising to the personal level all reactions to the value of 'the body and sex'... [it] is above all positive and creative 'from within,' not negative and destructive."[18]

A virtuous spouse, therefore, will "feel" differently about the marital act with his or her own spouse and about genital sex with another. He or she will recognize — not only intellectually but with his or her whole being as an emotional, affective, passionate person — that the choice to engage in the marital act is one that is good and that the pleasure and joy associated with it are good and noble too. And he or she will recognize — not only intellectually but with his or her whole being — that whatever delight there might be in genital sex with another person is specious, that it does not crown an act that is beautiful and ennobling but rather one that fails to respect the goods perfective of human persons. And virtuous single persons "feel" differently about having sex outside of marriage. They know that this is unworthy of the dignity of human persons not only with their minds but also with their hearts.

Of course, no one achieves the fullness of chastity swiftly without some struggle and effort. For many people, the effort to be chaste is a long struggle with recalcitrant emotion. For these people, there is not the peace and joy of mature chastity. Even here, however, the effort is not without real rewards, for there is an anticipation of the joy of chaste living, a recognition of the goodness of self-possession, and a nobility in seeking goods one cannot fully experience. Moreover, even here the struggle is not an attempt to overcome or suppress emotion but an effort to integrate one's personality in a way that is really rewarding. Thus, even the efforts of the imperfectly chaste are not to be seen as battles in an endless struggle but as the efforts to begin a life of inner tranquility and self-possession.

The virtue of chastity is one that all human beings need if they are to open themselves to integral human fulfillment and to the precious goods that perfect human existence and human persons. And chastity in no way deadens or repudiates sexuality. Rather, chastity, by freeing love from the utilitarian attitude,[19] enlivens it so that, being "vitally integrated into the person," it "makes the subject capable, on the plane of his passional life, of the self-determination and self-control which characterizes a mind."[20]

Moreover, as the *Catechism of the Catholic Church* reminds us, the virtue of chastity "blossoms in *friendship*... notably in friendship with one's neighbor."[21] Because this is so, "chastity... also involves a *cultural effort*... [and] presupposes respect for the rights of the person."[22]

Jesus, the complete human, provides a striking model of chastity. He is a sexual being, a virile yet affectionate male. His life was full of close and affectionate friendships with men and women alike. Yet Jesus was a celibate, a virgin because of the demands of his personal vocation as redeemer of the world. His example teaches us that the chaste person is the one who has his or her priorities right, who intelligently loves the goods of human nature and integrates his or her affective life into the vocation by which each one of us is called by God to pursue these goods.

In subsequent chapters the requirements of chastity both for married persons and for unmarried persons will be set forth in some detail. Here, the general outline of chaste Christian life will be sketched out by considering how the basic vocations of Christian life promote and protect the goods of human sexuality.

II. Christian Marriage: A Vocation of Chastity

The Christian vocation of marriage provides an important frame of reference for the understanding and development of the virtue of chastity. This vocation is the context within which God calls most men and women to holiness; and even those who are not called to this vocation know from the lives of married friends and relatives that this is a special locus for God's work in saving mankind. Moreover, marriage is the context in which the use of genital sexuality has its proper role in God's plan. So, it is within marriage that the goods to which human sexuality is ordered are properly realized. Since these goods are the basis for chastity, an understanding of marriage is indispensable for understanding chastity.

The Nature of Marriage. To understand chastity within marriage, it is necessary to understand the nature of marriage itself, for the nature of marriage is designed by God to enable people to integrate their sexuality into the service of self-giving and new life. Thus, marriage enables what could degenerate into a selfish and enslaving force to become instead a full and integral part of a life in which the greatest goods of human persons are served, and the love which is God himself is revealed.

Marriage is one of the most profound and important aspects of human social existence. Its depths of human meaning and supernatural significance are suggested by the attention it receives in Scripture, by the great theologians, and in the teaching of the Church. The discussions in the first three chapters of this book only begin to explore what faith teaches about this wonderful and mysterious reality. Here, it is possible only to summarize those aspects of Christian reflection on marriage which are necessary for understanding its special role as a vocation of chastity.

All human societies have some institutionalized framework for the begetting and raising of children. Perhaps "marriage" could be used as the name for any of these social arrangements. But the biblical and Christian understanding of marriage does not accept any such arrangements as marriage, for not just any arrangement for having and raising children is conducive to their genuine well-being, or for a promotion of the kind of relationship between men and women that will foster real love and respect between them. The God who reveals himself as our Father, whose love for us is like that of our mother but never failing, will not tolerate just any arrangement for begetting and raising children. So marriage is an institution, but unlike most institutions it does not depend simply on human convention or decision. God himself is the author of marriage. As Pope Pius XI said, reflecting the entire tradition going back to Genesis:

> Let it be repeated as an immutable and inviolable fundamental doctrine that matrimony was not instituted or restored by man but by God: not by man were the laws made to strengthen and confirm and elevate it but by God, the Author of nature and by Christ our Lord by whom nature was redeemed, and hence these laws cannot be subject to any human decrees or to any contrary pact even to the spouses themselves. This is the doctrine of Holy Scripture; this is the constant teaching

of the Universal Church; this is the solemn definition of the sacred Council of Trent, which declares and establishes from the words of Holy Writ itself that God is the Author of the perpetual stability of the marriage bond, its unity and stability.[23]

But what is the God-given character of marriage? It is the union of one man and one woman, who mutually give themselves to each other so that they may share an intimate partnership of the whole of their lives until death. Their marital union, which is brought into being by their personal act of irrevocable consent, is, of its own inner dynamism and nature, ordered to "the good of the spouses," the procreation and education of children, and to the fostering of a special and exclusive kind of love — marital or spousal or conjugal love. As spouses, moreover, husband and wife form the single subject of a shared sexual life, and their marital union is fittingly expressed in and by an act proper and specific to them, the marital act. In this act they become "one flesh," and come to "know" one another in a unique and unforgettable way. Through it, spouses symbolize and support all the activities in which they share intimately their lives with each other and communicate the gift of life to new human persons.[24]

This divine plan for marriage was obscured and damaged by the sin described in Genesis 3, with the result that divorce and polygamy disfigured the human reality that God had in mind in bringing marriage into being (cf. *Gaudium et Spes*, no. 47); but this divine plan has been restored in an incomparably marvelous way by our Lord and Savior, Jesus Christ.

Although God is the author of marriage and gives to this human reality its defining characteristics and intrinsic conditions of existence, its coming-into-being in a particular instance depends on the free, personal choice of the man and woman who give themselves to each other in marriage. Nothing can take the place of their act of mutual consent. It is this act that brings their marriage into being and makes them husband and wife. In and through this self-determining act they give to themselves a new identity: the man becomes the woman's husband, and she becomes his wife, and together they become spouses.[25] Prior to this act of irrevocable free consent in which they forswear all others to bestow themselves upon each other, the man and the woman live their own independent lives; in and through it they unite their lives, forming a community of sharing that is so intimate and all-encompassing that they can be said to have one common life and to be one flesh.

The paramount significance of this act of marital consent is eloquently expressed in the Yahwist account of the creation of marriage in Genesis 2. There we read that the man, Adam, on seeing the person equal to himself, whom the Lord had fashioned for him, cried out: "Here at last is bone of my bone and flesh of my flesh.... For this reason a man shall leave father and mother and cleave to his wife, and the two shall become one flesh" (Gen 2:23-24).[26] In his perceptive analysis of this passage from Genesis, Pope John Paul II noted: "The formulation of Genesis 2:24 itself indicates not only that human beings, created as man and woman, have been created for unity, but also that precisely this *unity, through which they become 'one flesh' has right from the beginning the character of a union derived from choice.* We read, in fact, 'a man will leave his father and mother and unite with his wife.' While the man, by virtue of generation, belongs 'by nature' to his father and mother, 'he unites,' by contrast, with his wife (or she to her husband), by choice."[27]

Since marriage is brought into being through an act whereby the spouses give and receive the "word" or person of the other,[28] it is unconditioned, irrevocable, and dependent for continuation in its being only on the continuation in being of the spouses themselves. Thus, both by reason of its God-given nature and the intention of the spouses, marriage is a relationship which lasts until death.

Moreover, in consenting to be spouses, a man and a woman consent to marriage and to all that it entails. Since marriage is an institution for the procreation and education of children, marital consent involves a commitment to this worthy enterprise. Similarly, they commit themselves to fostering the special love of those who would share a common life and hand on that life to their children. Thus, spouses consent to the special expression of marital love — the self-giving of marital intercourse.[29] All of these commitments are expressed in the consent whereby spouses take each other for richer or for poorer, in sickness and in health, unto death.

This brief account of the nature of marriage reveals the essential goods to which human sexuality is ordered; these are the three goods of marriage articulated by St. Augustine — (1) the bond of unity between the spouses, (2) children, and (3) marital fidelity. The requirements of faithful service to these goods provide much of the concrete fabric of chastity, but even the most general characteristics of Christian marriage just considered indicate some basic aspects of this virtue. First, they show that sexuality is not created for the sake of the satisfaction of individuals on terms they can themselves arbitrarily set. Rather, it serves great human goods which they can personally appreciate, goods they must share in to fulfill their own lives. Sexuality is for the sake of human relationships — precious relationships whose excellence must enlighten and guide our sexual desires, and which have an objective, God-given character.

Second, the essential role of mutual consent in the actualization of a marriage shows that these relationships are fundamentally a matter of the commitment of the whole person. The implication is that desire, affection, and emotion must serve commitment, and are enriched and made more satisfying by doing so. The reality of marriage is in the selves constituted by the mutual commitment to be spouses. The feelings of the spouses should be integrated into this commitment. They are not themselves constitutive of the fundamental reality of the relationship.

Chastity and the Goods of Marriage

As already noted, even the briefest account of the nature of marriage makes clear that marriage is meaningful because it is the context in which very important human relationships can be realized and basic human goods fostered and protected. It is in service to these goods — the goods of marriage first articulated by Augustine[30] — that the fabric of chastity takes shape. A brief review of these goods and their implications for chastity will provide some understanding of that shape.

The good of the sacrament — that is, the indissoluble unity of husband and wife — is the good which constitutes the reality of marriage itself, the bond of union between the spouses. Without this union there is no marriage, no marital giving and receiving, and so the tradition regards it as the most essential of the goods of marriage.[31] The centrality of this good is closely tied to its sacramental character.

The feature of this good that is morally most important is the indissolubility of the marriage bond. Indissolubility imposes a moral obligation on spouses not to attempt another marriage as long as their partner is alive. This obligation holds even if it is necessary to separate, even if one is deserted[32] — for marriage, as we saw above, is a total joining of two lives into one; the marital commitment is necessarily for life.

In fact, the indissolubility of marriage not only imposes an obligation not to attempt remarriage, but it also makes remarriage in the case of sacramental marriages literally impossible, for the bond of marriage is a reality, not a matter of human convention. When that bond is created in the life of two Christians, it simply cannot be broken. This bond is intended by God to symbolize the love of Christ for his Church, and as a sacrament of the new covenant it partakes of that divine and human love. And that love cannot be broken by any power in the universe.[33] Thus, as Vatican II teaches, marriage comes to be through the choice of the spouses; but once it has come to be, it does not depend on any choice whatsoever.[34] A spouse can no more become an ex-spouse than a father can become an ex-father, or a mother an ex-mother. They may cease to love each other as spouses should, but they are spouses until death.

In virtue of its being a sacrament of the new covenant, marriage is a special source of grace. A sacrament is a sign which represents a supernatural reality and in some way participates in the reality it signifies. Thus, a sacrament is a means for receiving the grace it signifies.[35] Marriage, therefore, is a means for the sanctification of the spouses.[36]

The marriage of those who give and receive each other "in the Lord"[37] has present within it not only the power of the spouses themselves but also the power of Christ's love. By virtue of this love their marriage not only can respect the precious goods it is bound to honor, it can also be the bearer of a greater and more healing kind of love. Thus, the marriage of Christians both signifies the love of Christ for his Church and participates in this love. It draws from this love so that it is capable of revealing it in the lives of the spouses.[38]

Christian marriage is capable of being a sacrament in this sense because the partners are already incorporated in Christ in virtue of their baptism. As Pope John Paul II said: "Indeed by means of baptism, man and woman are definitively placed within the new and eternal covenant, in the spousal covenant of Christ with the Church. *And it is because of this indestructible insertion* that the intimate community of conjugal life and love, founded by the Creator, is elevated... and enriched by his redeeming power"[39] (emphasis added).

The act of marrying of baptized persons, therefore, is an act of the Church and a sacrament of the new covenant to which Christ himself is party. As such, marriage enables the love of the spouses to be caught up "into divine love and is directed and enriched by the redemptive power of Christ and the salvific action of the Church, with the result that the spouses are effectively led to God."[40]

Non-Christian marriages are not sacramental in this full sense; but they are not totally separated from its saving reality, for whenever people seek earnestly the human goods of marriage, there is an openness to supernatural blessings not explicitly recognized. Thus, we can say that even the marriages of non-Christians are touched by grace, for the goods sought in such marriages "come from God the creator and are integrated in an inchoative way into the spousal love of Christ for His Church."[41]

The implications for chastity of the indissoluble bond of marriage and its supernatural significance as a sacrament of the new covenant are easy to grasp, for this bond points to the fact that our sexuality is meant to serve a lasting and unbreakable relationship with another person — a relationship that is meant to join the spouses in a common life together. It cannot do this if sexual feelings are not penetrated and guided by intelligent love. Thus, the principle for the use of sexuality is not the exigence of sexual desire or of romantic affection but the demands of lasting commitment. The sacramental character of this bond makes clear that the self-transcendence of marriage is not simply a self-transcendence of each of the spouses for the sake of the common life of their marriage but a contribution to the saving work of Jesus. Thus, their union should be a vocation in which they seek to contribute to the work of Jesus. In particular, their vocation is to signify the great saving union between Christ and the Church. So, chastity is shown to have a vocational, ecclesial dimension.

The procreative good — the good of children — also perfects marriage and generates requirements of chastity but in a way very different from the bond of marriage itself, for the procreative good is one of the goods which fulfills the life of married couples, and toward which marriage is ordered. This good — fulfillment and orientation

— is present even when couples are not actually blessed with children. The orientation toward procreation and education of children is implicit in the very fertility of sexuality and in the institutional significance of marriage.[42] Thus, spouses undertake a mission to serve life when they join together in marriage. This service is the natural effect and embodiment of their common life, so perfectly expressed in marital intercourse. Thus, children are "the supreme gift of marriage, and greatly contribute to the good of the parents themselves."[43] Of course, the inherent human significance of procreation is transformed in sacramental marriages, for children are not simply the next generation of the human species, they also are images of God, persons for whom Christ died and rose so that they might become citizens of his kingdom and children of God.[44]

The implications of this good for chastity are perhaps not as easy to see as those of the indissoluble bond of marriage; but they are far-reaching, for the procreative good introduces a new, social dimension to chastity. This good requires a dimension of responsibility for the use of sexuality which goes beyond what is required by the bond of unity alone, for procreation entails responsibility for very dependent persons who made no choice to be a member of a given family. Moreover, this good requires that human sexual activity remain open to new life, and that it be used in such a way as to preserve the delicate balance of community between parents and children.

The third good of marriage is the fidelity of the spouses. This good includes not only the literal fidelity — abstention from adultery — required by the nature of the marital bond and by the procreative good, but it also includes the development of the special love and friendship of the spouses. So, this good is required for the realization of the other goods of marriage but is not simply instrumental to their realization, for the love of spouses is good in itself, a wonderful form of human communion.[45]

Vatican II described marital love as eminently human, inwardly capable of being merged with the divine love of Christ, and utterly distinct from mere erotic attraction. The Council Fathers added that marital love is properly expressed in the chaste union of marital intercourse, that it is faithful and exclusive, and ready for self-sacrifice.[46] In short, this is a love in which all the goods of marriage are realized and celebrated.

The special implications for chastity of the good of fidelity and, in particular, of the love between spouses center on the need for sexuality to serve the needs of others. Genuine love must be ready for self-sacrifice, the antithesis of the self-gratification of sexual indulgence.

The distinctive expression of marital love is the act of marital intercourse. But it would be a mistake to think that marital intercourse is the only expression of marital love. Mutual help, support, and cooperation are also very important. Thus, chastity requires that we order and integrate all of our desires, affections, and aspirations so as to serve the love between spouses that is the foundation of family life. It follows from this, as from the good of procreation, that chastity cannot be limited to the sexual dimension in the narrow sense. All of our familial existence — our entire relationship with our children and our spouses — pertains to chastity. Marital chastity, therefore, affects in some way the entire existence of husbands and wives, for every part of the life of spouses must be integrated around these basic commitments of married life.

Conjugal intercourse is the act proper and exclusive to spouses. It is an act that singularly expresses conjugal love. It is the act in and through which the spouses *chastely* and intimately, as the Fathers of Vatican II remind us, become one.[47] As marital, this act is open to the goods or blessings of marriage, namely, faithful conjugal love and the procreation and education of children. Indeed, as St. Thomas teaches, the marital act, when chastely and honorably engaged in, participates in the good of the sacrament and can thus be called a "holy" act.[48]

As a marital act, it is a shared act of the spouses. Thus, it is the action which actualizes their common life — realizes their bond of unity. It is the act whereby they literally become one flesh, and come to know each other in the special way of spouses.[49] Since conjugal intercourse is the common act of persons irrevocably committed to each other, it fosters the love and fidelity of marriage, and signifies in a concrete way the union of Christ and his Church.[50]

Marital intercourse also realizes the goods of fidelity and of children. It can do this only insofar as it is truly conjugal, for only thus will it involve the self-giving needed for the responsibilities of parenthood and the common life of spouses.

This self-giving has several aspects that are essential for chastity. First, there must be an openness to children in sexual activity. Without this openness, the lovemaking of the spouses cannot be the full sharing of a common life, for it rejects the embodiment and responsibility of that life. This aspect of marital chastity will be considered more fully in Chapter 7. Second, self-giving must fully respect the person of the other. It must systematically avoid treating the other as an object for one's sexual gratification. Third, self-giving requires that the spouses have possession of their sexual desires so that they can freely offer themselves in marital intercourse. If their lovemaking is simply a response to sexual desire, if, in other words, it is activity to which they are driven rather than one chosen freely as an act of love, it cannot have the essential features of a gift. Something that must be done to satisfy exigent desire cannot be a gift, for a gift must be freely given and therefore must be within one's power to withhold. Thus, periodic voluntary abstinence from marital intercourse can also be an essential part of the self-giving of marital love. This is especially so when the full realization of the goods of marriage requires that the couple forgo intercourse.[51]

These aspects of the self-giving that should characterize marital intercourse are, of course, normative features which are not always realized. In fact, they are difficult to realize in the lives of many couples; but they are the goal toward which all couples must strive if their sexual relationships are not to degenerate into mere pleasure-seeking or to the pretense of genuine love.

III. Marriage, the Christian Family, and Chastity

The family rooted in the marriage of Christian spouses is, as Vatican II reminds us, "a church in miniature" (*Ecclesia Domestica*).[52] Thus, the Christian family, as Pope John Paul II insists, "is called upon to take part actively and responsibly in the mission of the Church in a way that is original and specific, by placing itself, in what it is and what it does as an 'intimate community of life and love,' at the service of the Church and society."[53]

The Christian family provides the home where new human life can take root and develop as it ought to develop. It is, indeed, the "sanctuary of life," whose role in building a culture of life and a civilization of love is, John Paul II says, "decisive and irreplaceable."[54]

Husbands and wives are the primary educators of their own children.[55] As such, they have the obligation, as Vatican II emphasizes, "to give suitable and timely instruction to young people, above all in the heart of their own families, about the dignity of married love, its role and its exercise, so that, having learned the value of chastity, they will be able at suitable age to engage in honorable courtship and enter upon a marriage of their own."[56]

Parents must keep in mind that God never obliges them to the impossible. Thus, they can confidently rely on him for help in carrying out their educational responsibilities toward their children. They can, with God's help, succeed in giving their children, especially through their own example and chaste love of each other, an understanding of "sex that is truly and fully personal," leading them to recognize that "sexuality is an enrichment of the whole person — body, emotions, and soul — and it manifests its inmost meaning in leading the person to the gift of self in love."[57]

IV. Chastity and the Life of Consecrated Virginity

Marriage is an especially important vocation of Christian life for putting the demands of chastity into perspective. Of course, it is not the only vocation of Christian life, nor is it the only one that helps put chastity into proper perspective. The life of consecrated virginity in which a person completely forgoes marital and familial life for the sake of witness to the kingdom is also important for understanding Christian chastity. It may seem that the life of consecrated virginity presupposes values quite opposite to those of marriage. In particular, it may seem that this life rejects the values of sexuality for the sake of higher values. These appearances are misleading, for the two vocations are in fact complementary. Pope John Paul II has explained part of this relationship as follows:

> Virginity or celibacy for the sake of the Kingdom of God not only does not contradict the dignity of marriage but also presupposes it and confirms it. Marriage and virginity or celibacy are two ways of expressing and living the one mystery of the covenant of God with his people. When marriage is not esteemed, neither can consecrated virginity or celibacy exist; when human sexuality is not regarded as a great value given by the Creator, the renunciation of it for the sake of the Kingdom of Heaven loses its meaning.[58]

Because marriage is so good, its renunciation can reveal how truly wonderful is the life of the kingdom to which the virginal life testifies in a special way; but the relationship works the other way as well. The life of consecrated virginity throws light on the character of Christian marriage, for the life of virginity is a response to the unconditioned demands of Christ's kingdom. This makes clear that marriage as a human reality is subordinate to the demands of Christ's kingdom; the basis for judging marriage, as for judging everything else in this world, is this kingdom.[59] Only as a vocation contributing to his kingdom does marriage have an absolute claim on his followers. The desires for gratification and earthly happiness must give way in the face of these demands, and nowhere are these more clearly manifested than in the response to the call to renounce all for the kingdom, for only in Christ's kingdom can each of us and all of us together realize full human perfection, and full sharing of goods with other human beings and God himself in loving communion.

Thus, the full meaning of Christian marriage requires an appreciation of the life of consecrated virginity. As Edward Schillebeeckx has said: "It is no longer possible within the Christian order of salvation, to define marriage perfectly without at the same time calling upon total abstinence for the sake of the kingdom of God as a correlative possibility.... Christianity will never be able to close its ears to the authentic biblical call to total abstinence as a possibility which forms an intrinsic and essential part of Christianity itself."[60]

Those who answer the call to the life of consecrated virginity in no way repudiate the goods of married life. Such goods are perfectly realized in the kingdom of Christ to which their lives attest. Moreover, such persons stand as a constant reminder that we can come into full possession of our sexuality without engaging in genital activity, and that we can reasonably engage in sexual activity only within a vocation in which the precious goods of human sexuality are fostered and respected.

V. The Single Life and Chastity

Some men and women, as we saw in the previous section, have the vocation to the consecrated life of virginity. There are, however, many men and women who sincerely desire to marry but unfortunately are never able to do so, and there are others, as the *Catechism of the Catholic Church* reminds us, who "forgo marriage in order to care for their parents or brothers or sisters, to give themselves more completely to a profession, or to serve other honorable ends. They can contribute greatly to the good of the human family."[61]

All these people are, like every human person, called to be chaste. While some of them are involuntarily celibate and have not freely chosen to be celibate either in order to enter the religious life or to serve "other honorable ends," they must all respect and honor the great goods of human sexuality and of human persons in their lives. In a sense, celibacy has chosen them.[62]

Indeed, in contemporary society, such single men and women have an especially important and indispensable role to play in the development of a civilization of love. They are called to show others that chastity is indeed a liberating virtue, one that enables a person to "maintain the integrity of the powers of life and love placed in him."[63] They are called to show the world that happiness in human life is not contingent upon the number of sexual experiences one has but rather on the respect one has for the goods of human existence and of human sexuality.

To sum up this chapter: chastity is an essential virtue of Christian life. It is the virtue by which our sexual dimension is integrated into our lives as followers of Christ. Through this virtue, we are able to reasonably order and direct our sexual desires and emotions so that they serve and do not hinder the vocation to which God calls each of us. Thus, chastity is not a matter of suppressing sexuality but of ordering and integrating so that it can be part of a life of Christian service. In marriage, the marital act, which is exclusive and proper to spouses, is a chaste act, one honoring the precious goods of human sexuality. In the other vocations of Christian life, genital activity is sacrificed for the sake of the goods which will be harmed and distorted because they cannot truly be realized outside of marriage. In these vocations, a person's sexuality is not denied but lived in different ways. In all the vocations of Christian life, chastity guarantees a life of self-possession in which the demands of following Christ are seen clearly, without the fog of disordered passion. In the subsequent chapters of this book we will see in a more specific way what chastity requires, and why the intelligent love of the followers of Christ makes these seemingly difficult demands.

ENDNOTES FOR CHAPTER SIX

1. See John Paul II, *Christifideles Laici,* no. 58. See in particular Germain Grisez and Russell Shaw, *Personal Vocation: God Calls Everyone by Name* (Huntington, IN: Our Sunday Visitor, 2003) for an excellent development of this central truth. See also Grisez's *The Way of the Lord Jesus,* vol. 1, *Christian Moral Principles* (Chicago: Franciscan Herald Press, 1983; now available from Alba Books), ch. 23, for an explanation of the concept of personal vocation and its role in Christian moral life.

2. John Paul II, *Familiaris Consortio,* no. 11.

3. Congregation for Catholic Education, *Educational Guidance in Human Love* (November 1, 1983), p. 5.

4. Pope John Paul II, *Man and Woman He Created Them: A Theology of the Body,* translation, Introduction, Index by Michael Waldstein (Boston: Pauline Books & Media, 2005), General Audience of January 16, 1980, 15.1, pp. 385-386. "15" refers to the 15th general audience or catechesis, "1" refers to the first numbered section of this catechesis, and the passage cited in the text is from pp. 385-386. Hereafter references to this book by John Paul II will be to Waldstein *TOB,* General Audience number, the numbered section of that catechesis, and page number or numbers.

5. On the nature of the complementarity between males and females see the following: Waldstein *TOB,* 13.1-15.5, pp. 178-190; Robert E. Joyce, *Human Sexual Ecology* (Washington, DC: University Publications of America, 1980), especially ch. 5, pp. 63-87; David L. Schindler, "Catholic theology, gender, and the future of Western civilization," *Communio* 20 (1993): 200-239; William E. May, *Marriage: The Rock on Which the Family Is Built,* 2nd ed. (San Francisco: Ignatius Press, 2009), ch. 2, "Marriage and the Complementarity of Male and Female."

6. Karol Wojtyla, *Love and Responsibility* (New York: Farrar, Straus, Giroux, 1981), pp. 45-54 .

7. On sensuality and concupiscence and the difference between them, see ibid., pp. 147-160.

8. On sentiment and sentimentality, see ibid., pp. 151-153. Wojtyla's analyses of sensuality and sentiment (or affectivity) in *Love and Responsibility* are brilliant and most helpful. He calls these profound

emotional responses the "raw material of love," but this raw material must be integrated into authentic love — rooted in an act of the will and not as a spontaneous emotional feeling. And the person integrates them into love in and through the virtue of chastity. But Wojtyla emphasizes that the emotional responses of sensuality and sentiment are as such natural and not evil; indeed, he insists that "an exuberant and readily roused sensuality is the stuff from which a rich — if difficult — personal life may be made" (p. 109).

9. Pontifical Council for the Family, *The Truth and Meaning of Human Sexuality: Guidelines for Education Within the Family* (December 8, 1995), no. 16.

10. The *Catechism of the Catholic Church* affirms that virtues "are firm attitudes, stable dispositions, habitual perfections... that govern our actions, order our passions, and guide our conduct according to reason and faith. They make possible ease, self-mastery, and joy in leading a morally good life. The virtuous man is he who freely practices the good" (no. 1804).

11. Albert Plé, *Chastity and the Affective Life* (New York: Herder and Herder, 1965), p. 117.

12. Thomas Aquinas, *Summa Theologiae*, II-II, q. 32, a. 1, ad 1.

13. Romanus Cesario, *Moral Virtues and Theological Ethics* (Notre Dame, IN: University of Notre Dame Press, 1991), pp. 52-57. See also Plé, *Chastity,* pp. 118-119.

14. Plé, *Chastity*, pp. 117-119.

15. Aquinas, *Summa Theologiae*, II-II, q. 141, c.1, ad 1; see also q. 151, aa. 1, 2. See also Wojtyla, *Love and Responsibility*, pp. 147-159, 200-210.

16. See Aquinas, *Summa Theologiae*, II-II, q. 142, a. 1; see also Plé, *Chastity*, p. 125.

17. See Aquinas, *De Virtutibus in Communi*, q. 4. a. 4, ad 15; see also Plé, *Chastity*, pp. 125-126.

18. See Wojtyla, *Love and Responsibility*, p. 171.

19. See ibid., p. 170.

20. Plé, *Chastity*, pp. 126-127.

21. *Catechism of the Catholic Church*, no. 2347.

22. Ibid., no. 2334.

23. Pius XI, *Casti Connubii*, in Liebard's *Love and Sexuality*, p. 24. For other magisterial teaching, see DS 1797-1800, for Trent; *Gaud-*

ium et Spes, nos. 47-52; Paul VI, *Humanae Vitae,* nos. 4, 6-8; John Paul II, *Familiaris Consortio,* nos. 11-16.

24. See *Gaudium et Spes,* no. 48; *Codex Juris Canonici* (Vatican City: Libreria Editrice Vaticana, 1983), Canon 1055.

25. The Church has constantly taught that the free consent of the man and woman to live together is what makes their union a marriage. See Edward Schillebeeckx, *Marriage: Human Reality and Saving Mystery* (New York: Sheed and Ward, 1965), pp. 287-302, for a history of this teaching. The Council of Florence taught that "the efficient cause of marriage is the mutual consent duly expressed in words relating to the present" (DS 1327). Pius XI in *Casti Connubii* taught that "each individual marriage . . . arises only from the free consent of each of the spouses; and this free act of the will, by which each party hands over and accepts those rights proper to the state of marriage, is so necessary to constitute the marriage that it cannot be supplied by any human power" (Liebard's *Love and Sexuality,* p. 24). See also Vatican Council II, *Gaudium et Spes,* no. 48; 1983 *Codex Iuris Canonici,* Canon 1057.

26. See Walter Brueggemann, "Of the Same Flesh and Bone (Gn 2.23a)," *Catholic Biblical Quarterly,* 32 (1970): 532-542; Brueggemann shows that the formula used in Genesis is a covenantal formula common in the Old Testament. Thus, it has strong connotations of fidelity.

27. Waldstein *TOB,* 10.3, p. 168.

28. See John L. McKenzie, "Toward a Biblical Theology of the Word," in his *Myths and Realities: Studies in Old Testament Theology* (Milwaukee: Bruce, 1963), for a discussion of the "word" in biblical thought.

29. See Aquinas, *Summa Theologiae,* Supplement, q. 48, a. 1, for an account of how marital consent implicitly contains consent to the marital act.

30. The teaching of Augustine on this point is detailed in Chapter 3 of this work. Pius XI, *Casti Connubii,* in Liebard's *Love and Sexuality,* pp. 26-31, says that in Augustine's teaching on the goods of marriage "is contained a splendid summary of the whole doctrine of marriage." *Gaudium et Spes,* no. 48, cites Pius XI and Augustine. Leo XIII, *Arcanum Divinae Sapientiae,* in Liebard's *Love and Sexuality,* p. 9, emphasizes that even the marriages of the unbaptized participate

218 | CATHOLIC SEXUAL ETHICS

in the goods of marriage and can be called the sacrament of marriage. See also Augustine Reagan, C.Ss.R., "The Perennial Value of St. Augustine's Theology of the Goods of Marriage," *Studia Moralia* (1981): 351-377.

31. See Aquinas, *Summa Theologiae*, Supplement, q. 49, a. 3, for an account of the good of the sacrament as the most essential of the goods of marriage.

32. See Augustine, *De Nuptiis Adulterinis*; also Schillebeeckx, *Marriage*, pp. 218-287.

33. See Schillebeeckx, *Marriage*, pp. 141-142, for an account of the biblical roots of the patristic and medieval teaching on the indissolubility of marriage. See also John Lucas, "The *Vinculum Conjugale*: A Moral Reality," *Theology*, 78 (1975): 225-230, for an account of the indissolubility of marriage by a non-Catholic.

34. See *Gaudium et Spes*, no. 48. It should be noted that the Church does "dissolve" the marriages of some non-Christians when one partner becomes a Christian and the other refuses to allow the first to carry out the obligations of the conversion, and it dissolves some nonconsummated marriages. In both cases the dissolution is done with the authority of God himself, and by no human authority. In the former case there is no implication that marriage is not naturally indissoluble. Likewise in the latter, for the dissolution is possible only because the marriage is not, as it were, fully completed by consummation. See Schillebeeckx, *Marriage*, pp. 155-168, 287-302.

35. See Council of Trent, Session 7, March 3, 1547, "Decree on the Sacraments, Canons on the Sacraments in General" (DS 1601-1608).

36. See Leo XIII, *Arcanum Divinae Sapientiae*, in Liebard's *Love and Sexuality*, p. 5; Gaudium et Spes, no. 48.

37. See Schillebeeckx, *Marriage*, pp. 133-140.

38. See ibid., p. 137: "Experience of marriage 'in the Lord' does not imply any extrinsic addition to secular; that is, the making Christian... of marriage, of its natural and human interrelationships... is an entirely intrinsic process."

39. John Paul II, *Familiaris Consortio*, no. 13; see also Schillebeeckx, *Marriage*, pp. 167-170.

40. *Gaudium et Spes*, no. 48; see also John Paul II, *Familiaris Consortio*, nos. 13, 49-64. See Michael F. McAuliffe, *Catholic Moral Teaching on the Nature and Object of Conjugal Love* (Washington, DC:

Catholic University Press, 1954), for a survey of Catholic teaching on this matter.

41. International Theological Commission, *Thèses de Doctrina Matrimonii Christiani*, in *Gregorianum*, 3.4 (1978): 453-464, at 450; English translation in *Origins: NC Documentary Service*, 8.12 (1975).

42. See John Paul II, *Familiaris Consortio*, no. 11.

43. *Gaudium et Spes*, no. 50; see also Germain Grisez, "Marriage: Reflections Based on St. Thomas and Vatican II," *The Catholic Mind*, 64 (1966): 5-19.

44. See Aquinas, *Summa Theologiae*, Supplement, q. 49, a. 5, ad 1.

45. See Pius XI, *Castii Connubii*, in Liebard's *Love and Sexuality*, p. 30: "This conjugal faith, which is most aptly called by St. Augustine the 'faith of chastity,' blooms more freely, more beautifully, and more nobly, when it is rooted in that more excellent soil, the love of husband and wife which pervades all the duties of the married life and holds pride of place in Christian marriage. For matrimonial faith demands that husband and wife be joined in an especially holy and pure love... as Christ loved the Church."

46. *Gaudium et Spes*, no. 49. See also Paul VI, *Humanae Vitae*, no. 9; John Paul II, *Familiaris Consortio*, nos. 11-14, 20-21, 28.

47. *Gaudium et Spes*, no. 49.

48. See St. Thomas Aquinas, *Summa Theologiae*, Supplement to Third Part, q. 49, a. 4. On the truth that the marital act is not simply an act between persons who merely "happen" to be married but is rather an act participating in and open to the goods of marriage, see William E. May, *Marriage: The Rock on Which the Family Is Built*, 2nd ed. (San Francisco: Ignatius Press, 2009), pp. 2-4, 12-14, 82-85.

49. See Waldstein *TOB*, 21 and 22 in full, pp. 205-218.

50. See John Kippley, *Birth Control and the Marriage Covenant* (Collegeville, MN: The Liturgical Press, 1976), pp. 105-113; Dietrich von Hildebrand, *In Defense of Purity* (New York: Sheed and Ward, 1935), pp. 54-76; Mary R. Joyce, *Love Responds to Life* (Kenosha, WI: Prow Press, 1970), pp. 8-26.

51. Paul VI, *Humanae Vitae*, no. 13. On this see Germain Grisez, Joseph Boyle, John Finnis, and William E. May, "'Every Marital Act Ought to Be Open to New Life': Toward a Clearer Understanding," *The Thomist* 52 (1988): 390-399.

52. *Lumen Gentium*, no. 11; *Apostolicam Actuositatem*, no. 11.

53. Pope John Paul II, *Familiaris Consortio*, no. 50.

54. Pope John Paul II, *Evangelium Vitae*, no. 92. See Pope John Paul II, *Centesimus Annus*, no. 39.

55. Among the documents of the Church dealing with the rights and duties of parents as educators are the following: Pope Pius XI, *Divini Illius Magistri;* Vatican Council II, *Gravissimum Educationis; The Charter for Families.*

56. *Gaudium et Spes*, no. 49. See also *Catechism of the Catholic Church*, no. 1632.

57. Pope John Paul II, *Familiaris Consortio*, no. 37. See also Pontifical Council for the Family, *The Truth and Meaning of Human Sexuality: Guidelines for Education within the Family* (December 8, 1995); Pontifical Council for the Family, *Preparation for the Sacrament of Marriage* (May 13, 1996).

58. John Paul II, *Familiaris Consortio*, no. 16.

59. See Schillebeeckx, *Marriage*, pp. 105-110, 123.

60. Ibid., p. 131.

61. *Catechism of the Catholic Church*, no. 2231.

62. See Roger Balducelli, O.S.F.S., "The Decision for Celibacy," *Theological Studies*, 36 (1975): 219-242. On celibacy and virginity for the kingdom, see also Raniero Cantalamessa, O.F.M. Cap., *Virginity: A Positive Approach to Celibacy for the Sake of the Kingdom of Heaven* (Staten Island, NY: Alba House, 1995).

63. *Catechism of the Catholic Church*, no. 2338.

CHAPTER SEVEN

Chastity and the "Obligations" (Love-based Demands) of Married Persons

I changed the title of this chapter because I thought the earlier title, "The Requirements of Chastity Within Marriage," although good in many ways, did not explicitly show that these "requirements" or "obligations" are not legalistic norms imposed from without but are expressions of marital love. I have also shortened considerably the lengthy discussion on contraception because of recent developments, and I have now added a section dealing with condom use by spouses as a means to prevent transmission of HIV/AIDS. After this introductory material, the chapter will consider: I. Adultery; II. Contraception; III. Natural Family Planning; IV. Sterilization; V. Other Violations of Marital Chastity; VI; Artificial Insemination and *In Vitro* Fertilization; and VII. Spousal Use of Condoms to Prevent HIV/AIDS.

God made men and women as sexual beings, and he blessed marriage. Sexual activity in marriage, when it is faithful to the great goods for which marriage was instituted, is very good. It is natural and excellent, and ennobles human life. Such activity is rooted in the unique kind of love meant to exist between husbands and wives, "marital" or "spousal" love. This is the love "uniquely expressed and perfected by the exercise of the acts proper to marriage. Hence the acts in marriage by which the intimate and chaste union of the spouses takes place are noble and honorable; the truly human performance of these acts fosters the self-giving they signify and enriches the spouses in joy and gratitude" (*Gaudium et Spes*, no. 49).

By the choice to marry, a man and a woman commit themselves to participate in the goods for which marriage was instituted. In pursuing faithful love and its extension and embodiment in children, spouses pursue goods naturally desired by human persons; in participating in the sacramental good, they take part in the most sublime ends of marriage and marital union. In Chapter 6 we already described the beauty of married life and of marital acts marked by a commitment to the goods of marriage.

But sex, like every good gift of God to man, can be abused. Married persons can engage in sexual activity in unreasonable and sinful ways; they can fail to respect the values that must be honored in sexual activity. Following the guidance of Scripture and Christian tradition, the Church urges the faithful to avoid those kinds of human acts that are irresponsible and wrong. It does so not to focus their attention on sin but to hearten them toward a more faithful and human living of their married vocation. As noted above, in this chapter we consider ways in which spouses can fail to meet the requirements of chastity, the demands of faithful and life-giving love. First we consider adultery, which fails to honor the good of faithful love. Then we treat contraception and sterilization, which attack the procreative good. Next, we take up artificial reproductive techniques, which separate the unitive and procreative goods. Finally, we treat other violations of marital chastity, including the use of condoms as a means of avoiding contracting the AIDS virus.

I. Adultery

Adultery was proscribed in the Decalogue, or Ten Commandments (Ex 20:14; Deut 5:18). In a patriarchal society such as existed at the beginning of God's moral revelation, there was emphasis on the rights of the husband, and a focus on external deeds.[1] But the Decalogue was concerned with more than the external act and rights externally violated. It explicitly noted the wrongness of *coveting* one's neighbor's wife (Ex 20:17; Deut 5:21), an inner act by which the heart of the sinner is harmed.

The malice of adultery was frequently recalled in the Old Testament. As the revelation given to Israel developed, marriage itself came to be seen as a faithful and loving covenant between man and woman, symbolizing the covenant of grace and fidelity between Yahweh and his people.[2] Implicit in this understanding of marriage is the realization that adultery violates far more than the rights of the husband. It attacks the heart of the marriage covenant itself, and strikes at every person guarded by that covenant. Pope John Paul II, commenting on the significance of the story of human origins in Genesis, properly sums up the teaching of the Old Testament: "Adultery... means a breach of the unity by means of which man and woman only as husband and wife can unite so closely as to be 'one flesh.'"[3]

Jesus clearly taught that not only the external deed of adultery is sinful but the desire for it as well (Mt 5:28).[4] Although Jesus forgave the woman caught in adultery, he cautioned her not to sin any more (Jn 8:11). He likewise made it quite clear that adultery violates the rights of both husband and wife, and that it desecrates the covenant of marriage (Mk 10:11-12; Mt 19:9).[5] By adultery he clearly meant sexual union with a person other than one's spouse.[6]

Paul saw sexual union between man and woman in marriage as very good. It is a communion in being, a "one-flesh" unity, symbolizing the intensely personal union between Christ and his bride the Church (Eph 5:25-33).[7] He taught that a Christian becomes one body with Christ in baptism.[8] And he stressed that the body of the Christian — that is, his whole person[9] — is a temple of the Holy Spirit (1 Cor 6:19), a "vessel" to be held in honor as a God-given and sacred reality (1 Thess 4:3-5).[10] Thus, precisely because sexual activity and the body are so meaningful and precious, Paul taught that any act of sexual immorality was an act of desecration, for in such an act the person who had already become one body with Christ, the Holy One of God, was taking something holy — his or her own person now living in Christ — and defiling it. He therefore pleaded with his brothers and sisters in the Lord to "control his own body in holiness and honor" (1 Thess 4:4) and exclaimed: "Do you not know that the unrighteous will not inherit the kingdom of God? Do not be deceived; neither the immoral, nor idolaters, nor adulterers, nor homosexuals, nor thieves, nor the greedy, nor drunkards, nor revilers, nor robbers will inherit the kingdom of God" (1 Cor 6:9-10). Adultery is wicked not only because it desecrates the living temple of the Holy Spirit but also because it does violence to a unique and exclusive kind of love, a love divinely intended to signify and partake of the love between Christ and his Church.

This brief summary makes it evident that the New Testament considered adultery — that is, sexual union with a person other than one's spouse — an evil, a desecration completely incompatible with the life of a Christian. Its teaching is admirably summed up in the Letter to the Hebrews: "Let marriage be held in honor among all, and let the marriage bed be undefiled; for God will judge the immoral and adulterous" (Heb 13:4).

The plain sense of this biblical teaching is faithfully proclaimed by the Church. The Fathers and the great medieval moralists, the approved authors of recent centuries, and the magisterium in all cases speak with one voice condemning adultery. In fact, the wrongness of adultery follows so immediately from what is central to the Christian view of marriage and marital relations that it is commonly taken to be obvious.[11] Adultery is therefore considered by many Christians as a clear example of an inherently wrongful act, and it is used as a reference point to elucidate the malice of other sins.[12]

Given the attack on the Christian doctrine of marriage and sexuality in recent decades, it is not surprising that the magisterium has reaffirmed and proclaimed the traditional teaching on adultery. Thus, Pius XI explicitly condemned adultery in *Casti Connubii*;[13] the Fathers of Vatican II stressed its incompatibility with the fidelity demanded by spousal love (*Gaudium et Spes*, no. 49); the American bishops clearly rejected it as gravely sinful in their pastoral on moral values;[14] and John Paul II branded it as a terrible breach of covenantal love.[15] The *Catechism of the Catholic Church* teaches that the spouse who commits adultery "fails in his commitment... does injury to the sign of the covenant which the marriage bond is, transgresses the rights of the other spouse, and undermines the institution of marriage by breaking the covenant on which it is based [and] compromises the good of human generation and the welfare of children who need their parents' stable union" (no. 2381).

This teaching cannot be set aside as culturally conditioned and therefore no longer normative.[16] The living body of the faithful, guided by the Holy Spirit and aware not only of cultural differences but of the unity through time of the Church, knows that every deliberate act of adultery is seriously wrong.

The grounds for this constant teaching of the Church on adultery are readily discernible. Only a brief account of these grounds is necessary here. Adultery is radically inconsistent with the proper pursuit of the goods of human sexuality and of human persons. Although all the goods honored in marriage — the procreative good, the good of friendship between the spouses, and the good of indissoluble unity — are violated by adultery, it is marital friendship which adultery primarily and immediately harms.

The inconsistency between adultery and marital friendship becomes clear if the special character of this friendship — one described in detail in Chapter 6 — is understood. Like many other friendships, marital friendship is a good thing, valued for its own sake. But this friendship differs from other types of friendship in a number of ways. It is rooted in the covenant of irrevocable personal consent, a consent that establishes the man and the woman as irreplaceable and nonsubstitutable spouses, as husband and wife. It is, therefore, a friendship that is exclusive of others in the sense that husband and wife pledge to be with and for each other fully until death, and aspire to a unity of personal intimacy, to a communion in being.[17] It is a friendship that involves an intimate sharing of life and love, a sharing so complete that it naturally leads to new life.[18] Marital friendship is essentially related to the most basic and intimate of human communities, the family. This friendship, unique among all kinds of human friendships, is the ground of the family and is nourished and expressed in the life of the family.[19] The intimacy of this friendship, so fittingly expressed in the conjugal act,[20] the unity of spouses in a common life, and the open-ended demands of procreating and raising children, require that marital friendship be the permanent and exclusive relationship that Christian teaching holds marriage to be.

Adultery obviously inflicts great harm on spouses and on their children. Moreover, as St. Thomas Aquinas and Pope John Paul II both have emphasized, a husband can commit adultery with his own wife (and she with him) if he looks on her with concupiscent desire, with lust even if he may "say" to her while having sex that he "loves" her; this is a lie, for what he loves is the pleasure he can take from her; he is in no way giving himself to her in an act of self-giving love.[21] The deep personal hurt and betrayal experienced by the victims of infidelity, the breaking of the bonds of trust and love, the painful effects of divorce — all these evils and many more are the commonly known effects of adultery. These obvious evils do not arise in each and every case of adultery; but evils of this type are the natural consequences of the harm to marital friendship that is necessarily involved in every act of adultery. The unfaithful spouse is ordinarily deceiving himself or herself when he or she thinks the act of adultery will cause no great harm. These evil effects are, therefore, useful signs of the inherent evil of this desecrating deed.

The argument is sometimes made that adultery can be consistent with the overall values of marriage and of family life if it is a necessary means to avoid great evils or to achieve great goods. Thus, under some circumstances adultery is said to be justified as therapy for sexual dysfunction, or a necessary way of avoiding loneliness and frustration when the spouses are separated, or as a way of gaining favors or avoiding harms — especially where the favors sought or the harms avoided affect one's family or spouse in a profound way. For example, a woman commits adultery with a concentration-camp guard so that she will become pregnant and be returned to the family who desperately needs her.[22] Arguments like these, however, are specious. They are essentially consequentialist and assume that the evil immediately brought about by adultery can be balanced by the good an individual hopes to achieve by it. As we saw in Chapter 4, this assumption is false.[23] In this area, as in all areas of life, one's life is disastrously wounded if one is willing to do evil so that good may come about.

Finally, we must consider the argument that sexual intercourse with a person other than one's spouse, if done with the consent of one's spouse, ought not to be called adultery or at any rate ought not to be considered adultery in a morally pejorative sense.[24] This line of reasoning assumes a subtle form of dualism, for it seems to hold that a man and a woman can continue to give themselves (that is, their conscious minds) to each other uniquely and exclusively even as they give their bodies (now regarded as distinct from their "selves") to another. This fallacious Gnostic assumption forgets the unity of the human person and promotes self-deception.

This argument also involves the false assumption that spouses' rights concerning each other's sexual activities are analogous to property rights or to other rights that can be waived. The mutual rights of spouses with respect to each other's sexual activities are not analogous to property rights or to other transferable rights. Rather, these rights are rooted in the marital covenant and in the marriage itself, in the giving and receiving of the *person* of the other. These realities are not subject to manipulation by the spouses; they come into being in the lives of the spouses from their mutual consent to marriage. But once the marriage comes to exist, it is governed by divinely established norms to which married persons must conform. Consensual adultery, therefore, *is* adultery, as Pope Innocent XI taught long ago.[25]

II. Contraception

The sexual revolution is closely related to the development of contraceptives.[26] At the beginning of the twentieth century the common moral position — not simply of Catholics but also of other Christians, of Jews, and of other religious groups and even of nonreligious people — was that sexual activity had to be responsibly related to marital promises and to the obvious purposes of sex. Contraception was viewed as an abuse of sexual activity, shameful and wrong. In it spouses abused each other, and they abused a significant kind of human action by failing to respect one of its obvious and humanly very important purposes. For very many it still seemed highly desirable to have large families. Even in circumstances in which more children were undesirable, the use of contraception to limit families was judged the use of an evil means. As a matter of fact, from the time of the Church Fathers, through the Middle Ages, during the Protestant Reformation and the Catholic Church's great ecumenical council, the sixteenth century's Council of Trent for renewing the Church, and until the twentieth century, *all* Christian churches regarded contraception as an *anti- or contra-life kind of act analogous to homicide*.[27] In 1930 the Lambeth Conference of the Anglican Church accepted contraception by married couples and only for serious reasons. This provoked Pope Pius XI to reaffirm most strongly the Church's teaching that contraception is intrinsically evil in his 1930 encyclical *Casti Connubii*.

In recent times many elements of modern life seemed to join together to commend having smaller families. Urbanization was one factor. In city life the economic cost of having large families could be seriously burdensome, surely in ways in which they had not been in rural life. Time and time again false claims that a "population bomb" was about to explode and cause utter chaos to all of us were made by those who wished to promote new moral visions — visions incompatible with Christianity. Limited social resources as well as limited family resources were presented as urgent reasons to control the family and the general population.[28]

Theoretically this control could have been managed by various kinds of self-discipline and sexual abstinence. Because of the cultural climate in the United States and Western World, many people of high moral standards who instinctively judged that sex was meaningful and sacred did not see clearly the reasons why contraception was not a humanly satisfactory solution to these problems. When the commercial interests favoring contraception and the moral revolutionaries proposing a new secular ethics portrayed in glowing terms the advantages of contraception, many failed to see the moral and social problems that a contraceptive mentality would create. The terrible harms that have been caused by the widespread use of contraception as a way of exercising "responsible parenthood" have been catalogued by many competent scholars.[29]

Certainly contraception was convenient. It enabled people to reach what had clearly become a desirable end by means that were effective and, moreover, required little self-discipline and no sexual abstinence at all. Everyone could have sex whenever it was desired without the inconvenience of unwanted pregnancies. (Many at first naïvely thought only married couples would take advantage of this.) This convenience led to a rapid progress toward broad social acceptance of what had earlier been recognized as immoral. Even various religious groups came to commend the contraception they had once sharply condemned. The desirability of the end pursued by contraceptionists was so clear that many failed to question sufficiently the morality of this precise means toward that end.

Pressure to change the Catholic teaching on contraception became very great. It became especially intense in the 1960s, when the "sexual revolution" was gaining steam. Nevertheless, Pope Paul VI, emphasizing that he was reaffirming the received teaching of the Christian faith on an important question, refused to alter the Church's stand against contraception. He affirmed in very clear language that contraception is seriously wrong. In doing so he was not denying the importance of family planning and responsible parenthood.[30] His concern was with the moral character of the means used to achieve this end.

During his pontificate, Pope John Paul II had repeatedly reaffirmed the teaching of Paul VI — and of the entire Catholic tradition and magisterium — on the intrinsic evil of contraception.[31] Pope Benedict XVI has also again and again reaffirmed the teaching of the Church on contraception as an intrinsically evil act, especially in many addresses given throughout the world in 2008, the fortieth anniversary of *Humanae Vitae*.

The Meaning of Contraception. Contraception, as the word itself suggests, is action aimed at preventing conception. But it is necessary to begin with a clear definition of "contraception" to make unmistakable the precise nature of the acts to which moral judgments about contraception are intended to apply.

In his encyclical *Humanae Vitae*, Paul VI gave an exact account of the nature of contraceptive actions. A contraceptive act is committed whenever one does something which is intended precisely to act against the procreative good of an act of coition, i.e., to prevent this good from being realized in and through the act of coition or intercourse. "Every act that intends to impede procreation [the official Latin text reads *"ut procreation impediatur, intendat"*] must be repudiated, intending this either as the end or means used, whether it is done in anticipation of marital intercourse, or during it, or while it is having its natural consequences."[32] Those who contracept, reasonably believing that a freely chosen act of intercourse is the sort of act through which new human life can be given, choose to do something, prior to, during, or subsequent to this freely chosen act precisely *to impede procreation*, i.e., to prevent the conception of the child who might otherwise be conceived in and through this act of intercourse. Thus it is more accurate to speak of "contracepted" intercourse than of "contraceptive" intercourse. Intercourse is the chosen object of one human act, whereas contraception or the impeding of procreation is the chosen object of another human act, namely, the contraceptive act.

Thus there are various ways in which intercourse can be contracepted: through the use of various barriers (e.g., condoms or diaphragms), by the use of spermicides or withdrawal, by the use of anovulant pills,[33] by surgical sterilization, and the like. Ordinarily,[34] in contracepted intercourse, a person or couple chooses, first, to engage in sexual intercourse. While choosing to have intercourse, which is known to be essentially related to the procreation of new human life, and precisely because one does not want that act of intercourse to flower into the fruitfulness it can have, one performs the contraceptive act. This act is aimed precisely against the procreative good. The coming-to-be of a new human life (which is in itself a great good, though one may perhaps reasonably desire not to realize it here and now) is treated as an evil, something to be prevented and opposed. The precise point of the contraceptive act, as we shall show more fully below, is to act directly against the great human good of procreation, of human life in its coming-to-be, and to treat it as if it were here and now an evil, not a good.

Contraception or contracepted intercourse, therefore, is not identical in meaning with birth control or family planning. Plainly there are other ways to control births and to plan one's family than by engaging in contracepted intercourse. One can control or prevent births by means far worse than contraception — by abortion, for instance. And one can plan one's family by means that are in themselves thoroughly good — that is, by natural family planning.

With this understanding of the meaning of contracepted intercourse (or contraception) in mind, we now propose to examine the Church's teaching on this subject and to develop the basic argument to show that this activity is immoral.

In the First and Second Editions of this book at this point there was a discussion of three objections and difficulties raised against this teaching by some Catholic thinkers from the late 1950s through the 1960s and beyond. The first objection, raised by theologians like Louis Janssens of the Belgian Universitet de Leuven, was that the birth control "pill," which differed from contraceptives such as condoms, diaphragms, and spermicidal jellies that interfered with "the naturalness" of sexual intercourse, thus seemed in some ways "natural" and morally acceptable. This issue was the precise question originally given to the celebrated Papal Commission on the Regulation of Birth that Pope John XXIII established at Vatican Council II; it was a question not formally addressed by the Council. But this Committee, a majority of whose members, as we have seen, urged Pope Paul VI to change Church teaching and accept contraception, quickly agreed that the "Pill" was indeed a contraceptive. That takes care of the first problem. A second major objection, still raised by theologians and others who reject magisterial teaching, claims that that teaching is "physicalistic" or "biologistic" and subordinates persons to "biological" or "physical" laws and is hence demeaning. This view, as noted, is still championed by dissenting theologians, among whom the most prominent is Charles E.Curran.[35] A third objection was that Church teaching on contraception was derivative and secondary, in the context of more important and substantive teaching on, for example, the pessimistic heresy of Manicheism that regarded procreation as sinful.[36]

We have already shown that the famous pro-contraception Committee established by Pope John XXIII and enlarged by Pope Paul VI in effect showed the first objection ridiculous and readily agreed that the "Pill" is contraceptive. In endnote 35 we referred to some theological literature showing how wrong is the criticism that Church teaching on contraception is "physicalistic." But of greater significance than the work of theologians is the trenchant reply to this criticism that Pope John Paul II gave to the charge that Church teaching is physicalistic in *Veritatis Splendor*. There he wrote:

> This [claim, that Church teaching on sexual issues, etc., is "physicalistic"] does not correspond to the truth about man and his freedom. It contradicts the "Church's teachings on the unity of the human person," whose rational soul is "per se et essentialite" the form of his body [with a footnote reference to Ecumenical Council of Vienne, Constitution "Fidei Catholicae": DS, 902; Fifth Lateran Ecumenical Council, Bull "Apostolici Regiminis": DS, 1440]. The spiritual and immortal soul is the principle of unity of the human being, whereby it exists as a whole — "corpore et anima unus" [with reference to *Gaudium et Spes,* 14] as a person. These definitions... remind us that reason and free will are linked with all the bodily and sense faculties. "The person, including the body, is completely entrusted to himself, and it is in the unity of body and soul that the person is the subject of his own moral acts." The person, by the light of reason and the support of virtue, discovers in the body the anticipatory signs, the expression and the promise of the gift of self, in conformity with the wise plan of the Creator. It is in the light of the dignity of the human person — a dignity which must be affirmed for its own sake — that reason grasps the specific moral value of certain goods towards which the person is naturally inclined. And since the human

person cannot be reduced to a freedom which is self-designing, but entails a particular spiritual and bodily structure, the primordial moral requirement of loving and respecting the person as an end and never as a mere means also implies, by its very nature, respect for certain *fundamental goods* [emphasis added], without which one would fall into relativism and arbitrariness. A doctrine which dissociates the moral act from the bodily dimensions of its exercise is contrary to the teaching of Scripture and Tradition. *Such a doctrine revives, in new forms, certain ancient errors* [emphasis added; he is referring to different forms of Gnosticism of which Manicheism was one] which have always been opposed by the Church, inasmuch as they reduce the human person to a "spiritual" and purely formal freedom. This reduction misunderstands the moral meaning of the body and of kinds of behavior involving it (cf. 1 Cor 6:19). Saint Paul declares that "the immoral, idolaters, adulterers, sexual perverts, thieves, the greedy, drunkards, revilers, robbers" are excluded from the Kingdom of God (cf. 1 Cor 6:9). This condemnation — repeated by the Council of Trent [Sess. VI, Decree on Justification "Cum Hoc Tempore," Chap. 15: DS, 1544] lists as "mortal sins" or "immoral practices" certain specific kinds of behavior the willful acceptance of which prevents believers from sharing in the inheritance promised to them. In fact, "body and soul are inseparable": in the person, in the willing agent and in the deliberate act, "they stand or fall together."[37]

Thus the first two objections against Church teaching on contraception have now been answered. According to the third, magisterial teaching on contraception is simply not of central significance, but is of secondary and derivative importance relative to much more important issues such as repudiation of heresies, etc. In part this has also been answered. Of crucial significance is the "good" of marriage, and its "goods" (the procreation and education of children, the deepening of conjugal love) are substantive or basic goods, as indicated above in the citation from *Veritatis Splendor,* where emphasis was placed on the words "fundamental goods" of the human person. These are the "goods" of human persons at stake with respect to contraception.

The Church's Teaching

Fully aware of these doubts, and in fact, largely to remove them, Paul VI strongly reaffirmed the received teaching of the Church on contraception. In 1968, after painstakingly deliberating over the matter and taking into account the arguments that had been advanced to support the moral permissibility of contraception, he reaffirmed in his encyclical *Humanae Vitae* the constant teaching of the Church that contraception is intrinsically a serious moral disorder. Although this encyclical met with dissent, and even, at times, contempt, the teaching set forth in it has since been firmly proclaimed by the magisterium from that time on until today, as matter already cited in this chapter shows. Thus, we have already noted that time and time again throughout his pontificate John Paul II had vigorously reaffirmed and defended the teaching that contraception is gravely immoral and that Benedict has done this too. John Paul had himself developed a strong, personalist argument against contraception by married persons as an act that violates their marital union (this argument will be summarized below). He had, furthermore, emphasized the crucial significance, both moral and anthropological, between the use of contraception and periodic abstinence as ways of meeting parental responsibilities and expressing conjugal love, affirming, indeed, that these two practices are based, ultimately, on "irreconcilable concepts of the human person and of human sexuality."[38]

Moreover, and this is most important, both the First and Second Vatican Councils clearly taught that the bishops of the Church teach infallibly when they propose matters of faith and morals in ways that reveal that they are acting as decisive witnesses to the teaching of the faith.[39] The Church proposes truths of both faith and morals infallibly in its ordinary magisterium, when that teaching has the characteristics noted in *Lumen Gentium*, no. 25.

Distinguished moralists have pointed out that the Church's teaching on contraception seems clearly to have been proposed by the ordinary magisterium in precisely this way.[40] At the very least, these considerations show that the received teaching must be accepted as a practical norm for preachers, confessors, and married people. Moreover, these considerations show that what is at issue is a teaching of the Church concerning morals and not a mere rule or policy. Thus, to "dissent" from this teaching is not simply to disregard commands of prelates but rather it is to attack what the Church presents as confirmed by divine teaching. Most Catholics are not willing to disregard truths closely related to their faith. The apparent disregard of the Church's teaching on contraception by many Catholics shows that the connection between this teaching and Catholic faith needs to be better understood.

It is true that among the faithful much confusion has been generated. There is not now evident the clear and morally unanimous support of the received Catholic teaching, which is the desired sign of Catholic unity. But dissent does nothing to cancel out the testimony of the whole Church, teachers and believers alike, over all the centuries. Some dissenters like to argue that the Holy Spirit is guiding their dissent. But, even though they may have noble intentions, their claim of support from the Holy Spirit is very far from proved. There are many other active forces, not identical with the Holy Spirit, that have led the massive social drive toward contraception; and these motives appear to have influenced some Catholic thinkers too.

Moreover, there is a striking testimony of the faithful in our time in support of the received teaching. Despite the immense propaganda favoring contraception, despite the failure of local teachers of faith to present intelligently and persuasively the position the Catholic faith has always taught, there has been great faithfulness on the part of vast numbers of the faithful. The astonishing growth of the Natural Family Planning (NFP) movement, with its joyful discovery of how valuable the Catholic teaching is, and how it is both livable and able to enrich married life, presages a happy return to a fuller acceptance of Catholic teaching everywhere. The terrible disadvantages of the contraceptive movement are becoming more visible, even in our environment, and it is evident that NFP provides in more human and nobler ways the goods that contraception was seeking to reach.

Theological Argument

The Catholic moral tradition contains a number of arguments against contraception. Catholic certainty in matters of morals is, of course, not dependent simply upon such arguments. The testimony of faith is much firmer, but such moral reflection is important for the family of faith.

Different theological arguments have been advanced to show the truth of the Church's teaching on the intrinsic evil of contraception.[41]

Here we will first summarize the argument developed by Pope John Paul II in *Familiaris Consortio* and other papal documents; we will also summarize the argument against contraception he advanced in his 1960 book *Love and Responsibility*. We will then develop an argument that follows the principled pattern of moral reasoning sketched above in Chapter 4.

John Paul II's major argument as pope to show that it is always gravely immoral for a married couple to contracept is rooted in a profound appreciation for the meaning of the marital act as an act of self-giving love on the part of husband and wife. It is an act fully open to the love-giving, live-giving union of man and woman. Thus, John Paul II writes:

> When couples, by means of recourse to contraception, separate these two meanings that God the Creator has inscribed in the being of man and woman and in the dynamism of their sexual communion, they act as "arbiters" of the divine plan and "manipulate" and degrade human sexuality — and with it themselves and their married partner — by altering its value of "total" self-giving. Thus the innate language that expresses the total reciprocal self-giving of husband and wife is overlaid, through contraception, by an objectively contradictory language, namely, that of not giving oneself totally to the other. This leads not only to a positive refusal to be open to life but also to a falsification of the inner truth of conjugal love, which is called upon to give itself in personal totality.[42]

Earlier, as Karol Wojtyla, John Paul II had advanced a different argument to show that contraception is immoral in *Love and Responsibility*, in a section concerned with "justice towards the Creator." In this section Wojtyla wrote:

> In the world of persons... the sexual urge passes, so to speak, through the gates of the consciousness and the will, thus furnishing... the raw material for love. At a truly human, truly personal level, the problems of procreation and of love cannot be resolved separately. Both procreation and love are based on the conscious choice of persons. When a man and a woman consciously and of their own free will choose to marry

and have sexual relations, they choose at the same time the possibility of procreation, *choose to participate in creation* (for that is the proper meaning of the word "procreation"). And it is only when they do so that they put their sexual relationship within the framework of marriage on a truly personal level.... a human being is a person, so that the simple natural fact of becoming a father or a mother has a deeper significance, not merely biological but also a personal significance. Since marital intercourse is, and must be, a manifestation of love... at the personal level, we must find the proper place for parenthood too within the limits of love. *Sexual relations between a man and a woman in marriage have their full value as a union of persons only when they go with the conscious acceptance of the possibility of parenthood* [emphasis added]. This is a direct result of the synthesis of the natural and the personal order. The relationship between husband and wife is not limited to themselves but necessarily extends to the new person, which their union may (pro)create.... Hence when a man and a woman capable of procreation have intercourse their union *must be accompanied by awareness and willing acceptance of the possibility that "I may become a father" or "I may become a mother"* [emphasis added]. Without this the marital relationship will not be internally justified.[43]

Obviously, if the couple is using contraception to impede procreating a new person, they are not willing to become parents and are acting immorally. It is also instructive to note that within this section of his book, Wojtyla explicitly states that "responsibility for love is complemented by responsibility for life and health, a combination of *fundamental goods* [emphasis added] which together determine the moral value of every marital act."[44] From this is it reasonable to conclude that Wojtyla is surely open to the understanding that contraception is, in addition to being an anti-love kind of act, an anti- or contra-life kind of act. It is this argument that will now be presented.

This argument, we hope to show, is one way in which the Church's teaching on contraception is an authentic application of the sexual morality rooted in the Scriptures. Like that of Scripture itself, the Church's teaching on contraception is integrally pro-life.[45]

In contracepted intercourse one chooses both to have sexual intercourse and to prevent the act from being procreative. The contraceptive element is aimed precisely and directly against the possible coming-to-be of human life. As the American bishops note, such a prevention is a rejection of the "life-giving meaning of intercourse"; and "the wrongness of such an act lies in the rejection of this value."[46]

Three major steps can be noted in the argument to establish this point. First, the procreative good is intrinsically and always good. Second, a contraceptive deed acts directly against this good, and of itself does nothing but assail that good. Third, it is always immoral to so act directly against a basic human good.[47]

Consider the first point: the procreative good is of its very nature always a good. To say this is not, of course, to suggest that in every case it would be wise or right to promote the procreative good. In the concrete conditions of life every kind of real good can be intermingled with serious evils and harms. Truth is a good; but one ought not to publish every truth, to the useless harm and embarrassment of others, or in neglect of duties of secrecy. Life itself is good, but one might be wrong to fight simply to sustain another's life (by extraordinary means) when further living cannot be dissociated from excessive pain and humiliation. Similarly, the realization of the procreative good might in a given case involve great dangers to the health of the mother, the stability of the family, or the like. But truth, life, and the procreative good remain in themselves great goods.

The Second Vatican Council and other Church teachings have made clear that Christian teaching honors the procreative good.[48] The teaching of the Church on this matter is clearly based on Scripture, which constantly celebrates the passing on of human life as a great and wonderful thing. To be able to have children is a great good and joy to human persons: a great progeny was among the chief blessings promised to Abraham. Our Lord himself pointed to the great joy that spontaneously follows childbirth; it is good when a child is born into the world.

And what Scripture witnesses is what everyone knows. All who are parents know this quite directly and immediately. Others see it as a desirable possibility — to have a child of one's own would be a good thing. Or if for some special reason they should not have a child, they know that this is not because a child is not a good thing and that having children is not desirable, but because in these circumstances such a good would involve also harms that they wish to avoid.

To acknowledge the intrinsic goodness of procreation is to recognize that human life is good and that its transmission is also good. As Christians, we are able to see reproduction as procreation — that is, as cooperation with God in his act of creating another image of himself, another member of the kingdom, another person called to be an adopted child of God.[49]

We shall weave together our treatment of the next two points: a contraceptive act of its very nature always strikes directly against the procreative good, and such an attack on an intrinsic human good is always wrong in every area of life.

The second point: a contraceptive act of its very nature as a freely chosen act is specified by the choice here and now to impede procreation, i.e., the coming to be of a new human person. This is the moral "object" of the act.

To do a contraceptive deed is to perform an action that in itself and directly has only one objective: to keep an act of intercourse from being fruitful, to see to it that a new human life does not come to be in and through an act of the kind in which new human life can come to be. The contraceptive act is directly aimed against the realization of the procreative good. One is not simply declining to promote that good; one is choosing to do something whose morally specifying object is precisely to impede this good which, concretely, is a new human person. One is choosing precisely to make the sort of act that, of its very nature, is open to the transmission of new life to be closed to this good. As Pope John Paul II said in *Veritatis Splendor,*

> The morality of the human act depends primarily and fundamentally on the "object" rationally chosen by the deliberate will [with a reference to St. Thomas, *Summa Theologiae,* I-II, Q. 18].... In order to be able to grasp the object of an act which specifies that act morally, it is therefore necessary to place oneself in the perspective of the acting person. The object of the act of willing is in fact a freely chosen kind of behavior.... By the object of a given moral act, then, one cannot mean a process or an event of the merely physical order, to be assessed on the basis of its ability to bring about a given state of

affairs in the outside world. Rather, *that object is the proximate end of a deliberate decision which determines the act of willing on the part of the acting person* [emphasis added].[50]

Continuing, John Paul II declared:

> Reason attests that there are objects of the human act which are by their nature "incapable of being ordered" to God, because they radically contradict *the good* [emphasis added] of the person made in his image. These are the acts which, in the Church's moral tradition, have been termed "intrinsically evil" (*intrinsece malum*): they are such "always and per se," in other words, on account of their very object, and quite apart from the ulterior intentions of the one acting and the circumstances.[51]

In a contraceptive act, one freely and deliberately chooses to attack a great human good. The motive for this act may be upright; one may wish to avoid for oneself and others the harms that would be inseparable from the untimely realization of that good. But there are many ways in which those harms, e.g., terrible financial burdens, the fear that the child may be afflicted with a dreaded and lethal genetic disease, the very life of the mother, can be avoided, as we will see, without choosing freely to impede the fundamental good of procreation, of handing life on to a new human person, cooperating with God in the great work of procreating new human persons made in his image.

The third point: such an attack on an intrinsic or basic human good is always wrong in every area of human choice.

The principle — that one ought not to do evil so that good may come about and that therefore it is always wrong intentionally to damage, destroy, or impede an intrinsic human good and its flourishing in any of our neighbors — is of critical importance in every area of Christian morality. As we have seen already, in the early debates over contraception, defenders of received Catholic teaching taught that those who permitted contraception in order to achieve the "greater good" or avoid the "greater evil" were adopting a principle (proportionalism) that would make any kind of sexual activity (fornication, masturbation, homosexual acts) permissible or good if done so that these good consequences would come about. To allow contraception one must deny either that procreation is a good, or assert that it is sometimes permissible to act directly against a basic human good. Either of these is sufficient to justify masturbation, sodomy, and so on. If the procreative good is not a basic good that must always be respected as such, there is no decisive moral barrier to actions like masturbation, sodomy, or adultery. If one can justify acting against a good for overriding reasons, then one can not only act against the procreative good by contracepting a freely chosen genital act, but also by acting against the good of children-to-be-born by generating them through acts of fornication, adultery, and making babies in the laboratory and treating them not as persons but as products that either measure up to certain standards or are discarded. And one can also choose freely to deprive innocent persons of the good of life, whether these persons are unborn or born, senile and suffering, etc.

Our argument has shown why the approval of contraception contributes to acceptance of abortion. Contraception is an attempt to prevent the handing on of life, and one who is willing to do an act aimed directly against life as it is passed on is likely to remain ready to act directly against life if, contrary to his or her expectations, the unwanted new life begins.[52] Those who act directly against a good to prevent its realization have only too frequently proved ready to take the next step. If the resolve to prevent a child from coming to be is so strong that one is willing to act deliberately and directly against that good, then one will be more disposed to act directly against the acquired life of the child if its conception is not successfully prevented.

III. Natural Family Planning

We turn now to a consideration of the difference between periodic continence and contraception. The Church has taught that couples may morally regulate the size of their families by methods that do not involve contraceptive acts. These methods have several forms; generically they may be called "natural family planning," or NFP.

Great strides have been made in recent years in perfecting NFP. While earlier forms were less effective, the best contemporary methods are quite reliable, not only for women with regular cycles but for all women. NFP is a genuine, practicable option; it avoids the harmful physical and moral effects of contraception, and it has many important good effects of its own.[53]

Despite Church teaching that contraception is intrinsically wrong and NFP is not, some have insisted that NFP does not differ in morally significant ways from contraception. Some claim that NFP is *natural* "contraception," whereas the use of drugs and mechanical devices is *artificial* "contraception."[54] Some argue that NFP and contraception have precisely the same purpose (that is, the avoidance of conception) and that therefore they must be morally the same. But this contention involves a fallacy of elementary logic.[55] Two acts — or one act and one deliberate omission — each of which has the same generically stated purpose need not be morally the same. One can get money to feed one's family by acts of stealing or by honest labor. Though they have exactly the same end, these acts are obviously not morally the same. The purpose of one's acts and policies is not the only factor relevant for determining the morality of these acts and policies. *What one does,* as well as one's reason for doing it, is morally relevant.

It is clear that NFP achieves its purpose in a way essentially different from contraceptive intercourse. NFP involves no choice to treat the procreative good as an evil and to act directly against it, whereas contraceptive intercourse does.[56] Some analogies can help show this. Thus to commit perjury (i.e., knowingly and freely choosing to lie under oath) in order to protect a secret is completely different from keeping silence in order to do so. Again, to kill a person "mercifully" is a morally bad act, but it is not morally bad to withhold or withdraw a treatment if the treatment is "extraordinary" or "disproportionate" because it is either useless or unduly burdensome even if one foresees that the person will die as a result of withholding or withdrawing the treatment.[57]

In practicing NFP, a couple adopts a policy to have sexual intercourse at infertile times and to refrain from intercourse at fertile times if they have serious reasons to avoid a pregnancy. Refraining from intercourse is not contracepted intercourse, since it is not intercourse at all. Moreover, refraining from intercourse has a different intentional relation to the good of procreation than contracepted intercourse has. In contracepted intercourse one does what one knows to be a potentially procreative act and one also acts to ensure that the procreative potential of that act is not realized. This is acting against the procreative good. In NFP, however, one's intention to avoid a pregnancy is achieved by abstaining from an act one reasonably believes will cause a pregnancy, not to engage in an act of genital sex that one has contracepted by intentionally impeding the beginning of a new human life.

Contraception, although unreasonable and gravely immoral, is a rational, purposeful act, and one does not contracept if one is playing tennis or abstaining from genital sex. There is a sense in which a couple practicing NFP in order to avoid causing a pregnancy when there is a good reason not to cause the wife to become pregnant (e.g., a serious threat to her life) do not, like a couple who contracepts, want to have a baby. But there is a crucial difference between the couple rightly practicing NFP and the contracepting couple. If there is a serious reason to avoid causing the wife to become pregnant (e.g., she has been told that a pregnancy might seriously threaten her life), the NFP couple chooses to *abstain* from the conjugal act because they believe, reasonably, that it is the kind of act that could cause her to become pregnant. The contracepting couple, even if they have some serious reason to avoid causing a pregnancy, do *not* choose to abstain from an act that they reasonably think could cause this but instead choose to do something prior to, during, or after their act of intercourse, to impede the beginning of a new human life.[58]

Choosing not to act so as to cause a child to come to be is a different choice than choosing an act known to be the cause of the child's coming to be, and taking further, contraceptive, steps to prevent that outcome.

Thus, the refraining from intercourse which is involved in NFP does not involve the anti-procreative intention of contracepted intercourse. Neither do the acts of intercourse in which a couple engages during infertile periods have this intention. Nothing is done to any of them to render them infertile, since nature itself has made them infertile. The other goods of marriage are quite legitimately pursued in these acts.

Moreover, the whole spirit and style of life promoted by NFP is radically different. As Pope John Paul II has said in *Familiaris Consortio*:

> In the light of the experience of many couples and of the data provided by the different human sciences, theological reflection is able to perceive and is called to study further *the difference, both anthropological and moral*, between contraception and recourse to the rhythm of the cycle: it is a difference which is much wider and deeper than is usually thought, one which

involves in the final analysis two irreconcilable concepts of the human person and of human sexuality [emphasis added].[59]

NFP therefore is not contraceptive. Moreover, it not only does not hinder but even promotes the other goods of marriage. The sexual life of the couple using NFP is controlled by chastity. The efforts of self-control must be mutual; thus couples living by NFP are given a motive to unite in a common effort of will. This chaste union obviates the temptation for couples to treat each other as instruments for sexual gratification and allows their sexual expression to be an expression of human communication, of their marital covenant, and of the love of Christ for the Church.[60]

Of course, there will be difficulties in the practice of NFP, just as the Lord has promised us that there would be difficulties of discipleship in other areas of life, for he spoke about carrying the cross daily. Cooperation between spouses in a moderate amount of self-restraint is necessary; but contraception's failure to respect the full meaningfulness of sex, to treat the sexual act as unrelated to the goods that give it its profound meaning, is ultimately destructive. The substitution of easy technological (and immoral) solutions for human ones is a common temptation of our age. But those who persist in finding temperate and human solutions to this problem in NFP testify that this is not only a morally good solution but in many ways enriches the lives of those who follow that path.

IV. Sterilization

Today, partially because of the dangers of the pill and IUD's (intrauterine devices), more and more people are resorting to sterilization as a means of preventing conception. Those who justify contraception as a way of avoiding pregnancy use the same basic moral justification for sterilization. Since sterilization, however, is for all practical purposes irreversible, some hold that a much more serious "proportionate reason" is necessary to justify the choice to sterilize.[61] Frequently, sterilization is advocated as the most appropriate way to cope with the problems faced by a couple who are the bearers of a recessive genetic defect of a serious nature, such as Tay-Sachs disease or sickle-cell anemia. For such couples, there is a 25 percent chance that any child they conceive will suffer the crippling disease. Sterilization is also recommended at times for women whose health may be seriously threatened were they to become pregnant.[62] It is frequently urged for couples whose families are now judged to be complete.

The Church has constantly taught that contraceptive or direct sterilization is intrinsically immoral.[63] The Church, along with theologians faithful to her teaching, distinguishes between direct or contraceptive sterilization and "indirect" sterilization. Direct or contraceptive sterilization is an act whose sole and immediate purpose is to destroy the procreativity of the person sterilized, whereas indirect sterilization is a medical procedure whose immediate purpose and direct intent is to remove pathological reproductive organs or to inhibit the natural functioning of such organs when such functioning (for example, abnormal hormonal production) aggravates a pathological condition within the person.

The Church condemns direct or contraceptive sterilization for the same reasons that she condemns contraception. The act in question is one that directly attacks a basic human good. One does evil for the sake of some good to come. Moreover, one could achieve the desired ends reasonably through other means, such as NFP. The Church teaches that indirect sterilization is often justifiable. The principle of totality indicates that a person is permitted to undergo a mutilating operation necessary to protect the life and health of the person, even if sterility results as a side effect of the operation.[64]

Some theologians[65] have attempted to claim that the principle of totality can be extended to justify contraceptive sterilization. They have argued that doing so will prevent a future pregnancy that may be hazardous to the life of the mother or that may result in the birth of a child suffering from a genetically induced disability, and in this way contribute to the total well-being of the person thus sterilized and to his or her family.[66] The argument, basically, is that some hoped-for-good-to-come-about can justify the deliberate intention to act directly against a good here and now.

This effort to extend the principle of totality merges, it can be seen, with the attempts of some recent theologians to argue that it is morally permissible to intend to do what they call premoral or nonmoral or ontic evil for the sake of a proportionately greater premoral or nonmoral or ontic good.[67]

Many theologians, as well as decisive Church statements, have vigorously rejected this attempt to justify contraceptive sterilization.[68] The revisionary effort is ultimately based on the belief that we may willingly and directly do evil for the sake of a good-to-come, as long as the good-to-come is "greater" than the good we deliberately and directly repudiate in doing the evil. But, as we have seen, such a position strikes at the heart of Christian morality.

Moreover, the threat of great social evils implicit in such an expanded principle of totality is obvious.[69] There are many who argue that for the good of society as a whole — and indeed for the good of the persons immediately affected — it is right to sterilize the mentally retarded, the indigent, and all those who fail to exercise "responsibility" in begetting.

The temptation to sterilize is perhaps understandable in a technological culture because sterilization appears to be an efficient way of realizing some worthwhile goals. Yet a technically efficient means may not be the morally right means. A sterilizing act performed precisely to remove a pathology or prevent the spread of disease can be morally justifiable; sterilization, substituted for personal control and reasonable self-discipline, cannot be.

V. Other Violations of Marital Chastity

The Church's teaching on contracepted intercourse and contraceptive sterilization applies not only to the use of contraceptive devices but also to any acts done with the intention of preventing a complete genital act between spouses from being a potentially life-giving act. Thus, mutual masturbation, oral and anal sex, and similar acts in which orgasms are sought apart from natural intercourse, are gravely wrong. The argument developed in the section against contraception applies very closely to these acts when done with contraceptive intent, as well as to acts of contracepted intercourse in the sense we have defined it.[70]

Moreover, such acts between spouses are not properly ordered to the goods of married life even if they are not done with contraceptive intent. The discussion of masturbation and sodomy, which will be given in the following chapter, will make it clear that the goods of marriage cannot be properly pursued in masturbatory, oral, and anal sexual activity on the part of married couples.[71]

The Church's teaching that natural intercourse open to procreation is the only legitimate form of complete sexual expression, even between spouses, does not imply that mutual genital stimulation other than intercourse is forbidden for spouses as part of the preliminaries to marital intercourse according to several moral theologians noted for their orthodoxy. [72]

Marriage is a mutual commitment in which each side ceases to be autonomous, in various ways and also sexually: the sexual liberty in agreement together is great; here, so long as they are not immoderate so as to become slaves of sensuality, nothing is shameful, if the complete acts — the ones involving ejaculation of the man's seed — that they engage in are true and real marriage acts.

But the qualification in this statement is important. The activities of spouses must be moderate, and the danger of becoming "slaves of sensuality" is real. Pope Pius XII warned against this danger by criticizing an anti-Christian hedonism that encourages "the pursuit of the intensest possible enjoyment" in the preliminaries to marital intercourse and in its consummation, as though in this sphere the moral law enjoined nothing more than that the act itself be accomplished normally, and as though the rest, in whatever manner done, could be justified as being an expression of mutual love which is sanctified by the sacrament of matrimony and deserves praise and reward in the eyes of God and conscience. Unfortunately, the dignity of the human being, the dignity of the Christian, which sets a check on sexual excess, can be left out of account.[73]

Spouses are required to seek the moderation and self-restraint necessary to preserve their lovemaking from becoming the pursuit of the shallow and apparent good of isolated sexual pleasure, rather than the authentic good of human love, sexually expressed in shared joy. There are no hard and fast rules for avoiding the immoderate pursuit of sexual pleasure, given that the life-giving and person-uniting goods of marriage are respected. Nevertheless, there are certain marks of immoderation and certain broad guidelines for marital chastity that spouses and confessors may refer to: a preoccupation with sexual pleasure, succumbing to desire in circumstances in which it would be wise to refrain, and insisting against serious reluctance of one's spouse. One has hardly acquired sufficient self-possession if one could not accept peacefully a few weeks or a few months of abstinence in case of real need.[74]

Spouses should avoid also the danger of insensibility and unjustified abstention. These also can be sins against moderation and can violate the reasonable expectations of the other spouse.[75] Marital intercourse should be a gladly agreed-upon activity, but under certain circumstances one is obliged to accede to the reasonable desires of one's spouse. Unreasonable refusal to have sexual intercourse can harm the person-uniting aim of marriage, and such refusal is often inconsistent with the demands of conjugal justice and charity.

VI. Artificial Insemination and *In Vitro* Fertilization

A basic principle of Christian sexual ethics, as we have seen, is that the goods toward which sexuality is ordered must not be separated from unitive and life-giving acts. There is an "inseparable connection established by God" between the unitive meaning and the procreative meaning of the conjugal act.

This intrinsic connection between the goods of marriage is relevant for understanding many of the contemporary challenges to the Christian ideal of family life. Two such challenges extensively discussed at the present time illustrate the far-reaching character of the Church's teaching on marriage.

The moral issues raised by new technologies for generating human life outside the marital act were faced by Pope Pius XII, who taught that human life, according to God's wise and loving plan, ought to be given only in the marital act because of the inherent relationship between marriage, the marital act, and the begetting of children.[76]

Because of advances made in these new reproductive technologies and the serious problems they raised for married couples naturally desiring to have children of their own and experiencing difficulties in achieving conception, the magisterium, through the Congregation for the Doctrine of the Faith, provided for the faithful and all persons of good will a carefully reasoned study, entitled *Instruction on Respect for Human Life in Its Origin and on the Dignity of Procreation* (*Donum Vitae*). Released in February 1987, this important document offered three major lines of reasoning to show why it is not morally right to generate human life outside the marital act, whether by artificial insemination or by *in vitro* fertilization, whether the gametic cells used were provided by the spouses themselves (called "homologous" insemination and *in vitro* fertilization) or provided by a person or persons other than the spouses ("heterologous" insemination and *in vitro* fertilization).

The first line of reasoning was based on the inseparability of the unitive and procreative meanings of the conjugal act. According to this line of thinking, fertilization is sought rightly only when it is the result of a "conjugal act which is *per se* (of itself) suitable for the generation of children to which marriage is ordered by its nature and by which spouses become one flesh." From the moral point of view, procreation is deprived of its true meaning when it is sought, not as the fruit of the conjugal act, the one-flesh unity of the spouses, but as a result of technological procedures.

The second kind of argument was based on the "language of the body." The spouses' one-flesh unity in the conjugal act speaks eloquently of the love-giving, life-giving nature of their marital union. The child is, as it were, the "word" they conceive in giving themselves to each other. This rich meaning is entirely lacking when the origin of new life is no longer linked to the bodily/spiritual union of husband and wife.

The third line of reasoning is rooted in the nature of these technologies of reproduction as forms of "making," of "producing." When a child is "begotten" in the marital act, it comes into being as a gift crowning the gift of husband and wife to each other. It is "begotten," not made. But when a child comes to be by recourse to the new technologies of reproduction, it comes into being as a "product" of human artifice. But to treat a human child as a product is to violate its dignity as a person.[77] The teaching of *Donum Vitae* on this matter was reaffirmed and extended to new methods of generating human life in the laboratory (e.g., intracytoplasmic sperm injection and cloning) in the Congregation for the Doctrine of the Faith's 2008 document, *Dignitas Personae* ("The Dignity of the Person").[78]

Several theologians have developed sound arguments against the artificial reproduction of human persons, some of them seeking to develop the lines of reasoning found in the Vatican *Instruction*.[79]

Artificial insemination, *in vitro* fertilization, and other ways of generating human life by laboratory means cannot be proper parts of sacramental marriage nor can they be proper parts of marriage as a natural institution because they leave out the marriage act itself —

the act in which the goods of marriage are pursued in their inseparable unity. Human life should come to be only in an act of human love, associated with God's creative act of love. This brief discussion is meant to show that the Church's teaching on marriage is a unified doctrine that directs not only the sexual conduct of individuals and spouses but also the most basic institutions and interpersonal relations of mankind. It is the wisdom of a God who loves us and who wills that we be members of his own Trinitarian family that directs us to be at the same time chaste, loving, and open to new life in our use of the sexual nature the Lord has given us.

VII. Spousal Use of Condoms to Prevent HIV/AIDS

In the late fall of 2010, Pope Benedict XVI wrote *Light of the World*. In answering one question his interviewer, Peter Seewald, posed, the pope said, "the secular realm has developed the so-called ABC Theory: Abstinence-Be Faithful-Condom, where the condom is understood only as a last resort, when the other two points fail to work. This means that *the sheer fixation on the condom implies a banalization of sexuality,* which . . . is precisely *the dangerous source of the attitude of no longer seeing sexuality as the expression of love, but only a sort of drug*" (emphasis added). Benedict went on to say, "There may be a basis in the case of some individuals, as perhaps when a male prostitute uses a condom, where this can be a first step in the direction of a moralization, a first assumption of responsibility, on the way toward recovering an awareness that not everything is allowed, and that one cannot do whatever one wants. *But it is not really the way to deal with the evil of HIV infection. That can really only lie in a humanization of sexuality*" (emphasis added).[80] Seewald then asked: "Are you saying, then, that the Church is actually not opposed in principle to the use of condoms?" To which Benedict replied: "She *of course does not* (emphasis added) regard it as a real or moral solution, but, in this or that case, there can be nonetheless the intention of reducing the risk of infection, a *first step* (emphasis added) in a movement toward . . . a more human way of living sexuality."[81]

I believe it is obvious, in light of the passages emphasized above, that Pope Benedict in no way said that the use of condoms to prevent HIV/AIDS is morally good and acceptable. Quite to the contrary. But some

Catholic theologians, among them Edward J. Vacek, S.J., and Jim Martin, S.J., commenting on Benedict's remarks, claimed that the Church now approved spousal condom use to prevent HIV/AIDS. Vacek said that a married man "can use a condom to prevent the spread of disease to a spouse. The intention makes the difference. A condom can be used if the intention is to combat disease, though not if intended to prevent conception." Martin said it was a "lesser evil" and permitted.[82]

What does the magisterium teach about this use of condoms?

So far as I know or can discover, the most authoritative teaching of the Congregation for the Doctrine of the Faith on this matter was probably set forth by Joseph Cardinal Ratzinger, then prefect of the Congregation for the Doctrine of the Faith, in a letter, authorized by Pope John Paul II, to Archbishop Pio Laghi, at that time the papal pronuncio to the United States, on May 29, 1988, after the "lively discussion," widened and sometimes distorted by the press worldwide, which followed the publication of the NCCB Administrative Board's well-known document, *The Many Faces of AIDS*, a document in which this issue was considered, but in a way that was not too clear. Confronting this precise issue head-on, Cardinal Ratzinger wrote as follows:

> I want to draw attention to the clarification which appeared in the March 10 edition of *L'Osservatore Romano*, in an unsigned article entitled "Prevention of AIDS: Christian Ethical Aspect," and I quote, "To seek a solution to the problem of infection by promoting the use of prophylactics would be to embark on a way not only insufficiently reliable from the technical point of view, but also and above all, *unacceptable from the moral aspect* [emphasis added]...." In the case here under discussion, it hardly seems pertinent to appeal to the classical principle of tolerance of the lesser evil on the part of those who exercise responsibility for the temporal good of society. In fact, even when the issue has to do with educational programs promoted by the civil government, one would not be dealing simply with a form of passive toleration but rather with *a kind of behavior which would result in at least the facilitation of evil* [emphasis added].

Ratzinger then wrote: "The problem of educational programs in specifically Catholic schools and institutions requires particular attention. These facilities are called to provide their own contribution for the prevention of AIDS, *in full fidelity to the moral doctrine of the church* [emphasis added].... the church's responsibility is to give that kind of witness which is proper to her, namely an unequivocal witness of effective and unreserved solidarity with those who are suffering and, at the same time, *a witness of defense of the dignity of human sexuality which can only be realized within the context of moral law* [emphasis added]." In closing his letter, Ratzinger emphasized that Pope John Paul II fully supported this teaching.

Do any later magisterial documents disagree with the teaching set forth in this 1988 letter of the CDF? The answer, in my judgment, is that none do. I have already argued that Pope Benedict XVI's comments on this matter in *Light of the World* in no way indicate that the Church's teaching has changed on this matter. Moreover, John Paul II himself in numerous homilies and addresses throughout the world, particularly in Africa, reaffirmed this teaching again and again. Moreover, Father John Flynn, L.C., in an article published in Zenit (February 11, 2008), cited several texts from Pope Benedict XVI affirming the same doctrine. For example:

> Benedict XVI addressed the HIV/AIDS issue in a couple of recent speeches made when receiving the credentials of new ambassadors. On Dec. 13, in his address to Peter Hitjitevi Katjavivi from Namibia, the Pope recognized the urgent need to halt the spread of infections. "I assure the people of your country that the Church will continue to assist those who suffer from AIDS and to support their families," the Pope stated. The Church's contribution to the goal of eradicating AIDS, the Pontiff continued, "cannot but draw its inspiration from the Christian conception of human love and sexuality." This vision sees marriage as a total, reciprocal and exclusive communion of love between a man and a woman, Benedict XVI explained.

None of the statements thus noted, however, seem to be intended as definitive judgments. Those bishops, philosophers, and theologians, who argue the contrary, at any rate, do not think that this matter has been definitively decided. And those married couples, legitimately afraid that they might harm their spouse by engaging in intercourse with them, and naturally longing to manifest spousal love by uniting bodily in the marital act, are acting in good faith and with the understanding that eminent members of the hierarchy (e.g., Carlo Cardinal Martini, emeritus archbishop of Milan) support their acting in this way.

Nevertheless, I am convinced that when spouses use condoms as a means of preventing HIV/AIDS they change the act they perform from one of true marital union (the marriage act) into a *different kind of act*. Why? To show why this is so, we must be clear about the "object" morally specifying human acts. As we have seen already in *Veritatis Splendor*, no. 78, Pope John Paul II had clearly identified what this "object" is: "In order to be able to grasp the object of an act which specifies that act morally, it is therefore necessary to place oneself in the perspective of the acting person. The object of the act of willing is in fact a freely chosen kind of behavior.... that object is the proximate end of a deliberate decision which determines the act of willing on the part of the acting person." For example, the "object" of an act of adultery is having intercourse with someone who is not one's spouse or with the spouse of another. This is *what* adultery is.

In using condoms to prevent HIV/AIDS the "object" freely chosen and primarily specifying the spouses' act is precisely to put on a condom while engaging in intercourse; this is also the "immediate" or "proximate" end. The "further" or "more remote" end for whose sake the couple chooses to use condoms while engaging in intercourse is the hoped-for benefit of not harming a spouse by transmitting HIV/AIDS. This further end is good; but the act freely chosen as the means to this end has as its morally specifying object the use of condoms while having intercourse. This "object" is different from the "object" morally specifying a *marital or spousal act*. In that act the spouses are choosing here and now to give and receive each other in a bodily act that is the *only* bodily act "apt" for generating new human life, even if one or the other is not fertile. And even if one does not "intend" to impede procreation but rather the disease, the use of the condom impedes the unitive meaning of the marital act.

Much more could be said about this issue. I have myself carefully studied this matter since 1988 when it was first suggested that married couples might legitimately use condoms as a means of preventing AIDS, perhaps contracted by a husband while undergoing a blood transfusion.[83] The many attempts to distort Pope Benedict's comments in *Light of the World* generated a host of articles pro and con on the use of condoms to prevent transmission of a disease, many in different blogs and online e-mail. I will return to this use of condoms in the following chapter where we consider the love-based responsibilities of non-married persons with respect to the exercise of their power to generate human life.

ENDNOTES FOR CHAPTER SEVEN

1. For the exegesis of these Old Testament passages, see Friedrich Hauck, "Moicheuo, ktl.," in *Theological Dictionary of the New Testament*, ed. Gerhard Kittel, tr. Geoffrey W. Bromiley (Grand Rapids, MI: Eerdmans, 1967) 4.730-731. See Elaine Adler Goodfriend, "Adultery," *Anchor Bible Dictionary*, ed. David Noel Freedman et al. (New York: Doubleday, 1992), 1.82-86; John L. McKenzie, "Adultery," *Dictionary of the Bible* (Milwaukee: Bruce, 1965). See also the essays in *Reading the Decalogue Through the Centuries,* ed. Timothy Larsen and Jeffrey Greenman (Grand Rapids, MI: Brazos Press, 2010).

2. On this see Gordon Paul Hugenberger, *Marriage as a Covenant: A Study of Biblical Law and Ethics Governing Marriage Developed from the Perspective of Malachi.* Supplements to Vetus Testamentum, 52 (Leiden: Brill, 1994); F. C. Fensham, "The Marriage Metaphor in Hosea for the Covenant Relationship Between the Lord and His People (Hos 1:2-9)," *Journal of Northwest Semitic Languages* 12 (1984): 71-78; see also Edward Schillebeeckx, *Marriage: Human Reality and Saving Mystery* (New York: Sheed and Ward, 1965), pp. 31-63, 89-91.

3. John Paul II, *Man and Woman He Created Them: A Theology of the Body,* translation, Introduction and Index by Michael Waldstein (Boston: St. Paul Books & Media, 2005), General Audience ("Catechesis") of April 23, 1980, 25.1-5, pp. 229-233 ("25" signifies the 25th General Audience, "1-5" the numbered paragraphs within that Audience). Hereafter reference is to Waldstein *TOB,* followed by numbers and pages.

4. An excellent commentary on the significance of lustful desire as a rupturing of the covenant with God and the introduction of the "world" opposed to God spoken of by John (1 Jn 2:15-16) in place of the "world" of Genesis 1 and 2 that was "good" in the sight of God is provided by John Paul II in Waldstein *TOB,* 26.1-5, pp. 234-238.

5. On this, see Schillebeeckx, *Marriage*, pp. 141-155. See also Hauck, "Moicheuo, ktl."

6. This is evident from the fact that Jesus considered as adulterous the union of a person who divorced and remarried. This indeed is the sense in which the term *adultery* is understood by users of ordinary language. Yet it seems necessary to make this point explicit inasmuch as some contemporary moralists (for example, Richard A. McCormick, S.J., in his "Notes on Moral Theology," *Theological Studies*, 39 [1978]: 93) use the term to describe coition with the "wrong" person, leaving open for further judgment whether the "wrong" person is someone who is not one's spouse.

7. Contemporary scholars debate whether Ephesians was written by Paul or not. Even those who believe it to be the work of another writer agree that the teaching in it on the significance of sexual union is Pauline, for it is in conformity with the teaching of 1 Corinthians 6. On the deep significance of Ephesians 5, see Pope John Paul II, Waldstein *TOB*, General Audiences ("Catecheses") 87-102, pp. 465-529. See also Hans Urs von Balthasar, "Ephesians 5:21-33 and *Humanae Vitae*: A Meditation," in *Christian Married Love*, ed. Raymond Dennehy (San Francisco: Ignatius Press, 1981), pp. 55-74.

8. See, for instance, 1 Corinthians 6. For an excellent commentary on this central theme in Pauline theology, see George T. Montague, S.M., *Maturing in Christ: St. Paul's Program for Growing in Christ* (Milwaukee: Bruce, 1964). See also Manuel Miguens, O.F.M., "Being a Christian and the Moral Life: Pauline Perspectives," in *Principles of Catholic Moral Life*, ed. William E. May (Chicago: Franciscan Herald Press, 1981), pp. 89-111. See also the excellent study of O. Larry Yarbrough, *Not Like the Gentiles: Marriage Rules in the Letters of Paul*, Society of Biblical Literature Dissertation Series 80 (Atlanta, GA: Scholars Press, 1985), pp. 89-121.

9. For the meaning of *body* in Paul, see John A. T. Robinson, *The Body: A Study in Pauline Theology* (London and Naperville, IL: SCM Press and A.J. Allen, 1961). Although written 50 years ago, Robinson's study remains perhaps the best study of "body" in Pauline theology as Edward T. Oakes, S.J., professor of biblical theology at the University of St. Mary of the Lakes, Mundelein, IL, notes in his essay, "The Body in St. Paul and Pope Benedict XVI," *First Things,* November 20, 2006,

http://www.firstthings.com/onthesquare/2006/11/oakes-the-body-in
-st-paul-and-.

10. The meaning of the term *skeuos* in 1 Thessalonians 4:4 has been disputed. Literally it means "vessel," "container," or "dish." Some exegetes believe that in this passage it means "wife," whereas others hold that it means one's own "body." Among those who hold that it means "body" are: J. Terence Forestell, C.S.B., "The Letter to the Thessalonians," *The Jerome Biblical Commentary*, 1st ed., eds. Raymond E. Brown, S.S., Joseph Fitzmyer, S.J., and Roland E. Murphy, O.Carm. (Englewood Cliffs, NJ: Prentice Hall, 1968), 48. Other scholars hold that it means "wife," among them O. Larry Yarbrough, *Not Like the Gentiles: Marriage Rules in the Letters of Paul*, p. 68ff. Some others hold that it refers to the male organ; see Yarbrough for a discussion of the different interpretations.

11. Thus, the reference to adultery in the condemnations of laxism by Innocent XI in 1679 assumes the serious wrongness of adultery and makes clear that the consent of one's spouse does not make an extramarital sexual act nonadulterous. See DS 2150.

12. See Cyprian (*De Ecclesiae Catholicae Unitate*), PL 4.507, who compares the embracing of false doctrine to adultery.

13. Pius XI, encyclical *Casti Connubii*, no. 73.

14. National Conference of Catholic Bishops, *To Live in Christ Jesus: A Pastoral Reflection on the Moral Life* (Washington, DC: U.S. Catholic Conference, 1976), p. 19.

15. See text cited above in endnote 3.

16. The view that the condemnation of adultery in Scripture, Christian tradition, and by the magisterium is culturally conditioned is advanced by Anthony Kosnik et al., *Human Sexuality: New Directions in American Catholic Thought* (New York: Paulist Press, 1977), pp. 17-29. More recently several well-known Catholic authors have claimed that sex with someone else's wife can be and frequently is justifiable as a "personal commitment" not necessarily lasting for life. For these authors, in addition, pleasure is something *good in itself* and is indeed a *key component* in most personal sexual experiences. Among these writers the following are typical: Margaret Farley, S.M., *Just Love: A Framework for Christian Sexual Ethics* (New York: Continuum, 2006), especially pp. 159-193, 223-236; Todd Salzman and Michael

Lawler, *The Sexual Person: Toward A Renewed Catholic Anthropology* (Washington, DC: Georgetown University Press, 2008), Chapter Six, pp. 192-212, especially pp. 210-212; Joseph Selling, editor, *Embracing Sexuality: Authority and Experience in the Catholic Church* (London: Ashgate, 2001), 11 essays challenging magisterial teaching on sexual morality, including sex with someone who is another person's wife.

17. Waldstein *TOB*, 9.1-10.4, pp. 161-169, General Audiences ["Catecheses"] of November 14 and 21, 1979.

18. *Gaudium et Spes*, no. 50: "… It must be said that true married love and the whole structure of family life which results from it is directed to disposing the spouses to cooperate valiantly with the love of the Creator and Savior, who through them will increase and enrich his family from day to day."

19. John Paul II has written profoundly on the relationship between spousal friendship and the giving of new life within the family. See, in particular, Waldstein *TOB*, 13.1-4, pp. 177-181 (General Audience ["catechesis"] of January 2, 1980) and 20, 1-5 (General Audience ["catechesis"] of March 5, 1980). See also his analysis in *Love and Responsibility*, tr. H. T. Willetts (New York: Farrar, Straus, and Giroux, 1981), pp. 224-237.

20. *Gaudium et Spes*, no. 49.

21. For St. Thomas Aquinas, see *Summa Theologiae*, Supplementum ad Partem Tertiam, Q. 41, a. 4: "Si autem extra matrimonii bona [vir] efferatur, ut scilicet cum quacumque muliere id facere proponeret, est peccatum mortale." "But if [the husband] is carried outside the goods of marriage so that he propose to do this [have genital sex], this is mortal sin." For Pope John Paul II, see Waldstein *TOB*, 43.2 (General Audience ["catechesis"] of October 8, 1980), pp. 297-298.

22. This case was made famous by Joseph Fletcher, *Situation Ethics: The New Morality* (Philadelphia: Westminster, 1966), pp. 164-165. It was also used by Anthony Kosnik et al., *Human Sexuality in Our Day: New Directions in Catholic Thought* (New York: Paulist Press, 1978).

23. See Paul Ramsey, *Deeds and Rules in Christian Ethics* (New York: Scribner's, 1967), pp. 145-225, for a detailed critique of Fletcher's consequentialism.

24. See, for example, the view of Richard McCormick as set forth in endnote 6 above.

25. For the teaching of Innocent XI, see DS 2150; for Karol Wojtyla/John Paul II, see *Love and Responsibility*, pp. 221-222.

26. On this, see, as an example of a classic work on this matter, Ashley Montagu, *Sex, Man, and Society* (New York: Putnam's, 1969), ch. 1. See also the recent and revealing book by Elaine Tyler May, *America and the Pill: A History of Promise, Peril, and Liberation* (New York: Basic Books, 2010), a book written to celebrate the 50th anniversary of the discovery of "The Pill."

27. Representative texts from the Fathers of the Church, St. Thomas Aquinas, canon law from the 12th through the early 20th century, Protestant Reformers such as John Calvin, and the Council of Trent are the following: John Chrysostom, *Homily 24 on the Epistle to the Romans*, PG 60.626-627: "Why do you sow where the field is eager to destroy the fruit? Where there are medicines of sterility? Where there is murder before birth? You do not even let a harlot remain only a harlot, but you make her a murderess as well. Do you see that from drunkenness comes fornication, from fornication adultery, from adultery murder? Indeed, it is something worse than murder and I do not know what to call it; for she does not kill what is formed but prevents its formation. What then? Do you contemn the gift of God, and fight with his law? What is a curse, do you seek as though it were a blessing? Do you make the anteroom of birth the anteroom of slaughter? Do you teach the woman who is given to you for the procreation of offspring to perpetuate killing?" Cited by John T. Noonan, Jr., in his *Contraception: A History of Its Treatment by Catholic Theologians and Canonists* (Cambridge, MA: The Belknap Press of Harvard University, 1965), p. 98; St. Thomas Aquinas, *Summa contra gentiles*, Bk. 3, chap. 122: "Nor, in fact, should it be deemed a slight sin for a man to arrange for the emission of semen apart from the proper purpose of generating and bringing up children... the inordinate emission of semen is incompatible with the natural good of preserving the species. Hence, *after the sin of homicide whereby a human nature already in existence is destroyed, this type of sin appears to take next place, for by it the generation of human nature is impeded;*" the "Si aliquis" canon, which was integrated into the canon law of the Church in the *Decretum Greg. IX*, lib. V, tit., 12, cap. V, and was part of the Church's canon law from the mid-13th century until 1917: "If anyone for the

sake of fulfilling sexual desire or with premeditated hatred does something to a man or a woman, or gives something to drink, so that he cannot generate or she cannot conceive or offspring be born, let him be held as a murderer;" John Calvin, in his commentary on the sin of Onan in Genesis 38, had this to say: "Onan not only defrauded his brother of the right due him, but also preferred his semen to putrefy on the ground.... The voluntary spilling of semen outside of intercourse between man and woman is a monstrous thing. Deliberately to withdraw from coitus in order that semen may fall on the ground is doubly monstrous. For *this is to extinguish the hope of the race and to kill before is born the hoped-for offspring*.... If any woman ejects a foetus from her womb by drugs, it is reckoned a crime incapable of expiation, and deservedly Onan incurred upon himself the same kind of punishment, infecting the earth by his semen in order that Tamar might not conceive a future human being as an inhabitant of the earth." *Commentaries on the First Book of Moses Called Genesis*, ch. 38:9, 10; quoted in Charles D. Provan, *The Bible and Birth Control* (Monongahela, PA: Zimmer Printing, 1989), p. 15. Provan points out that the editor of the *unabridged* series of Calvin's Commentaries, published by Baker Book House, has omitted the commentary on these two verses of Genesis; and the *Roman Catechism*, popularly known as *The Catechism of the Council of Trent*, declared: "Whoever in marriage artificially prevents conception, or procures an abortion, commits a most serious sin: the sin of premeditated murder" (Part II, chap. 7, no. 13).

28. A leading proponent of the claim that the "population bomb" was about to explode was Paul Ehrlich. The first edition of his book, *The Population Bomb*, appeared in 1968. In it he predicted that "India cannot possibly feed two hundred million more people by 1980." However, in 2010 India had almost 1.2 billion people, having nearly tripled its population from around 400 million in 1960. Its average fertility rate, about 2.7 babies per woman, has been at this level since 2004. That 2.7 rate means India's population is still growing rapidly because, due to the benefits of modern medicine (e.g., infant vaccines), the average death rate has declined from previous high levels. It is anticipated that the population of India will reach 1.7 billion by around 2050. In 2004, answering the question "Were your predictions in *The Population Bomb* right?" Ehrlich responded: "My basic

claims (and those of the many scientific colleagues who reviewed my work) were that population growth was a major problem. Fifty-eight academies of science said that same thing in 1994, as did the world scientists' warning to humanity in the same year. My view has become depressingly mainline!" For a magnificent rebuttal of these claims by Ehrlich and others, see Steven Mosher, *Population Control: Real Costs, Illusory Benefits* (New Brunswick, NJ: Transaction Publishers, 2008).

29. See the following; Elizabeth Marquart, *Between Two Worlds: The Inner Lives of Children of Divorce* (New York: Crown Books, 2006); W. Bradford Wilcox et al., *Why Marriage Matters, Second Edition: Twenty-Six Conclusions from the Social Sciences* (New York: Institute for American Values, 2005); Patrick McCrystal, *Who's at the Center of YOUR Marriage... The Pill or Jesus Christ? Contraception's Disintegrating Effect on Marital Harmony* (Dublin: Human Life International Ireland, 2009).

30. Pope Paul VI, encyclical *Humanae Vitae.*

31. John Paul II has explicitly taken up the issue of contraception, each time reaffirming vigorously the teaching that it is intrinsically immoral, in many places. Among the more important sources for his teaching are the following (listed chronologically): (1) his apostolic exhortation *Familiaris Consortio* (November 22, 1981), no. 32; (2) Waldstein *TOB,* 118.1-132, 6, pp.617-657; (3) his "Address to the II International Congress of Moral Theology," November 12, 1988, in *"Humanae Vitae": 20 Anni Dopo. Atti del II Congresso Internazionale di Teologia Morale* (Milano: Edizioni Ares, 1989), pp. 12-18; and (4) his encyclical *Evangelium Vitae,* no. 13.

32. Paul VI, *Humanae Vitae,* no. 14.

33. It should be noted that the anovulant pills now marketed in the United States may well be abortifacient in addition to being contraceptive. These pills first seek to prevent conception by inhibiting ovulation. Should ovulation, however, still occur, they seek to prevent conception by rendering the mucus of the cervix hostile to sperm. Should some sperm, however, survive and should one fertilize the ovum, these pills then act abortifaciently by changing the lining of the uterine wall, making it reject the developing embryo. On this issue, see Thomas Hilgers, M.D., "The New Technologies of Birth," in *New Technologies of Birth and Death,* ed. Donald McCarthy (St. Louis: The Pope John Center, 1981), pp. 29-55. See also Pope John

260 CATHOLIC SEXUAL ETHICS

Paul II, *Evangelium Vitae,* no. 13. Some more recent literature offering reasons to show that the anovulant pill now marketed *can* cause early abortions are the following: J. T. Finn, "'Birth Control' Pills Cause Early Abortion," *Pro-Life Facts on Abortion,* accessible at http://www .prolife.com/BIRTHCNT.html; Patrick McCrystal, "Do Contraceptive Pills Cause Abortion?" *Human Life International Ireland,* accessible at http://www.hliireland.ie/abortifacient_contraception.html.

34. We say "ordinarily" here because it is possible that one who is not choosing sexual intercourse can choose to make another's act of intercourse infertile. For instance, a young couple may live, for financial reasons, in the wife's family home. They are themselves totally opposed to contraception, would never choose to contracept their marital union, and are in fact anxious to have a child. But the young woman's father, who thinks that they ought not to have a child, puts some sterilizing agent into his daughter's food precisely to impede procreation. Whether this should be called "contraception" is perhaps disputed, but it surely shares the moral malice of any couple's choosing to make their own sexual intercourse contracepted. Such possibilities make clear the sense in which contraception is not itself a sexual act but an action taken in relationship to one's own or another's sexual acts. On this see Germain Grisez, Joseph Boyle, John Finnis, and William E. May, "'Every Marital Act Ought to Be Open to New Life': Toward a Clearer Understanding," *The Thomist* 52 (1988): 365-426, at 369-370.

35. Charles E. Curran, *The Moral Theology of John Paul II* (Washington, DC: Georgetown University Press, 2005). In this book Curran repeats incessantly the same arguments claiming that Church teaching on sexual issues is "physicalistic" and "biologistic," making persons puppets, that he made during the 1960s and '70s. For a substantive and extensive critique of this poorly researched, woefully biased work, which also falsely attributes to John Paul II positions he never took, see E. Christian Brugger and William E. May, "Charles Curran's Critique of Pope John Paul II's Moral Theology: A Review Essay," *The Thomist* 69.2 (April 2005): 279-312.

There is some good theological literature showing how false is the claim that magisterial teaching on contraception and other issues is "physicalistic." Some representative ones are the following: Stephen Theron, "Natural Law in *Humanae Vitae,*" in *"Humanae Vitae": 20 Anni*

Dopo: Atti del II Congresso Internazionale di Teologia Morale, Roma, 9-12 Novembre 1988 (Milano: Edizioni Ares, 1989), pp. 487-495; Giovanni Battista Guzzetti, "La naturalita del agire humano...," ibid., pp. 439-444. Other essays in the same volume also show that Church teaching is not physicalistic.

36. This objection was suggested by John T. Noonan, Jr., *Contraception: A History of Its Treatment by Catholic Theologians and Canonists* (Cambridge, MA: Harvard University Press, 1965), pp. 508-533.

37. Pope John Paul II, *Veritatis Splendor,* nos. 48-49.

38. Pope John Paul II, apostolic exhortation *Familiaris Consortio,* no. 32.

39. For the First Vatican Council's teaching on the infallibility of the ordinary magisterium, see Session IV (July 18, 1870), constitution *Pastor Aeternus,* c. 4, "De Romani Pontificis Infallibili Magisterio." See, in particular, DS 3069. For the Second Vatican Council's teaching on the infallibility of the pope and of the bishops united with the pope in the ordinary exercise of their teaching office, see *Lumen Gentium,* no. 25.

40. See Ford and Grisez, "Contraception and the Infallibility of the Ordinary Magisterium": 258-312.

41. In her book *Humanae Vitae: A Generation Later* (Washington, DC: The Catholic University of America, 1991), pp. 98-129, Janet Smith provides an account of many of these arguments. In *Contraception and Chastity,* Elizabeth Anscombe argues that contraception is not a proper act of intercourse because it is not an act that is the sort of act open to the transmission of life. Thus, it cannot be a true marital act, and sex acts that are not true marital acts are either mere lasciviousness or an inauthentic substitute for marital union. John Kippley, *Sex and the Marriage Covenant: A Basis for Morality* (Cincinnati: Couple to Couple League, 1991 — a revision of his older *Birth Control and the Marriage Covenant,* pp. 50-76, argues that contraception is inconsistent with the marriage covenant. Arguments emphasizing that contraception by married persons sever the bond between the unitive and procreative meanings of the conjugal act are developed by Mary R. Joyce, *The Meaning of Contraception* (Collegeville, MN: The Liturgical Press, 1969) and Dietrich von Hildebrand, *The Encyclical Humanae Vitae: A Sign of Contradiction* (Chicago: Franciscan Herald Press, 1969). In *Love and Responsibility,* pp. 224-237, Karol Wojtyla argues

that unless those who engage in sexual intercourse are willing and able to become fathers and mothers, and they are surely not if they practice contraception, they are violating the personalist norm. In *Contraception and the Natural Law* (Milwaukee: Bruce, 1964) and in "A New Formulation of a Natural Law Argument Against Contraception," *The Thomist* 30 (1966): 343-361, Germain Grisez developed an argument against contraception on the ground that it attacked the good of procreation, an argument then later developed by John Finnis, "Natural Law and Unnatural Acts," *Heythrop Journal* 11 (1970): 379-387. Grisez and Finnis, along with Joseph Boyle and William E. May, have developed, clarified, and strengthened this argument in "'Every Marital Act Ought to Be Open to New Life': Toward a Clearer Understanding."

42. Pope John Paul II, *Familiaris Consortio,* no. 32.

43. Karol Wojtyla, *Love and Responsibility,* trans. tr. H. T. Willetts (New York: Farrar, Straus, Giroux, 1981; reprinted San Francisco, CA: Ignatius Press), pp. 226-228.

44. Ibid., p. 225.

45. In what follows, we will summarize the argument developed by Grisez et al. in "'Every Marital Act Ought to Be Open to New Life': Toward a Clearer Understanding." In *Humanae Vitae: A Generation Later*, pp. 340-370, Smith claims that this argument, emphasizing the anti-life character of contraception, while essentially true, is "inadequate" chiefly because, she claims, it shifts attention from the objective act of contraception to subjective intentions. Smith, unfortunately, seriously misunderstands the argument and ignores totally the 16 pages of the essay devoted to showing why the choice to contracept is always wrong because it is contrary to *objective* norms of natural law. For an appreciative but critical assessment of Smith's study, see William E. May's review of her work in *The Thomist* 52 (1992): 155-161.

46. *To Live in Christ Jesus*, p. 18.

47. For a development of these points, see Grisez et al., "Every Marital Act Ought to Be Open to New Life."

48. *Gaudium et Spes*, nos. 49, 50; *To Live in Christ Jesus*, p. 18; John Paul II, "An Address to the U.S. Bishops," 289, and "'Stand Up' for Human Life," his homily on the Capital Mall, Washington, DC, October 7, 1979, in *Origins: NC Documentary Service*, 9.18 (October 18, 1979), 291.

49. On this, see Waldstein *TOB* 13.1-4, pp. 177-181, General Audience ("catechesis") of January 2, 1980; ibid., *TOB* 20.1-5 and 21 1-7, pp. 204-218 General Audiences ("catecheses") of March 5, 1980 and March 12, 1980.

50. Pope John Paul II, *Veritatis Splendor,* no. 78.

51. Ibid., no. 80. Among acts *"intrinsece malum"* by reason of their specifying object John Paul II includes contraception.

52. Here, it is instructive to note that frequently abortion is described as "post-conceptive" birth control. Moreover, some ethicists — among them David H. Smith ("The Abortion of Defective Fetuses: Some Moral Considerations," in *No Rush to Judgment: Essays in Medical Ethics* [Bloomington, IN: The Poynter Center, 1978], pp. 144-148) — argue that if people "responsibly" seek to prevent conception by the use of contraceptives which subsequently "fail," then abortion is morally justifiable. See also Judith Jarvis Thompson's influential and widely reprinted defense of abortion, "A Defense of Abortion," *Philosophy and Public Affairs* 1 (1972): 1-27. See more recent claims of this kind, e.g., David Boonin, *A Defense of Abortion* (Cambridge and New York: Cambridge University Press, 2002); see also the excellent critique of Boonin and others making the same claims in Christopher Kaczor's *The Ethics of Abortion: Women's Rights, Human Life, and the Question of Justice* (New York and London: Routledge, 2010).

53. On the benefits and effectiveness of natural family planning, see the following: Hanna Klaus, M.D., "Fact Sheet: Action, Effectiveness, and Medical Side-Effects of Common Methods of Family Planning," *Current Medical Research* (Washington, DC: National Conference of Catholic Bishops, 1993); R. T. Kambie, "NFP Use Effectiveness and Continuation," *Obstetrics and Gynecology* 165.6 (1991): 2041-2047; A. D. Nolasco, "Can Natural Family Planning Really Work?" *Population Forum* (1989) 1.13-16; Barbara Barnett, "Fertility Awareness Benefits Couples," *Network: Family Health International* 17.16 (1996): 1-20; Mary Shivanandan, "The How and the Why of Natural Family Planning," *Catholic Update,* ed. Father Jack Wintz, O.F.M. (Cincinnati: St. Anthony Messenger Press, 1995). More recent studies showing the effectiveness of NFP as a way of avoiding a pregnancy are the following: "Natural Family Planning Methods Are as Effective as Contraceptive Pills in Avoiding Causing a Pregnancy," *Science Today,* February 32, 2007; "Basic Information on Natural Family Planning,"

United States Conference of Catholic Bishops, 2010 update. A 14-year composite of five different studies over 14 years (from 1992-2006) had the following conclusion: "These studies, all utilizing life-table analysis and an objective assessment of pregnancies, reported the range of the method-effectiveness to avoid pregnancy at the 12th ordinal month to be 98.7 to 99.8 (with the five-study composite 99.5)." Accessible at: http://www.creightonmodel.com/effectiveness.htm.

54. This is a commonly voiced claim. Thus it was made by Kosnik et al. in *Human Sexuality in Our Time,* pp. 114, 292-295, and by many other writers, some Catholic and others secular.

55. Formally this is the fallacy of drawing an affirmative conclusion in a Figure II syllogism; the conclusion does not follow, as the following example shows:

From	All crows are birds.
and	All eagles are birds.
	All eagles are crows.
From	All contraceptive acts are for avoiding pregnancy
it does not follow that	All use of NFP is for avoiding pregnancy.
And therefore	
one cannot validly conclude	All use of NFP is contraceptive.

56. This is not to suggest that the only way one violates the good of procreation is by acting against it in contraceptive intercourse. Married couples ordinarily have an obligation to have some children if they can, because marriage is of its nature ordered to the procreation and education of children. To refuse to fulfill this obligation — even by use of NFP throughout one's fertile years — is ordinarily a violation of the procreative good. See Anscombe, *Contraception and Chastity,* p. 19, and William E. May, "Contraception, Abstinence, and Responsible Parenthood," *Faith and Reason,* 3.1 (1977): 46-49; Karol Wojtyla (John Paul II), *Love and Responsibility,* pp. 224-237.

57. For a development of relevant analogies, see Mary R. Joyce, *The Meaning of Contraception,* p. 41; and Anscombe, *Contraception and Chastity,* p. 20. Anscombe asks us to consider two types of protest by industrial workers who have a legitimate complaint against their employer. In one type of protest the workers act violently — for example, by destroying machinery in the factory. In the other they

"work to rule," by doing their job at a slow pace within the limits of minimal justice. Clearly there is a moral difference between the cases. If the protest is justified in the first place, the latter strategy is clearly justified but not the former. The use of contraception is analogous to the use of violent protest.

58. See Grisez et al., "'Every Marital Act Ought to Be Open to New Life,'" section VI: "NFP: Not Contra-Life." Moreover, couples use NFP in order to enhance the likelihood of achieving pregnancy; no one ever uses a contraceptive to do this.

59. John Paul II, *Familiaris Consortio*, no. 32. On this see William E. May, "Irreconcilable Concepts of the Human Person and Human Sexuality," in *The Catholic Faith* 3.1 (January-February 1997): 38-43; "A Profoundly Different Understanding," in Ibid. 3.2 (March-April 1997): 25-29.

60. See Janet Smith, *Humanae Vitae: A Generation Later*, pp. 118-128; Germain Grisez, "Natural Family Planning Is Not Contraception," *International Review of Natural Family Planning*, 1 (1977): 123-126; and Joseph Boyle, "Contraception and Natural Family Planning," in *Why Humanae Vitae Was Right*, pp. 407-418.

61. On this, see Charles E. Curran, "Sterilization: Exposition, Critique, and Refutation of Past Teaching," pp. 207-211; John Dedek, *Contemporary Medical Ethics* (New York: Sheed and Ward, Inc., 1975), pp. 113-120.

62. See, for instance, Bernard Häring, *Medical Ethics* (Notre Dame, IN: Fides, 1972), pp. 90-91.

63. See, for example, Paul VI, *Humanae Vitae*, no. 14; National Conference of Catholic Bishops, *Ethical and Religious Directives for Catholic Health Care Services* (Washington, DC: U.S. Catholic Conference, 1995), no. 53. See also the July 9, 1980 "Statement on Tubal Ligation" of the National Conference of Catholic Bishops, *Hospital Progress*, 61.9 (1980): 39.

64. A good presentation of magisterial documents and theological analysis of this matter is given by Gerald A. Kelly, *Medical-Moral Problems* (St. Louis: Catholic Hospital Association, 1955).

65. For example, Häring, *Medical Ethics*, pp. 90-91; John Boyle, *The Sterilization Controversy* (New York: Paulist Press, 1977).

66. Martin Nolan, "The Principle of Totality," in *Absolutes in Moral Theology?* ed. Charles E. Curran (Washington, DC: Corpus,

1968). For an incisive critique of this effort to extend the principle of totality, see Paul Ramsey, *The Patient as Person* (New Haven, CT: Yale University Press, 1971), pp. 178-181.

67. John Boyle, who agrees that contraceptive sterilization is justifiable on the grounds that it promotes the greater good, provides a good history of this position in *The Sterilization Controversy.*

68. The effort to justify contraceptive sterilization on the grounds of the principle of totality was explicitly rejected by the National Conference of Catholic Bishops in their "Statement on Tubal Ligation" July 9, 1980, in *Origins,* Vol. 10, No. 11 (August 28, 1980). The National Conference is now the United States Conference of Catholic Bishops. See also the 5th edition (2009) of the USCCB's *Ethical and Religious Directives for Catholic Health Care Services,* Directive 53.

69. Pius XII, "Address to the Delegates of the Eighth Congress of the World Medical Association," September 30, 1954, AAS 46.587-598.

70. Thus, Paul VI says in *Humanae Vitae* that any use of marriage must remain open (*per se destinatus*) to procreation. Anscombe (*Contraception and Chastity*), pp. 18-21, makes very clear the conceptual link between contraception and such acts as masturbation and sodomy. Her argument is that if contraception is permissible, then so are such acts. For this entire section, see Germain Grisez, *Living a Christian Life,* vol. 2, *The Way of the Lord Jesus* (Chicago: Franciscan Herald Press, 1992; now available from Alba House, Staten Island, NY), pp. 644-685.

71. See Pius XII, "Address to the Second World Congress on Fertility and Sterility," May 19, 1956, AAS 48.473. The English is from John C. Ford, S.J., and Gerald A. Kelly, S.J., *Contemporary Moral Theology*, vol. 2, *Marriage Questions* (Westminster, MD: The Newman Press, 1964), p. 212. Ford and Kelly discuss this and other relevant texts, pp. 188-234.

72. Among theologians approving such behavior are Heribert Jone and Benoit Merkelbach, O.P., in their manuals of moral theology (Jone's *Moral Theology,* 1956, reprinted by TAN Publishers 1993; Merkelbach, *Quaestiones de castitate et Luxuria,* 1933). But see St. Alphonsus de Liguori's *Theologia Moralis, De Sexto,* and John Kippley's *Sex and the Marriage Covenant* (Cincinnati: Couple to Couple League 1992), p. 47.

73. See Pius XII, "Address to the Midwives," October 29, 1951, AAS 43.835-854. See also the critique of hedonism given by Grisez et al., "'Every Marital Act Ought to Be Open to New Life'": 390-399.

74. Anscombe, *Contraception and Chastity*, p. 26; Ford and Kelly, *Marriage Questions*, pp. 228-230, suggest three principles for evaluating sexual behavior between spouses: conjugal justice, conjugal chastity, and Christian self-restraint. They make clear how prudent application of these principles helps not only in the avoidance of lustful immoderation but also in the efforts of mutual sanctification.

75. Anscombe, *Contraception and Chastity*, p. 26. See also Grisez et al., "'Every Marital Act Ought to Be Open to New Life'": 390-399.

76. See Pius XII, "Address to the Fourth International Congress of Catholic Doctors," September 29, 1949, AAS 41.557-561; "Address to Midwives," October 29, 1951, AAS 43.835-854; "Address to the Second World Congress on Fertility and Sterility," May 19, 1956, AAS 48.467-474. English translations of the latter two addresses are available in Liebard's *Love and Sexuality*, pp. 101-122, 173-179.

77. Congregation for the Doctrine of the Faith, *Instruction on Respect for Human Life in Its Origin and on the Dignity of Procreation*. See also *Catechism of the Catholic Church*, nos. 2373-2379.

78. Congregation for the Doctrine of the Faith, *Instruction "Dignitas Personae" on Certain Bioethical Questions*, nos. 14, 15, 17.

79. See William E. May, *Catholic Bioethics and the Gift of Human Life*, 2nd ed. (Huntington, IN: Our Sunday Visitor, 2008), ch. 3 (1st ed. 2000; a 3rd edition is being prepared); Donald DeMarco, *Biotechnology and the Assault on Parenthood* (San Francisco: Ignatius Press, 1991); Paul Ramsey, *Fabricated Man* (New Haven, CT: Yale University Press, 1970), pp. 104-160, and "Shall We 'Reproduce'?" *Journal of the American Medical Association* 220 (1972): 1346-1350, 1480-1485. The words of Pius XII in his "Address to Midwives" (translation from Liebard's *Love and Sexuality*, pp. 117-118) are instructive: "To consider unworthily the cohabitation of husband and wife, and the marital act as a simple organic function for the transmission of seed, would be the same as to convert the domestic hearth, which is the family sanctuary, into a mere biological laboratory.... There is much more than the union of two life germs, which can be brought about even artificially, that is, without the cooperation of husband and wife. The marital act, in the order of, and by nature's design, consists of personal

cooperation which the husband and wife exchange as a right when they marry."

80. Pope Benedict XVI, *Light of the World: The Pope, the Church, and the Signs of the Times: An Interview with Peter Seewald* (San Francisco, CA: Ignatius Press, 2010), pp. 118-119.

81. Ibid., p. 119.

82. Edward Vacek, S.J., "The Condom Question," *America* (January 3, 2011); accessible at http://www.americamagazine.org/content/article.cfm?article_id=12649. James Martin, S.J., "Lesser of Two Evils? Double Effect?" *America* blog (Sunday, November 28, 2011); accessible at http://www.americamagazine.org/blog/entry.cfm?entry_id=3601. In 2000, Jon D. Fuller, S.J., and James F. Keenan, S.J., in an article entitled "The Vatican's New Insights on Condoms for H.I.V. Prevention," insisted that remarks of Vatican officials clearly showed that the Church was now approving condom use to prevent HIV/AIDS, not only for male prostitutes but also for married couples (*America* [September 23, 2000]).

83. William E. May, "The Question of the Use of Condoms by Spouses to Prevent Use of Transmission of AIDS," in *Fellowship of Catholic Scholars Newsletter*, Vol. 11, No. 3 (June, 1988): 1-2.

CHAPTER EIGHT

Chastity and the "Obligations" (Love-based Demands) of Unmarried Persons

Chastity is not a virtue for married persons alone, for the goods at stake in human sexuality need to be cherished and reverenced in every person's life. The self-possession of a chaste person is necessary not only within marriage but also within every Christian vocation and, indeed, within every humanly satisfactory life. A proper regard for the human body, a wholesome respect for the handing on of the great good of human life, respect for the real integrity of intimate human relationships — all these are necessary not only for the married but for those who plan marriage, for all who choose the splendor of committed virginity for the sake of the kingdom, and for all whose lives should, however indirectly, support or image marriage and its goods. This includes every person.

Everyone is called to a love that binds persons together in ways that reflect the personal communion of divine love. Single persons exhibit chastity when in the service of human friendship they do not merely behave impulsively; when they do not permit unworthy pursuit of passing gratification to lead them to act in ways that fail to honor the real goods of human persons and not the pseudo-good of pleasure in and for itself. They act chastely when they refuse to depersonalize the human body by using it as though it is but an instrument for gratification. Of course, the lure of pleasure is great and the instincts of selfishness are strong, so that the demands of chastity for the unmarried can at times be difficult, as it can also be for the married. But the difficulty is none other than that of truly reverencing persons and the goods of persons in the actual conditions of our life. Like the other difficulties in living well, it can be made light by the grace of Christ.

In the preceding chapter we presented the most central obligations — or better, love-based demands — of chastity for married persons. Here, we present a similar moral analysis of the general requirements of chastity for those who are unmarried. Our special focus will be on those choices and acts which the Church has always taught to be unchaste kinds of acts, for these are acts which must be avoided if the personal and interpersonal fabric of the most basic of human relationships is to be protected from the ravages of lust and selfishness. We will first analyze premarital sex or fornication, then masturbation, followed by homosexuality and homosexual acts. We will conclude this chapter by considering bestiality, rape, incest, and sins of thought. In treating these issues, we draw upon the relevant teaching of Scripture, Christian tradition, and magisterial doctrine. We will note also some of the currently popular objections to, or difficulties with, received Catholic teaching.

I. Premarital Sexual Relations

Christian tradition, as we have seen above in Chapters 1, 2, and 3, has always regarded sexual intercourse between unmarried persons to be seriously wrong. The Church sees this prohibition as part of the natural law. This does not mean that in the turmoil of our sinful world everyone "naturally" grasps the truth of this norm. Nor does it mean that there will not be some who will even regard nonmarital sexual activity as being a good thing, for such actions can be very attractive and even seem to be good. We have seen already that in the final decade of the twentieth century and in the early years of the new millennium there has been an enormous cultural change in the United States and throughout the Western world, one characterized by live-in unmarried "lovers," an acceptance of a homosexual or gay lifestyle, and a demand to acknowledge the validity of same-sex marriage, etc. What the Church means in saying that sexual intercourse between unmarried persons violates the natural law is (1) that the malice of this kind of activity follows necessarily from a reflective understanding of the human goods at stake in sexual activity and the requirements of intelligent concern for these goods; and (2) that, as in other areas of human life, persons who fail to observe the requirements of intelligent concern for what truly perfects their human nature harm themselves and others.

The Church's teaching on the immorality of extramarital intercourse is also based on the conviction that God's revelation, as expressed in Scripture and tradition, unequivocally condemns it. For those who have faith, the word of God is an even surer guide to good living than arguments from the natural law. In making use of Scripture and tradition in this chapter as throughout this entire book, we are avoiding what is called a "proof-text" approach — that is, using isolated biblical texts as simple proof for a moral or theological belief, doctrine, or principle. Catholic doctrine on matters so long reflected upon and so constantly taught as these is not built upon superficial appeals to isolated fragments of Scripture. Rather, the basis for the Catholic conviction on specific moral questions is the integral vision of human persons and of human sexuality which, with the guidance of the Holy Spirit, is drawn from the word of God as understood, believed, and taught within the family of faith over the centuries. Thus, citation of a given scriptural text or magisterial teaching is meant to highlight statements in which the convictions of the faith are succinctly and powerfully brought to a focus.

Scripture. The Old Testament contains the roots of the Christian prohibition of extramarital intercourse, for within the Old Testament the values protected by this prohibition begin to be articulated. This is clearest in the Old Testament insistence on the virginity of women before marriage.[1] This insistence is not equally clear in the case of men — perhaps the patriarchal structure of Israelite society played a part here.[2] Despite this limitation, the Old Testament kept constantly before the eyes of the Chosen People the beauty of monogamous marriage as willed by Yahweh. The Wisdom literature is filled with warnings against sins of lust. Fornication, or *porneia*, is portrayed there as an apostasy from God and a devising of idols.[3]

By the first century A.D., the reflective faith of the Jewish community, instructed by the prophets and the authors of the Wisdom books, came to a remarkably full understanding of the significance of Old Testament teaching on extramarital intercourse. They understood the biblical injunction "Thou shalt not commit adultery" broadly to "prohibit various immoral sexual activities,"[4] and they valued chastity highly. The words of Philo Judaeus, a faithful Jew who lived in apostolic times, are typical of the attitude of first-century Judaism:

> We, the descendants of the Hebrews, have excellent customs and laws. Other nations allow their young men of fourteen years of age to go to prostitutes and to other women who sell their bodies. But according to our laws, all *hetairas* [kept women] are condemned to die. Until there can be legitimate relations, we do not have intercourse with a woman. Both parties enter marriage as virgins, and for us the purpose of marriage is not pleasure but the propagation of children.[5]

What is only pointed to in the Old Testament is clearly affirmed in the New Testament — namely, that all sexual intercourse outside of marriage, all fornication, is seriously wrong. This teaching is expressed in the numerous condemnations of *porneia*. This word is usually translated into English as "fornication." Not all of the uses of *porneia* and its cognates in these passages, however, refer directly and clearly to premarital sex. This is not surprising, since "*porneia*" (like the word "fornication" in English) did not refer merely to premarital sex.[6] This term does not simply mean uncleanness but refers to certain kinds of sexual activity which, like fornication in the narrow sense, fail to honor the goods that sexual activity should always respect.

Matthew and Mark report that Jesus includes *porneia* in a list of evil activities which make a person unclean (Mt 15:19; Mk 7:21).[7]

These brief indications of the mind of the Lord on this matter were greatly elaborated on in the evangelization and catechesis of pagans by the early Church. The Gentiles did not share the Jewish conviction about the importance of chastity, and so clear teaching was especially needed.

Thus, pagan converts were told bluntly that they must abstain from fornication (Acts 15:20, 29; 21:25). The Pauline literature, in particular, not only contains repeated references to fornication as a serious sin but also an explanation of why it is incompatible with Christian life.

The First Letter to the Corinthians contains much of what Paul says about fornication. Paul lists fornicators among those who will not inherit the kingdom of God (1 Cor 6:9). The body, he reminds the Corinthians, is not for fornication but for the Lord (1 Cor 6:13, 14). He then explains why sexual intercourse with prostitutes is wrong for Christians. The bodies of Christians are members of the body of Christ. The Christian who has intercourse with a prostitute joins his body to hers and becomes one flesh with her (1 Cor 6:15-17).

St. Paul goes on to say: "Keep away from fornication. All the other sins are committed outside the body; but to fornicate is to sin against your own body. Your body, you know, is the temple of the Holy Spirit who is in you since you received him from God" (1 Cor 6:18-19).

After proposing virginity as an ideal expression of Christian love, Paul notes that, because of the danger of fornication, in the ordinary case it is good for each man to have his own wife and each woman her own husband (1 Cor 7:2). He goes on to add a comment specifically directed at widows and the unmarried: "It is good for them to stay as they are, like me, but if they cannot control the sexual urges, they should get married, since it is better to be married than to be tortured" (1 Cor 7:8, 9).[8]

Thus, the Church has always understood extramarital sex to be gravely wrong — not only because specific scriptural texts teach this but also because of her understanding of the overall thrust of God's revelation concerning the meaning of love and sex, and of how the goods of sexuality should be honored. Scripture and tradition, as understood and interpreted by the Church, are at one in holding that premarital intercourse or fornication is seriously wrong. The *Catechism of the Catholic Church* sums this up accurately when it says that fornication "is gravely contrary to the dignity of persons and of human sexuality which is ordered to the good of the spouses and the generation and education of children. Moreover, it is a grave scandal when there is corruption of the young" (no. 2353).[9]

Why Extramarital Intercourse Is Immoral

The reasons why the Church condemns extramarital intercourse as seriously immoral are clearly set forth by Pope John Paul II in *Familiaris Consortio*. There, referring to "God's plan" for marriage and the family, John Paul II emphasizes that the human meaning of sexual activity is not merely biological, nor is it aimed at mere pursuit of pleasure. It "concerns the innermost being of the human person as such." Sexual intercourse is realized in a truly human way "only if it is an integral part of the love by which a man and a woman commit themselves totally to each other until death." When spouses give themselves humanly and generously to each other in marital intercourse, they signify a will to honor each other and to respect the goods each needs to fulfill his or her life. The self-giving in sexual intercourse is a lie if it fails to be "the sign and fruit" of this total and generous self-giving.

John Paul continued, explaining that this total self-giving is possible only within marriage, for marriage is the covenant of conjugal love by which man and woman freely unite their lives into an "intimate community of life and love willed by God himself." Outside of this covenant something is withheld. Instead, one reserves for oneself the possibility that in the future one might decide otherwise than to maintain the community of life and love. Thus, outside of marriage the self-giving is by definition not total. The pope concludes from this analysis that the limitation of sexual activity to marriage is not an unreasonable or arbitrary imposition on people's freedom but an "interior requirement of the covenant of conjugal love."[10]

Pope John Paul's statement draws out the point of the Church's teaching on extramarital intercourse. The Church believes that her absolute prohibition of this kind of activity is reasonable, that it is not simply an inexplicable taboo or ritual requirement for Catholics. The reasons presented by the Church are all related to the fact that extramarital intercourse bruises human persons, their intimate relationships, and their personal integrity. Moreover, since Christians are united with Christ in baptism, the relationships and integrity harmed are not just those of the parties involved but include the body of Christ, which is defiled by such actions.

The failure to respect these goods becomes clear if one carefully considers the different types of extramarital intercourse. Acts of fornication done solely for sexual pleasure obviously trivialize the act of sexual intercourse. In such acts the partners simply use each other and their sexual powers to grasp pleasure for themselves or to give each other pleasure. Such a use of a human person, even if there is mutual consent, is a violation of human dignity,[11] for human love is more meaningful than this. This kind of sexual intercourse totally fails to serve the genuine goods of human sexuality. The procreative good is ignored and the harm to children who might come into being through such relationships is overlooked. Indeed, today many children conceived in extramarital relations are killed within the womb, and many others are raised under deplorable conditions. The good of marital friendship and fidelity is set aside in favor of satisfying a craving for pleasure. The sacramental significance of sexual activity is absent entirely.

When fornication is chosen to promote and to express romantic affection or "love," the trivialization of human sexuality and its goods is not so apparent — but it is present nonetheless. The partners are not, of course, treating each other *merely* as sources of gratification. Still, substantial and necessary goods of human sexuality are ignored and undercut, and this kind of sexual activity abounds in self-deception and mutual exploitation. This becomes clear if one inquires as to the nature of the "love" expressed in "romantic" fornication, for clearly this is not the strong, genuine love of marriage in which spouses decisively commit themselves to each other without reservation.

Fornicators strongly desire to experience a bodily, personal communion, but they can achieve — and they know they can achieve — only the *illusion* of the personally rich communion proper to spouses, a communion made possible by a commitment to the authentic goods of human sexuality: self-giving spousal love and openness to the gift of human life.[12] The human disappointment and suffering that flow from sexual activity without love as complete and lasting as marital love is only too evident in our time.

The affection between fornicators can, no doubt, be deeply felt; but it is deeply flawed. It cannot be the love of Christian marriage. Marital love is in part constituted by an unconditional pledge of fidelity. Those who are not married have not made this commitment. Consequently, their love simply cannot be the intimate love of those who have joined their lives into one life together, who have made themselves "the single subject, as it were, of sexual life."[13] They have not given themselves to each other by an act of irrevocable, unconditional consent. It is profound self-deception for affectionate fornicators to think that their love is like that of married persons for each other.

Thus, the "love" of fornicators just cannot be the love of spouses. Then what sort of love is it? If it is not mere sentiment and affection ungrounded on a real union of lives, it must be some sort of sharing of life; but since it is not marital, it can be no more than a conditional or partial sharing of life. Their act of intercourse does not unite two persons who have made themselves irreplaceable in each other's life, and united in a common life in the pursuit of all the goods of marriage. Yet this union, this common life, this complete love, is what sexual intercourse is meant to symbolize; it is also what many romantic fornicators wish it to symbolize, even though they know at some level that their refusal to make the commitment of marriage makes this impossible. Thus, the self-deception — the "lie" of which John Paul II spoke.

The love of fornicators is therefore suspect. Authentic human love is a love grounded in full respect for the being of human persons and for the goods needed to fulfill human persons. And where sex is involved, such love demands respect for the good of procreation and for the irreplaceable value of the person to whom one chooses to disclose one's intimate self in coition. But the "love" of fornicators spurns these real goods of human persons and of human existence. Their union is not intended to be fruitful, since no care is taken for possible children — unless it is care not to have them. The conditions for responsible and fruitful love are not met; the commitment necessary for the sharing of a common life is deliberately not made. If the love which was expressed and promoted in such acts were the love it claimed to be, one could pledge oneself with the full love of marital commitment. Willingness to choose the appearances of marital love — the friendship, sexual intimacy, and sharing of life — while rejecting the substance of common commitment to common goals clearly indicates an unwillingness to make serious commitments to human goods. This unwillingness, in turn, is incompatible with the character traits needed to be a faithful partner, responsible parent, and follower of Christ. Thus, the truth as well as deep insight of the Church's teaching that sexual intercourse is a moral and human good only within marriage is based on a realistic appreciation of the meaning of sexual union and the irreplaceable value of human persons.

We could put matters this way. A man and a woman, in "giving themselves to one another" and in "receiving each other" in marriage, have made each other irreplaceable, non-substitutable, and non-disposable in their lives, and their act of marital or spousal intercourse unites them as irreplaceable, non-substitutable, and non-disposable spouses and in it they "give" their bodies to each other exclusively in an act that makes them literally to be "one flesh." Fornicators, however, precisely because they refuse to "give themselves to one another" and to "receive each other" in marriage, have failed to make each other irreplaceable, non-substitutable, and non-disposable, and their chosen acts of genital sex do not unite two irreplaceable, non-substitutable, and non-disposable spouses but rather join two individuals who are in principle replaceable, substitutable, disposable.[14]

Objections. There are many today, both in the general culture and within Christian communities (including the Catholic community), who reject this teaching. In the Second Edition of this book (1998), this section of Chapter 8 took up three objections widely voiced in the late twentieth century by writers like Philip Keane, S.S., Anthony Kosnik and his associates, the Quakers, the United Church of Christ, Bishop John A. Robinson and others.[15] These objections were characterized in that edition as "more serious objections" than the claims that the total rejection of extramarital intercourse was simply unrealistic or that sexual intercourse is really trivial and needs no justification. The "more serious objections" were (1) that sexual intercourse should always be in the context of an interpersonal relationship that involves some affection and commitment but that it need not be limited to the relationship of marriage; (2) that extramarital intercourse always has some ontic deformity but can be morally justified for serious reasons; and (3) that sometimes intercourse between the unmarried really is marital; it is not really premarital but only preceremonial, and pages 175-177 were devoted to a discussion of and rebuttal of these three objections. Many popular objections are based on the widespread contemporary idea that the prohibition of extramarital sex, whether adultery or fornication, is the remnant of a taboo mentality fostered by a patriarchal culture that refused to recognize the equality of women and, indeed, of persons of the same sex for intimate genital relationships.

A Note on "Preceremonial" Sexual Relations as in Reality Truly "Marital" in Nature. Although the idea promulgated by some Catholic theologians in the period between 1975-95 falsely made this claim, it is important to note that, in very rare cases, an affirmative answer is appropriate. It has always been the teaching of the Church that it is the consent between the man and the woman that brings marriage into being.[16] Moreover, during much of the Middle Ages the Church

278 | CATHOLIC SEXUAL ETHICS

recognized the validity of clandestine or secret marriages; but at the Council of Trent she decreed that from that time forward, *for Roman Catholics*, valid matrimonial consent could *not* be given unless this consent were given in the presence of the parish priest (or his duly appointed representative) and two witnesses.[17]

The decision was based on the fact that very great evils occurred because of clandestine or secret marriages, and there is no reason to think that such evils will not occur today if such unions are recognized as marriages. Marriage deserves protection by public safeguards. It is not a private affair between two isolated individuals but a public act of two persons in a society. The family is indeed the most basic and important community within society. The stability and legitimate constitution of the family are obviously important — for spouses, children, and society at large. Thus, the act which constitutes a family is a public act in which all society has a stake. Consequently, the Church may rightly insist, as the state ordinarily does, that the act in which one person marries another be public.[18] There could be instances in which two Catholics could validly and rightly exchange vows and make themselves thereby to be married persons without the witness of the priest and two witnesses, for example, if the persons involved lived in an area where no priest could reasonably be expected to come for a long time, or if the persons were in a concentration camp.

The Twenty-First-Century Situation. Today the situation has dramatically changed over the past fifteen years or so, i.e., over the final years of the last decade of the twentieth century and the first decade of the twenty-first. Dissenting Catholic theologians have in many ways gone beyond proportionalism or at any rate have widened in a practical sense its applications so that in large measure they are in agreement with the elitist views of Western culture (now making inroads elsewhere) that is atheistic, materialistic, and relativistic. This truth has been brilliantly developed by Archbishop Charles Chaput of Denver, who in one memorable address reminded his audience that the late John Courtney Murray, S.J., gave three talks, never published, to students in 1940, making the point that he, Chaput, was making, namely, that the dominant culture in the United States, promulgated by major media, is materialistic, atheistic, relativistic, making human persons the ones who determine morality, not God.[19] Citing Murray, whose theme he made his own, Chaput declared: "American culture, as it exists, is actually the quintessence of all that is decadent in the culture of the Western Christian world. It would seem to be erected on the triple denial that has corrupted Christian culture at its roots, the denial of metaphysical reality, of the primacy of the spiritual over the material, of the social over the individual.... Its most striking characteristic is its profound materialism.... It has given citizens everything to live for and nothing to die for. And its achievement may be summed up thus: It has gained a continent and lost its own soul."[20]

According to this elitist view, promulgated so persuasively by contemporary American media (TV, especially sitcoms; movies, major newspapers, and newsmagazines), what is most important in matters of sex is the *quality of the relationship* between sex partners; sexual relationships ought to be consensual, affective, pleasurable for both parties, etc. This view is definitely the one championed today by major dissenting Catholic theologians who repudiate magisterial teaching about marriage and sexual morality but who would not like to be called atheists. Among those dissenting Catholic theologians who hold this view of sexual relations are the following: Daniel Maguire, Eileen Silverman, Christine Gudorf, Margaret Farley, Joseph Selling and his associates and others, including Michael Lawler and Todd Salzman.[21] The Committee on Doctrine for the United States Conference of Bishops issued a lengthy criticism of their book *The Sexual Person: Toward a Renewed Catholic Anthropology.* Not only did the book claim that homosexual acts can sometimes be good, but, "applying a deficient theological methodology to additional matters, the authors reach erroneous conclusions on a whole range of issues, including the morality of pre-marital sex, contraception, and artificial insemination.... [T]he USCCB Committee on Doctrine has examined the moral methodology found in the book...." This Committee declared that this book "does not offer minor revisions to a few points of Catholic sexual ethics. Instead, the authors insist that the moral theology of the Catholic tradition dealing with sexual matters is now as a whole obsolete and inadequate and that it must be re-founded on a different basis. Consequently, they argue that the teaching of the Magisterium is based on this flawed 'traditional theology' and must likewise be substantially changed." According to the Committee, the authors accept a flawed dualistic view of the human person, make "experience" the primary criterion for moral judgments, and make other serious errors. The Committee concluded that the work is "seriously flawed and falls short of the goal of theological investigation, *fides quaerens intellectum*."[22]

Common to these authors is the claim that "pleasure" is a basic good of the person. This is the central theme of books on human sexuality by the authors of the books noted in endnote 21.

II. Masturbation

Definition and Summary of the Teaching of the Fathers, Medieval Schoolmen, and Theologians Until the Late Twentieth Century. Masturbation is the deliberate stimulation of the genital organs to the point of orgasm which is not a part of sexual intercourse.[23] Thus understood, masturbation can be done either by a person acting on himself or herself (thus, its frequent description as "self-abuse"), or by one person acting on another. Throughout her history the Church has consistently held that masturbation, when it is a freely chosen act, is seriously wrong, for it always involves a failure to respect the human goods which all sexual activity should take into account. The Fathers of the Church,[24] the medieval Scholastics, and all moral theologians[25] until most recent times have been unanimous in condemning every deliberate act of masturbation as a serious violation of the virtue of chastity.[26] This same teaching has been proposed by the magisterium of the Church from the time when it was discussed by Pope Leo IX in 1054 to the present.[27]

The Church's certainty that of its very nature masturbation is gravely wrong is first of all rooted in divine revelation. In the past, theologians frequently cited certain key texts as witnesses to the scriptural condemnation of masturbation — for example, the Onan text in Genesis 38:8-10, or 1 Corinthians 6:9, where St. Paul lists among those who are excluded from the kingdom the *malakoi* or the "soft," or Romans 1:24, where he points out that those who reject God come to dishonor their own bodies.

Contemporary scholars point out that these texts do not *unambiguously* refer specifically to masturbation.[28] But in condemning irresponsible uses of sex generally, Scripture certainly does include a condemnation of masturbation.[29] As the 1975 *Declaration on Certain Questions Concerning Sexual Ethics* states: "Even if it cannot be proved that Scripture condemns this sin by name [masturbation], the tradition of the Church has rightly understood it to be condemned in the New Testament when the latter speaks of 'impurity,' 'unchasteness,' and other vices contrary to chastity and continence."[30]

The Church has rightly understood Scripture to teach that genital activity should take place only within marriage in ways that rightly express marital love. From St. Paul (1 Thess 4:1-5; 1 Cor 6:15-20) Christians have learned that their bodies are the temples of the Holy Spirit, that their flesh has become one with the flesh of Christ. Our genital organs, Christians have thus rightly concluded, are not playthings or tools that we are to employ simply for pleasure. Rather they are integral to our persons, and our free choice to exercise our genital powers is thus to be in service of human persons and of the goods perfective of human persons. The goods to which sexual activity is ordered, as we have seen throughout this work, include procreation, marital friendship, and chaste self-possession. By respecting these goods when we use our genital powers, we honor the body that has, through baptism, become one body with Christ and a temple of his Spirit. When we do not respect these goods in our genital activity we act immorally, and we desecrate the temple of the Holy Spirit and abuse the body-person who has been purchased at such great price. It is this deeply biblical vision of human sexuality and of the human person that is at the heart of the Church's teaching on the immorality of masturbation.

Why Masturbation Is Seriously Evil. This vision does not exclude a more purely ethical analysis of the immorality of masturbation, for one who chooses to masturbate exercises his or her genital powers of sexuality in a way that does not take into account the precious human goods that these powers are meant to serve. These are life-uniting and life-giving powers. And in choosing to masturbate we use these meaningful powers in ways which ignore or disdain their life-uniting or life-giving meaning. Because they regard their own bodies merely as a means of bringing about a desired conscious state and do not respond as body persons to the real goods making human sexuality meaningful, masturbators violate the body's capacity for self-giving or what John Paul II calls its "spousal" or "nuptial" significance.[31] That is surely a basic "good" of the person that masturbation violates. Psychologists note that there is a sort of narcissism involved in such acts, a turning in on oneself, in the use of powers which should serve one to go beyond oneself.[32] This reason takes on added significance for the

Christian, who is to regard himself or herself as a "vessel" consecrated to the Lord and a temple of his Spirit. This argument to show why masturbation is seriously evil, matter for mortal sin if freely willed and chosen after sufficient reflection, should be kept in mind during the following presentation and refutation of objections leveled against the teaching of the Church by Catholic authors who reject magisterial teaching and by secularists who regard it as utterly outdated, a remnant of a taboo mentality, both in the decades following dissent from *Humanae Vitae* and more radically by both groups in the final decade of the 20th century and first decade of this one.[33]

Objections. In the First and Second Editions of this work there was here a multipage section considering the reasons "some recent moralists" gave for rejecting the Church's teaching on masturbation, along with a detailed response to their objections. Many of those "recent moralists," among them the Catholic theologians Michael Valente and Anthony Kosnik and secular moralists like James McCory, Helmut Katchedorian and Donald Lunde, Albert Ellis, and Eleanor Hamilton are no longer active, while others, including Charles E. Curran, have become more radical.[34] Here we will briefly note the three major objections and summarize the response given them and then take up the more radical views of those thinkers, both Catholics who repudiate Church teaching and secular moralists who regard that teaching as woefully outdated, rigoristic, and rooted in a taboo mentality.

The principal objections were: (1) the constant teaching of the Church that divine revelation condemns masturbation as seriously wrong is simply mistaken because it is based on a misreading of Scripture and is rooted in Stoicism;[35] (2) the Church is mistaken in teaching that all acts of masturbation are wrong, for only some masturbatory acts are really lustful; and (3) masturbation is of itself morally neutral and not in fact a bad kind of act.

In summary, replies to these objections are the following.

Reply to (1): This objection includes several unacceptable claims. The first is that Scripture does not condemn masturbation. This is altogether unacceptable, for it goes far beyond the denial that some specific texts unequivocally condemn masturbation, and proposes instead that the scriptural vision of man does not exclude masturbation. The Church, the authentic interpreter of Scripture, draws a contrary conclusion. The second unacceptable component of this objection is that the Church is radically mistaken in her most firm and insistent interpretations of Scripture. This overlooks the fact that the Church is guided by the Holy Spirit in proposing moral truths as part of what is necessary for salvation. A teaching so seriously proposed over so many centuries is certainly authoritative for believers. In fact, it would not be implausible to count her teaching on masturbation as part of the infallible exercise of the ordinary magisterium of the Church.[36] The third disputable component in this first objection is that the Church's teaching on masturbation is based on Stoicism and a version of Manichean mind-body dualism. This is simply erroneous and, as Pope John Paul II pointed out in *Veritatis Splendor*, nos. 47-49, especially no. 49, a dualism of a pernicious sort is what underlies the arguments which revisionists use to justify masturbation and other sexual activity that the received tradition has rejected.[37]

Nor is the Church's position based on a Stoic view that procreation is the only legitimate purpose of sexual activity. We have seen how the Church has grown in her explicit appreciation of the fact that sexual activity serves other human goods as well. The development of this appreciation has in no way been accompanied by any tendency to abandon her absolute prohibition of masturbation, for masturbation serves none of the great goods to which human sexuality is ordered, and fails, in its pursuit of pleasure, to respect any of them adequately.

Reply to (2): The second objection to the Church's teaching on masturbation was that it is not a grave moral disorder in some circumstances. Some, e.g., Kosnik et al., who made this objection in the 1970s and '80s, distinguished various kinds of masturbation — adolescent, compensatory, of "necessity," pathological, medically indicated, and hedonistic — and asserted that in most of these categories masturbation is not seriously wrong. The Church has always acknowledged that circumstances alter cases. To perform an act of masturbation in some circumstances may be far more reprehensible than in others. Moreover, the Church recognizes that not all acts of masturbation are done with the full consent and knowledge necessary for grave personal guilt. Nevertheless, the Church has consistently maintained that objectively every act of masturbation is seriously wrong. To distinguish several different kinds of masturbation is not to provide any reasonable ground for thinking that some forms of masturbation are not gravely wrong. But reflection on some of these kinds, such as pathological masturbation, does correctly suggest that masturbation is at times not a freely chosen voluntary human action but rather compulsive behavior. We must, however, distinguish between truly compulsive behavior, in which case there simply is no human act, and what can be called "quasi-compulsive" sins of weakness. With the latter there is indeed a true human act, freely chosen after deliberation, but one of which the agent is ordinarily immediately ashamed, the kind of behavior exhibited, for instance, by alcoholics.[38]

The designation of medically indicated masturbation as a medical act appears to be a rhetorical redefinition of the act based on the purpose of the masturbation. The inducing of orgasm seems to be of the essence of the act as a moral act — it is by inducing the orgasm that the sperm is procured. Thus, we have, in fact, a disordered sexual act — one directed toward orgasm outside of marital intercourse. The fact that there is a good purpose for such an act does not remove its disorder. Moreover, even if medically indicated masturbation could be shown to be a different sort of act than lustful masturbation — that it is simply an act of obtaining semen for medical purposes and not the performance of a distinctively sexual act — it still does not follow that acts of this type would be permissible. There are, after all, other effective and practical ways to procure sperm. This activity, even if not essentially directed toward sexual pleasure outside of marriage, ordinarily so stimulates such pleasure, and so inclines the agent to delight in sexual pleasure unrelated to the real goods of sexuality, that it may be an unreasonable way to pursue the medical end. Thus, Pope Pius XII's authoritative condemnation of medically indicated masturbation is realistic and well founded.[39]

Reply to (3): The third objection was that masturbation is objectively a neutral act which *by itself* lacks any moral disorder. There were two major versions of this thesis. One was that no *single* act of masturbation can be seriously wrong; if masturbation is wrong it is only because of the larger lifestyle in which it occurs.[40] Another version was that masturbation cannot be seriously wrong because masturbation is natural or normal, an inevitable phase in personal growth.[41]

Both these versions of this objection have already been shown to be erroneous by the arguments given already to show why masturbation as such is always gravely immoral and the fit subject of mortal sin if freely willed and chosen after deliberation; and it has already been shown that the Church recognizes that circumstances alter cases and that some acts of masturbation are the result of compulsive behavior and are not human acts at all. As John Paul II said: "clearly, situations can occur which are very complex and obscure from a psychological viewpoint, and which influence the sinner's subjective imputability. But from a consideration of the psychological sphere one cannot proceed to create a theological category, which is precisely what 'fundamental option' is, understanding it in such a way that it objectively changes or casts doubt upon the traditional concept of mortal sin."[42]

To sum up: the Church has always taught that masturbation is seriously wrong. Even though the Church recognizes that sins of this type are sometimes not fully imputable, and pastors have shown great gentleness and understanding in helping those who wish to overcome sins of this type, the Church has never qualified her authoritative teaching on the serious wrongness of masturbation. Moreover, the objections to this teaching are based on poor arguments or perspectives contrary to the received teachings of the faith. There is no doubt, therefore, that the Christian ideal of chastity excludes masturbation, and that it is possible for Christians to acquire the ability to live in accord with this teaching.

The More Radical Situation Today Among Secularist Authors and Some Catholic Authors

The radical re-constructing or re-evaluating of sexual morality that has taken place since the final years of the twentieth century and today has led some Catholic authors who repudiate magisterial teaching and secularist authors who judge it utterly irrelevant to consider masturbation as a good thing, as a way of "getting into touch with one's own body" and of experiencing the rapture one's body can give one. There are in fact "masturbation marathons" going on around the globe; these, one website informs us, "provide a supportive, encouraging environment where masturbation can be performed openly among young and old without embarrassment." Many others, in particular some Catholic theologians, consider masturbation as morally neutral in itself but an act that serves interpersonal relationships.

Catholic theologians who reflect this mentality are Margaret Farley, R.S.M., Christine Gudorf, Patricia Beatie Jung, and Rosemary Radford Ruether — in many ways the most radical of all. They all applaud the "dethronement of procreativity," make pleasure a fundamental good, and in particular approve of female masturbation and gay and lesbian unions.[43]

III. Incomplete Acts of Lust

The Church has regularly taught in her ordinary teaching that all lustful acts (though not all acts of immodesty) are objectively gravely sinful. This is true not only of complete acts, those aiming to complete sexual satisfaction through orgasm, but of all direct and deliberate acts of lust. Thus, solitary acts that would stir up sexual pleasure but not proceed toward complete sexual satisfaction, and acts of fondling or kissing aimed precisely at stirring up sexual arousal in oneself or one's partner even if one does not intend this to lead toward complete external sins, are objectively gravely sinful.[44]

There is always some difficulty in teaching these matters in balanced ways to young people. The sexual practices common even among persons glamorized in the media and the forms of kissing and fondling that are presented as entertainment may make it seem strange and excessively prudish to suggest that there could be grave immorality in conduct which seems so common. This problem has worsened since the Second Edition of this book. One need only think of the grotesquely offensive "sitcoms" now on major TV stations, of alleged "music" glorifying masturbation, demeaning women, and similar media forms to recognize this. Yet there is a profound inner consistency to the truth the Church teaches in her sexual ethics. Care, imagination, intelligence, and sensitivity are always necessary in teaching sexual ethics to the young. They need to realize that excluding deliberately lustful dimensions from the acts in which they show affection in no way means that they cannot be spontaneous and joyful in their expression of real affection. Intelligent teaching of all that the Church has learned of chaste and self-possessed love is liberating and bracing; it does not impoverish human life.

IV. Homosexuality and Homosexual Acts

Homosexuality

Here again pertinent and worthwhile literature, along with literature justifying homosexual activity and promoting "same-sex marriage" has proliferated since the publication of the Second Edition of this book. There are many today who claim that opposing homosexual acts is itself a form of "homophobia" or "hatred of homosexually oriented persons" and who want to make any criticism of homosexual activity a "hate crime." Some even hold that the freedom of exercise of one's religious faith guaranteed by the first amendment must today yield to the constitutional right of gays and lesbians to marry.[45] Some claim that the homosexual condition is genetically based and that therefore homosexuality is as "natural" as heterosexuality and that therefore justice requires recognizing the validity of same-sex marriage. But this claim, popularized at times in the media, lacks sound scientific support as will be shown below.[46] Homosexuality is a complex phenomenon, so much so that the researchers A. Bell and M. Weinberg entitled their massive study *Homosexualities* because they discovered great diversity in lifestyle and personality among the nearly one thousand homosexual men and women interviewed for their work.[47] It is not appropriate, however, to label a person "homosexual," even if he or she has this orientation, because there is something more fundamental about the person. Indeed, the Church "refuses to consider the person as 'heterosexual' or 'homosexual' and insists that every person has a fundamental identity: the creature of God and, by grace, his child and heir to eternal life."[48]

A person is said to have a homosexual orientation if he or she (1) is attracted physically and erotically by persons of his or her own sex; (2) usually has no similar attraction to the opposite sex; and (3) in many instances has a positive revulsion for sexual acts with a member of the opposite sex. It has traditionally been used to describe a "persistent and predominant attraction of a sexual-genital nature to persons of one's own sex."[49] The attribute common to all homosexuals, however divergent their lifestyles and personalities, is this persistent and predominant erotic attraction to persons of the same sex.[50]

Several consequences of this description of the homosexual condition should be noted. First, one may be homosexually oriented and not engage in homosexual acts,[51] and one may not be so oriented and nonetheless choose to engage in them. Thus, the prisoner or adolescent who engages in homosexual acts is not necessarily a homosexual; and persons with this orientation can, and do, live lives of perfect chastity. Second, as empirical studies show, the description allows for a spectrum of personality types going from a completely heterosexual orientation to a completely homosexual orientation.[52]

It is most important to distinguish between someone who is a "homosexual" and someone who is "gay." Joseph Nicolosi, a psychologist who has over eighteen years of practice, and who has treated over 400 homosexually oriented patients, informs us that a "homosexual" is anyone who experiences a sexual attraction to persons of the same sex. Only some homosexuals are gay. Homosexuals who regard their attraction as disordered and want to live chastely are not "gay" and do not want to be identified as "gay." A homosexually oriented person who identifies himself as "gay" chooses this way of self-identification and embraces the idea that homosexuality is as normal and natural as heterosexuality, and that homosexual acts are morally good and that gays are unjustly denied the right to marry. Nicolosi regards "gay" as a self-deceiving way of identifying oneself, a fiction invented to resolve painful emotional challenges. He calls it "the gay deception."[53]

What is most important to keep in mind is that the homosexual orientation itself is not freely chosen but is the result of an interplay of different factors, some hereditary "inclinations," other environmental factors in the life of a child, etc.[54] The homosexual condition may make certain acts appear to be attractive options, but this condition is not itself freely chosen — it is not an act. Nor, for many homosexuals, is the condition something that can be readily or even significantly altered. However, the claim that the homosexual orientation is irreversible cannot be sustained. There is now abundant evidence, attested to by competent professionals, both secular and religious, to support the "modest conclusion that some persons with a homosexual orientation can acquire a heterosexual one through a process of prayer, group support, and sound therapy. [But] this is not to say that everyone who seeks such a change is able to attain it."[55]

Homosexual acts, however, can be freely chosen and even when done without entirely free choice are frequently in some measure voluntary. These acts, therefore, are proper objects for moral evaluation; and the homosexual condition is morally relevant as part of the determination of the imputability of homosexual acts.

Homosexual Acts: Morality Of

The Church's constant teaching on the morality of homosexual acts is unequivocal: such acts are of their very nature seriously wrong. This teaching is clearly based on Scripture and is rooted in the biblical understanding of sexuality. The Bible teaches that the sexual differentiation of the human race into male and female is divinely willed, that male and female complement each other, and that marriage, rooted in the irrevocable consent of man and woman to be "one flesh" for life, alone respects the goods of human sexuality. Thus, Scripture teaches that marriage provides the normative condition for genital sexual expression; all other expressions of this kind, whether between man and woman or between members of the same sex, are to be evaluated in the light of this norm.[56]

In addition to this general scriptural account of human sexuality, there are specific biblical passages referring to homosexual acts, and in each of these passages such acts are unambiguously condemned. There are five clear references to male homosexual acts and one to female.[57] The reference in Romans 1:26-27 is, in some ways, the most telling, since homosexual behavior is regarded as a punishment for disbelief: "For this reason God gave them up to dishonorable passions. Their women exchanged natural relations for unnatural, and the men likewise gave up natural relations with women and were consumed with passion for one another, men committing shameless acts with men and receiving in their own persons the due penalty for their error."

Thus, the Church's constant and firm teaching that homosexual acts are seriously wrong is clearly rooted in Scripture. There is no doubt that the Church has taught and believed homosexual acts to be wrong. This is reflected in the writings of the classical theologians and in the approved authors of recent centuries.[58] The *Catechism of the Catholic Church*, speaking of homosexual acts, declares:

> Basing itself on Sacred Scripture, which presents homo-sexual acts as acts of grave depravity [with references to Gen 19:1-29; Rom 1:24-27; 1 Cor 6:10, and 1 Tim 1:10], tradition has always declared that "homosexual acts are intrinsically dis-ordered" [a citation from the Vatican *Declaration on Certain Questions of Sexual Ethics* (*Persona Humana*), no. 8]. They are contrary to the natural law. They close the sexual act to the

gift of life. They do not proceed from a genuine affective and sexual complementarity. Under no circumstances can they be approved [no. 2357].

Both the *Catechism* (no. 2358) and the Vatican *Declaration on Certain Questions of Sexual Ethics* (no. 8), which it cites approvingly in the passage quoted above, are careful to stress the distinction between the homosexual *inclination* or orientation and homosexual *acts*, noting that the former is not chosen. But since some persons, in their interpretation of the 1975 Vatican *Declaration* gave an "overly benign interpretation… to the homosexual condition itself, some going so far as to call it neutral or even good," the Congregation for the Doctrine of the Faith found it necessary, in 1986, to affirm that the homosexual inclination, "while not a sin, is a more or less strong tendency toward an intrinsic moral evil and thus the inclination itself must be seen as an objective disorder."[59]

But, and this is the critical matter, the *moral* judgment of the Church bears on homosexual *acts*, and, as has been shown, this judgment affirms that such acts are intrinsically evil, firmly condemned by Scripture, and contrary to natural law.

Finally, it is perhaps worth pointing out that the enemies of Christianity have noted the essential connection between Christian ethics and the condemnation of homosexual activity. As James Hitchcock has pointed out:

> Beginning at least as early as Victorian and Edwardian litterateurs like John Addington Symonds and E. M. Forster, intellectualized homosexuality in the modern West has consciously repudiated Christianity as a distorted, inhumane religion which snuffed out the joyous, guilt-free paganism of ancient times. The intent of this homophilia has been to re-create as far as possible the conditions of that ancient paganism, for which the destruction of Christianity as a cultural influence has been seen as an essential prerequisite. Such a view of history, which from the homosexual viewpoint is to a great extent correct, is continued into the present by, among others, Gore Vidal, the admirer of Julian the Apostate, who manifests both the obsessive anti-Christian sentiment and the contempt and hostility toward heterosexual values which seems characteristic of much of the homosexual subculture.[60]

Objections to Catholic Teaching: A. From 1960s to early 1990s

Despite the long-standing teaching of the Church on the objective immorality of homosexual activity, some Catholic writers have denied that homosexual activity is always wrong. These writers argued that (1) the biblical evidence is inconclusive and (2) homosexual activity between homosexually oriented persons, when this occurs within a relatively stable relationship, is either essentially good and natural, or is at least morally acceptable as the best that can be expected of persons with a homosexual orientation.[61] These writers argue, with respect to the biblical foundation for the teaching, that the story of Sodom and Gomorrah does not involve a condemnation of the homosexual practices of those cities but rather of their inhospitality.[62] Likewise, they claim that the condemnations of homosexual activity in the New Testament are condemnations of idolatrous homosexual acts or of homosexual acts chosen by heterosexuals.[63]

These objections based on the interpretation of Scripture were not well founded. They generally presuppose that the received position on homosexual acts is entirely dependent upon a few isolated proof texts. In fact, however, the Catholic teaching follows necessarily from the whole scriptural vision of what man and woman are, of what sexuality means, and of the nature of morality. If the classical texts on homosexual acts were to be removed altogether from Scripture, the immorality of such acts would still be an obvious implication of the biblical view of sexuality.

In 1980, a work cited by many to justify a "gay" lifestyle was John Boswell's *Christianity, Social Tolerance, and Homosexuality: Gay People in Western Europe from the Beginning of the Christian Era to the Fourteenth Century* (Chicago and London, 1980). This was very influential in the decades to follow. According to Boswell, the strong condemnation of homosexual acts in the book of Leviticus is motivated, not by the nature of these acts themselves, but rather by the role they played in pagan cult. Biblical scholars, however, have demonstrated how flawed Boswell's interpretation of this and other biblical texts is.[64] Boswell's claims about "gay" homosexuality in the Middle Ages have also been devastated by competent historians.[65]

Although today, as noted, and as will be shown in more detail below, the situation even for writers like John McNeill is much more radical and indeed celebrates the gay way of life, it will be useful here to reply to the objection McNeill and others (e.g., Kosnik et al.) leveled against Church teaching during the 1970s and '80s, namely, that homosexual acts within a relatively stable situation is either good or is at least the best that can be expected. Many excellent replies were given to that objection. Thus in the Second Edition this chapter included the following on pages 189-191:

> We have seen that Scripture celebrates sex as life-giving of its very nature. True, not every upright genital act will originate a new life; neither need one intend that it will. There are other worthy goals of sexual activity also. But the life-giving aspect of sexual activity must always be guarded and respected, or sex is trivialized and made inhuman. Genital activity must always be of a kind that does not assail or scorn the procreative good; it must not be structured in ways that rob it of its life-giving thrust. The life-giving meaning of human sexuality is always good and worthy of respect. An awe for this power and a love for the life it can give are essential for the human development of sexuality. But homosexual activity must leave altogether out of consideration this aspect of human sexuality which transcends the activity itself and is essential for its human significance.
>
> Genital activity, moreover, has a life-uniting or person-uniting dimension or meaning. Genital acts serve to join two persons, two lives, by a special kind of love. This is marital love — a love that has an exclusive and enduring quality about it, precisely because it has reference to the life-giving end or meaning of genital sexuality.[66] This is a love which opens those whom it unites to what is other than themselves, to a transcendent goal or good toward which they can commit themselves and their shared lives. But this sort of love is simply incapable of being expressed in homosexual activity.
>
> Many forms of homosexual life clearly seek the pleasure of orgasm isolated from any genuinely and authentically satisfying human good. To seek pleasure in good acts, acts that retain their ties to and further real human goods, is not morally wrong. But to organize one's life around the pleasure of orgasms in acts which separate sexual activity from its precious

human goods is unreasonable and immoral. Homosexual life is a bitter form of life, for it is founded on actions which pursue not the real goods of human persons but only the mere appearances of these goods. The unhappiness of many homosexuals is a sign that their lives are not properly oriented toward what is truly good.[67]

Many object that not all homosexuality is of this kind. Some homosexual relationships are relatively stable, and at times, perhaps, are as stable as the relationships between some faithful spouses. Homosexuals can love each other, and wish to share and unite their lives.

But even these homosexual relationships, if they involve homosexual actions, are deeply flawed. They do not and cannot have the inner dynamism toward permanence and fidelity which the marriage relationship can have. Homosexual activity is essentially disordered because it cannot be directed toward nor have a proper respect for the goods of human sexuality. Recall that the lovemaking of spouses is directed either toward having children, or is expressive of a love that essentially includes an orientation toward the fruitfulness of procreation. The love of spouses can and must be enduring because it is essentially related to enduring goods; but homosexual love simply is not ordered to any transcendent good that essentially requires of the partners utter self-giving and faithfulness until death. A marital kind of friendship cannot obtain among homosexuals; their sexual act cannot express a marital kind of love, for they cannot be what spouses are. Their sexual acts cannot be procreative and cannot express a love that is inherently fruitful and procreative.[68]

Some apologists for homosexual activity between partners in a stable relationship which they consider to be the moral equivalent of marriage argue that although homosexual unions cannot share in the good of procreation, the same is true of the genital union of married men and women who know that they are sterile.[69] This objection, however, is based on the false presupposition that the marriage of man and woman is merely an instrumental good for achieving an end that is intrinsically good, namely, the procreation and education of children. But this understanding of marriage is woefully inadequate. The marital act, which makes the spouses to be literally one body, the "single subject, as it were, of sexual life,"[70] is, of course, the sort of act fit for the gift of new human life. But the procreation of new human life is *not* some good extrinsic to the marriage itself but an intrinsic fulfillment of the good of marriage itself.[71] Children are not "products" that spouses make; rather they are "gifts, which, if all goes well, supervene on their acts of marital union."[72] The whole point of sex in marriage, fertile or not, is the good of marriage itself, considered as a two-in-one-flesh communion of persons consummated and actualized by "marital acts," i.e., acts intrinsically the sort apt to receive the gift of life. The coupling of same-sex persons through homosexual acts can in no way be regarded as the consummation and actualization of the marital union of husband and wife.[73]

There are many things homosexual lovers may share and which may form a basis for their life together. However, it is hard to see how their *sexual acts* could express or promote these common goods. To use genital activity, which is essentially ordered to indispensable and distinctive human goods, to serve an affection that cannot minister to such goods — to do these things is to distort radically the finality and sense of these important human acts. That is to say, homosexual acts are of their nature seriously immoral.

Objections to Catholic Teaching: B. From Early 1990s to the Present

From the 1960s on, some influential Protestant authors advocated the radical view now presented almost every day through the media, in particular so-called "sit-coms" on TV, the major newspapers (e.g., *The New York Times*, *The Washington Post*), and TV media. More notable among them were James B. Nelson and Norman Pittinger.[74] Since the early '90s (and even earlier) some Catholic writers had accepted this radical view of homosexuality. Some of the leading representatives of this position, which champions same-sex marriage, are Daniel Maguire, Margaret Farley, and Robert Nugent and Jean Gramick of New Ways Ministry. It is of interest to know that John McNeill (cited above), whose 1976 book, *The Church and the Homosexual,* was a very influential apologia for homosexual acts popular among dissenting theologians of that time, has now left the Jesuits and, apparently, the Church, and is as radical in celebrating gay and lesbian sex and is the author of a widely used book extolling this radical view.[75]

Immorality of Homosexual Acts. This subject has already been presented, and it has been shown why the Church, rooting her teaching in the Scriptures, as these have been and are understood by the Church, whose "book" the Scriptures are, condemns homosexual acts.

The Question of Same-Sex Marriage

We have noted this issue already. There is, unfortunately, a growing movement in the United States to recognize as "marriage" same-sex unions, and some states have already granted such recognition, and there is, as noted before, a movement among some elites to claim that the right of same-sex persons to marry takes precedence over the exercise of religious liberty found in the first amendment.

But persons of the same sex cannot marry simply because they cannot engage in the human bodily act, the marital act, which is of itself the kind of human bodily act, in fact, the only human bodily act, that is a procreative kind of act and remains such even if the spouses, through no fault of their own, are sterile and have not made themselves so by contraceptive sterilization.[76]

Conclusion

Persons of a homosexual orientation deserve the love and support of the Christian community. They are called to friendship with God and to holiness of life, as are all human persons; and they have distinctive heavy burdens to bear. If, as many homosexuals do, they carry their burdens with generous and chaste fidelity, they support and strengthen all Christians. They become witnesses to the nobility of making great personal sacrifices to guard the great human goods sexuality is ordered to. Should they fall in their human weakness, they should still receive the compassionate concern that all persons long for. It is precisely the purpose of Courage, founded by John Harvey, O.S.F.S., to help men who discover that they are homosexually oriented, to lead lives of chastity. Courage chapters are now found in many dioceses of the United States. Since Father Harvey's death at the end of 2010, Father Paul Check of the Diocese of Bridgeport is director of this organization in the United States.

The *Catechism of the Catholic Church* declares that homosexually oriented men and women "must be accepted with respect, compassion, and sensitivity. Every sign of unjust discrimination in their regard should be avoided. These persons are called to fulfill God's will in their lives and, if they are Christians, to unite to the sacrifice of the Lord's Cross the difficulties they may encounter from their condition" (no. 2358).

The moral judgment that homosexual acts are intrinsically disordered and "matter" of mortal sin in no way deprives homosexually oriented persons of their constitutional and civil rights.

V. Bestiality

Bestial acts are those in which a human being copulates with a nonrational animal.[77] Such acts are repulsive to most people and are fairly uncommon. Most people regard bestiality as seriously perverse, and this common opinion is confirmed by Scripture and Church teaching. In the Old Testament, bestiality is condemned as seriously wrong; its punishment was either death or exile.[78] Bestiality was universally condemned by the Catholic moral tradition as the worst of the unnatural sins against chastity.[79]

The reasons for this severe judgment are readily seen. In bestiality, sex is used in a way that totally thwarts its interpersonal dimensions. Moreover, there is a complete perversion of the order between man and nature intended by God. Sexual activity should express a sublime love for another person and respect for great human goods. To use sexuality to gratify oneself in ways that make personal relationships and shared care for great goods impossible is a gross abuse of one's sexuality.

VI. Rape

The grave immorality of rape seems almost universally admitted. Certainly it is condemned by the Church as a form of lustful behavior that is especially wicked because of the forced and unjust violation of the intimacy of another person.[80]

Rape is the extreme case — perhaps the paradigm case — of treating the person assailed, usually a woman, as a sex object. One of the least controversial objectives of the women's liberation movement has been the protesting of the treatment of women as sex objects, whether in the extreme form of rape, or in pornography, or in the attitude of those who regard women as little more than sources of amusement. The bodies of men and women are not things to be used; men and women are personal in all of their reality. The sexual dimension of a person is properly respected only if it is used in a personal way, in pursuit of a free and personal union.

Rape has become more frequent in recent years.[81] Many moral factors may be related to this fact. Many in our time consider masturbation morally harmless, and masturbation involves treating one's own body as a "sex object." Pornography is epidemic and recreational sex is widely approved. Both of these phenomena degrade women and treat them not as persons but as objects. Moreover, self-possession in chastity is widely mocked as prudery or as unhealthy repression. Our culture tends to forget that chastity is a necessary requirement for making sexual activity a personal relationship concerned with authentic human goods, and for guarding the world from the barbarism of crimes like rape.

The horror of rape and the trauma it frequently induces in its victims point to the personal and especially intimate depths of human sexuality. Rape is not only an unjust invasion of the person, it is an especially abhorrent invasion. It is altogether more offensive than other violent assaults. Why should this be, if our sexuality were simply another biological function, without inherent ordering to precious values, to be used as people like? The natural abhorrence of rape — even on the part of those who insist that there are no special moral norms in the area of human sexuality — makes clear that sexual activity has a special significance. It is not a routine human activity like taking a walk or eating a snack.[82]

The victim of rape is a victim, not an offender, and deserves sensitive care. Those threatened with rape are not required to offer resistance that is foreseen to be useless or perilous to their lives; but they have the right to resist violently, even if the life of the assailant is endangered. Their own dignity requires that they not cooperate willingly in this assault on their persons. Society has a grave duty to help establish conditions that minimize the occurrence of this crime.

The efforts of a woman to prevent the sperm of her assailant from fertilizing her ovum is not a contraceptive act.[83] To say that it is legitimate for her to seek to prevent conception in this way is not an exception to the universal prohibition of contraception. Contraception occurs when one who freely chooses to have sexual intercourse seeks to prevent the act from having its fruitful outcome.[84] But abortifacient procedures after a rape are morally of a very different nature; they are not defenses against an unjust invasion but attacks on an innocent person — that is, they are acts of abortion and therefore are not permissible.

VII. Incest

Incest is a sin of lust between two persons closely related by blood or affinity. Sexual intercourse or lustful fondling between parent and child or stepchild, or between siblings, would exemplify this sin. We are not here concerned to treat the reasons why marriage between close relatives is forbidden by divine and positive law. What we want to point out here is that there is a twofold malice in incest. It is a sin of lust, an act in which pleasure is irrationally pursued, with gross disregard for the values toward which, of its nature and of divine will, human sexuality is essentially ordered. But it is also ordinarily seen as sin against piety, a failure to give the special honor and love due to those bound together in the close ties of the family.[85]

Sins of incest seem to have become much more common than they once were. At one time the instinctive revulsion against this sin was strong and an effective repressant. But an age that has liberated lust and tended to enslave human persons more deeply to passion has blinded many to the cruelty of this deed, and the grave harm that it so regularly causes. The reasons *why* incest is wrong are parallel to those that explain the malice of other lustful acts, and a culture that fails to recognize the depth and value-relatedness of sexual activity generally needs great help to escape falling into the most inhuman excesses.

VIII. Purity in Thought and Modesty

Realistic moral thinking has always been concerned with purity of heart as well as of external action. The ninth precept of the Deca-

logue, "You shall not covet your neighbor's wife" (Ex 20:17) is illuminated by the saying of Jesus: "Every one who looks at a woman
lustfully has already committed adultery with her in his heart" (Mt
5:28). The inner life of a person — that is, the desires and inclinations
freely cultivated in the mind and imagination — is also important in
the moral life as it is taught by Catholic faith. Catholic morality is not
concerned only with achieving good effects in this world but in guiding men and women toward excellent lives through the free actions of
their lives — internal actions as well as external ones.[86]

Obviously, self-possession in thought, imagination, and desire has
considerable instrumental value for leading a chaste life. One who
so controls the inner life will find it much easier to avoid the evils
we have been discussing in this chapter and the last. However, the
value of internal chastity is not merely instrumental. To have a pure
heart and mind is itself an excellent and irreducibly important thing.
Without inner self-possession, not only will a person's whole life be in
moral disarray but the person's very self is fatally compromised.

Here, we note briefly basic guidelines that illumine the morality of
thoughts and desires concerning sexual activity.[87]

(1) Simply thinking about sexual matters is obviously not of itself
sinful. To think about sexual activity even of the most sinful kind
may be done innocently, even virtuously, when it is done for reasonable motives and with intelligent respect for all the values concerned,
including the values of one's own self-possession and integrity. Theologians, moral educators, artists, and many others often have important
reasons to reflect on matters that could easily stir up sexual passions.
A morally mature person knows ways to make the dangers of falling
into sin remote when responsibly reflecting on such matters.

(2) One may, however, entertain sexual thoughts in thoroughly
lustful ways as well. This is a matter not simply of "thinking about"
such matters but of choosing deliberately to direct the affections in
seriously disordered ways, irresponsibly disregarding the goods the
heart should cherish. Thus, a certain kind of evil desire is really lustful and seriously wrong — namely, the choice or resolve to do deeds
that are gravely wrong. Such an inner act is of the kind condemned
by the Lord in the Gospel (Mt 5:28). Another kind of inner act is also
lustful — namely, what might be called "deliberate complacency" in
unchaste thoughts. In choosing to take delight in inner representations

of things that are lustful, one is choosing in a disordered way, making oneself an unchaste person. Thus, if done with full deliberation, such choices are gravely sinful; when such delight is accepted with less freedom or deliberateness, the measure of guilt will be less, and when the delight is completely nonvoluntary there is no guilt at all.

(3) Those who entertain thoughts of a sexual nature that are likely to stir the passions and perhaps lead them to fall into external or internal sins of lust without the good reasons and care suggested in number 1 (above) — but also without the lustful choice noted in number 2 — may be said to be behaving in an *immodest* rather than in a strictly lustful way.

Modesty is a virtue that guards chastity. There are many kinds of actions that can be good or bad: kisses, embraces, forms of dressing and dancing, thoughts of sexual matters and the reading, conversations, forms of entertainment, and the like that stimulate such thoughts. Such actions can be virtuous; kisses and embraces, for example, can be excellent expressions of a right affection, or they can be strictly lustful, for example, when one engages in any of these activities as a prelude to lustful acts, or if they are now engaged in with lustful desires or complacencies.

One behaves immodestly when one's internal or external acts in matters that could lead toward sins of lust are not reasonable. Such acts can be objectively either grave or venial. If one engages in immodest thoughts or behaviors out of curiosity or playfulness — in circumstances in which there is no serious danger of falling into sins of lust, but some risk is present (and there is no reasonable ground for creating that danger) — one's sin is ordinarily venial. Behavior of a kind that ordinarily stimulates sexual passions vehemently, and is a proximate occasion of serious sin, is gravely wrong.

Since in questions of modesty we are not speaking of acts that are intrinsically wrong but of inner and outer acts whose morality is derived from their relationships to other factors, the concrete morality of immodest acts is derived from the circumstances of each case. Obviously, what constitutes modesty in dress, language, and the like is highly relative to time and circumstances. But this does not suggest that modesty is merely a matter of opinion; intelligent rules of thumb can be formulated which hold for most cases. It can be clear and certain that, in these given circumstances, to attend a certain obscene motion picture or to read a particular obscene book would be a grave offense against modesty, or even a direct offense against chastity itself. Parents, confessors, catechists, and other moral teachers need an intelligent grasp of the basic principles of Christian modesty such as they have been given in the ordinary teaching of the Church. Their own education in modesty is not derived merely from study but from the experience of acquiring self-possession and chastity, and from learning the need to guard chastity with intelligently lived modesty. We live in times in which it is difficult to give materially specific directives with clarity. Still, moral teachers must seek to give concrete guidance in these matters with sensitive and intelligent care, for a contempt for modesty is evident in much modern entertainment, literature, and advertising. The minds and imaginations of people can be corrupted, and their efforts to achieve self-possession in sexual matters can be undermined, if moral education does not include a bracing education in Christian modesty.

ENDNOTES FOR CHAPTER EIGHT

1. Friedrich Hauck and Siegfried Schulz, "Porne," in *Theological Dictionary of the New Testament*, vol. 6, ed. Gerhard Kittel, tr. Geoffrey W. Bromiley (Grand Rapids, MI: Eerdmans, 1968), pp. 585-586.

2. Ibid., p. 585.

3. Ibid., pp. 586, 587-588.

4. Raymond F. Collins, *Christian Morality: Biblical Foundations* (Notre Dame, IN: University of Notre Dame Press, 1986), pp. 184-186.

5. Philo, *De Josepho*, 9.

6. One of the best studies of the meaning of *porneia* in the New Testament and, in particular, in the thought of St. Paul is provided by Silverio Zedda, S.J., in his book *Relativo e Assoluto nella morale di San Paolo* (Brescia: Paideia Editrice, 1984), ch. 5. Zedda provides abundant evidence to show that this term, while having as some of its specific meanings "prostitution" and "incest," was used to designate any kind of sexual shamelessness, including intercourse outside of marriage and simple "fornication," or consensual coition by persons who are not married. See also Manuel Miguens, O.F.M., "Christ's

Members and Sex," *The Thomist*, 39 (1975): 24-48; Joseph Jensen, "Does *Porneia* Mean Fornication? A Critique of Bruce Malina," *Novum Testamentum*, 20 (1978): 161-184, and especially 179-181.

7. The only other mention of *porneia* in the Gospels is in the Matthean divorce texts (Mt 5:32, 19:9). Many contemporary biblical scholars tend to hold that the term *porneia* in these Matthean texts refers to incestuous kinds of relationships, termed *zenut* in Hebrew. See Joseph Fitzmyer, S.J., *To Advance the Gospel: New Testament Studies* (New York: Crossroad, 1981), pp. 79-111. This understanding of *porneia* in this text is disputed by others; but it clearly did not mean adultery because if the author of the Gospel wished to say that divorce is permissible because of adultery he would have used the precise Greek word for adultery, i.e., *moicheia*.

8. John J. O'Rourke, "Does the New Testament Condemn Sexual Intercourse Outside of Marriage?" *Theological Studies*, 37 (1976): 478-479, makes it clear that Paul is referring here to extramarital intercourse: "Obviously the Apostle is not speaking of idolatry, nor of marriages prohibited by law, nor of evil in general. He is not speaking of sacred prostitutes, an institution which at one time had flourished in Corinth, but which was most likely nonexistent in a Roman *colonia*. Surely he is not speaking of commercial prostitution. He is not saying that it is likely that a girl who remains unmarried and does not have the special gift which he possesses (see 1 Cor 7:7b) will become a whore, because the reason that he gives for both a man and a woman is the same: *dia tes porneias*. Thus the only possible understanding in context of *porneia* is illicit sexual intercourse (see also 1 Cor 7:9, where Paul says of the 'unmarried' [*agamoi*] and the widows, 'if they cannot exercise self-control, let them marry' [*ei de ouk egkateuontai gamesatosan*])." See also Jensen, "Does *Porneia* Mean Fornication?" pp. 181-182. In addition to the study by Zedda referred to in endnote 6 above, see also the excellent treatment of St. Paul's sexual ethics (which unequivocally repudiated any extramarital genital sex as incompatible with the Christian life) provided by O. Larry Yarbrough, *Not Like the Gentiles: Marriage Rules in the Letters of Paul*, Society of Biblical Literature Dissertation Series No. 80 (Atlanta, GA: Scholars Press, 1985), pp. 89-121.

9. See also Innocent IV, *Sub Catholica Professione*, March 6, 1254, in DS 835; Decrees of the Holy Office (September 24, 1665, DS

2045; March 2, 1679, DS 2148); Pius XI, *Casti Connubii,* December 31, 1930, AAS 22.558-559; Sacred Congregation for the Doctrine of the Faith, *Declaration on Certain Questions Concerning Sexual Ethics* (Washington, DC: U.S. Catholic Conference, 1976), no. 7.

10. John Paul II, *Familiaris Consortio,* no. 11.

11. See Karol Wojtyla (John Paul II), *Love and Responsibility,* tr. H. T. Willetts (New York: Farrar, Straus, and Giroux, 1981), p. 41, for a discussion of what he calls the "personalist principle": "This norm, in its negative aspect, states that the person is the kind of good which does not admit of use and cannot be treated as an object of use and as such the means to an end. In its positive aspect the personalist norm confirms this: the person is a good towards which the only proper and adequate attitude is love."

12. The argument briefly summed up here is cogently developed by Germain Grisez, *The Way of the Lord Jesus,* vol. 2, *Living a Christian Life,* (Quincy, IL: Franciscan Press, 1993), pp. 651-653 (now published by Alba House, Staten Island, NY).

13. Wojtyla, *Love and Responsibility,* p. 30.

14. On this, see William E. May, *Marriage: The Rock on Which the Family Is Built,* 2nd ed. (San Francisco: Ignatius Press, 2009), Chapter One.

15. See the following: Philip Keane, S.S., *Sexual Morality: A Catholic Perspective* (New York: Paulist Press, 1977), 92-113; Anthony Kosnik et al., *Human Sexuality in Our Day: New Directions in American Catholic Thought* (New York: Paulist Press, 1977), pp. 155-165; *Toward a Quaker View of Sex* (London: Friends Homes Service Committee, 1963); *Sex and Morality: A Report Presented to the British Council of Churches* (Philadelphia: Fortress Press, 1966); United Church of Christ, *Human Sexuality: A Preliminary Study* (New York: United Church Press, 1977); Joseph Fletcher, *Situation Ethics: The New Morality* (Philadelphia: Westminster, 1966); John A. T. Robinson, *Honest to God* (Philadelphia: Westminster, 1963).

16. On the history of this, see Edward Schillebeeckx, *Marriage: Human Reality and Saving Mystery* (New York: Sheed and Ward, 1965), pp. 37-102.

17. Council of Trent, Session 24, November 11, 1563; DS 1813-1816. The requirement of a canonical form was later incorporated into the 1917 *Codex Juris Canonici,* Canon 1098. In the 1983

revised *Codex* the relevant canon is Canon 1108. Canon 1116 spells out circumstances in which this form is not required. A new canon in the 1983 *Codex*, Canon 1117, declares that Roman Catholics who have by a formal act repudiated their Roman Catholicism may marry validly without this canonical form.

18. The essentially public character of marriage is clearly set forth in *Familiaris Consortio*, no. 11.

19. See the Most Reverend Charles Chaput, archbishop of Denver, "Life in the Late Republic: The Catholic Role in America After Virtue," a paper delivered to the Fellowship of Catholic Scholars, Baltimore, MD, September 26, 2010. This paper will appear later in the annual *Proceedings of the Fellowship of Catholic Scholars*.

20. John Courtney Murray, S.J., "The Construction of a Christian Culture." This was the title given to three talks Murray gave to students at Woodstock College, the theological center in Maryland where Jesuits of the Maryland and New York Provinces were taught theology. Woodstock was moved to New York City after Vatican Council II and is now closed; its famous library is now housed at Georgetown University. Murray's papers are part of that library, and one of the editors of the library put the three talks Murray originally called "The Concept of a Christian Culture" under the new title "The Construction of a Christian Culture." To download a copy of the edited address go to http://woodstock.georgetown.edu/library/murray/1940A.htm.

21. See Daniel Maguire, *Whose Church? A Concise Guide to Progressive Catholicism* (New York: The New Press, 2008); Rosemary Radford Reuther, *Sexism and God Talk: Toward a Feminist Theology* (Boston: Beacon, 1993), *Gaia and God: An Ecofeminist Theology of Earth Healing* (New York; Harper/Collins, 1994), *Goddesses and the Divine Feminine: A Western Religious History* (Berkeley and Los Angeles: University of California Press, 2005); Christine Gudorf, *Body, Sex, Pleasure: Reconstructing Christian Sexual Ethics* (Cleveland: Pilgrim Press, 1995); Margaret Farley, S.M, *Just Love: A Framework for Christian Ethics* (New York: Continuum, 2006), pp. 234-235; Patricia Beatie Jung and Joseph Andrew Corey, eds., *Sexual Diversity and Catholicism: Toward the Development of Moral Theology* (Collegeville, MN: A Michael Glazier Book published by Liturgical Press, 2001), an anthology of many essays which defend gay and lesbian relations, same-sex marriage, trial marriage, non-marital unions, etc.; Michael

Lawler and Todd Salzman, *The Sexual Person: Toward a Renewed Catholic Anthropology* (Washington, DC: Georgetown University Press, 2008); Joseph Selling, editor, *Embracing Sexuality: Authority and Experience in the Catholic Church* (London: Ashgate Publishing Group, 2001). See also Patricia Beatie Jung, "Christianity and Human Sexual Polymorphism: Are They Compatible?" in *Ethics and Intersex*, ed. S. Sytsma (The Hague: Springer, 2006), pp. 293-309.

22. Committee on Doctrine of the USCCB, "Inadequacies in the Theological Methodology and Conclusions of *The Sexual Person: Toward a Renewed Catholic Anthropology* by Todd A. Salzman and Michael G. Lawler," in *Fellowship of Catholic Scholars Quarterly*, 33.4 (December 2010): 4-22.

23. See Joseph J. Farraher, S.J., "Masturbation," *New Catholic Encyclopedia* (New York: McGraw-Hill, 1965), 9.438, for a general discussion; for a more thorough discussion with several classical definitions, see *Dictionnaire de Théologie Catholique*, ed. A. Vacant, E. Manganot, and A. Amann (Paris: Librairie Letouzy et Ane, 1902-1905), 15 vols., 9.1346-1347. See also Marcellinus Zalba, S.J., *Theologiae Moralis Compendium*, vol. 1, (Madrid: Biblioteca de Autores Cristianos, 1958), pp. 771-775, for a modern definition and discussion. Zalba defines pollution as the complete, separate use of the generative faculty. By *complete* he means to orgasm, by *separate* he means outside of sexual intercourse. He goes on to argue that all directly and perfectly voluntary pollution is intrinsically a grave sin.

24. See, for instance, Augustine, *Opus Imperfectum Contra Julianum*, 4, 11, 10 (PL 44.74) il 3, 20, 38 (PL 44.72) and *De Nuptiis et Concupiscentia*, 2, 26, 42 (PL 44.460). The penitentials in use from the sixth through ninth centuries strongly condemned masturbation. See, for example, *Paenitentiale Aquilonale* (Canon 2) and *Luci Victoriae* (Canon 8), cited in Josef Fuchs, S.J., *De Castitate et Ordine Sexuali*, 2nd ed. (Rome: Gregorian University, 1960), p. 49. See also the references in John T. Noonan, Jr., *Contraception: A History of Its Treatment by Catholic Theologians and Canonists* (Cambridge, MA: Harvard University Press, 1965), pp. 70-77, for a discussion of patristic and Jewish views on masturbation.

25. For medieval thought, see, for instance, Thomas Aquinas, *Summa Theologiae*, II-II, q. 154, a. 5. Zalba and Fuchs, cited above in notes 23 and 24, are representatives of the manualist tradition.

26. It should be noted that not only in the Catholic theological tradition has masturbation been regarded as seriously immoral but also in the whole Christian tradition until relatively modern times. For Protestant thought on this subject, see references given by Derrick S. Bailey, *The Male-Female Relationship in Christian Tradition* (New York: Harper and Row, 1968).

27. See Leo IX, Epistola "Ad Splendidum Nitentis" ad Petrum Damiani, 1054, DS 687-688; Alexander VII, "Errores Doctrinae Moralis Laxioris," September 14, 1665, DS 2044; Innocent XI, "Errores Doctrinae Moralis Laxioris," March 2, 1679, DS 2149; Pius XI, "Decree of Holy Office on Masturbation," July 24, 1929, DS 3684; addresses of Pius XII, October 8, 1953, AAS 45.677-678; May 19, 1956, AAS 48.472-473; Sacred Congregation for the Doctrine of the Faith, *Declaration on Certain Questions Concerning Sexual Ethics*, no. 9; Sacred Congregation for Catholic Education, "Educational Guidance in Human Love," November 1, 1983, no. 98. This teaching was reaffirmed in 1975 by the Congregation for the Doctrine of the Faith in its *Declaration on Certain Questions Concerning Sexual Ethics*, no. 9. It was also reaffirmed in the *Catechism of the Catholic Church,* no. 2352, where the relevant text from the CDF's 1975 document was cited twice.

28. See John L. McKenzie, "Onan," in his *Dictionary of the Bible* (Milwaukee: Bruce, 1965).

29. In *Relativo e Assoluto nella morale di San Paolo*, pp. 115-119, Zedda argues that relevant Pauline texts (e.g., 1 Thess 4:4, 1 Cor 7:2-9, 2 Cor 7:1), especially if read in the light of the Greek text of Sirach 23:17, which speaks of the "man who lusts after his own body" (*anthropos pornos en somati sarkos autou*), surely support the conclusion that autoeroticism is among the vices on which St. Paul pronounces, as a teacher of the faith, a judgment of reproval.

30. *Declaration on Certain Questions Concerning Sexual Ethics*, no. 9.

31. For John Paul II on the "spousal" meaning of the body see his *Man and Woman He Created Them: A Theology of the Body*, translation, Introduction, and Index by Michael Waldstein (Boston: Pauline Books & Media, 2006), 13.1-15.5, pp. 178-190. In the reference, "13" refers to catechesis number 13 in this translation, "1" refers to the first numbered paragraph in that catechesis, "15" to catechesis number 15, and "5" to the fifth numbered paragraph in that catechesis, while the

page numbers, of course, refer to the pages in which all this material appears. On the Holy Father's teaching on this matter see Grisez, *Living a Christian Life*, pp. 649-651.

32. See Gerard van den Aardweg, *On the Origins and Treatments of Homosexuality* (New York: Praeger, 1986).

33. I personally consider the argument rooted in John Paul II's understanding of the "spousal" meaning of the body to be the best argument against masturbation — and, indeed, against all forms of non-marital genital sex. In endnote 22 I referred to the articles of Farraher, Zalba, and of the famous *Dictionnaire de Théologie Catholique* on masturbation. More recent articles by theologians on this subject are John Harvey, O.S.F.S., "The Pastoral Problem of Masturbation," *The Linacre Quarterly* (May 1993): 25-49; Janet Smith, "Masturbation," *Our Sunday Visitor Encyclopedia of Catholic Doctrine*, ed. Russell Shaw (Huntington, IN: Our Sunday Visitor, 1998).

34. Curran in many ways simply repeats criticisms of Church teaching he made in the 1960s and '70s, but he now has become a radical feminist in theology, referring to God as "she," and being even more radical than before in rejecting Church teaching on sexual issues such as masturbation and sodomy. In 2005 he published a work severely attacking the moral theology of John Paul II — a theology he simply misrepresents grotesquely. On this see his *The Moral Theology of Pope John Paul II* (Washington, DC: Georgetown University Press, 2005) and the critique of that book by E. Christian Brugger and William E. May, "John Paul II's Moral Theology on Trial: A Reply to Charles E. Curran," *The Thomist*, 69.2 (April 2005): 279-312. See also John Michael McDermott's magnificently detailed critique of Curran's entire corpus of writings up to 2007, "Charles Curran's Moral Theory: Foundational Sexual Ethics," in *Anthropotes: Rivista di Studi sulla Persona e Famiglia*, 23 (2007): 167-226.

35. See, for example, Michael Valente, *Sex: The Radical View of a Catholic Theologian* (New York: Bruce-Macmillan, 1970).

36. See John C. Ford, S.J., and Germain Grisez, "Contraception and the Infallibility of the Ordinary Magisterium," *Theological Studies*, 39 (1978): 263-277, for an exposition of the conditions under which the ordinary magisterium teaches infallibly; these conditions are set out in *Lumen Gentium*, no. 25. In the remainder of this article Ford and Grisez apply these conditions to the teaching on contraception;

some of this material is directly relevant to the teaching on the morality of masturbation. Their analysis suggests that a similar argument can be made concerning the received teaching on masturbation.

37. On the dualism underlying the charge of "physicalism," see Germain Grisez, "Dualism and the New Morality," *Atti del Congressa Internazionale Tommaso D'Aquino nel Suo Settimo Centario*, vol. 5, *L'Agir Morale* (Naples: Edizione Domenicane, 1977), pp. 323-330. This was the pre-eminent objection to Church teaching on sexual issues from the end of the '60s through the mid-'90s, with exponents including Charles E. Curran in many writings; John Dedek, *Contemporary Sexual Morality* (New York: Sheed and Ward, 1976); Kosnik et al., *Human Sexuality* (New York: Paulist Press, 1977); John Boyle, *The Sterilization Controversy* (New York: Paulist Press, 1977); Philip Keane, S.S., *Sexual Morality: A Catholic Perspective* (New York: Paulist Press, 1978).

38. On the difference between truly compulsive behavior and "quasi-compulsive" sins of weakness, see Germain Grisez, *Christian Moral Principles* (Staten Island: Alba House, 2005 reprint), ch. 17, questions D through F, pp. 419-427.

39. Pope Pius XII, Address to Delegates at the Twenty-sixth Congress of Urology, October 8, 1955, and Address to the Second World Congress of Fertility and Sterility, May 19, 1956, explicitly condemned "medically indicated masturbation," confirming a directive from the Holy Office (now Congregation for the Doctrine of the Faith), August 2, 1929. Pornography is also frequently used with this type of masturbation and others.

40. See Kosnik et al., *Human Sexuality*, pp. 227-229; Charles E. Curran, "Masturbation: An Objectively Grave Matter?" in *A New Look at Christian Morality* (Notre Dame, IN: Fides, 1968), pp. 200-221.

41. See Charles E. Curran, *Contemporary Problems in Moral Theology* (Notre Dame, IN: University of Notre Dame Press, 1970), pp. 159-188; Keane, *Sexual Morality*, pp. 62-68.

42. Pope John Paul II, *Veritatis Splendor*, no. 70, citing his own *Reconciliatio et Paenitentia*, no. 17.

43. See their works cited in endnote 21. Donna Steichen, *Ungodly Rage: The Hidden Face of Catholic Feminism* (San Francisco: Ignatius, 1992) provides trenchant criticisms of the writings of Farley, Gudorf, and Ruether.

44. See *Summa Theologiae*, II-II, q. 154, a. 4; this is the standard reference for the common teaching of the manuals.

45. This is the position presented by Chai Feldblum, with some "exceptions" that would *not* protect Catholic organizations and schools, in *Same-Sex Marriage and Religious Liberty: Emerging Conflicts*, edited by Douglas Laycock, Anthony R. Picarello, Jr., and Robin Fretwell Wilson (Washington, DC: The Becket Fund and Rowman & Littlefield Publishers, 2008).

46. Examples of the way this claim is made by influential media are provided by Jeffrey Satinover, "The Biological Truth About Homosexuality," in *Same-Sex Attraction: A Parents' Guide*, eds. John Harvey, O.S.F.S., and Gerard V. Bradley (South Bend, IN: St. Augustine's Press, 2007), pp. 9-24. On pp. 9-10 Satinover writes: "On July 15, 1993 National Public Radio reported a new study in *Science* due to be released the next day. The tenor of the report was to celebrate the so-called discovery of the gene that causes homosexuality. Near the end, the necessary caveats were quickly added, but most laymen would have turned off the radio thinking that homosexuality is genetically determined. Print media reinforced this impression. The *Wall Street Journal* headlined their report the next day 'Research Points Toward a Gay Gene.' A subheading of the *Journal* article stated 'Normal Variation,' leaving the casual reader with the impression that the research led to this conclusion [although it did not]."

47. A. Bell and M. Weinberg, *Homosexualities* (New York: Simon and Schuster, 1978).

48. Congregation for the Doctrine of the Faith, *Letter to Bishops of the Catholic Church on the Pastoral Care of the Homosexual Person*, October 1, 1986, no. 16.

49. See John Harvey, O.S.F.S., *The Homosexual Person: New Thinking in Pastoral Care* (San Francisco: Ignatius Press, 1987), p. 27. Harvey adds that he uses the term "*predominant* to indicate that there may be a lesser degree of erotic interest in the other sex," and the term "*persistent* to indicate that these erotic feelings toward someone of the same sex have persisted beyond the adolescent phase." In subsequent pages Harvey judiciously reviews and discusses the descriptions of homosexuality provided by contemporary researchers, in particular Dr. Gerald van den Aardweg and Dr. Elizabeth Moberly. Harvey, the founder of Courage, an organization now active in many

dioceses of the United States whose purpose is to help homosexually oriented men to lead chaste lives, died at the end of 2010. More recent studies by Harvey or edited by him include *Same-Sex Attraction: A Parents' Guide,* edited with Gerard V. Bradley (South Bend, IN: St. Augustine's Press, 2003) and *Homosexuality and the Catholic Church: Clear Answers to Difficult Questions* (Westchester, PA: Ascension Press, 2007). The work edited with Bradley contains essays by Harvey ("Questions and Answers for Parents of Persons With Same-Sex Attraction"), Bradley ("Same-Sex Marriage: Our Final Answer?"), and essays by others concerning scientific studies on the etiology of the homosexual orientation (e.g., Satinover's article cited in endnote 46), on the teaching of Scripture, on the intrinsic disorder of the homosexual orientation, and on law and homosexuality. Reference will be made to several of these studies in responding to recent claims made by those seeking to claim that homosexuality is as normal as heterosexuality because it is determined genetically, to justify same-sex marriage and homosexual acts.

50. It is very necessary to distinguish between "*transitory homosexuality,* which may be a phase of development, especially during adolescence, and *chronic homosexuality,* the latter being the type of homosexuality that is generally meant when one uses the term" (Gerald van den Aardweg, *On the Origins and Treatment of Homosexuality* [New York: Praeger, 1986], p. 1, cited by Harvey, *The Homosexual Person,* p. 27).

51. As van den Aardweg puts it, "the criterion lies in one's feelings, not in one's manifest behavior." Ibid. See also Satinover, "The Biological Truth About Homosexuality."

52. Other distinctions among types of homosexuality are those between *compulsive, symptomatic,* and *episodic* homosexuality. On this see Jeffrey Keefe, O.F.M. Conv., "Key Aspects of Homosexuality," in John F. Harvey, O.S.F.S., *The Truth About Homosexuality: The Cry of the Faithful* (San Francisco: Ignatius Press, 1996), pp. 54-61.

53. Joseph Nicolosi, Ph.D., "The Gay Deception," in *Same-Sex Attraction: A Parents' Guide,* pp. 25-32. See also Alan P. Medinger, "Calling Oneself 'Gay' Clouds One's Self-Perception," in ibid., pp. 170-189. See also Samuel McCracken, "Are Homosexuals Gay?" *Commentary* (January 1979): 19-29. He shows by a critical analysis of data published in pro-homosexual books that the claim that

homosexuals are as happy as other people has not been established; in particular, he points to data which show that suicide attempts are significantly higher among homosexuals than among others — for example, 3 percent for white non-homosexual males, 18 percent for white homosexual males. He cites the following statistics: 14 percent of homosexual males studied and 38 percent of females lived in an equivalent of a "happy marriage." But 84 percent of the males studied "cruised" at least once a month, 42 percent at least once a week. Half the males in the study cited had at least 500 sexual partners. More recent studies, too, have similarly indicated the higher incidence of physical and mental health problems for persons with a homosexual inclination.

54. On this see the studies of van den Aardweg, Moberly, Bell and Weinberg, and others. The orientation is brought about principally because of environmental factors affecting psychosexual development, although there may well be, at least in some cases, some *predispositions* of a genetic origin. A judicious review of relevant research on this question is given by Jeffrey Keefe, "Key Aspects of Homosexuality," pp. 32-54.

55. John F. Harvey, *The Truth About Homosexuality*, p. 114. This statement appears at the end of a chapter (pp. 69-114) dealing with the possibility of changing a homosexual orientation to a heterosexual one. In his survey of relevant literature, Harvey first reviewed and noted both the limitations of the empirical data in and a priori assumptions governing the work of authors claiming that such a change is not possible (C. A. Tripp, Robert Bidwell, Richard Green, and Laura Reiter). He then turned to the clinical psychologists and psychiatrists (Gerald van den Aardweg, E. Mansel, Myrna Loy Pattison, George Rekers, Charles Socarides, Ismond Rosen, Lawrence Hatterer) and religious counselors with professional knowledge and experience (Elizabeth Moberly, Leanne Payne, Andy Comiskey, William Consiglio, Joe Dallas, Bob Davies, Lori Rentzel, and Frank Worthen) who testify to the possibility of such a change. Concluding, Harvey says: "All these professional men and women present evidence that their counselees have been able to make the journey from homosexuality to heterosexuality. [Indeed] some of these counselors... were homosexual in orientation themselves.... They make it clear that they were able to make the transition by the help of God's grace" (p. 114).

56. This is the Church's constant understanding of the relevant teaching of the Scriptures on this subject. See Kevin E. Miller, "Scripture and Homosexuality," in *Same-Sex Attraction: A Parents' Guide,* pp. 53-74. See also these older works: Pierre Grelot, *Man and Wife in Scripture* (New York: Herder and Herder, 1965), pp. 34-37, and Edward Schillebeeckx, *Marriage*, pp. 14-16, 20-21. See also John L. McKenzie, "Human Origins," in *The Two-Edged Sword: An Interpretation of the Old Testament* (New York: Doubleday, 1966), where McKenzie makes the point that Genesis 1 and, in particular, Genesis 2 — the story of the creation of mankind as male and female and of marriage — is also the story of the creation of marriage. See also the article on sex in *The Interpreter's Dictionary of the Bible* (Nashville, TN: Abingdon, 1966). See also Roger Shinn, "Homosexuality, Christian Conviction, and Enquiry," *The Same Sex*, ed. Ralph Weltge (Philadelphia: Pilgrim Press, 1969), p. 26: "The Christian tradition over the centuries has affirmed the heterosexual, monogamous faithful marital union as normative for the divinely given meaning of the intimate sexual relationship."

57. On male homosexuality, see Leviticus 18:22, 20:13; Romans 1:27; 1 Corinthians 6:9-10; 1 Timothy 1:9-10; on female homosexuality, Romans 1:26-27.

58. See *Summa Theologiae*, II-II, q. 154, aa. 11-12; Salmanticenses, tr. XXVI, C.VII, 109; Zalba, 1, pp. 780-781.

59. Congregation for the Doctrine of the Faith, *Letter to Bishops of the Catholic Church on the Pastoral Care of the Homosexual Person*, no. 3. John Finnis, "'An Intrinsically Disordered Inclination,'" in *Same-Sex Attraction: A Parents' Guide,* pp. 89-99, presents a superb argument to show why the inclination is indeed intrinsically disordered.

60. James Hitchcock, Catholicism and Modernity: Confrontation or Capitulation? (New York: Seabury, 1979), p. 207.

61. See, for example, John McNeill, S.J., *The Church and the Homosexual* (Kansas City, MO: Andrews and McMeel, 1976); Kosnik et al., *Human Sexuality*, pp. 186-218.

62. See McNeill, *The Church and the Homosexual*, pp. 42-53. See also Kosnik et al., *Human Sexuality*, pp. 191-192. For a counterargument that this story definitely includes a reference to homosexuality, see Manuel Miguens, O.F.M., "Biblical Thoughts on 'Human Sexuality,'" in *Human Sexuality in Our Time*, ed. George A. Kelly (Boston:

Daughters of St. Paul, 1979), pp. 112-115. It is important in this connection to note that the Epistle of Jude (v. 7) refers to Sodom and Gomorrah, and indicates their sin as unnatural vice.
63. McNeill, *The Church and the Homosexual*, pp. 53-56.
64. See the following: Lynn C. Boughton, "Biblical Texts and Homosexuality: A Response to John Boswell," *Irish Theological Quarterly*, 58 (1992): 142-150. See also Kevin E. Miller, "Scripture and Homosexuality," in *Same-Sex Attraction . . .*, pp. 53-73, at 57-60.
65. See Glenn Olsen, "The Gay Middle Ages: A Response to Professor Boswell," *Communio: International Catholic Review*, 8 (1981): 131-156.
66. See John M. Finnis, "Natural Law and Unnatural Acts," *Heythrop Journal* 11 (1979): 384-385.
67. See Paul Cameron, "A Case Against Homosexuality," *The Human Life Review*, 4.3 (1978): 17-49. Cameron is a psychologist and argues effectively on the basis of the empirical data that homosexual activity undercuts the values required for stable family life and society because of its direction to immediate sexual gratification. See also Samuel McCracken, "Are Homosexuals Gay?" *Commentary* (January 1979): 19-29, for further convincing documentation of the almost exclusive orientation toward pleasure on the part of most homosexuals, and of their consequent irresponsibility; two quotes from homosexuals are most revealing:

> . . . Gay people have more fun than your average married guy in a home with two or three kids. You have more time and money. You don't have the responsibilities. . . . I can lavish . . . presents . . . on my nephews and take them to the zoo and have a great old time. When they get tired and cranky I take them back to mommy and dad — you know, dad has just finished paying two hundred bucks for their teeth.
> . . . It's so hard to be a straight man, harder than to be a faggot, because the rewards are so stupid — the rewards that you are told you can have. Whereas if you're a faggot, I guess you can make up your own rewards. . . . It's more fun to be a faggot because nobody expects anything of us."

More recently, Stanley Kurtz has noted the lack of monogamy on the part of homosexuals in "Beyond Gay Marriage: The Road to

Polyamory," *Weekly Standard*, August 4/August 11, 2003, http://www
.weeklystandard.com/Content/Public/Articles/000/000/002/938xpsxy
.asp?page=3.

68. McCracken, ibid., 27: "The fact is that homosexuality generally entails a renunciation of responsibility for the continuance of the
human race and of a voice in the dialogue of the generations. This is
a renunciation made also by some heterosexuals and indeed by some
married heterosexuals. There is, however, a still greater renunciation
made by homosexuals, and that is of the intricate, complicated, and
challenging process of adjusting one's life to someone so different
from oneself as to be in a different sex entirely."

69. See Stephen Macedo, "Homosexuality and the Conservative
Mind," *Georgetown University Law Journal* 84 (1995): 261ff.

70. Karol Wojtyla, *Love and Responsibility*, p. 30.

71. This truth is developed at length by Germain Grisez in *Living
a Christian Life*, pp. 555-584. In developing this truth he shows that
the magisterium of the Church, particularly in the teaching of Vatican Council II and in the many writings of John Paul II on marriage,
clearly holds that marriage is something good in itself and not merely
good as an instrument for generating life.

72. See *In Vitro Fertilization and Public Policy: Evidence Submit-
ted to the Government Committee of Inquiry Into Human Fertilization
and Embryology by the Catholic Bishops' Joint Committee on Bio-Ethical
Issues, on Behalf of the Bishops of Great Britain* (May, 1980).

73. Here it is worth noting that in his encyclical *Humanae Vitae*,
Pope Paul VI made it clear that the marital act renders spouses *fit* or
worthy to generate human life according to laws inscribed into their
very nature as man and woman. The Latin (official text) says that the
marital act *"eos (spouses) idoneos (fitting or worthy) facit."* The English
text, unfortunately, mistranslates the text and says that the marital
act makes the spouses "capable" of generating human life. But what
makes spouses capable of doing so is a genital act, one of which fornicators and adulterers are capable.

74. See Norman Pittinger, *A Time for Consent: A Christian's
Approach to Homosexuality* (London: SCM Press, 1970); James B.
Nelson, *Embodiment: An Approach to Sexuality and Christian Theol-
ogy* (Minneapolis, MN: Augsburg Press, 1978); more recently Nel-

son wrote another work in which gay sex is celebrated, *Body Theology* (Louisville, KY: Westminster/John Knox Press, 1992).

75. Maguire in 2006 published a pamphlet, *A Catholic Defense of Same-Sex Marriage*, in which he advocates this radical position; he in fact sent copies of his pamphlet to all the bishops of the United States, along with another pamphlet, *The Moderate Catholic Position on Contraception and Abortion*, prompting them to issue a statement declaring his views completely incompatible with Catholic teaching. See also Maguire, "The shadow side of the homosexuality debate," in *Homosexuality in the Priesthood and the Religious Life*, Jean Gramick, ed. (Hyattsville, MD: New Ways Ministry, 1989), pp. 36-55. For Farley, see her "An Ethic for Same Sex Love," in Robert Nugent, ed., *A Challenge to Love: Gay and Lesbian Catholics in the Church* (New York: Crossroad, 1987). Nugent and Gramick have published many anthologies through their New Ways Ministry defending this radical acceptance of the gay lifestyle. For McNeill's later work see his *Taking a Chance on God: Liberating Theology for Gays, Lesbians, and Their Lovers, Families, and Friends* (Boston: Beacon Press, 1988).

76. On this see Gerard V. Bradley, "Same-Sex Marriage: Our Final Answer?" in *Same-Sex Attraction: A Parents' Guide*, pp. 119-145; William E. May, "Same-Sex Marriage: Impossible," *Faith* 36.5 (September 2004); William E. May, "On the Impossibility of Same-Sex Marriage," *National Catholic Bioethics Quarterly* 2.2 (Summer 2006): 303-316.

77. See *Dictionnaire de Théologie Catholique*, 14, 4.1350, for an elaboration and explanation of this definition.

78. See Leviticus 18:23, 29; 20:15-16; Exodus 22:19. See the commentary on these passages in *The Jerome Biblical Commentary*, ed. Raymond Brown, S.S., Joseph A. Fitzmyer, S.J., and Roland E. Murphy, O.Carm. (Englewood Cliffs, NJ: Prentice-Hall, 1968), pp. 60, 78-79.

79. See *Summa Theologiae*, II-II, q. 154, a. 12, ad 4; Marcellinus Zalba, S.J., *Theologiae Moralis Compendium*, vol. 1, pp. 781-782. Some modern thinkers, however, such as the atheist and utilitarian bioethicist Peter Singer, are willing to justify bestiality.

80. For a standard statement of the Catholic theological tradition, see *Summa Theologiae*, II-II, w. 154, a. 6.; Zalba, *Theologiae Moralis Compendium*, vol. 1, pp. 765-766.

81. In 1976 Sharon L. McCombie et al. reported as follows: "Development of a Medical Center Rape Crisis Intervention Program," *American Journal of Psychiatry*, 133.4 (1976), 418-421, at 418: "It is the fastest rising violent crime in the United States: the FBI reported a 68% increase in rape (from 31,000 to 51,000 cases) between 1968 and 1973, and police records in Boston show a 43.5% increase between 1972 and 1973." It is common knowledge also that many cases of rape are not reported. See L. S. McGuire et al., "Survey of Incidence of and Physicians' Attitude Toward Sexual Assault," *Public Health Report*, 91.2 (1976): 103-109. More recent statistics are given by the Internet Encyclopedia *Wikipedia* (see http://en.wikipedia.org/wiki/Rape_statistics#United_States). A summary of the incidence of assault by rape in the United States provided there is the following: The U.S. Department of Justice reported 191,670 victims of rape or sexual assault reported in 2005. But only 16 percent of rapes and sexual assaults are reported to the police. One of 6 U.S. women has experienced an attempted or completed rape, according to Colorado Coalition Against Sexual Assault. From 2000-2005, 59 percent of rapes were not reported to law enforcement. One factor relating to this is the misconception that most rapes are committed by strangers. In reality, according to the Bureau of Justice Statistics, 38 percent of victims were raped by a friend or acquaintance, 28 percent by "an intimate" and 7 percent by another relative, and 26 percent were committed by a stranger to the victim. About 4 out of 10 sexual assaults take place at the victim's own home. In short, rape has become increasingly widespread in a sex-crazed culture.

82. Here the words of Dietrich von Hildebrand, *In Defense of Purity* (New York: Sheed and Ward, 1935), pp. 12-14, are instructive: "Sex... as contrasted with other departments of bodily experience is *essentially* deep. Every manifestation of sex produces an effect which transcends the physical sphere and, in a fashion quite unlike the other bodily desires, involves the soul deeply in its passion.... It is characteristic of sex that in virtue of its very significance and nature it tends to become incorporated with experiences of a higher order, purely psychological and spiritual. Nothing in the domain of sex is so self-contained as the other bodily experiences, e.g., eating and drinking. The unique profundity of sex... is sufficiently shown by the simple fact that a man's attitude toward it is of incomparably

greater moral significance than his attitude to the other bodily appetites. Surrender to sexual desire for its own sake defiles a man in a way that gluttony, for example, can never do. It wounds him to the core of his being.... Sex occupies a central position in the personality.... Sex can indeed keep silence, but when it speaks it is no *obiter dictum*, but a voice from the depths, the utterance of something central and of utmost significance. In and with sex man, in a special way, gives himself."

83. For a well-argued defense of this position see Grisez, *Living a Christian Life*, p. 512.

84. See National Conference of Catholic Bishops, *Ethical and Religious Directives for Catholic Health Care Services*, 5th ed. (Washington, DC: United States Catholic Conference, 2009), Directive 36.

85. See *Summa Theologiae*, II-II, q. 154, a. 9.

86. Keane (*Sexual Morality*), pp. 58-59, misses this important point. He says, "... It can thus be said that in most cases sexual thoughts and fantasies do not deeply involve the average person; they are not very significant as an area of moral concern." This statement is ambiguous; he may be saying that most sexual thoughts are such that they never become an object of choice. This is contrary to common experiences; sex is important, and when a person is self-consciously dealing with sexual matters deliberation is triggered and choice is required. Keane may, of course, simply mean that sexual thoughts are not a morally serious matter. We have argued otherwise, and his position is simply inconsistent with the common teaching of the Church and with ordinary common sense.

87. For a fuller account, see *Dictionnaire de Théologie Catholique*, 9.4, "Luxure," 1352-1354, for the standard classification. See also Zalba, *Theologiae Moralis Compendium*, vol. 1, pp. 786-789. For an account in English, see Henry Davis, S.J., *Pastoral and Moral Theology*, pp. 218-221. A more recent and most helpful treatment of this is given by Grisez, *Living a Christian Life*, pp. 737-741. See also Pontifical Council for the Family, *Preparation for the Sacrament of Marriage*, 1996.

Pastoral Conclusion

Sexual morality must be taught in the Church in the spirit in which Christ taught.[1] In the preceding chapters we have spoken of "the biblical foundations, the ethical grounds, and the personalistic reasons" that underlie Catholic teaching in sexual ethics.[2] We have pointed out that the Church's insistent teachings in sexual morality are entirely faithful to Gospel teaching, are true and good, and that they liberate the human spirit by guiding us to live in ways that are truly good.

But this splendid and saving teaching must be proclaimed in a very flawed world in which cultural conditions can make it very difficult to follow even necessary precepts. It must be presented to people who are very weak. It must be spoken to contemporary men and women who frequently find acceptance of Catholic doctrine in this area difficult because of the pervasive pressures of the world, and even because of the halfhearted support of — or in some cases, dissent from — this teaching on the part of many in the Church herself.

The aim of pastoral theology, and the purpose of pastoral labors, is to help the faithful actually live their lives in accordance with the teachings of faith, and so to grow in love and in the grace of God. By no means is pastoral theology concerned with replacing the excellent and necessary teachings of the Gospel with more lenient maxims, which undermine essential respect for human values and weaken personal resolve to live in accord with the authentic requirements of love.

In this concluding part of the book, we can only sketch the most basic elements of a pastoral stance that flows from Catholic teaching. We stress the following points:

(1) The importance of teaching Catholic sexual morality faithfully, intelligently, and attractively;

319

(2) The need to make clear the objective truth of Catholic moral teaching in sexual ethics, its seriousness, and also the reasons why those who perform acts that are objectively gravely sinful are often not guilty of grave sin;

(3) Finding ways to give the faithful practical assistance in living in accord with the excellent standards of Catholic faith;

(4) Helping all see how Christ assists his people to bear the burdens of chaste living without excessive stress.

I. Teaching Sexual Ethics Faithfully, Intelligently, Attractively

Teaching Faithfully. Catholic teachers — bishops, priests, parents, religious educators — have the privilege and the duty of teaching faithfully and clearly the Catholic vision of sexuality and its authentic moral teachings. They must not excuse themselves on the pretext that in our time Catholic teachings on chastity are too difficult, or that people of our time have rejected what faith teaches in this area. For Catholics have a right to Catholic teaching in this very important matter, and they need the light of the Gospel to come to appreciate the truth and goodness of what faith teaches about chaste love.[3]

We must teach the precepts that guard pure love persistently. For the faithful are daily battered by the voices of the world, with its teachings about sexuality that are incompatible with Christian life. They will suffer great harm if they are not fortified by the saving teaching of the Gospels.

Teaching as Jesus Taught. Jesus strengthened and heartened the people to whom he preached by speaking with authority (Mt 7:29). He spoke as one who knew with certainty what is true and truly good. And he spoke out of a life of such excellence that his hearers realized that he was in fact teaching the truth their hearts longed for and needed.[4] Even when he taught difficult precepts, he enabled his hearers to realize that he spoke in defense of their lives and of their greatest good.

Over the centuries the Church has spoken with authority in the name of Jesus on questions of sexual morality, as she has in all essential areas of moral life. The Church has spoken with a bracing authority, because in a bewildered and suffering world, she has known with certainty important and saving truths, and has recognized that forceful teaching is necessary to support persons in their weakness (cf. 1 Cor 14:8).

Our Times Require Excellent Teaching. Even in the midst of the spiritual confusion of our time, the pastoral leader must teach the sexual ethics of the Church with the merciful firmness of Christ. The duty to teach the doctrine of the Church in this area is certain,[5] and the harm done to the faithful when this doctrine is not faithfully proclaimed is all too clear. Public-opinion surveys reveal that many Catholics do not accept the sure teachings of the Church in this area. As a result, many tend to live in ways that assail the most precious values, and fail to respect the human goods that must be honored if we are to have a fulfilled and happy life on earth, and live in the love of God with a secure hope for eternal life.

Though a life of self-possession and of disciplined love is ultimately far happier than a life wounded by lust, the young and the weak do not know this through their own experience. In many ways the world around them (and sometimes even Catholic educators) tends to deceive them, by telling them that the excellent ways of Christ are too difficult, or that what seems so attractive to the flesh must be right for them. Consequently, if pastoral leaders within the Church seem uncertain whether the sexual morality always proclaimed by the Church is true, they undermine whatever resolve the weak and the young can muster.

Teaching With One Voice. Recent popes have regularly reminded scholars and pastoral leaders of their duty to teach with one voice the truth about marriage and sexual morality which has constantly been taught in the family of faith.[6] The fact that there has been an unprecedented outburst of illegitimate dissent from this teaching in our time, the fact that the modern media induce many of the faithful to accept the unhappy ethics of shallow hedonism, the fact that those who proclaim the teaching of the Church on these matters can be subjected to a measure of ridicule and loss of popularity — all these things do not remove the duty to proclaim faithfully the teaching of the Church on sexual morality.[7] For the faithful have a right to receive all the authentic teaching of the Church.[8]

The faithful are not receiving the teaching of the Church about sexual morality unless they are given that teaching in a fully Catholic way. Thus, they must not simply be told that the Church "officially" teaches this or that. For to say simply that does not help the faithful realize that the Church teaching is true and good, that it proposes the way the Lord wills us to live, and that, consequently, they have a grave duty to believe it and live by it. Only the sound conviction that the Church's teachings are true and that they can be lived gladly with the help of God's grace will provide the strength needed by one who is tempted to commit fornication or to enter an invalid marriage. Those who speak for the Lord must do all they can to provide this strength, and to do this they must speak his truth as what it is — the way to live in Christ.

II. Teaching Compassionately and Truthfully

Pastoral care must seek to be honest and charitable in its assessment of the measure of subjective guilt incurred by those who lapse into behavior that objectively is mortally sinful. Catholic faith teaches that sins of lust are objectively so gravely disordered that those who perform them freely and with a sufficient understanding of their malice do commit mortal sins. They tragically separate themselves from the love of Christ and endanger their eternal salvation. Moreover, the Church teaches that, while passion and ignorance frequently lessen or take away the personal guilt of sexual sins, people can and do commit mortal sin by lustful thoughts and actions. It is useful to list here some of the considerations essential for a balanced pastoral approach to this question.

1. *Activities That Are Objectively Gravely Wrong Are Not Always Subjectively So.* To say that lustful actions, such as acts of fornication or masturbation, are objectively gravely sinful is certainly not to say that every person who engages in behavior of these kinds necessarily incurs personally the guilt of grave sin.[9] Ignorance and antecedent passion can lessen or remove such guilt. The lives of many are lived in such difficult conditions, subject to utter poverty and grave injustices, and in the midst of gravely scandalous provocations, that it can be very difficult for them to grasp the serious nature of sins of lust. Psychological impediments (for example, in the case of compulsive actions) may remove responsibility considerably — or, in some cases, entirely — from lustful behavior. Those who are told by trusted teachers and advisers that it is permissible to do kinds of actions that faith

has regularly condemned as always objectively gravely wrong may at times follow this bad advice with some real measure of good faith. Those who are deeply troubled by bad actions they have performed — while influenced by scandal, injustice, false teaching, or compulsions of which they were victims — deserve gentle, strong, and competent pastoral care.

2. *Sexual Sins Are Often Subjectively Grave Sins.* In some individual cases a spiritual guide may have specific reasons for judging that a particular person has not sinned by indulging in sexual acts which are objectively gravely immoral. This may be true, for example, if the action in question seems compulsive to the point that it is not within the person's control. But there is no reason whatever for assuming that people who engage in such behavior virtually always escape the guilt of personal mortal sin. People can and do commit mortal sins by lustful deeds and by deliberately indulging in lustful desire.[10] Nor is it right to suggest that a person who wishes to live his or her life generally in ways pleasing to God, but engages occasionally in lustful deeds of a kind common enough in worldly society, would retain a fundamental stance of faithfulness to God — that one does not lose grace or endanger eternal salvation by deliberately engaging in such acts.[11] Single gravely wrong acts (normally preceded by less grave sins) can be formal mortal sins, for if one is prepared to do, and chooses to do, an action that is gravely evil and known to be opposed to the demanding will of God (or does not know this precisely because of a gravely culpable unwillingness to learn the truth), then one does not maintain a faithful love of God. Rather, one thus expresses the spirit of one who does not in fact love God in even the minimum measure required to live in his grace (cf. Jn 14:15).[12]

3. *Ignorance and the Gravity of Sins.* The fact that one does not know or believe that it is mortally sinful to engage deliberately in a particular lustful act is very relevant. But it does not always indicate that one has not incurred personally the guilt of formal mortal sin,[13] for ignorance in this matter can itself be deliberate and gravely sinful. Self-deception is only too easy for us human beings. One who culpably maintains ignorance of truths that God has made very accessible (by the gift of public revelation and by the graces that make the assent of faith possible) can sin mortally without honestly acknowledging any responsibility. In fact, those who commit mortal sins in any area

are only too ready to seek to persuade themselves that what they choose to do is reasonable and right for them. Thus, they add to their sin by acting against the truth that has been made accessible to them.

4. *Passion and the Gravity of Sins.* Antecedent passion and the reality of human weakness are important considerations in assessing subjective guilt. But the fact than an objectively grave act was done out of weakness and with some influence of passion is no certain sign that mortal sin was not committed. As long as the person maintains substantial freedom, knows that a proposed action is gravely wrong (or is gravely culpable in his ignorance of that fact), and in choosing to act or not act retains essential self-mastery, one is capable of grave sin, and of meritorious fidelity to God.[14] Christians are bound to be faithful to God, and to lead morally good lives, even when it is difficult to do so. God's grace makes faithfulness very possible.

5. *Principles for Spiritual Guidance.* In evaluating subjective guilt, the role of those who have any kind of teaching or advising role is different from that of casual acquaintances and friends. Ordinarily, it is quite proper to have a generous interpretation of other people's conduct. It is inappropriate to judge that our friends and acquaintances have in fact formally sinned, even if it is manifest that some of their conduct exhibits behavior of a kind that the Church teaches to be gravely wrong.

But teachers and advisers have special duties; frequently, they have the duty to help others escape self-deceit. Thus, any general presumption that those who are doing things which the Catholic faith teaches to be gravely wrong should be assured that they are in good faith is a serious mistake. False assurances of this kind can be extremely harmful. They can support forms of malice that directly imperil the salvation of the one advised, and they can imperil also the salvation of the adviser.

In giving spiritual direction, an adviser must have profound concern for the truth. When one is morally certain that grave sin has been committed, or that it has not, his advice should follow his considered judgment. When it is far from clear whether or not mortal sin has been committed (in forming judgments in these matters, the guidance of those moralists and spiritual authors whose work has faithfully mirrored received Catholic positions is to be followed), advice must reflect the uncertainty of the situation. Grace is a most precious gift; mortal sin is a terrible evil. One who may have committed a mortal sin, or may yet be entangled in a practice or actions that are objectively mortally sinful, needs the help of his advisers to find his way toward a better state.

6. *Witnesses to What Is Truly Good.* In certain rare cases and for special reasons it may be right for confessors or spiritual directors to be silent about the objective immorality of actions that a penitent or someone whom they advise has engaged in. Divine revelation, however, was given to the Church concerning moral matters because it is good for us to know the truth about how we should live to gain eternal life. Hence Catholic pastoral leaders would fail gravely in their duties if they did not make publicly known the full malice of sexual sins. When, moved by grace, a person asks about the morality of sinful behavior that he or she has engaged in or proposes to engage in, that person is to be answered truthfully; and one must not routinely suppose that even habitual sinners or very weak persons will be unable or unwilling to respond to the calls of grace. Human lives are made far better when the light of truth and the many supports of faith are made richly accessible. To be quiet about Catholic teachings concerning sexual morality in order to escape conflicts with those who brazenly deny these teachings, or out of a fear of mockery from worldly forces, or because of a mistaken judgment that the less the faithful know about the truth God has revealed, the less likely they are to commit sins — this is not the stance of pastoral love. Rather, "to diminish in no way the saving teaching of Christ constitutes an eminent form of charity for souls."[15]

7. *Sinful Kinds of Acts Do Harm Even When Innocently Done.* Pastoral care is, of course, concerned with more than subjective guilt or innocence in this matter. Catholic moral teaching about sex speaks the truth about basic human goods and is concerned about what really is good for human persons. Lustful actions are really bad for human beings. They are not merely "forbidden." They harm those who engage in them, even if they do not know that they are evil acts, and even when these acts are not morally imputable to the one performing them. Hence the pastoral teacher and adviser must be concerned to help people know what is good in these matters, and assist them to walk in ways that really serve their human fulfillment and their salvation.

8. *The Power of God's Grace.* The remembrance that human beings can and do commit mortal sins should not lead to despair or excessive sadness. All teaching and guidance in sexual ethics is to be carried out in a spirit of faith and with trust in divine mercy. Difficult and excellent things are commanded in the New Law. Human weakness could be inclined to fear that what faith teaches is too difficult. But it is a commonplace in Catholic teaching that the accessibility of God's grace must be remembered here. Indeed, the entire fulfillment of the moral law would be impossible for fallen humankind without the assistance of the grace and mercy of God. Advisers who have experienced how true it is that God enables very weak persons to do what he has required of them can speak with realistic encouragement to even the weakest sinners.

III. Giving Practical Assistance for Living the Truth

The Christian teacher must not only teach the excellence of the ways in which the Lord would have his people walk. He is also called upon to give the many forms of practical assistance which they need to live as they are called to live.

Instilling a Desire for Holiness and a Love of Chastity. The Second Vatican Council stressed at length the essential need in the Church for stirring up a hunger for holiness. To lead good lives we must seek to grow in faith, hope, and love, and in living with entire faithfulness to the demands of love. Thus, pastoral leaders must seek to help the faithful to live in those excellent ways which make this life happy in the midst of trials, and which make the people of God worthy of eternal life. Holiness of life is not the special goal of a certain elite within the Church. Each one of God's people is called to holiness and can fulfill his or her vocation only by pursuing generous love faithfully. Education in chastity must be carried on in the context of this duty to pursue holiness. Thus, chastity is not to be taught in abstraction from other virtues. It is to be grasped as a necessary ingredient in a holy, free, and good life.

Revealing the Goodness and Attractiveness of Chaste Love. In the confusion of our time, pastoral leaders must see to it that the faithful are taught well the meaning of chastity. Chastity is not an irrational form of repression. It is an essential part of temperance and self-possession, for it gives to the emotions, affections, and passions themselves an orderly direction, so that the human desire for sexual pleasure is itself wisely directed only toward pleasures which are properly related to authentic human goods. Thus, the chaste person finds it easy to forgo pleasure which it would not be wise or good to pursue. The full realization of chastity is different, therefore, from that type of continence in which many people struggle more or less constantly against serious sexual temptation. They genuinely want to be chaste, but they have not succeeded in fully integrating their personalities and sexual desires around their morally good choices. They have not been assisted to the generous acquisition of a full possession of the virtue of chastity — which makes living chastely much easier and much more satisfying. Those who, through faithful concern to act chastely, and through prayer and the help afforded in the sacraments, come to a solid possession of the virtue of chastity acquire with it peace and self-possession, and escape from the burden of constant struggle and temptation.

Profound Importance of Chastity. It is true that chastity is far from the greatest of virtues. St. Thomas Aquinas — along with much of Catholic tradition — teaches that chastity is a form of temperance, which is the least excellent of the cardinal virtues.[16] Nevertheless, Catholic tradition has also emphasized the indispensable importance of this lowly virtue. For the self-control and tranquillity it provides are necessary conditions for the full development of the more exalted virtues. The moral tradition of the Church often pointed out how disastrous are the spiritual fruits of unchastity. The "offspring of lust," that is, the bitter fruits which the tradition perceived as flowing from lives lived unchastely, are indeed formidable. The tradition lists them as: "blindness of mind, lack of balanced consideration, inconstancy, precipitation, love of self, hatred of God, excessive clinging to the present world, and horror or despair of the world to come." These are the bitter and disastrous fruits of a life that lacks self-possession and the will to live chastely.[17]

Pastoral leaders must then take very seriously the problems created when a culture tends to lead great numbers of the faithful into sins of impurity. Experience shows how those who fall into sins of lust begin to find faith and the practice of faith uninteresting. In any place where the pastors do not seriously seek to guard chastity, we must expect to see a corresponding decline in faith and in efforts to live a life of charity.

Formation for Teachers of Chastity. Pastoral leaders must see to it that those who educate the young in chastity have themselves not merely learned the ways of Christ theoretically but are themselves seeking to lead chaste and good lives. They must have tasted for themselves how true it is that temperance and chastity can be achieved even in a sinful world. They must be persons who firmly and fully believe the truth of Catholic teaching about marriage and sexual morality, and who have tasted in their lives the joy and freedom of living chastely. Those who have experienced the ways in which self-possession is happily achieved can give heart and encouragement to beginners in the school of Christ.

Chastity and Freedom. Central to their efforts, as Pope John Paul II has pointed out, must be education in the true sense of freedom.[18] True sexual liberation is not achieved by pretending that each person may without fear do any kind of act toward which he or she is actually inclined, whether it serves real human goods and the authentic fulfillment of life or not. It is not achieved in the life of one dominated by one's passions, without faith-enlightened concern for what is required by love of oneself and of others. It is achieved when one's passions are mastered: that is, not repressed, but governed by generous love. Then one can freely choose to live as one needs to live to acquire in joy what a person must possess to achieve his or her entire fulfillment, and to serving the common good of one's friends in the family of God.[19]

Removing the Impediments That Make Chastity Difficult. Pastoral care must not only make clear the excellence of chastity but also assist in removing the impediments to chaste living and in providing the natural and supernatural supports needed to make chastity flourish in the Christian community.

Social Conditions and Chastity. Many people in the world "lack both the means necessary for survival, such as food, work, housing, and medicine, and the most elementary freedoms." In wealthier countries "excessive prosperity and the consumer mentality, paradoxically joined to a certain anguish and uncertainty about the future," deprive the faithful of the courage and generosity needed to pursue holiness and self-possession.[20] People everywhere are wounded by the invasions of the mass media, which bring into every home solicitations to live lives patterned on ways of thinking entirely alien to the Gospel. Realistic education in chastity cannot be carried out without awareness of these evils, and without serious efforts to overcome them as far as possible.

It is not necessary, however, to overcome every social evil before inviting the faithful to holiness of life. Still, the faithful are heartened when they see that their leaders are aware of the burdens under which they labor to serve Christ, and when they can see that pastoral leaders are earnestly helping them in visible and realistic ways.

Strong Christian community life must be built up to assist the faithful in countering social pressures toward accepting the many forms of lust that appeal to fallen man. It is essential to avoid that despair which judges that in the circumstances of our time young people will fall into fixed practices of masturbation or fornication, that the married will adopt a contraceptive mentality and practice, and that adultery will be commonplace. For this kind of despair leads to compromising sound pastoral practice and even to rejecting Catholic teaching. Since on this view pastoral practice can really do nothing to guard people from the inevitable triumph of sexual immorality, there is a temptation to downplay the importance of sexual sins and to seek a Christianity that accepts gravely sinful practices as a normal part of a good Christian life. From the time of the Church's birth Christians have known that these counsels of despair are entirely wrong. The fire of the early Christians, love, their pursuit of perfection despite their weaknesses and the corruptive influences of the life of the Roman Empire, enabled them to build communities in which chastity flourished. Certainly grave sin did not leave these communities entirely, as they will not leave ours; but Christian communities whose members cherish and nourish chastity make it possible for all those willing to respond to God's grace to grow in the freedom and strength of virtue.

Specific Alternatives to Sinful Practices. Many Catholic people today engage in behavior that is objectively mortally sinful because they have difficult problems and are not aware of realistic and not excessively burdensome ways of resolving them. Many Catholic spouses practice contraception, even in ways that are at times in fact abortifacient,[21] or choose the gravely sinful alternative of sterilization, because they do not know any effective and morally acceptable ways of limiting family size. Often this decision leads them to resentment of the Church and to a kind of despair.

Making Natural Family Planning Accessible. But much of this sorry condition could be removed if pastoral leaders carried out their duties in the way John Paul II has pointed out. A virtuous decision concerning a difficult problem can be made much easier if pastoral leaders see to it that contemporary forms of natural family planning — which are secure and safe, and which are strong supports for marital love — were really made accessible to all Catholic people in every place. The faithful are helped when excellent preaching makes it clear why the use of natural family planning and the use of contraception manifest radically different philosophies of life, and involve "in the final analysis two irreconcilable concepts of the human person and of human sexuality."[22] In this matter the Church *must*, Pope John Paul II points out, offer "practical help." "Every effort must be made to render such knowledge [of natural family planning] accessible to all married people and also to young adults before marriage, through clear, timely, and serious instruction."[23]

The Practical Importance of Supernatural Helps. Faith calls us to live in the ways of love — which does often make great demands. But it is necessary to walk in these ways for life to become human and happy. Divorce is bitterly painful to both spouses and children; yet to live in faithful love of one partner until death, in shared love of the goods that can make life together happy, requires serious efforts not likely to be sustained without the assistance of grace. The distinctive gift of Christ, our teacher, is that he gives those who believe in him not only knowledge of what is good but also "power to become children of God" (Jn 1:12). Things that would be beyond human power are possible to those who seek assistance from the Lord in confident prayer and in devout use of the sacraments, especially the sacrament of reconciliation and the Eucharist. Those turning aside from bad habits, or seeking in young years to acquire self-possession and chastity, benefit greatly by finding a confessor whose spiritual assistance will give them light and encouragement, and who can strengthen their resolve to acquire that purity of heart which supports faithful and generous love.

Pastoral Care for the Family. The family itself is the "little church," the first school of virtue for the young, the community in which love and the requirements of love must first be learned. But the Christian family is assaulted in many ways by the materialistic and hedonistic forces that are so powerful in our culture, and so pervasive in their influence through the mass media. The many forms of care which the Church owes to the family were pointed out by the Synod of Bishops in 1980, and summarized by John Paul II in his apostolic exhortation *Familiaris Consortio.* All these need to be put into effect to help the family of our time to be the school of human values. No other group can replace the family in doing its proper and indispensable tasks. Unless the family flourishes, both civil society and the Church suffer deeply, and the healthy personal growth of young people is deeply endangered. When families seem to be too weak to carry out their proper roles, one should not have immediate recourse to other social structures to achieve what is desired. Rather, every effort must be made to strengthen the family itself, and enable the family to become what it must be. For nothing can replace the family. "Parents are the first and most important educators of their children, and they also possess a fundamental competency in this area: they are educators because they are parents."[24]

Pastoral leaders should be familiar with the many recent Church documents which make it clear that support of the family must be the central focus of pastoral efforts today. Many families today are deeply wounded, and need strong help; and the pastoral life of the Church generally cannot flourish without the presence of strong families given freedom and the resources to carry out their indispensable role. It must be the primary pastoral care of the Church to aid parents and families, for the Church herself cannot prosper if families do not prosper. Families can flourish in grace and become holy even in times like our own; and unless they are helped to do so, the Church herself cannot flourish.[25]

Preparation for Marriage. If education in Catholic faith and in Christian living is to flourish, homes must be strong and parents must be enabled to carry out their indispensable tasks in the face of all the obstacles our culture creates.

Many young couples who approach the Church with the intention of marrying in the Church, and of establishing families, have been deeply wounded by the circumstances of the times. Many of them are not practicing Catholics. Often they know their faith only poorly, and do not have possession of good reasons for believing what faith teaches.

332 | CATHOLIC SEXUAL ETHICS

It is especially important at this time for the Church to provide a really excellent immediate preparation for the sacrament of marriage.

Fortunately, the Holy See has prepared an excellent set of guidelines to govern preparation for marriage in our time.[26] Surely we ought not fall into discouragement, or believe that in our time people simply cannot prepare suitably for Christian marriage. The time of immediate preparation for marriage is a time of grace. The young people are ordinarily in love, and this gift of sincere human love, with its great hopes, can itself prove a singular blessing. Those about to marry have earnest hopes that their marriages will endure. Their experience of honest love can help them realize that the cynical and selfish spirit of the world ought not dominate their spirits. They are often prepared to learn freshly of Christ, and of the great love to which he calls all, and the special love he has for those entering marriage.

We can expect much of marriage-preparation programs, if the leaders and instructors in the program approach it wisely. Certainly, as the *Instruction* urges, they must have a great love for the young people they are assisting. They must also have a good doctrinal and personal formation, so that they reveal to the young the full Catholic vision of marriage and marital love, and permit them to see how earnestly they love all that faith teaches, and how earnestly they themselves are seeking to live their lives in Christ. There must be a strong evangelizing element in marriage preparation. The engaged couples must be taught the meaning of marriage, the greatness of this vocation, the Catholic understanding of marital love, and the goodness and wisdom of its moral requirements. Many kinds of assistance must be offered to each couple: helps toward communicating well and learning generosity in their new life, and helps to understand why natural family planning liberates couples from the bitter burdens of contraception, and the deeply flawed understanding of love that it serves.

Pastoral Care for Young People. In the world today it can be very difficult for young people to grow up enjoying a profound personal possession of their Catholic faith, and with a sound understanding of the goodness of Catholic moral teaching. The education in chastity given to the young must be intelligently and faithfully shaped. Since parents are the first and most indispensable teachers of pure love for their children, the Church owes them assistance to become able to carry out their responsibilities. From their earliest years, children must be helped to experience the greatness of love, to desire to have generous love, and to acquire that self-possession that is needed to grow in love. They must be helped to experience the joy of overcoming that selfishness which is the enemy of true love, and to feel the freedom of being liberated from overwhelming needs to act as immediate pleasure suggests.[27]

Other realistic helps must be given to the young if the Christian community seriously wishes to make chastity a reality for many of them. They must be educated in ways of critically evaluating what the mass media and modern forms of entertainment make popular, so that they may appreciate and enjoy those aspects of popular culture that are suitable and learn not to be harmed by those elements that are harmful. The community must also assist them to find forms of creative play and experiences of beauty which are in full harmony with their Christian vision of life.

Education of Young People in Chastity. Education in the Christian vision of sexuality and in chaste living for the young is primarily the responsibility of parents. They are uniquely qualified to give such instruction, because of their close knowledge of their own children, and their special love for them. If in some respects and under certain circumstances, others assist parents in this matter, education in the Catholic vision of sexuality and in chaste love must still be carried out under the attentive guidance of parents. And these programs must be penetrated with the spirit of pure love that shines in the Gospel.[28]

Many secular forms of sex education assume that most young people will adopt the lustful practices so common in our society — masturbation, fornication, and the like; and they seek not so much to guide people away from immoral activity and the great harm that does to their inner lives, as to protect them from the most visible effects of immoral activity: sexually transmitted diseases and unwanted pregnancies. Often these programs assume the hedonistic attitudes of our time, and consequently set up sexual-education programs so as to help people realize for themselves and others as much pleasure as possible, in ways that do not "hurt" others. But reflection on the harm that is done by separating interest in sexual activity from the indispensable human goods toward which that activity should be essentially ordered tends to be entirely neglected in such programs.

Pastoral leaders have the duty to see to it that no inappropriate forms of sexual education are tolerated in Catholic contexts, and the duty to assist parents who rightly wish to protect their children from such programs when they are thrust upon their children in public schools or in other public contexts. They must see to it also that only excellent programs in teaching chaste love are permitted in Catholic contexts, and that those who direct or teach in Catholic programs sincerely believe Catholic teaching in the whole area of sexuality, so that they may genuinely help the young to grow in the love of chastity.

Chastity, Justice, and Peace. Christian life cannot be taught in fragmented segments; it is a living whole, and neglect of any essential elements redounds to the harm of every part. In recent years some groups of Catholics have stressed too exclusively the importance of the social teaching of the Church with its concern for justice and peace, and others have stressed too exclusively the importance of personal holiness, or guarding life and attending to purity of mind and body. Different stresses can, of course, be acceptable, for it is not possible for everyone to focus energies on all things. But there must be real respect on everyone's part for all the essential goods which fulfill human life. All must be concerned both with matters of social justice, matters of personal morality, and holiness of life.

It would be fatal to a Catholic pursuit of justice and peace to count it unimportant if the faithful should reject Catholic teaching on chaste love. For the fruits of lust — as we have seen above — lead to disorder in every moral area. They lead to a contempt for that love and concern for others' rights that may interfere with the satisfaction of one's own undisciplined desires. Chastity is far from being the greatest virtue, but the greatest virtues, such as justice, are not possible without chastity. Nor may those who struggle to support personal holiness of life minimize the importance of caring for a just social order. For one who promotes chastity — but not the social conditions that favor it and flow from it — fails to appreciate the essentially social character of the entire fabric of Christian life. Self-possession without love for others is not the Christian virtue of chastity.

IV. Making the Burdens of Chastity Light

The Christian teacher wishes to share the gladness of living in Christ with his beloved students and friends. He should have a special desire to assist those who fear that the ways of chaste and generous love may be too difficult to follow. The leaders of the Church have sought to show great concern and compassion for such people. The bishops taking part in the 1980 Synod on marriage took great care to make clear that they understood well how the circumstances of life today make faithfulness to the teachings of faith on contraception, divorce and remarriage, and fidelity within marriage so difficult for many people. And in his apostolic exhortation on the family, summing up the work of the synod, Pope John Paul II spoke with great gentleness on the pastoral care of the family in very difficult cases.[29]

Compassion and Faithfulness to Principle. The Church's sensitivity to these difficulties should not be understood as an acceptance of what are in fact counsels of despair. One must compassionately understand what leads many into invalid marriages, into habitual fornication, toward practices of contraception or to sterilization. But proper compassion for persons should not lead to an approval of sin, however reluctant. For when men and women — pressed by hard circumstances — solve their problems in ways that are objectively gravely evil, they are doing deeds that deepen the wounds and sorrows of their lives.

They are creating disorder and pain in the world in which they live. For sexual sins are not simply violations of arbitrary precepts. They are, rather, attacks on the basic human values that are indispensable for authentically human lives. Deeds that are in fact base and sinful are never reasonable solutions, even to tragic problems.

False "Pastoral" Solutions. That is why the Church has always rejected allegedly "pastoral solutions" which in fact involve approval of kinds of actions that the Church knows always to be immoral. When John Paul II presented the received Catholic teaching concerning persons who are living as spouses in invalid marriages, contracted after civil divorces, he revealed a sensitive understanding of the difficulty of their position. But he did not pretend for a moment that it could be good to tell such people that if they "really think" that it is good for them to perform within invalid marriages actions that are in fact adulterous, then these are good acts for them. He insisted (as the received teaching of the Church always has) that persons who are living in unions that are in fact adulterous may not be told that it is permissible for them to receive the Eucharist.

He readily understands (as every compassionate person would) how extremely difficult it is to be faithful to Catholic teaching in some circumstances. Consider the case of a woman who has been abandoned by her husband and who has several children. She is suffering from loneliness and poverty, and has the opportunity to "marry" an attractive man who is deeply devoted to her and her children. But the Church, illumined by the Gospel, teaches that she ought not attempt marriage again in such circumstances. To attempt to marry anew while the one to whom she is yet bound in marriage is alive is in itself a bad kind of action. The prohibition may seem at first a brutal exercise in legalism. Some may be tempted to find a "pastoral solution," that is, to tell her that in this case to enter into a union which the Church knows to be in fact adulterous would be permissible.

The Holy Father presents a much different answer. There is a pastoral duty to help the woman understand that it is not shallow legalism but concern for faithful love and for spouses and children everywhere that requires faithfulness to the teaching of Christ. She must be helped to see that her pain is not meaningless and cruel, and that she is able to transform the loneliness and suffering into a generous witnessing of the importance of faithful love, even when we have ourselves been treated badly. Her heroic decision not to enter an invalid marriage becomes a reminder to everyone of the duty to be faithful to the values that serve every home and every family. Such faithfulness is a support of spousal love and of children everywhere. Meanwhile the community has great duties to her, and should assist her in bearing the burdens she carries for the sake of all.

Not Doing Evil to Achieve Good. Pastoral love does not propose solutions that are opposed to the true and healing teachings of faith. For when one commends evil kinds of deeds in hopes of achieving a better life, one enters into a hopeless path. If the revelation of God together with the faith of the Catholic Church is true, objectively evil deeds wound both the world and the inner lives of those who perform them. It is often only by difficult ways that one can save one's life, maintain its integrity, and ultimately its blessedness.

Grace and Love Make Light and Easy What Otherwise Would Be Too Burdensome. Christ never hid from his disciples the excellence and the difficulty of his teaching concerning marriage and sexual morality. The Gospels portray him as not at all surprised when the apostles themselves found his teaching on divorce difficult to believe (see Mt 19:10). He assured them, however, that this excellent but sometimes seemingly harsh teaching (in fact indispensable for guarding faithful love and the procreative good in this broken world) would indeed be made bearable by the gift of God. Even more, Christ insisted that the whole burden of his teaching was an easy burden, that the yoke he imposes on his own (for their sake) would be a light one for those who draw near to him (cf. Mt 11:30).

There are many paradoxes in Christian morality. By dying we come to life. By the cross we come to joy. The hard way is easy but walking the easy path leads to unbearable sorrow. To come to the viewpoint and to the experience of faith is not an easy task. But the conversion of heart this requires is indispensable for the saving of both human and divine goods in our lives.

Those who wish to live chaste lives, faithfully respecting every human value in their choices, will experience trials and stress but also great comfort and consolation. Contemporary literature and experience reveal that those who deliberately engage in lustful deeds in the hope of escaping pain and stress tend to fall into even greater anxieties and strains. The ways of living taught by faith work. The paths of intelligent love are often difficult, but to abandon these paths always proves tragic.

St. Thomas Aquinas asks pointedly whether the New Law, with its sublime and demanding moral teaching, might not in fact be more difficult to observe than the Old Law itself. He responds, with the voice of tradition and the experience of Christianity, that it is not.[30] He acknowledges that in one sense the new law is more difficult than the old. It requires a form of life that is intrinsically more demanding because it is more excellent. Yet it is made easy in a number of ways. Those who with devoted hearts accept the graces that invite them to life in Christ receive from the Holy Spirit gifts that make bearable, even light and pleasant what otherwise would certainly have been too difficult and even unsupportable. God's great mercy, and his grace, make the best ways of living also light and easy. To walk the ways of intelligent love is to choose a life surrounded with countless blessings and great peace.

ENDNOTES FOR PASTORAL CONCLUSION

1. The fundamental principles of pastoral theology are exemplified in the pastoral visits John Paul II has regularly made to many

nations. Pastoral theology has an integrative and immediately practical thrust: in sincere charity it seeks to understand the situation of
those to whom the Gospel is taught; it offers encouragement and
assistance; it is compassionate in the face of weakness but firm in its
concern to proclaim the saving truth in its fullness, and to hearten the
faithful to follow Christ generously. The American bishops outlined
the fundamental principles of a pastoral approach to moral questions
in two pastorals: *To Teach as Jesus Taught* and *To Live in Christ Jesus: A
Pastoral Reflection on the Moral Life* (Washington, DC: U.S. Catholic
Conference, 1975 and 1976).

2. John Paul II, *Familiaris Consortio*, no. 31.

3. Thus, John Paul II stresses how important it is to offer practical
assistance in observing the moral precepts that express the requirements of love in *Familiaris Consortio*, no. 35, and in his concern to
help pastoral leaders to see how great are the problems they must help
the faithful to overcome (see Parts I and IV of *Familiaris Consortio*).

4. The Church insists that her teachings on morality are not merely
authoritative declarations or rulings but express the truth entrusted to
the Church by God; see Vatican Council II, *Dei Verbum*, ch. 1; John
Paul II, *Redemptor Hominis*, no. 12. In his apostolic exhortation *Reconciliatio et Paenitentia* (December 2, 1984), John Paul II speaks of
the duty of all teachers in the Church to avoid subjective views and
seek to proclaim in moral matters the truth found in the word of God
as interpreted by the magisterium (cf. no. 25). See also his encyclical
Veritatis Splendor (August 6, 1993), esp. nos. 114-117.

5. The primacy of the duty of teaching the faith, including its
moral aspects, is clear in the recent teaching of the Church. See
Vatican Council II, *Lumen Gentium*, no. 25; *Christus Dominus*, nos.
12-13; on the right of the faithful to have the whole of the faith proclaimed to them, see John Paul II, "Address at Catholic University to
Presidents of Catholic Universities and Colleges," October 7, 1979, in
Pilgrim of Peace (Washington, DC: U.S. Catholic Conference, 1979),
pp. 166-167. See also *Code of Canon Law* (1983), Canons 747, 760. See
also *Veritatis Splendor*, nos. 114-117.

6. See the moving appeal of John Paul II to theologians in *Familiaris Consortio*, no. 31. See also Paul VI, *Humanae Vitae*, nos. 28-30.

7. John Paul II reminded American bishops that this duty remains
foremost for bishops, even when it becomes painful: "The bishop must

announce to the young and the old, to the rich and the poor, to the powerful and weak the fullness of truth, which sometimes offends, even if it always liberates.... Precisely because he cannot renounce the preaching of the Cross, the bishop will be called upon over and over *to accept criticism*, and to admit failure in obtaining a consensus of doctrine acceptable to everyone." See "The Bishop — A Living Sign of Jesus Christ," September 5, 1983, in *Ad Limina Addresses: April 15-December 3, 1983* (Washington, DC: U.S. Catholic Conference, 1984), p. 18.

8. This is an insistent theme in contemporary Church documents in catechesis and pastoral theology, confronting tendencies to be silent about authentic teachings that some scholars reject, or to present a vision of the faith that fails to proclaim the excellent and saving but demanding requirements of the Gospel. See Paul VI, *Humanae Vitae*, no. 29; *Evangelization in the Modern World* (December 8, 1975), no. 78.

9. See Sacred Congregation for the Doctrine of the Faith, *Declaration on Certain Questions Concerning Sexual Ethics*, nos. 9-10.

10. See Pius XII, "Address to Psychotherapists," AAS 45.278-286; see also *Declaration on Certain Questions Concerning Sexual Ethics*, no. 10.

11. On grave inadequacies in some forms of fundamental option theory, see Pope John Paul II, encyclical letter *Veritatis Splendor (The Splendor of Truth)*, (1993), nos. 65-68.

12. See *Declaration on Certain Questions Concerning Sexual Ethics*, no. 10. For a presentation of "fundamental option" theories in accord with authentic Catholic teaching, and a critique of extreme views, see Ronald Lawler, O.F.M. Cap., "The Love of God and Mortal Sin," and Joseph M. Boyle, Jr., "Freedom, the Human Person, and Human Action," in *Principles of Catholic Moral Life*, ed. William E. May (Chicago: Franciscan Herald Press, 1981), pp. 205-215, 237-266. See also Germain Grisez, *The Way of the Lord Jesus*, vol. 1, *Christian Moral Principles* (Chicago: Franciscan Herald Press, 1983), ch. 16, qs. B through E.

13. See Grisez, *Christian Moral Principles*, ch. 17, q. A.

14. See ibid., ch. 17, qs. C through F.

15. John Paul II in *Familiaris Consortio*, no. 33, quotes this passage from Paul VI, *Humanae Vitae*, no. 29.

16. Thomas Aquinas, *Summa Theologiae*, II-II, q. 141, a. 8.

17. See ibid., II-II, q. 153, a. 5.

18. Pope John Paul II commends contemporary concern for freedom, and notes the importance of understanding freedom in authentically human and Gospel ways in *Veritatis Splendor*, nos. 31-34.

19. See John Paul II, *Familiaris Consortio*, no. 37.

20. Ibid., no. 6.

21. That some of the most popular forms of birth control, notably IUD's and most contemporary forms of the birth control pill, permit conception (and so the coming-to-be of a new human being) and then cause the destruction of that person is well known. See Kevin Hume, "Latest Research Findings: The Pill and the I.U.D.," *Proceedings of the First International Congress for the Family* (Madras: Office of the Congress, 1983), pp. 86-95. For a theological reflection on these facts, see Germain Grisez, *Abortion: The Myths, the Arguments, and the Realities* (Washington, DC: Corpus, 1970), p. 344.

22. John Paul II, *Familiaris Consortio*, no. 32.

23. Ibid., no. 35.

24. Pope John Paul II, *Letter to Families* (*Gratissimam Sane*), (1994), no. 16.

25. Pope John Paul II's *Familiaris Consortio* is the basic document. Also to be noted are the Holy See's *Charter of Rights for the Family* (1967) and Pope John Paul II, *Letter to Families* (1994). See also: Pontifical Council for the Family, *The Truth and Meaning of Human Sexuality* (1995). See especially, Pontifical Council for the Family, *Instruction: Preparation for Marriage* (1996).

26. Ibid.

27. Ibid.

28. On providing a suitable education for young people in the Christian vision of love and sexuality, see *Familiaris Consortio*, no. 37; Pontifical Council for the Family, *The Truth and Meaning of Human Sexuality* (1995); Congregation for Christian Education, *Educational Guidance in Human Love* (1983). A number of programs have been prepared for education in chastity for the young in the spirit of these documents, for example, *The Catholic Vision of Love* (Huntington, IN: Our Sunday Visitor, 1996), prepared by the Diocese of Pittsburgh.

29. See *Familiaris Consortio*, nos. 77-85.

30. Aquinas, *Summa Theologiae*, I-II, q. 107, a. 4.

Index

Aardweg, Gerald van den, homosexuality, 309ff

abortion, sequence of failed contraception, 263

Albert the Great, arguments against nonmarital and "unnatural" sex acts, 107

Albigensians, medieval Gnostics repudiating procreation, 89

Alexander VII, condemnation of masturbation, 306

Alphonsus Liguori, goodness of marital act, 100, legitimate foreplay, 266.

American bishops, adultery condemned, 224, 255; binding norms, 172f, 190; conscience, duty to follow rightly formed, 162, 189; conscience, moral teaching of Church, 172f, 190; contraception, 237, 262; critique of M. Lawler and T. Salzmann, 279, 305; duty to follow magisterial teaching, 172, 190; duty to teach in union with pope, 321, 338f; sterilization, 265; treatment of rape victims, 317.

anal and oral sex, gravely immoral, 245

anamnesis, central anthropological and ontological meaning of conscience, 165

Anscombe, G. E. M. (Elizabeth), link between contraception and masturbation/sodomy, 266; need for abstinence in marriage, 267

Apostolicam Actuositatem, universal call to holiness, 219

Aquinas, Thomas, see Thomas Aquinas

Aristotle, critique of hedonism, 123, 144; nature of good, 143; understanding of pleasure, 97.

artificial insemination/fertilization, 247ff

assent, religious, of will and mind, 26

Athanasius, encouraged virginity, 80,

Athenagoras of Athens, marriage for sake of children, 80

Aubert, Jacques Marie, infallibility of ordinary exercise of magisterium. 45

Augustine, Christ, the founder of virginity, 80; detailed presentation of teaching on marriage, 82ff, 104ff; evil of masturbation, 305; nature of concupiscence, 83f, 105; pleasure in marriage and marital act, 84, 106; threefold good of marriage: proles, fides, sacramentum, and marital act, 84ff, 106f, 205; Sermon on the Mount, the perfect pattern of the Christian life, 73; sexual intercourse before the fall, 81, 83,105

Baal myth of human origins vs. biblical account, 53, 67

Báez, Silvio José, biblical meaning of "bone of my bone, flesh of my flesh," 70

Bailey, Derrick S., history of sex in Christianity, 102; Protestant thought on masturbation, 306

Baldanza, G., sacramental grace in Trent, 46

Balducelli, Roger, decision for celibacy, 220

Barnet, Barbara, NFP's effectiveness, 263

Bauer, Johannes, monogamy willed by God, 56, 71; *porneia* in Mt 19:9 and so-called "exception clause," 63, 74, 45

Bell, A., homosexualities, 287, 309

Benedict XVI, conjugal love, the "epitome of love," 35; *Deus Caritas Est*, on marriage, 37; significant addresses on marriage 2005-2007, 48f; teaching on marriage, 12, 35ff; use of condoms to prevent HIV/AIDS, 249ff; see also Ratzinger, Joseph Cardinal

Benoit, Pierre, indissolubility of marriage and no divorce in Paul, 65, 75

344 | CATHOLIC SEXUAL ETHICS